CLIMATE RISK AND RESILIENCE IN CHINA

Edited by Rebecca Nadin,
Sarah Opitz-Stapleton and Xu Yinlong

Schweizerische Eidgenossenschaft
Confédération suisse
Confederazione Svizzera
Confederaziun svizra

Embassy of Switzerland in China
瑞士驻华大使馆

Routledge
Taylor & Francis Group

LONDON AND NEW YORK

First published 2016
by Routledge
2 Park Square, Milton Park, Abingdon, Oxon OX14 4RN

and by Routledge
711 Third Avenue, New York, NY 10017

Routledge is an imprint of the Taylor & Francis Group, an informa business

British Library Cataloguing-in-Publication Data
A catalogue record for this book is available from the British Library

Library of Congress Cataloging-in-Publication Data
Climate risk and resilience in China / edited by Rebecca Nadin, Sarah
Opitz-Stapleton and Yinlong Xu.
  pages cm
  Includes bibliographical references and index.
  1. Climatic changes–Government policy–China. 2. Climate change
  mitigation–China. 3. Environmental policy–China. I. Nadin, Rebecca.
  II. Opitz-Stapleton, Sarah. III. Xu, Yinlong.
  QC903.2.C5C55 2016
  363.738′745610951–dc23   2015006415

ISBN: 978-1-138-81882-8 (hbk)
ISBN: 978-1-138-81884-2 (pbk)
ISBN: 978-1-315-74498-8 (ebk)

Typeset in Bembo
by Wearset Ltd, Boldon, Tyne and Wear

Printed and bound in Great Britain by
TJ International Ltd, Padstow, Cornwall

CONTENTS

FIGURES

TABLES

BOXES

CONTRIBUTORS

Ai Hui, Climate Center of Guangdong Province.

Ao Renqi, Institute of Sociology, Inner Mongolia Academy of Social Sciences.

Bao Lu, Inner Mongolia Development Research Center.

Anna Barnett, Red Pen of Justice Editing Services.

Scott Baum, Centre for Environment and Population Health, Griffith University.

Chen Chen, Department of Agrometeorology, College of Resources and Environmental Sciences, China Agricultural University.

Chen Xiaohong, Department of Water Resources and the Environment, Sun Yat-Sen University.

Cordia Chu, Centre for Environment and Population Health, and Peking University-Griffith University International Collaborating Centre for Development, Environment, and Population Health.

Declan Conway, Grantham Research Institute on Climate Change and the Environment, London School of Economics and Political Science.

Dong Wanlin, College of Resources and Environmental Sciences, China Agricultural University.

Du Fenglian, School of Economics and Management, Inner Mongolia University.

Du Yaodong, Regional Climate Center of South China; Sun Yat-Sen University; South China Agricultural University; and National Strategy of Climate Change Adaptation of China.

Fan Jianmin, Ningxia Economic Research Center.

Fan Jianrong, Ningxia Economic Research Center.

Fang Shuxing, Ningxia Hydraulic Research Institute.

Gao Xuejie, National Climate Center, China Meteorological Administration.

Hang Shuanzhu, Inner Mongolia Development and Reform Commission and Inner Mongolia Development Research Center.

He Jian, Climate Center of Guangdong Province.

Hu Mengjue, Guangdong Provincial Institute of Public Health, Guangdong Provincial Center for Disease Control and Prevention.

Hu Yanan, Institute of Environment and Sustainable Development in Agriculture, Chinese Academy of Agricultural Sciences.

Huang Cunrui, School of Public Health, Sun Yat-Sen University.

Jia Wei, INTASAVE Asia-Pacific, China.

Jessica M. Keralis, Freelance writer and copy editor; International Health Section, American Public Health Association.

Samantha Kierath, South China Morning Post.

Krystal Lair, Daybreak: Asia.

Li Kuo, Institute of Environment and Sustainable Development in Agriculture, Chinese Academy of Agricultural Sciences.

Li Qiuyue, Department of Agrometeorology, College of Resources and Environmental Sciences, China Agricultural University.

Lin Hualiang, Guangdong Provincial Institute of Public Health, Guangdong Provincial Center for Disease Control and Prevention.

Liu Jinhuan, Climate Center of Guangdong Province.

Liu Qiyong, State Key Laboratory for Infectious Diseases Prevention and Control, National Institute for Communicable Disease Control and Prevention, Chinese Center for Disease Control and Prevention.

Liu Tao, Guangdong Provincial Institute of Public Health, Guangdong Provincial Center for Disease Control and Prevention.

Luo Yuan, Guangdong Provincial Institute of Public Health, Guangdong Provincial Center for Disease Control and Prevention.

Ma Jianyong, Institute of Environment and Sustainable Development in Agriculture, Chinese Academy of Agricultural Sciences.

Ma Wenjun, Guangdong Institute of Public Health.

Ma Zhongyu, College of Environment, Remin University of China.

Meng Huixin, Institute for Urban and Environmental Studies, Chinese Academy of Social Sciences.

Rebecca Nadin, INTASAVE Asia-Pacific.

Esther Onyango, East African Institute, Aga Khan University; Centre for Environment and Population Health, Griffith University.

Sarah Opitz-Stapleton, INTASAVE Asia-Pacific; Institute for Social and Environmental Transition; Staplets Consulting.

Pan Jiahua, Research Centre for Urban and Environmental Studies, Chinese Academy of Social Sciences.

Pan Jie, Institute of Environment and Sustainable Development in Agriculture, Chinese Academy of Agricultural Sciences.

Pan Xuebiao, Department of Agrometeorology, College of Resources and Environmental Sciences, China Agricultural University.

Shan Ping, Inner Mongolia Development Research Center.

Shi Shangbai, Institute of Urban & Environmental Studies, Chinese Academy of Social Sciences.

Roger Street, Adaptation Science, UK Climate Impacts Programme, Environmental Change Institute, Oxford University.

Su Hao, Institute of Sociology, Inner Mongolia Academy of Social Sciences.

Wang Changgui, PRECIS System Manager, Hadley Centre, Met Office, United Kingdom.

Wang Dandan, Department of Disaster Assessment and Emergency Response, National Disaster Reduction Center of China, Ministry of Civil Affairs.

Wang Guoqing, Nanjing Hydraulic Research Institute, Research Center for Climate Change, Ministry of Water Resources.

Wang Jianwu, Urban Development and Environment Institution of Chinese Academy of Social Sciences.

Wang Jing, Department of Agrometeorology, College of Resources and Environmental Sciences, China Agricultural University.

Wang Mingjiu, College of Ecology and Environmental Science, Inner Mongolia Agricultural University.

Wang Xi, Department of Disaster Assessment and Emergency Response, National Disaster Reduction Center of China, Ministry of Civil Affairs.

Wang Zhanjun, Ningxia Ecological Office.

Wei Yurong, Inner Mongolia Ecology and Agricultural Meteorology Centre.

Andreas Wilkes, Values for Development Limited.

Wu Xiaoxuan, Climate Center of Guangdong Province.

Xiao Jianpeng, Guangdong Provincial Institute of Public Health, Guangdong Provincial Center for Disease Control and Prevention.

Xie Xinlu, Institute of Urban & Environmental Studies (IUE), Chinese Academy of Social Sciences.

Xu Yinlong, Climate Change Lab, Institute of Environment and Sustainable Development in Agriculture, Chinese Academy of Agricultural Sciences.

Yuan Yi, Department of Disaster Assessment and Emergency Response, National Disaster Reduction Center of China, Ministry of Civil Affairs.

Zeng Weilin, Guangdong Provincial Institute of Public Health, Guangdong Provincial Center for Disease Control and Prevention.

Zeng Yunmin, Guangdong Academy of Social Sciences.

Zhang Xiaoyu, Ningxia Institute of Meteorological Sciences.

Zheng Dawei, College of Resources and Environmental Sciences, China Agricultural University.

Zheng Yan, Climate Change Economics Department, Institute for Urban and Environmental Studies, Chinese Academy of Social Sciences.

Zhou Hongjian, Department of Disaster Assessment and Emergency Response, National Disaster Reduction Center of China, Ministry of Civil Affairs.

Zhou Liguang, Financial Centre for Scientific Research of Inner Mongolia.

Zhu Furong, Ningxia Economic Research Centre.

Zhu Zhongyuan, Water Conservancy and Civil Engineering College, Inner Mongolia Agricultural University.

ACKNOWLEDGEMENTS

This book is the result of multiple new and continuing research collaborations around adaptation planning, from assessments to policy, within China. Compiling and organising the contributions of so many authors would not have been possible without the dedicated assistance of:

Krystal Lair – Editorial assistant
Jessica M. Keralis – Copy editor
Guo Feifei – Book coordinator assistant
Elaine Odlin – Graphic designer
Huang Wei – Graphic designer
Rebecca Shadwick – Copy editor
Jia Wei – Supporting research
Sophie Lashford – Supporting research and coordination
Jessie Liu – Supporting coordination
Zhang Xi – Translator
Samantha Kierath – Writer for 'China Voices'
Du Yaodong – Interviewer for 'China Voices'
Luo Yuan – Interviewer for 'China Voices'
Su Hao – Interviewer for 'China Voices'
Zhu Furong – Interviewer for 'China Voices'
Zhang Lei – Interviewer for 'China Voices'

The book, and much of the research contained within, was produced under the auspices of the Adapting to Climate Change in China Phase I (ACCC I) programme. ACCC I was supported by the UK Department for International Development (DfID), UK Department for Energy and Climate Change (DECC) and the Swiss Agency for Development and Cooperation (SDC).

DISCLAIMER

The analysis, views and policy recommendations of this book do not necessarily reflect the views of the Editors, DfID, SDC or DECC. The designations employed and the presentation of material on the maps in the book do not imply the expression of any opinion whatsoever on the part of the Editors, DfID, SDC or DECC concerning the legal status of any country, territory, city or area or its authorities, or concerning the delimitation of its frontiers or boundaries.

INTRODUCTION

Rebecca Nadin and Sarah Opitz-Stapleton

This book, *Climate Risk and Resilience in China*, aims to provide the reader with a broad overview of climate risk[1] and adaptation planning in China, from climate vulnerability and risk assessments to adaptation policy and actions. It introduces China's complex development context through the lens of climate change and the resulting subsequent adaptation challenges. As a country with a large, economically and culturally diverse population, regional disparities in socio-economic development, and varying topography, China is facing a number of challenges and opportunities in responding to and anticipating possible climate change impacts and risks.

China's economic and social development context is complex. Rapid urbanisation, rural to urban migration, historical economic development and reform pathways, and significant pollution and ecological degradation have combined to make different groups of people and sectors face disparate climate risk. Large segments of the rural population are abandoning agriculture and migrating to urban areas for different opportunities (Wang *et al.*, 2011; Mullan *et al.*, 2011), but they often remain excluded from urban health and social security benefits, making them less resilient to climate shocks. Ecosystem degradation and pollution resulting from agricultural practices, natural resource extraction, urbanisation and industrialisation are making China's diverse ecosystems less resilient to climate changes and changing socio-economic pressures (Song *et al.*, 2013; Zhang and Crooks, 2012). In this already complex development context, policy makers must now begin to effectively manage climate risk, formulate policies that take into account climate change and implement adaptation measures. For a country the size of and with the diversity of China, this is a considerable challenge.

China has already experienced significant agriculture, water resource, public health and ecosystem impacts related to vulnerabilities arising from previous development pathways and a changing climate. Growing awareness of the increasing severity of these impacts and the threat they pose to China's continued economic development has prompted its policy makers and researchers to develop a number of climate adaptation research programmes and policy initiatives.

The National Development and Reform Commission (NDRC) 2014 annual report, *China's Policies and Actions on Climate Change*, introduces the various policies and actions carried out by China to address climate change, including both mitigation and adaptation to date. Of these recent policies, perhaps the most important piece of adaptation policy is the *National Adaptation Strategy* (NAS). The NAS provides the macro-level policy framework for assessment research and adaptation policy priorities on the national and provincial level. It was publicly released in November 2013 at the United Nations Framework Convention on Climate Change 19th Conference of Parties.

The NAS has three primary work areas: strengthening capacities to address climate change risks in the priority sectors of agriculture, water resources, forestry and ecological systems, tourism, public health, coastal zones and maritime waters and industries; elevating the importance of, and capacity building in, disaster risk reduction and mitigation; and reducing economic losses and human and asset damages triggered by extreme weather events and shifting climate. China has a long history of using pilot projects to test programmes and policies in some areas before modifying and scaling them to the rest of the country. The NAS continues this tradition with select provinces – including Chongqing (Three Gorges area), Guangdong, Guangxi, Hainan, Heibei, Heilongjiang, Inner Mongolia, Jiangxi, Jilin, Ningxia, Shanghai, Sichuan and Xinjiang – testing different research approaches, investigating vulnerabilities and climate risks to the priority sectors pertinent to that province and trialling policies and actions.

The 2014 NDRC annual report (p. 59) also makes specific reference to the Adapting to Climate Change in China Project (ACCC I). To date, ACCC I is the most comprehensive adaptation research to support policy project of its kind in China, providing a wealth of quantitative and qualitative vulnerability and climate risk information. In particular, ACCC I[2] was designed to contribute to the NAS, as well as to the development of a national- and provincial-level adaptation programme. Some of the most recent research and policy formulation experiences from the ACCC I programme have been referenced and included in this book. The chapters herein draw also on adaptation assessment and policy research from a wide range of academic institutions in China.

The book is organised along thematic lines, with chapters grouped according to theme. The themes are: adaptation planning processes and challenges; sector-based climate risks for disaster risk reduction, water resources, agriculture, grasslands management and public health; social vulnerability and climate risks for three provinces (Ningxia, Inner Mongolia and Guangdong); and adaptation policies and policy directions. The themes and chapter foci reflect adaptation policy priorities and concerns within China.

This book should not be considered a technical report or manual. In order to show the human dimension of climate change, many of the chapters' introductions contain excerpts of interviews with Chinese citizens – for example, a herder, farmer, public health researcher or ecosystem manager – who have been impacted by increasing climate variability and change. They were compiled in order to understand how real individuals face climate challenges and to hear how they think they might be impacted by climate change. Their stories exemplify that – while research investigates macro-level vulnerabilities, climate risks and adaptation activities – it is individuals, families and livelihoods that suffer. Adaptation policy and planning processes are often implemented at business or community to national-level scales, but individuals and households have a strong, yet poorly understood, role to play.

Part I Introduction to adaptation processes and China's development context

The first part of this book focuses on evolution in adaptation policy and planning processes, experiences in international programmes, and emerging adaptation challenges and opportunities. The latest IPCC assessment notes 'adaptation to climate change is transitioning from a phase of awareness to the construction of actual strategies and plans in societies' (Minura *et al.*, 2014, p. 871).

Chapter 1 examines general adaptation planning processes and concepts that have developed from experiences in adaptation programmes in multiple countries. It also examines common adaptation challenges and what makes adaptation a 'wicked problem'. Climate is not the only thing that is changing; societies, economies and ecosystems are also evolving. Successful adaptation must account for the linkages and dependencies between all of these processes. Because of the challenges encountered in early and current adaptation experiences, adaptation is increasingly seen as a continuous and iterative learning and action process (PROVIA, 2013). In this chapter, Street *et al.* explore good practice and challenges in adaptation planning as a process, and help to provide context for subsequent chapters.

The second chapter provides a background on socio-economic and environmental conditions in which the country's climate response must take place. These conditions make different groups of people and economic sectors more vulnerable (likely to suffer harm) as the climate changes. Nadin *et al.* discuss how all of these processes combine to create climate risks for China's peoples and economic development. This complex context makes it challenging for China's decision makers to craft adaptation policies and choose development pathways that are robust and flexible in adapting to changing conditions. Chapter 2 should be read as the context for understanding the sector-based risks described in the chapters of Part II and the social risks discussed in Part III.

Part II Climate change risks in five key sectors

The chapters in Part II highlight the climate risks occurring in five of China's policy priority sectors: climate disaster risk reduction and management; water resources; agriculture; grasslands; and public health. Burgeoning demand in both rural and urban areas, changing socio-economic preferences and conditions, agricultural and industrial intensification leading to pollution and difficulties around implementing and enforcing national policies at local levels are among some human behavioural factors that have led to increasing vulnerability in these sectors. Climate variability and change are two more challenges being added to these volatile and dynamic conditions.

In Chapter 3, Zhou *et al.* examine shifts in the frequency, intensity and distribution of extreme weather-related events (e.g. typhoons and flooding) and slow-onset shifts (e.g. droughts, sea level risk and changing seasons) that China is experiencing because of climate variability and change. Disasters have taken a heavy human and financial toll as climate change has intersected both population and economic growth and land use change. This chapter also looks at China's recent approaches to predicting, mitigating, responding to and reducing climate disaster risks through practical and policy measures, while outlining the challenges that the country still faces in mainstreaming climate change considerations into disaster risk reduction planning and management.

Chapter 4 discusses where rising and changing human demand intersects with climate variability and change to produce risks in China's water resources sector. Wang *et al.* begin with an overview of China's history of water management and vulnerability, including a discussion of the trends in slow-onset and extreme weather events over the past few decades and their impacts on water supply. The chapter then explores China's recent investigations of potential future climate change impacts and risks in light of projected demand on water supplies. It closes with a discussion on remaining barriers in adaptation planning in the water sector and policy directions China is exploring.

The fifth chapter provides an overview of China's efforts to date in developing adaptation measures to help its agricultural sector cope with climate variability and change. In Chapter 5, Li *et al.* discuss recent impacts on agriculture and food security, including a biophysical impacts assessment of climate risk for three of China's staple crops – rice, maize and wheat. The authors conclude the chapter by outlining remaining pressing needs and challenges in adapting agriculture to changing social, environmental and climate conditions and describing some of the policy measures that the central and provincial governments have been taking to build agricultural resilience.

Grasslands cover more than 40% of China's land area (Zhang, 2000) and sustain its livestock production and livestock-related industries (Liu, 2012), making it one of the priority sectors of concern in government adaptation efforts. Chapter 6 gives an overview of recent historical management and development trends in China's grasslands, and climate impacts and risks. Pan *et al.* then summarise relevant policies and related concerns for mainstreaming adaptation considerations into grassland management.

The final chapter in Part II examines the range and magnitude of climate change impacts on human health in China. Chapter 7 provides a brief overview of trends in climate change, vector-borne diseases and health, drawing from an extensive literature review of contemporary Chinese research. While vector-borne diseases are a concern under climate change, as Ma *et al.* highlight in a case study on public health impacts in Guangdong Province, heat stress and significant morbidity and mortality associated with disasters (e.g. flooding deaths) also have the potential to be exacerbated by climate change. The chapter closes with current public health policy responses in China at national and provincial levels and outlines some existing response challenges.

Part III Social vulnerability and climate risks in three provinces

While understanding sector-based climate risks is important, impacts to these sectors are felt most acutely at the local level. Communities, households and their livelihoods face differentiated vulnerabilities and capacities that shape their options for preparing for, recovering from and responding to socio-economic, policy, environmental and climate change processes. The chapters in Part III are dedicated to understanding the social vulnerability and climate risk disparities for different populations in Ningxia, Inner Mongolia and Guangdong provinces. The research presented in these chapters offers an important contribution in efforts to understand the benefits and trade-offs in policies and targeted actions, in particular around impacts for specific groups – farmers, herders and ecological and economic migrants. The three chapters represent case study snapshots of current conditions in each of the provinces and project future risks.

Chapter 8 highlights Ningxia province, an arid region of China with a largely agriculture-based economy and areas of severe environmental degradation. Zheng *et al.* discuss how shifting socio-cultural values and environmental and economic pressures, coupled with greater drought incidence, are leading to differentiated vulnerabilities and climate risks for Ningxia's farmers. The chapter also looks at the province's ecological migration programmes as an adaptation measure. Ningxia has been experimenting with ecological migration programmes – moving populations from severely degraded areas that can no longer support farming – but these programmes have not necessarily considered climate change or the socio-economic implications of moving people. The chapter concludes with adaptation-related policies in Ningxia and the challenges the province faces in mainstreaming climate change and development implications into long-term planning.

Chapter 9 examines the implications of climate change and grassland impacts on pastoralists' lives, traditions and livelihoods. While Chapter 6 focuses primarily on biophysical impacts, Hang *et al.* examine things from herders' perspectives. Economic, social, environmental and climate change processes are dramatically and rapidly altering the lifestyles, livelihoods and traditions of the peoples of Inner Mongolia, creating feedback loops exacerbating grassland destruction and desertification. The research in this chapter highlights one of the first studies within China to integrate regional-scale climate projections with participatory assessment research on social vulnerability and adaptation planning at the pastoralist household level.

The tenth chapter explores the disparities in vulnerability and climate risk between the rural and urban areas of Guangdong Province, with a discussion on its economic migrants. As Du *et al.* discuss, the economic boom in Guangdong's urban areas have attracted large numbers of rural migrants seeking better options. This population growth, socio-economic disparity and concentration of assets and infrastructure make Guangdong more vulnerable to suffering harm due to typhoons, flooding and sea level rise, while changing its climate risks. Chapter 10 discusses potential changes in climate, socio-economic and development processes that could exacerbate or decrease Guangdong's future vulnerability and climate risk.

Part IV Adaptation planning and policy in China

The book closes with an overview of adaptation assessment and policy within China, including a more detailed discussion of its adaptation challenge. As Nadin *et al.* note in Chapter 11, China has undertaken multiple iterations of adaptation planning, from assessments to developing policy and recommending actions. It examines key adaptation policies China has instituted at national and provincial scales in light of previous research and ongoing priorities, such as those covered in the previous chapters. The book concludes with an evaluation of recent developments in China's assessment research and adaptation policy directions at the end of Chapter 11.

Detailed research on adaptation, which links impact projections with decision-making and policy processes, is now starting to emerge in China. There is open acknowledgment by China's policy makers and researchers that more detailed and integrated assessments of biophysical and socio-economic impacts on livelihoods, production, infrastructure and the planning and construction of major projects are needed to inform and prioritise potential response strategies. Adaptation is increasingly being integrated in national and sub-national policy frameworks including impact assessments and sector plans in a variety of areas such as water, agriculture, development and transport. Through inclusion in the *Twelfth Five Year Plan*, China has started to make significant progress in mainstreaming climate change adaptation into economic development planning. While significant challenges remain to the successful development and implementation of national and provincial adaptation policy and plans, new opportunities are also emerging. As we will see throughout this book, China is one country with disparate adaptation needs, profiles and responses.

Notes

1 Climate risk is often described as the likelihood and severity of certain impacts occurring, given underlying vulnerabilities and the likelihood of occurrence and severity of a climate hazard (Noble *et al.*, 2014; Agard *et al.*, 2014).
2 ACCC I was developed as a trilateral adaptation research to policy collaboration between China, Switzerland and the United Kingdom, building upon prior collaborations. The programme investigated the conditions contributing to vulnerability to existing climate hazards in three provinces – Guangdong, Ningxia and Inner Mongolia – and their evolving climate risks. These provinces were chosen because they reflect the diversity of China and a wide range of climate hazards and risks, vulnerabilities and response strategies. It also examined biophysical impacts and climate risks in five of China's priority sectors: disaster risk reduction; water resources management; agriculture; grasslands and livestock production; and public health. The ACCC I programme represents an iteration of adaptation planning processes and efforts within China. Some of the most important outcomes of ACCC I include the development of relationships between physical and social science researchers, and the beginning of dialogue and collaboration between researchers and policy makers. Recommendations to China's NAS and to the provincial and national level *Five Year Plans* could not have been made without such dialogue and other forms of engagement, particularly the involvement of the National Development and Reform Commission.

References

Agard, J., Schipper, E.L.F., Birkmann, J. *et al.* (2014) Annex II: Glossary. In: Barros, V.R., Field, C.B., Dokken, D.J., Mastrandrea, M.D., Mach, K.J., Bilir, T.E., Chatterjee, M., Ebi, K.L., Estrada, Y.O., Genova, R.C., Girma, B., Kissel, E.S., Levy, A.N., MacCracken, S., Mastrandrea, P.R. and White, L.L. (eds), *Climate Change 2014: Impacts, Adaptation, and Vulnerability. Contribution of Working Group II to the Fifth Assessment Report of the Intergovernmental Panel on Climate Change.* Cambridge University Press: Cambridge, United Kingdom and New York, New York, USA.

Liu, J. (2012) *Small Grass, Large Sector.* Guizhou People's Press: Guiyang.

Minura, N., Pulwarty, R.S., Duc, D.M., Elshinnawy, I., Redsteer, M.H. *et al.* (2014) Adaptation planning and implementation. In: Field, C.B., Barros, V.R., Dokken, D.J., Mach, K.J., Mastrandrea, M.D., Bilir, T.E., Chatterjee, M., Ebi, K.L., Estrada, Y.O., Genova, R.C., Girma, B., Kissel, E.S., Levy, A.N., MacCracken, S., Mastrandrea, P.R. and White, L.L. (eds), *Climate Change 2014: Impacts, Adaptation, and Vulnerability. Part A: Global and Sectoral Aspects. Contribution of Working Group II to the Fifth Assessment Report of the Intergovernmental Panel on Climate Change.* Cambridge University Press: Cambridge, United Kingdom and New York, New York, USA.

Mullan, K., Grosjean, P. and Kontoleon, A. (2011) Land tenure arrangements and rural–urban migration in China. *World Development.* 39 (1). pp. 123–133.

Noble, I.R., Huq, S., Anokhin, Y.A., Carmin, J., Goudou, D. *et al.* (2014) Adaptation needs and options. In: Field, C.B., Barros, V.R., Dokken, D.J., Mach, K.J., Mastrandrea, M.D., Bilir, T.E., Chatterjee, M., Ebi, K.L., Estrada, Y.O., Genova, R.C., Girma, B., Kissel, E.S., Levy, A.N., MacCracken, S., Mastrandrea, P.R. and White, L.L. (eds), *Climate Change 2014: Impacts, Adaptation, and Vulnerability. Part A: Global and Sectoral Aspects. Contribution of Working Group II to the Fifth Assessment Report of the Intergovernmental Panel on Climate Change.* Cambridge University Press: Cambridge, United Kingdom and New York, New York, USA.

PRC National Development and Reform Commission (2014) *China's Policies and Actions on Climate Change (2014).* PRC National Development and Reform Commission: Beijing, People's Republic of China.

PROVIA (2013) *PROVIA Guidance on Assessing Vulnerability, Impacts and Adaptation to Climate Change. Consultation Document.* United Nations Environment Programme: Nairobi, Kenya.

Song, W., Chen, B. and Chen, L. (2013) Soil heavy metal pollution of cultivated land in China. *Research of Soil and Water Conservation.* 20 (2). p. 297.

Wang, X., Huang, J., Zhang, L. and Rozelle, S. (2011) The rise of migration and the fall of self employment in rural China's labor market. *China Economic Review.* 22. pp. 573–584.

Zhang, Q. and Crooks, R. (2012) *Toward an Environmentally Sustainable Future: Country Environmental Analysis of the People's Republic of China.* Asian Development Bank: Mandaluyong City, Philippines.

Zhang, X. (2000) Eco-economic function of grassland and its paradigm. *Science and Technology Review.* 65 (8). pp. 3–7.

PART I

Introduction to adaptation processes and China's development context

1

CLIMATE CHANGE ADAPTATION PLANNING TO POLICY

Critical considerations and challenges

Roger Street, Sarah Opitz-Stapleton, Rebecca Nadin, Cordia Chu, Scott Baum and Declan Conway

Introduction

While climate change is a global phenomenon, the activities that contribute to climate change and its impacts are inherently local. Accumulating evidence within national and UN Intergovernmental Panel on Climate Change (IPCC) assessments (IPCC, 2013 and 2014), special reports (IPCC, 2012) and from recent extreme events indicates that all countries have elements of society, economy and environment that are vulnerable to a variable and changing climate. According to the IPCC, global surface temperature change for the end of the twenty-first century is likely to exceed 1.5°C relative to pre-industrial levels, with warming projected to continue beyond 2100. Warming and precipitation changes will be much more pronounced at different locations (IPCC, 2013). Continued variability, shifts in seasons, and climate extremes – such as heat waves and more frequent and intense precipitation events – will continue to cause harm.

Climate change manifests through two different time dimensions: those over the long-term and those that occur abruptly. While it is easier to investigate the potential impacts of climate hazards and extreme weather events (acute hazards such as typhoons, heat spells or severe storms that last only for a short period), slow-onset events (long-term, gradual changes to an area's average precipitation, temperature and seasons) such as drought and sea level can be just as detrimental or beneficial as the more flashy events. These types of changes can exceed thresholds, sensitivities and coping mechanisms for a group of people or system, and cause a cascade of impacts detrimental or beneficial to other groups or systems. The impacts of these projected changes are expected to be many and serious for both natural and human systems. The core systems (e.g. agriculture, electricity generation and water, among others) upon which humanity depends for livelihoods, safety and well-being are exposed and sensitive to being affected by climate variability[1] and change. Around the world, socio-economic development has sometimes increased vulnerability. This is due to increasing demographic pressures and ageing populations, as well as resource-use pressures and previous policy choices made in pursuit of economic growth and development.

This chapter provides an overview of current ideas and practices around adaptation planning processes, as well as the movement from these to develop adaptation policies and actions. The primary goals of adaptation planning processes are to be able to develop policies and actions that meet stakeholder-agreed criteria and values – e.g. equity, feasibility and minimisation of environmental impact or economic development – while trying to avoid maladaptation. As such, the chapter also discusses the common challenges and difficulties researchers, practitioners, businesses and policy makers are facing in moving from understanding vulnerabilities and climate risks to actually being able to decide what policies and actions are required and implementing them. Even with growing scientific knowledge about the likely impacts of climate change, moving forward with adaptation planning, policies and actions has not been easy, and levels of action on national to global scales are relatively slow (Brown *et al.*, 2011).

The chapter is structured around core concepts and steps in adaptation planning that have been developed through trial-and-error experiences in disaster risk reduction, sustainable livelihoods and development and climate adaptation programmes. These concepts and steps in planning are evolving and are intended to assist in addressing the many challenges and common barriers that slow or prevent adaptation policies and actions, which are also discussed in this chapter.

Knowing some of the common barriers to adaptation provides context to the monumental challenges facing China in continuing to improve the lives and livelihoods of its people. Like many other developing countries, the critical question facing China is how to develop adaptation policies and mechanisms in the context of an already complex development environment that has already led to severe environmental degradation. The challenge for China, an emerging world power, is to address the risks and opportunities presented by climate change while also addressing long-term socio-economic needs and, in particular, the needs of diverse rural and urban vulnerable populations in more sustainable ways in an uncertain climate future.

This chapter also serves as a guide which can be used to interpret the other chapters of this book. As with many nations, China has begun adaptation planning – a flexible, reflective step-by-step process – with the intent of understanding its complex vulnerabilities and moving toward policies and actions aimed at building resilience to an uncertain future. This chapter describes emerging concepts and phases in adaptation planning processes, how these ideally lead to policies and action, and the challenges in making adaptation happen. China is finding it difficult to identify, prioritise and implement comprehensive guiding policies on provincial and national levels that enable actions at the local level, similar to adaptation planning efforts in other countries and shares many of the adaptation challenges described by this chapter. Many of the chapters in this book describe either the social vulnerabilities of China's diverse peoples (Chapters 8, 9 and 10) or the biophysical impacts of climate change on key sectors like water or agriculture (Chapters 4 to 7). The chapters also discuss the various policies that China has instituted in various sectors to begin addressing climate change. They acknowledge the challenges and difficulties China is facing in moving from often conflicting and sector-siloed policies to implementable actions.

The need for adaptation

There are many interrelated problems facing humanity, including growing and ageing populations, ecological systems under stress, socio-political differences around managing economies, energy and natural resources, and climate change. The problem of climate change itself is due to the combination of these dynamic development processes that have been driven by fossil fuel based economies and livelihoods, with the emissions from industrialisation, urbanisation and modernisation trapping heat in the atmosphere and oceans.

Growing recognition of these problems is leading to a plethora of planning processes, dialogues, policies and some actions at international to local scales. These activities are often broadly characterised as mitigation – strategies and measures to reduce greenhouse gas sources and enhance sinks – and adaptation – those that help human and natural systems to cope, adjust and shift strategies as conditions change. Adaptation is defined as 'the process of adjustment to actual or expected climate and its effects. In human systems, adaptation seeks to moderate harm or exploit beneficial opportunities. In natural systems, human intervention may facilitate adjustment to expected climate and its effects' (IPCC, 2012, p. 5). This chapter focuses largely on adaptation processes.

Adaptation can fall into three broad categories (IPCC, 2014): *autonomous*, which refers to adaptation in response to experienced climate and its effects, without planning explicitly or consciously focused on addressing climate change (also referred to as spontaneous adaptation); *incremental adaptation*, or adaptation actions where the central aim is to maintain the essence and integrity of a system or process at a given scale; and *transformational adaptation*, which refers to adaptation that changes the fundamental attributes of a system in response to climate and its effects.

Effective adaptation seldom consists of a single measure; it is dependent upon linking policies and actions and building capacity to implement them, all while recognising the trade-offs between actions. For instance, many coastal cities, like

Guangzhou on China's Pearl River Delta in Guangdong Province, are seeking ways to protect their growing populations, expanding infrastructure and assets from existing hazards like tropical cyclones and storm surges. Climate change is likely to exacerbate the frequency and intensity of such hazards, while continued urban growth is putting more people and assets in harm's way and changing flood risk patterns. Guangzhou has been upgrading its flood-control infrastructure – a network of dams, dikes and sea walls – yet these very flood control infrastructure measures, along with development, have been implicated in increasing flood risk (Cui, 2003; Zhang *et al.*, 2008). The Guangdong provincial government is also beginning to restore some critical wetlands and tidal flats (Li *et al.*, 2006), which offer better floodwater dissipation and protection against storm surges and tides than infrastructure alone. Provincial governments have also issued their own policy frameworks. For example, in 2011, Guangdong released its provincial *Climate Change Programme*, which outlines some of the priority areas and makes a number of recommendations for action, including extreme event, risk management (including urban and riparian flood prevention measures) and measures to monitor and respond to impacts on human health (see Chapters 7 and 10). These types of actions and policies are helping to lay the foundation for more comprehensive adaptation actions, but the city still has a long way to go, and the consequences of current flood policies and actions on future resilience have yet to be examined.

Adaptation as a process ideally involves a number of steps, from identifying what particular group of people or sector to focus upon and assessing vulnerabilities and risks to using this information to craft policies and implement actions, and then reflecting upon what is working or not and triggering another iteration. Processes and frameworks are being developed and trialled in national programmes, and policy formation, local government actions, development and resilience programmes are being promulgated by non-governmental organisations and various private sector actors and communities (Preston *et al.*, 2011; Agrawal, 2008; Measham *et al.*, 2011; Berrang-Ford *et al.*, 2014).

Introduction to adaptation planning processes and frameworks

Early and ongoing experiences around adaptation planning at different scales and in various contexts have led to the recognition that there are some critical steps (or phases) that should be included in the process, as well as good practice considerations. Yet, one of the most important lessons from multiple programmes is that there is no single 'correct' adaptation planning process, and no step-by-step instructions exist for how to conduct such processes. While numerous frameworks, manuals and toolkits from adaptation and disaster risk reduction programmes around the world are emerging, none of them can (or should) prescribe exactly what should be done (PROVIA, 2013; UKCIP, 2014; Snover *et al.*, 2007; MacClune *et al.*, 2013). They instead offer advice and case studies of different approaches, methods and process elements that have succeeded or failed in specific contexts.

Experiences are also indicating that adaptation planning processes should incorporate the following good practice considerations (PROVIA, 2013; Street and Opitz-Stapleton, 2013):

- Adaptation planning processes should be inclusive and participatory. All members of society will be impacted by climate change, but some will be affected more than others. A single adaptation process cannot address the vulnerabilities and risks of everyone or every sector in a country, or involve all stakeholders – individuals or groups influenced by, and with the ability to significantly impact, the adaptation process (Glicken, 2000) – in every step of every phase. Stakeholders can include policy makers, community groups, non-governmental organisations, researchers and businesses, among others. Who is included depends on the purpose and scale of the process. A successful adaptation planning process engages sets of stakeholders at critical points in the process for clearly-defined purposes so that all may share and co-learn from the knowledge and expertise of each stakeholder group.
- Adaptation planning processes are circular and iterative, emphasising that adaptation is a continuous improvement process that builds on previous stages and decisions and the need to revisit these decisions in the light of new evidence. Adaptation planning cannot be tackled as a one-off task, and a single assessment is unlikely to yield a complete set of relevant knowledge required to make the necessary adaptation decisions. Feedback and iterations are necessary to develop robust decisions. This includes refining the problem, objectives and decision-making criteria, as well as further identifying and assessing adaptation options.
- The adaptation planning process and information derived from it must be useable, implementable and embeddable into the policy, socio-economic and decision context. In other words, it must be presented in an accessible format for decision makers that accounts for their needs and decision priorities. Otherwise, it is largely a research exercise, although this may be the desired outcome. The purpose of the process must be decided by stakeholders.

A number of frameworks have been developed to help conceptualise and operationalise adaptation planning processes. The UKCIP Risk, Uncertainty and Decision-Making Framework (Willows and Connell, 2003) and the Adapting to Climate Change in China I (ACCC I)[2] Programme Adaptation Framework (Street and Opitz-Stapleton, 2013) are two examples of such frameworks (Figures 1.1 and 1.2). The basic phases of each are similar, and they both incorporate the good practice considerations listed above. Yet they are both different, in order to reflect the variable contexts in which they were formed and implemented. This enables different approaches to be adapted to specific

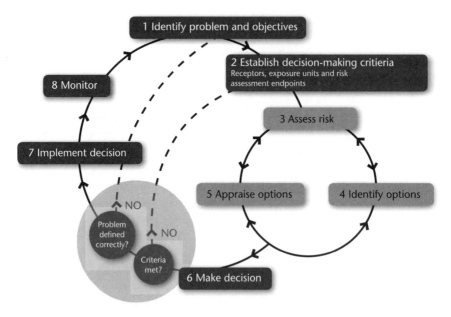

FIGURE 1.1 The UKCIP Risk, Uncertainty and Decision-Making Framework (source: Willows and Connell, 2003)

contexts, supports the particular priorities, learning and needs of involved stakeholders, and facilitates an increased understanding of the breadth of adaptation required. From each phase of any framework and process, from scoping and problem definition to monitoring and evaluation, there are key issues that decision makers should consider and questions that should be answered.

General phases of adaptation planning

The primary goals of adaptation planning processes are to be able to develop policies and actions that meet stakeholder-agreed criteria and values – e.g. equity, feasibility, minimising environmental impact or economic development – while trying to avoid maladaptation. Additionally, the process should try to ensure that policies and actions remain flexible as climate and socio-economic conditions change. To meet these goals, experiences indicate that adaptation planning (and frameworks) should include four general phases: scoping; assessments; identification, appraisal and implementation of policies and actions; and monitoring and evaluation.

Scoping

The first phase of an adaptation process involves *scoping* – making initial decisions about what problems to investigate, assigning stakeholder responsibility

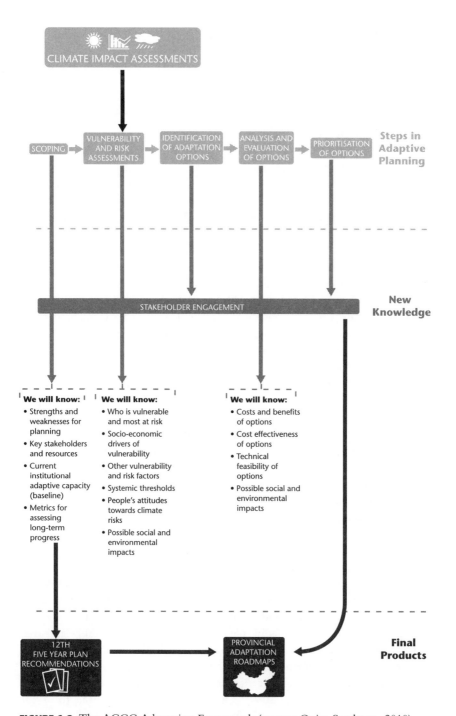

FIGURE 1.2 The ACCC Adaptation Framework (source: Opitz-Stapleton, 2010)

throughout the process and crafting an initial set of objectives to guide the process, as well as articulating the reasons for undertaking certain kinds of work and defining expected outcomes. The scoping phase is crucial because it provides the foundation that informs and guides the rest of the adaptation process.

During this first phase, researchers, decision makers and other stakeholders begin building relationships (initial engagement) and develop an initial understanding of the institutional, social and developmental contexts within which they think adaptation should take place. Information is gathered from previous efforts on hazards and disasters, vulnerability and risk, and policy and governance to find out what has already been done and identify potential barriers, and to develop an initial picture of the area's context(s). Stakeholders should discuss policy cycles, priorities, types of information needed to support decisions and the criteria by which decision makers will accept information, as well as their understanding and tolerance of uncertainty around impacts and adaptation responses. This includes a discussion of where and why there may be potential conflicts around objectives and desired outcomes.

The framing of the issue(s), the initial stakeholder engagement and the agreement of decision priorities by initial stakeholders during the scoping phase greatly influences the rest of the adaptation planning process. During the scoping phase, important elements of the subsequent phases are decided, such as: the stakeholders that need to be engaged, for what reasons, how and during what phases of the process; the methods and tools that will be used to conduct various assessments and analysis; a common language and appropriate communication strategies; the way in which the information and outcomes from the assessment phase will be presented and discussed with different stakeholders; the guiding principles, stakeholder values and decision-making criteria (e.g. targeting the most vulnerable groups or bolstering environmental protections), and how these all can be used to assess adaptation options; and some of the possible programmes, organisational activities or policies that should be studied or considered. Decision priorities and timing are also clarified.

Assessments

Adaptation does not take place within a static climate nor within a static socio-economic, environmental or political environment. *Assessments*, as part of an adaptation process, help provide the data and information needed for forming adaptation policies and actions by identifying current vulnerabilities and risks and providing plausible scenarios of future vulnerability and risk.

There are different approaches that can be used to assess vulnerability and risks and provide the broader evidence base for supporting and making decisions (Carter *et al.*, 2007; Füssel, 2009). One approach, often referred to as the 'bottom-up' approach, begins with understanding existing vulnerability, usually socio-economic vulnerability (Figure 1.3). A social vulnerability approach

Box 1.1 Scoping in an adaptation programme in China

The ACCC I programme represented an iteration of initial adaptation planning processes and efforts in China, and many of the chapters in this book contain insights and information about climate vulnerability and impacts from that programme. ACCC I brought together a diverse set of researchers including economists, climate scientists and physical scientists, each with different methodological practices, terminology and research interests. For many of the researchers, the adaptation planning research process, beginning with scoping and initial stakeholder engagement before moving to vulnerability and risk assessments, was a new concept. Few of the research partners had experienced engaging with policy makers or formulating their research to support decision-making criteria and priorities.

Partners held a number of scoping workshops at the project's inception to map the process and begin learning about other methodologies. They were introduced to the importance of stakeholder engagement, which was a new way of doing work in China, and began to learn about vulnerability assessments. Following the scoping workshops, provincial teams conducted preliminary research and began engagement to gain a basic overview of the policy landscape in each province. This information was compiled into provincial scoping reports that were shared with other ACCC I partners so that each might learn from the others and exchange ideas for moving forward. It took quite a bit of time for partners to become comfortable with the new methodologies, stakeholder engagement and working across disciplines as introduced during the scoping phase, which is quite normal in all adaptation planning processes.

At the same time, ACCC I engaged with national- and provincial-level policy makers to ensure that all information was relevant and usable in China's *Five Year Plan*. The National Development and Reform Commission is the main governmental agency in charge of developing and implementing China's policies on socio-economic and land development. The ACCC I Project Management Office worked with the Commission at all stages of the project and included them in training workshops and project meetings.

involves examining who or what (e.g. a specific community or livelihood base) is vulnerable to climate and other disruptions, the nature of that vulnerability (e.g. how severe, or how changing with time), the underlying factors or reasons for this vulnerability (like income or gender) and an estimation of how projected socio-economic, environmental and climate processes will impact future vulnerability. A social vulnerability-based approach is comprehensive and

Box 1.2 Climate assessment terminology

There are many definitions of terms like 'vulnerability' and 'risk' in use by different members of the climate adaptation community. Below are some of the most common terms from the IPCC assessment reports (Agard *et al.*, 2014).

Adaptive capacity is defined as the ability of systems, institutions, humans and other organisms to adjust to changes in climate – extremes, shifts in means, increasing variability, etc. – to moderate potential damages, to take advantage of opportunities, or respond to the consequences. Adaptive capacity is influenced by social, physical, environmental and human factors.

Exposure refers to the presence of people, livelihoods, environmental services and resources, infrastructure, or economic, social or cultural assets in places that could be adversely affected.

Maladaptive actions (or *maladaptation*) are actions that may lead to increased risk of adverse climate-related outcomes, increased vulnerability to climate change or diminished welfare, now or in the future.

Risk describes the potential for consequences when something of value is at stake and when the outcome is uncertain, recognising the diversity of values. Risk is often represented as probability of occurrence of hazardous events or trends multiplied by the impacts if these events or trends occur. It results from the interaction of vulnerability, exposure and hazard.

Sensitivity is the degree to which a system or species is affected, either adversely or beneficially, by climate variability or change. The affect may be direct (e.g. change in crop yield in response to a change in mean, range or variability of temperature) or indirect (e.g. damages caused by an increase in the frequency of coastal flooding due to sea level rise).

Vulnerability refers to the propensity or predisposition to be adversely affected. It encompasses a variety of concepts and elements including sensitivity or susceptibility to harm and lack of capacity to cope and adjust.

challenging because it focuses on the wider context beyond climate change, examining the underlying determinants (economic, cultural, built environment, social, etc.) that contribute to a group of people's or a community's adaptive capacity or vulnerability to climate change.

A second approach, often called an impacts assessment or 'top-down' approach, starts with multiple climate change scenarios and how these lead to particular impacts for sectors or ecosystems such as crops or water resources. The biophysical impact approach typically follows the standard IPCC assessment approach (Carter *et al.*, 1994) used in the first three reports. They are typically conducted on regional to national scales and are model-intensive, feeding

'Top-down' and 'bottom-up' approaches used to inform climate adaptation policy

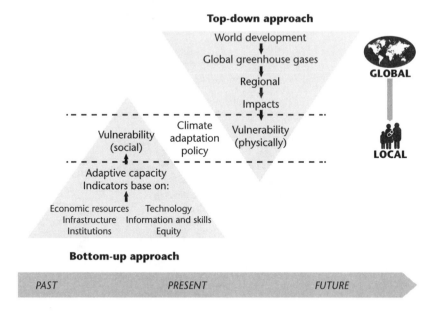

FIGURE 1.3 A conceptualisation of vulnerability assessment approaches (source: adapted from Dessai and Hulme, 2004)

selected global climate projections, which have been downscaled to regional levels, into biophysical impact models to identify impacts on such sectors as agriculture, productivity or health. Estimates of future climate risk – the severity of certain impacts happening given the probability of particular hazards occurring in the future – are often then derived from the results of the impacts models by comparing them with impacts and probabilities of occurrence over a baseline (historical) period. Adaptation measures may then be suggested that will reduce or counter the model-projected risks and maximise identified benefits.

The two approaches and their resultant information are ideally integrated together during the assessment phase to provide policy makers and other stakeholders with a more holistic picture of the interdependencies of vulnerability determinants and risks. Integration supplies necessary information and data on how changes in ecosystems, crops or water supply (biophysical systems) might contribute to the overall vulnerability or adaptive capacity of a particular community, city or region (see Figure 1.4). It is important to note that a focus only on impacts can miss potential opportunities associated with climate change that should be explored, such as the ability to plant two rice crops in one year or improving access to health services that also builds immediate disaster resilience, as well as longer-term resilience.

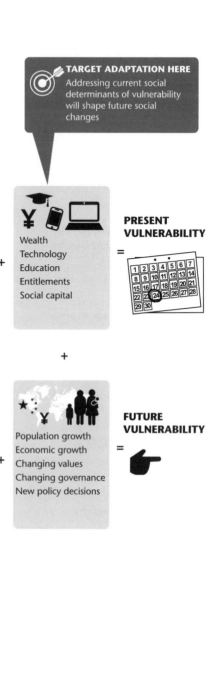

FIGURE 1.4 Relationships among current and future determinants of vulnerability and the appropriate targets for adaptation (source: adapted from Preston and Stafford-Smith, 2009)

In most adaptation programmes and planning processes, assessments have historically focused on biophysical impact assessments. In China, this has also tended to be the case for decision makers and physical scientists (hydrologists, agricultural researchers, etc.) in trying to understand sector vulnerabilities and impacts. All of the chapters in Part II of this book highlight possible climate change impacts on some of China's key sectors using a biophysical impacts approach. Yet China and other countries are increasingly recognising the importance of social vulnerability assessments and the need for participatory research processes to begin documenting the voices and experiences of some of the most vulnerable populations, and the opportunities and constraints they face that guide the autonomous adaptation actions they take. Chapters 8 and 9 employed social vulnerability approaches, quite novel to China, to examine farmers' and pastoralists' differentiated vulnerabilities. China is still working to integrate the information from the two different assessment approaches to inform the development of polices and adaptation actions.

Identification, appraisal and implementation of options

The *identification, appraisal and implementation* phase often involves several iterations and requires significantly broader stakeholder engagement to identify, appraise, prioritise and implement policy, cultural, institutional, socio-economic and technological adaptation options. The identification of different adaptation options and their initial appraisal in terms of potential benefits or harm prevented may arise during the vulnerability and risk assessment phase. Ideally, identified options are appraised according to the criteria and values, such as costs and benefits or social equity, defined in the scoping phase and refined during the assessment as interdependencies become apparent.

As the magnitude and likelihood of potential impacts and future vulnerabilities are investigated during the assessment, stakeholders will have to decide what types of actions are required and within what time frame they should be implemented. The interconnected nature of environmental, socio-economic, political and cultural systems leads to interdependencies both in terms of the risks and opportunities being addressed, and in the resulting adaptation actions being implemented. As a result, identifying, appraising and deciding which options to implement raises the potential of having to deal with conflicts requiring multiple trade-offs and synergies. This risk prioritisation should be done through expert consultation and broader stakeholder engagement, including using the results of these to inform a further assessment if it becomes apparent that more analysis is needed. Broad stakeholder engagement around all phases and steps of the adaptation planning process, including risk prioritisation, is more likely to lead to the identification of a more robust range of adaptation options than without engagement.

There are various tools and methods available to appraise and prioritise options, such as threshold analysis, social preference ranking and scenario

---

Box 1.3 Option identification and prioritisation in ACCC I

Although limited, some of the ACCC I research did progress to the identification and appraisal of certain policies and actions, like plans for more efficient irrigation or continued government resettlement of communities out of areas with severe environmental degradation. Researchers worked with policy makers involved in the development of the *Twelfth Five Year Plan*, in drafting the *National Adaptation Strategy*, and with stakeholders at the community level. China is grappling with the fact (as are many other countries) that at a practical level, it can be difficult to understand, categorise, prioritise and implement the different types of policies and options. There is a tendency to focus on those options that are within direct control, particularly infrastructure or engineering solutions. Another challenge is that policy makers and experts at different levels (e.g. provincial and community), although generally consistent in their identification and assessment of options, tend to rank the importance of various options differently based on experiences and priorities. Resolving how to prioritise options and which policies and actions to pursue is part of China's ongoing adaptation challenge. Because of this, the chapters in this book offer general recommendations for adaptation policies and actions, many of which have yet to be formally appraised or implemented.

---

building, multi-criteria evaluation, costing and environmental impact assessment (de Bruin *et al.*, 2009; Withycombe *et al.*, 2012). The appropriate tools or set of methods chosen depends greatly on how stakeholders defined the issues during the scoping phase and the information available from the assessments. As an initial set of options is identified and appraised, it may be necessary to do another, more in-depth iteration of the vulnerability and risk assessments. An important aspect of this phase is considering an implementation plan – who will implement various options and policies and how and when to facilitate an investigation of the benefits and reduced harm as things are put in place. This should also include linking into the next phase, monitoring and evaluation.

Monitoring and evaluation

Establishing a *monitoring and evaluating* process is critical for assessing how well adaptation measures and the broader plan are addressing the identified vulnerabilities, meeting stakeholder criteria and values, handling unidentified surprises and unintended outcomes and building overall adaptive capacity. The seeds of an effective monitoring and evaluation process are sown during the scoping phase, during which the criteria and values were identified that would guide the overall adaptation planning process. Some of these criteria and values can serve as monitoring and evaluation indicators. Additional indicators, both qualitative and quantitative, for measuring the performance of implemented adaptation measures may also emerge during the identification, appraisal and implementation phase. There are a number of tools and approaches for monitoring and evaluation, including logical frameworks, outcome mapping and results-based management (Anderson, 2013; Ayers *et al.*, 2012; Olivier *et al.*, 2012; Pringle, 2011).

The monitoring and evaluation phase should also provide the basis for identifying when it is necessary to restart the adaptation planning process as conditions have changed sufficiently that the previously implemented measures are no longer sufficient. As such, monitoring and evaluation should provide the means for learning from and building on the lessons and experiences of the previous iteration of the full adaptation process. These four general phases form the core of current adaptation planning processes.

Developing and implementing adaptation policy and plans must be a continuous learning process for policy makers, communities and businesses, among others. This is because adaptation must take place in the context of changing physical, socio-economic and political circumstances, as well as knowledge and technological advances in which uncertainties are inherent. The learning process should be based on introducing systematic adjustments in response to new information and changing circumstances, and it can often result in the identification of alternative development pathways. Successful adaptation necessitates a monitoring and evaluation approach capable of identifying a system's critical thresholds and interdependencies with other systems or evolving conditions. Adaptation planning includes the flexibility to change strategies and pathways as new information and changing circumstances become known (Moss and Martin, 2012).

While the previous section described why adaptation is necessary and what it should constitute, there are a number of barriers and challenges at a variety of scales that make it difficult to move from assessing vulnerabilities and risks to actual policy and action and the monitoring and evaluation of these (Brown *et al.*, 2011). What are some of these barriers and challenges?

Adaptation challenges: moving from planning to policy and action

Adaptation presents policy makers, practitioners, businesses and individuals with a 'wicked problem'[3] or a 'wicked adaptation challenge' as seen in Figure 1.5. It is dependent on characterising and understanding constantly evolving vulnerability and risk, with high uncertainty. It is also dependent on what happens at multiple spatial scales and across time. A country may promulgate agricultural

INTERACTIONS:
- Requires coordination and cooperation of many organisations
- Interdependencies and trade-offs

SOLUTIONS:
- No clear endpoints or solutions
- Multiple options needed, not just science and technology
- Can lead to unforeseen consequences, cascading effects

LEARNING ITERATION

WICKED
ADAPTATION
CHALLENGE

TRIAL AND ERROR

REQUIREMENTS:
- Involve changing behaviours
- Strong political, economic, ecological, ethical and moral dimensions
- Complex judgements

UNCERTAINTY:
- Limited data
- Lack of experience in accounting for multiple uncertainty
- Difficulty framing the problem and process

FIGURE 1.5 The many challenges that make adaptation a 'wicked problem'

adaptation policies, but the effectiveness of these will be influenced by external factors, such as trends in food preferences within the country, international demand, markets or trade pacts enforced by organisations like the World Trade Organization. Short or low-quality historical records for variables such as rainfall, temperature, demographics or hazard losses and damages make it difficult to characterise vulnerability and risk. Additionally, many policy makers do not necessarily have the capacity to interpret certain types of information and data. Furthermore, it cannot be solved by technology and physical sciences (like engineering) alone. It must account for and result from political, economic, social, cultural and ecological processes that decide the role of policies and actions, including technology.

Adaptation does not have endpoint solutions. Humanity does not adapt to a single, known future climate, but rather to continually changing and uncertain socio-economic, environmental and climate conditions. It is also inconvenient because it requires solutions – policies and actions – that do not sit conveniently within any one discipline, or within the mandate of a single organisation or government agency. This makes it difficult to appoint responsibility for identifying, assessing and implementing solutions, as well as subsequent monitoring and evaluation and revision. Adaptation may require transformational solutions that involve changes in personal and social behaviour. Shifting economies to less-intensive fossil fuel use and moving them in directions that are less-resource intensive and less reliant on the consumption of physical goods challenge current political and social structures. All adaptation solutions require consideration of conflicts, trade-offs and synergies. Finally, adaptation requires recognition that there might be some future situations to which we cannot currently adapt. Climate scientists are warning that current greenhouse gas emission, land use change and population trajectories may lead to a global average warming beyond 4°C, causing certain ecosystems upon which humanity depends to collapse.

Adaptation planning for policy making is resource intensive, making it hard for many developing countries. It involves trade-offs between certain actions and, even with the best information and intent, can lead to adaptation policies and actions that create maladaptive futures. As discussed in the next chapter, and in other chapters of this book, adaptation policy and planning at any level must occur within a complex development environment that is constantly changing.

Vulnerabilities, impacts and risk are evolving with time and at different spatial scales, which makes it difficult to develop adaptation policies and actions. Vulnerability, impacts and climate risk are shaped by socio-economic, political, environmental and cultural processes, among others, and the linkages between them. Impacts are dependent upon previous development choices and how these have altered the functioning of ecosystems upon which humanity depends. Understanding vulnerability and climate risk requires examination and anticipation of the interactions, drivers and multiple pathways of causality between human and environmental systems. Vulnerabilities at the local level, in a small village or a megacity, are partially shaped, and in turn influenced, by processes occurring at the national and international scales. Vulnerabilities and risks evolve over time and are dependent upon previous development pathways and policy choices. These complexities in vulnerability and risk dependencies and feedbacks require that adaptation consider the synergies, potential conflicts and trade-offs of proposed actions and policies across numerous sectors and for different populations.

Another fundamental challenge is that uncertainty about the future is inherent and sometimes used to avoid making policies or taking action. There is uncertainty in any estimate of future socio-economic, environmental, cultural and political systems and in projections of future climate, although most attention is focused on the uncertainty in climate models. Ironically, a large portion of the uncertainty in climate model projections is actually due to uncertainty in the scenarios of future population, energy sources and demands, land use change and greenhouse gas emissions. There is also quite a bit of uncertainty in characterising current and future vulnerability, adaptive capacity and risk, and the trade-offs and synergies of different adaptation strategies. Estimates of future risk under a changing climate are not yet adept at incorporating considerations of confounding factors like global economic depressions, large-scale conflicts or impacts of trade negotiations and pacts. Yet uncertainty, whether in data or in estimates of future vulnerability and risk, has to be acknowledged in adaptation planning processes and activities in order to develop sound decisions and policies that can flexibly respond to changing conditions.

Data limitations and lack of capacity in knowing how to understand, interpret and incorporate evidence into decisions hampers adaptation. In all countries, from Germany to China, data limitations – short or incomplete records, discrepancies in data collection and analysis methods between groups, inaccessibility, giving more importance to quantitative data over qualitative, etc. – hamper efforts to understand vulnerability, impacts and risk or describe how these are changing. Historical weather observations of less than 60 years often cannot capture the natural climate variability an area experiences and makes it difficult to make localised projections of future climate; some areas may require an even longer period of record to attribute trends. Low spatial distribution of weather stations, the cost of maintaining stations and training personnel to quality control the data all mean that high quality weather records of sufficient length are lacking in many developing countries. For instance, some of the more remote and rural provinces of China have low station density and short records, making it difficult to assess current changes and nearly impossible to detect historical trends. Low scientific capacity, funding and access to computational resources also prohibit many developing countries from generating country-specific or even high-resolution projections of climate change that could be used in assessments. Access to only a few projections from a small number of global or regional climate models makes it difficult to describe to policy makers the potential range of future climate change; relying on only a single model may lead to a gross underestimation of future climate risk and to maladaptation.

Quantitative and qualitative data issues beyond weather and climate information – having reliable and current demographic and land use data, for example – can challenge adaptation planning processes. How assessments are conducted can shape what vulnerability and risk information and data are available to policy makers and other stakeholders concerned about adaptation. Social vulnerability and biophysical impact approaches each have their particular strengths and weakness, and they provide different types of information and data to inform adaptation policy and action identification, appraisal and implementation. Both approaches encompass quantitative measurements of vulnerability and risk, but social vulnerability assessments also incorporate qualitative analyses that allow for a more comprehensive vulnerability and risk context and profile than is possible with strictly quantitative impact assessments.

A solely quantitative social vulnerability approach is inadequate for capturing the diversity of causes of vulnerability, and ultimately risk. Quantitative social vulnerability data, like reliable and long records of demographics data, or household-level or community-aggregated asset data may not be available at the appropriate spatial or temporal scales in many countries. Other quantitative data for determining risk, such as asset loss or damage data or human morbidity and mortality data associated with particular historical climate hazards, can also be lacking. Furthermore, quantitative data cannot provide the context or histories describing why particular groups are more vulnerable than others or face greater risks. For these reasons, qualitative evidence and contexts collected through storylines, interviews and other methods must be developed. Their development can be challenging because it can be time-consuming to collect stories, experiences and local knowledge through household surveys and interviews (among other techniques), but is necessary as an evidence base.

Impacts assessments, as a source of evidence to support decisions, have a long history in decision and policy making within the public and private sectors. However, this so-called 'predict and provide' assessment of suggesting adaptation measures designed to reduce model-projected impacts often only leads to marginal, incremental adaptation suggestions (Downing, 2012). Such an approach does not easily consider socio–economic, political and cultural interdependencies and challenges. Yet, integrating qualitative information and quantitative data to inform decisions is often difficult, because many physical scientists and policy makers want to reduce data to numbers. Not all evidence required is quantitative. Evidence should come from a variety of sources and disciplines, including information from experts, practitioners and vulnerable populations.

Ignoring qualitative evidence will have a detrimental impact on the decisions and resulting policies, including reducing their acceptability to intended recipients and relevance to adaptation goals. Experience in integrating qualitative and quantitative evidence in climate change assessments is limited and very challenging; many adaptation programmes are still grappling with this issue. As will be seen in the other chapters in this book, biophysical impacts and social vulnerability assessments have not been well integrated in China; all of the chapters in Part II of this book, with the exception of Chapter 7, employed biophysical impact assessment techniques that were not integrated with social vulnerability approaches. The chapters in Part III predominantly employed a social vulnerability approach. Researchers and policy makers in China are working on processes for improving this situation in subsequent rounds of adaptation planning.

Many government entities, from the country to the local level, still lack a clear understanding of how climate change will impact their human and natural systems and, as a result, do not understand their associated physical and social vulnerabilities (Baker *et al.*, 2012). Scientific assessments of vulnerability and risk often take a long time and are not always able to produce data and information in the time frame that policy makers require. These data limitations challenge policy formation and action. In many instances, climate adaptation policies are formulated with limited scientific evidence (Moser, 2010). Many policy makers are not necessarily used to evaluating, or have the capacity to account for, multiple sources of uncertainty in climate risk data. In addition, policy makers often pay more attention to short-term adaptation needs rather than longer-term considerations. This limited approach increases the risk that the identified and implemented adaptation measures will be maladaptive and have longer-term socio-economic implications and costs.

Policy makers in both developing and developed countries often want to address climate adaptation through technology and engineering solutions, in part because of the data issues mentioned, and because it is easier to demonstrate to the public that actions are being taken with concrete (e.g. infrastructure) steps than through community-outreach and education programmes. Yet, technology and engineering solutions alone will not lead to sufficient adaptation. Considering adaptation solely in the context of reducing harm – minimising or eliminating impacts, reducing vulnerabilities, and enhancing resilience – can be problematic. Although this is a laudable goal, it often leads to a consideration only of technical and engineering solutions in the context of adaptation. This framing often fails to consider the socio-economic, political and other dependencies that influence impacts and need to be considered in the adaptation response (Walker *et al.*, 2013; Preston *et al.*, 2011). Technology or physical science alone cannot address or suggest courses of actions for these other dependencies. Such measures frequently do not include win–win options like improving health care, insurance and financing mechanisms, access to and improved education or transparency in governance or decision-making.

In addition to these challenges, different strategic approaches have been and can be taken when defining the adaptation problem to study during the adaptation planning process. The approach adopted can have implications for the scope and nature of the adaptation policies and measures identified during and after the assessments (McEvoy *et al.*, 2013). There are four basic, overlapping approaches (Walker *et al.*, 2013):

- building resistance by planning for the worst possible case or future conditions;
- building resilience by planning for quick recovery of the system whatever the future (accept short-term negative performance, but focus on recovery);
- static robustness, or reducing vulnerability under the largest possible range of conditions; and
- dynamic robustness (flexibility), or planning to learn and change as conditions change.

Frequently, policies and actions tend to focus on building resistance and resilience – the 'ability of a social or ecological system to absorb disturbances while remaining the same basic structure and ways of functioning, the capacity for self-organisation, and the capacity to adapt to stress and change' (Carter *et al.*, 2007, p. 880). Framed this way, adaptation is often treated as incremental policies and steps, related to those measures that are needed to avoid disruptions to systems, like the energy grid, in specific locations under climate variability and extremes. Developing and implementing adaptation measures across multiple scales of governance remains limited (Swart *et al.*, 2009) and often leads to a focus on technological and engineering solutions alone.

Even with the best of knowledge, and political and social will, there are limits to adaptation. Human and natural systems often have tolerance thresholds which, if exceeded, will lead to a fundamental change in the functioning and nature of that system. The potential for climate change, in conjunction with other socio-economic and political changes, to exceed systems' sensitivities and thresholds has led to recognition that there are limits to incremental change. Current adaptation practices and policies may not be sufficient in some locations, particularly as it becomes clear that mitigation efforts are unlikely to limit global warming to the 2°C level associated with dangerous climate change (Jordan *et al.*, 2013). Transformational adaptation may be needed in which whole economic sectors or economies must change, shifts in management of resources and development thinking are needed, or policies and actions must be implemented at a much wider scale (Kates *et al.*, 2012).

The need for transformational change includes difficult policy and social shifts, such as a rapid move away from fossil fuels toward more renewable energy sources while encouraging societies (individuals) to consume less. Some examples include conflicts over dwindling water supply, such as those emerging between cities, farmers, ranchers and states in the arid western United States that may require renegotiation of water compacts and rethinking existing water laws. Changes in personal behaviour will require more than recycling, composting or turning down the heat or air conditioning in homes and businesses. Individuals and households in countries with widespread vehicle ownership, and cities and lifestyles designed around the car, may have to give up some notions of mobility on demand. These examples and others, such as moving away from materials consumption-based economies or curbing population growth, threaten the current political and economic structures of countries like the United States, Canada or China, where fossil fuel extraction and use underpin the economy.

Adaptation to an uncertain future requires new ways of thinking and acting, especially in moving away from treating adaptation as a series of incremental actions to some clearly defined endpoint. Experiences around trying to mainstream adaptation into development policies and plans in a variety of contexts indicate that there are a number of adaptation challenges. The very same experiences are beginning to indicate that some of those challenges may be overcome in time by treating adaptation as a continual learning process that must necessarily span political cycles, sectors and disciplines. Stakeholder engagement is necessary throughout the adaptation process, especially in building strong foundations for socially relevant and acceptable interventions. Yet, it is not easy due to a variety of issues, from including multiple perspectives and voices (which can challenge socio-political power structures) to stakeholders speaking different languages (e.g. climate scientists, sociologists, financiers and policy makers have different terminology) and therefore not understanding each other.

Summary

China is one country with many different adaptation needs and profiles, and the responses for dealing with its complex and regionally disparate development contexts, some of which will be unpacked in the next chapter, will vary. At a time when China is going through rapid social and economic transformation, proper planning to deal with the impacts of climate change is essential if the most vulnerable sectors and groups in society are to avoid the greatest hardship, and environmental degradation stopped to ensure continued and sustainable development. All of these issues, and how China is grappling with them within its adaptation planning processes, are discussed in this book.

The chapters in this book provide a broad overview of various adaptation challenges and planning phases and policies currently underway in China. The disparate impact and social vulnerability assessments, myriad of provincial- to national-level policies and adaptation plans and pilot adaptation activities discussed in each chapter reflect the very real adaptation challenges mentioned in this chapter that are also being encountered in other locations and countries. Thus, the contributions of the researchers and policy makers to this book should be viewed in light of the adaptation challenges discussed here and, as such, should form an integral part in the iterative, circular, learning and participatory adaptation planning processes that China is beginning to undertake at a variety of scales.

Notes

1 Climate variability comprises the natural, day-to-day, seasonal, yearly and sometimes decadal variations that an area's climate experiences. It may be thought of as the departure of a variable above or below the long-term mean; for instance, one July's average daily maximum temperature being 1.5°C warmer than the average of all previous Julys for the last 40 years. Climate change is measured through changes to the overall, long-term behaviour of an area's climate (e.g. summers may be 2°C to 4.1°C warmer in the 2050s when compared with summers over 1961–1990) or extreme event statistics (e.g. by the 2060s, an area may experience ~20 more days per year with temperatures exceeding 45°C than it did over the period 1970–2000).
2 The Adapting to Climate Change in China Project Phase I (ACCC I) was a 'research into policy' project that focused on the development of robust interdisciplinary research and its inclusion into Chinese policy-making processes to result in evidence-based planning. The project aimed to improve international knowledge on the assessment of climate impacts and risks, and to develop practical approaches to climate change adaptation by helping China integrate climate change adaptation into the development process to reduce its vulnerability to climate change and by sharing this experience with other countries.
3 A 'wicked problem' is term that was first used by social scientists to describe socio-political problems that are extremely difficult to address because of many of the challenges described in Figure 1.5. These challenges are discussed in terms of adapting to climate change; they are also similar to the challenges policy makers face shifting social attitudes and behaviours in areas like economic development or social equity.

References

Agard, J., Schipper, E.L.F., Birkmann, J. *et al.* (2014) Annex II: Glossary. In: Barros, V.R., Field, C.B., Dokken, D.J., Mastrandrea, M.D., Mach, K.J., Bilir, T.E., Chatterjee, M., Ebi, K.L., Estrada, Y.O., Genova, R.C., Girma, B., Kissel, E.S., Levy, A.N., MacCracken, S., Mastrandrea, P.R. and White L.L. (eds), *Climate Change 2014: Impacts, Adaptation, and Vulnerability. Contribution of Working Group II to the Fifth Assessment Report of the Intergovernmental Panel on Climate Change.* Cambridge University Press: Cambridge, United Kingdom and New York, New York, USA.

Agrawal, A. (2008) The role of local institutions in adaptation to climate change. In: *Papers of the Social Dimensions of Climate Change Workshop.* 5–6 March 2008. World Bank: Washington, DC, USA.

Anderson, S. (2013) *TAMD: A Framework for Assessing Climate Adaptation and Development Effects.* IIED Briefing. [Online] Available from: http://pubs.iied.org/pdfs/17143IIED.pdf. [Accessed: 2 December 2014.]

Ayers, J., Anderson, S., Pradhan, S. and Rossing, T. (2012) *CARE Participatory Monitoring, Evaluation, Reflection and Learning (PMERL) for Community-Based Adaptation: A Manual for Local Practitioners.* CARE and IIED. [Online] Available from: www.care climatechange.org/files/adaptation/2012_PMERL.pdf. [Accessed: 8 April 2015.]

Baker, I., Peterson, A., Brown G. and McAlpine, C. (2012) Local government response to the impacts of climate change: An evaluation of local climate adaptation plans. *Landscape and Urban Planning.* 107. pp. 127–136.

Berrang-Ford, L., Ford, J.D., Lesnikowski, A., Poutiainen, C., Barrera M. and Heymann, S.J. (2014) What drives national adaptation? A global assessment. *Climatic Change.* 124. pp. 441–450.

Brown, A., Gawith, M., Lonsdale, K. and Pringle, P. (2011) *Managing Adaptation: Linking Theory and Practice.* UK Climate Impacts Programme: Oxford, United Kingdom.

Carter, T.R., Jones, R.N., Lu, X., Bhadwal, S., Conde, C., Mearns, L.O., O'Neill, B.C., Rounsevell, M.D.A. and Zurek, M.B. (2007) New assessment methods and the characterisation of future conditions. In: Parry, M.L., Canziani, O.F., Palutikof, J.P., van der Linden, P.J. and Hanson, C.E. (eds), *Climate Change 2007: Impacts, Adaptation and Vulnerability. Contribution of Working Group II to the Fourth Assessment Report of the Intergovernmental Panel on Climate Change.* Cambridge University Press: Cambridge, United Kingdom.

Carter, T.R., Parry, M.L., Harasawa, H. and Nishioka, S. (eds) (1994) *IPCC Technical Guidelines for Assessing Climate Change Impacts and Adaptations. Report of Working Group II of the Intergovernmental Panel on Climate Change.* University College London and Center for Global Environmental Research, National Institute for Environmental Studies: London, United Kingdom and Tsukuba, Japan.

Cui, W. (2003) *Issues and Countermeasures on Mudflat Wetland Protection in the Pearl River Estuary.* International Conference on Estuaries and Coasts, 9–11 November 2003: Hangzhou, People's Republic of China.

de Bruin, K., Dellink, R.B., Ruijs, A., Bolwidt, L., van Buuren, A., Graveland, J., de Groot, R.S., Kuikman, P.J., Reinhard, S., Roetter, R.P., Tassone, V.C., Verhagen, A. and van Ierland, E.C. (2009) Adapting to climate change in the Netherlands: An inventory of climate adaptation options and ranking of alternatives, *Climatic Change.* 95 (1/2). pp. 23–45.

Dessai, S. and Hulme, M. (2004) Does climate adaptation policy need probabilities? *Climate Policy.* 4 (2). pp. 107–128.

Downing, T.E. (2012) Views of the frontiers in climate change adaptation economics. *WIREs Climate Change.* 3. pp. 161–170.

Füssel, H.M. (2009) *Review and Quantitative Analysis of Indices of Climate Change Exposure, Adaptive Capacity, Sensitivity and Impacts.* Background note to the World Development Report 2010. Potsdam Institute for Climate Impact Research: Potsdam, Germany.

Glicken, J. (2000) Getting stakeholder participation 'right': A discussion of the participatory processes and possible pitfalls. *Environmental Science and Policy.* 3. pp. 305–310.

IPCC (2012) *Managing the Risks of Extreme Events and Disasters to Advance Climate Change Adaptation.* A Special Report of the Intergovernmental Panel on Climate Change Working Groups I and II (Field, C.B., Barros, V., Stocker, T.F., Qin, D., Dokken, D.J. *et al.* [eds]). Cambridge University Press: Cambridge, United Kingdom and New York, New York, USA.

IPCC (2013) *Climate Change 2013: The Physical Science Basis. Contribution of Working Group I to the Fifth Assessment Report of the Intergovernmental Panel on Climate Change* (Stocker, T.F., Qin, D., Plattner, G.K., Tignor, M., Allen, S.K., Boschung, J., Nauels, A., Xia, Y., Bex, V. and Midgley, P.M. [eds]). Cambridge University Press: Cambridge, United Kingdom and New York, New York, USA.

IPCC (2014) *Climate Change 2014: Impacts, Adaptation, and Vulnerability. Part A: Global and Sectoral Aspects. Contribution of Working Group II to the Fifth Assessment Report of the*

Intergovernmental Panel on Climate Change [Field, C.B., Barros, V.R., Dokken, D.J., Mach, K.J., Mastrandrea, M.D., Bilir, T.E., Chatterjee, M., Ebi, K.L., Estrada, Y.O., Genova, R.C., Girma, B., Kissel, E.S., Levy, A.N., MacCracken, S., Mastrandrea, P.R. and White, L.L. (eds)]. Cambridge University Press: Cambridge, United Kingdom and New York, New York, USA.

Jordan, A., Raynor, T., Schroeder, H., Adger, N., Anderson, K., Bows, A., Le Quére, C., Joshi, M., Mander, S., Vaughan, N. and Whitmarsh, L. (2013) Going beyond two degrees? The risks and opportunities of alternative options. *Climate Policy*. 13 (6). pp. 14–39.

Kates, R.W., Travis, W.R. and Wilbanks, T.J. (2012) Transformational adaptation when incremental adaptations to climate change are insufficient. *PNAS*. 109 (19). pp. 7156–7161.

Li, X., Yeh, A., Liu, K. and Wang, S. (2006) Inventory of mangrove wetlands in the Pearl River Estuary of China using remote sensing. *Journal of Geographical Sciences*. 16 (2). pp. 155–164.

MacClune, K., Tyler, K., Opitz-Stapleton, S., Hawley, K. and Khan, F. (2013) *Climate Resilience Framework: Training Materials*. ISET-International: Boulder, Colorado, USA.

McEvoy, D., Fünfgeld, H. and Bosomworth, K. (2013) Resilience and climate change adaptation: The importance of framing. *Planning Practice and Research*. 28 (3). pp. 280–293.

Measham, T.G., Preston, B.L., Smith, T.F., Brooke, C., Gorddard, R., Withycombe, G. and Morrison, C. (2011) Adapting to climate change through local municipal planning: barriers and challenges. *Mitigation and Adaptation Strategies for Global Change*. 16 (8). pp. 889–909.

Moser, S.C. (2010) Now more than ever: The need for more societally relevant research on vulnerability and adaptation to climate change. *Applied Geography*. 30 (4). pp. 464–474.

Moss, A. and Martin, S. (2012) *Flexible Adaptation Pathways*. ClimateXChange: Edinburgh, United Kingdom.

Olivier, J. Leiter, T. and Linke, J. (2012) *Adaptation Made to Measure: A Guidebook to the Design and Results-Based Monitoring of Climate Change Adaptation Projects*. Deutsche Gesellschaft für Internationale Zusammenarbeit (GIZ) GmbH: Bonn and Eschborn, Germany.

Opitz-Stapleton, S. (2010) *Theoretical Framework: Adaptation Planning as a Learning Process*. ACCC I Methods Meeting, 8–12 June 2010, Xilinhot, Inner Mongolia, People's Republic of China.

Preston, B. and Stafford-Smith, M. (2009) *Framing Vulnerability and Adaptive Capacity Assessment: Discussion Paper*. CSIRO: Clayton South, Victoria, Australia (Climate Adaptation National Research Flagship Working Paper No. 2).

Preston, B.L., Westaway, R.M. and Yuen, E.J. (2011) Climate adaptation planning in practice: An evaluation of adaptation plans from three developed nations. *Mitigation and Adaptation Strategies for Global Change*. 16. pp. 407–438.

Pringle, P. (2011) *AdaptME: Adaptation Monitoring and Evaluation*. UKCIP: Oxford, United Kingdom.

PROVIA (2013) *PROVIA Guidance on Assessing Vulnerability, Impacts and Adaptation to Climate Change*. United Nations Environment Programme: Nairobi, Kenya.

Snover, A.K., Binder, L.C.W., Kay, J., Sims, R., Lopez, J., Wilmott, E., Wyman, M., Hentschel, M. and Strickler, A. (2007) *Preparing for Climate Change: A Guidebook for Local, Regional, and State Governments*. Center for Science in the Earth System

(The Climate Impacts Group), University of Washington Joint Institute for the Study of the Atmosphere and Ocean & King County, Washington: Oakland, California, USA.

Street, R. and Opitz-Stapleton, S. (2013) *ACCC Resource Manual: Reflections on Adaptation Planning Processes and Experiences.* DfID-China: Beijing: People's Republic of China.

Swart, R., Biesbroek, R., Binnerup, S., Carter, T.R., Cowan, C., Henrichs, T., Loquen, S., Mela, H., Morecroft, M., Reese, M. and Rey, D. (2009) *Europe Adapts to Climate Change: Comparing National Adaptation Strategies.* Partnership for European Environmental Research: Helsinki, Finland (PEER Report No. 1).

UKCIP (2014) *Adaptation Wizard.* [Online] Available from: www.ukcip.org.uk/wizard/. [Accessed: 23 October 2014.]

Walker, W.E., Haasnoot, M. and Kwakkel, J.H. (2013) Adapt or perish: A review of planning approaches for adaptation under deep uncertainty. *Sustainability.* 5. pp. 955–979.

Willows, R.I. and Connell, R.K. (eds) (2003) *Climate Adaptation: Risk, Uncertainty and Decision-Making.* UKCIP: Oxford, United Kingdom (UKCIP Technical Report).

Withycombe, G. *et al.* (2012) *Prioritising Coastal Adaptation Development Options for Local Government: Project Summary Report,* Sydney Coastal Councils Group, Oak Ridge National Laboratory and University of the Sunshine Coast: Sydney, Australia.

Zhang, H., Ma, W.C. and Wang, X.R. (2008) Rapid urbanization and implications for flood risk management in hinterland of the Pearl River Delta, China: The Foshan Study. *Sensors.* 8. pp. 2223–2239.

2

UNDERSTANDING CHINA'S ADAPTATION CHALLENGE

Rebecca Nadin, Sarah Opitz-Stapleton and Jia Wei

Introduction

China is facing a number of key challenges in reducing poverty and maintaining economic growth whilst moving toward and ensuring sustainable development. Its economic growth has been achieved in a challenging context: China now feeds one-seventh of the world's population using just 9% of its total arable land and just 6% of the world's renewable water resources (UN, 2014; ICID, 2011; Gleick, 2013; Faurès, 1997; Chapters 4 and 5 of this volume). Many of China's natural resources are under pressure. Significant pollution of water and soil resources, soil erosion, land degradation, and ecosystem and habitat loss are common; they are due to a complex interplay of previous development pathways and current local to international socio-economic pressures and preferences. Rapid urbanisation, rural-to-urban migration and industrial development are creating economic opportunities and improved standards of living for some while leading to increased socio-economic inequality for others. At the same time, international pressures (e.g. trade deals and market forces) also influence China's development strategies. The linkages between these dynamic and shifting environmental and development processes are culminating in diverse vulnerabilities and increasing the exposure of its people, assets and infrastructure to natural and technological disasters, leading to heightened risks.

Vulnerability (the propensity of a group of people or sector to suffer harm) due to climate variability, extremes and climate change is determined by the complex interplay between socio-economic, political and environmental processes occurring at multiple scales, from the local level to international arenas. It is more than just exposure to a particular hazard;[1] different groups of people and sectors within China face disparate levels of vulnerability due to regional variations in historical development pathways. At this time, the mid-2010s, when China is going through rapid social and economic transformation, increasing climate variability and change are mounting pressures that are altering climate risks throughout the country. The frequency and intensity of extreme weather events like heavy rain or heatwaves appear to be shifting, as are the seasons, though the rates and types of change are highly disparate in various regions (discussed in other chapters in this volume). Climate risk – the likelihood and severity of certain impacts occurring given underlying vulnerability, as well as the likelihood of a hazard occurring – is also dynamic and spatially uneven throughout China. This is a reflection of the regional vulnerability differences and how China's many climates are changing. Figure 2.1 is a conceptualisation of the interaction between vulnerability and hazards that give rise to risk.

Climate variability and change are challenging development and adding to the pressures on China's natural resources. China has already experienced significant health, agriculture, water resource and ecosystem impacts related to the interactions between increasing climate variability and change and underlying vulnerabilities. These have the potential to slow and disrupt the strides it has made in improving the lives of its people. Because of the marked regional disparities in development and changing climates, a one-size-fits-all approach to assessing vulnerabilities and climate risks is unlikely to adequately capture the deepening differences in economic development and social disparity or lead to holistic, yet targeted, adaptation policies and actions.

China is perceived as an economic powerhouse and an emerging superpower, frequently defined by its sheer size (in terms of both landmass and population) and the breakneck speed of its economic growth over the past 30 years. It is also a country of contradictions and paradox. With rapid economic growth and development, the expectation by many Western countries and the other G77[2] nations is that China's economy and society are well-equipped to build resilience to climate change. Yet, China's adaptation policies and actions must address the needs and vulnerability of both highly urbanised and underdeveloped rural areas simultaneously, while finding more environmentally sustainable ways to do so. China is one country with many disparate adaptation needs and profiles, and different responses are required for dealing with these issues. At a time when China is going through rapid social and economic transformation, proper planning and policies, and implementation of these to deal with the impacts of climate change, is essential if the most vulnerable sectors and groups in society are to avoid the greatest hardship. A single all-encompassing approach to adaptation is unlikely to deliver the range of adaptation options China urgently needs to avoid extensive economic and social costs.

This book examines some of the core issues China is facing as it tries to adapt to climate change. This chapter provides an overview of the country's evolving socio-economic diversity and disparities in light of policies and natural resource bases. These, when combined with regional pollution and environmental

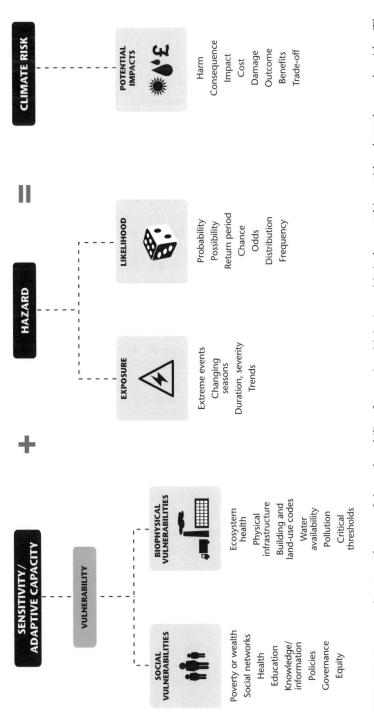

FIGURE 2.1 Conceptualisation of some of the vulnerability factors (sensitivity/capacities) that combine with a hazard to make risks. The overall vulnerability of a sector or a group of people, and the severity of the hazard to which it is exposed, determine the impacts it experiences. Climate risk is a description of the impacts and their likelihood

degradation issues, create China's complex development environment. It is within this rapidly changing context that China's policy makers must craft adaptation policies and measures – this is China's adaptation challenge. The evolution of adaptation planning and policies within China is covered in the last chapter of the book in light of all the previous chapters and China's complex development context and trajectories.

The complex face of modern China

Before examining how China as a whole is responding to climate change, it is important to have some understanding of what is meant by 'modern China'. There are many generalisations about China, which often seem made upon the assumption that China is an homogenous unit with evenly dispersed socio-economic development, a coherent state-economy model, a single culture, uniform thinking and unvarying topography and climate (Horesh, 2013; Bhalla and Luo, 2012; Ferchen, 2013; Chen and Goodman, 2012).

In the past 30 years, China's social, economic and cultural fabric has undergone a dramatic transformation from a largely rural agrarian society to a modern manufacturing giant. In addition, the very landscape upon which this rapid development has taken place has also been dramatically altered by new infrastructure developments and geo-engineering projects such as the Three Gorges Dam and the South–North Water Transfer Project, in turn changing society.[3] The following section provides a short introduction to the complex geographic, socio-economic, institutional and climate contexts in which China must develop and implement adaptation strategies and plans.

Topography, climate and natural resources

China covers a vast geographic area, approximately 9,569,000 km^2, with its topography and landscapes varying greatly from south to north and west to east. It is partially encircled by some of the tallest mountain ranges in the world, the Pamir and Himalaya ranges, in its western and south-western-most provinces. The 'Rooftop of the World', the Tibetan Plateau, encompasses most of Qinghai Province and the Tibet Autonomous Region. As one moves from the west to the east, the mountains give way to hilly regions, grasslands and desert in parts of Ningxia and Inner Mongolia Autonomous Region before descending into the broad semi-arid to arid plains of the north and north-east in which cities like Beijing and Harbin lie. The dramatic mountains of western China meld into lower elevation in Yunnan, Guizhou and Sichuan Provinces, finally evening out into undulating hills in central and south-eastern China before opening onto the coastal alluvial plains of the Pearl River Delta.

This diverse topography shapes the large spatial and temporal variability of China's multiple climate zones. In general, the East Asia Summer Monsoon

(EASM) dominates precipitation patterns around the country, with approximately 60% to 85% of annual precipitation falling during the monsoon season of May to September. The presence of the Tibetan Plateau directly influences the uneven spatial distribution of the EASM's precipitation, with the north-west, north and portions of the north-east being more arid than the southern provinces of the country (Liu and Yin, 2002; Wu et al., 2007). Topography also influences the diverse temperature ranges experienced across the country, with the north typically experiencing cold and dry winters while the south generally has a much more mild climate; southern provinces ranging from humid subtropical to tropical. The large spatial diversity of China's landscapes and climates directly influence the distribution of certain natural resources like grasslands, groundwater and surface water distribution, wetlands, forests and arable land.

People and political geographies

It is perhaps not surprising that with such a large landmass and uneven spatial distribution of resources, China's population is also unevenly distributed. China is currently the world's most populous country, with around 1.37 billion people, which accounts for around one-seventh of the world's total population. China is often perceived as a culturally homogeneous unit with evenly dispersed socio-economic development. In fact, China's population is composed of 56 officially recognised ethnic groups with distinct cultures and histories, in addition to the majority Han population (which in turn is significantly diverse in culture and dialect) (NBS, 2013; UN, 2014). China's cultural diversity ranges from the polytheistic Hani peoples living in Yunnan Province to the predominantly Muslim Hui ethnic group throughout north-western China (mostly in Ningxia and Qinghai provinces) or the historically famous Mongol peoples throughout northern China. Each of these 56 officially recognised ethnic groups, and a few others without official status, have diverse languages, customs and histories that have been shaped by China's varied landscapes and climates. They have helped to shape China's rich history and have been impacted by the previous development pathways that have led to China's current complex and dynamic development context.

This diversity is also reflected in the political geography of China. Administratively, mainland[4] China is divided into 31 provinces, autonomous regions and municipalities, which are directly under the control of the central government (Figures 2.2 and 2.3). In order to appreciate some of the challenges and issues facing China's leadership in building a society resilient to the impacts of climate change, it is important to understand the national, regional and municipal structures that govern and administer China. Each administrative level has different capacities, resources and mandates for crafting and administering policy, which as will be seen in subsequent chapters, have profound implications for dealing with China's adaptation challenges at different scales.

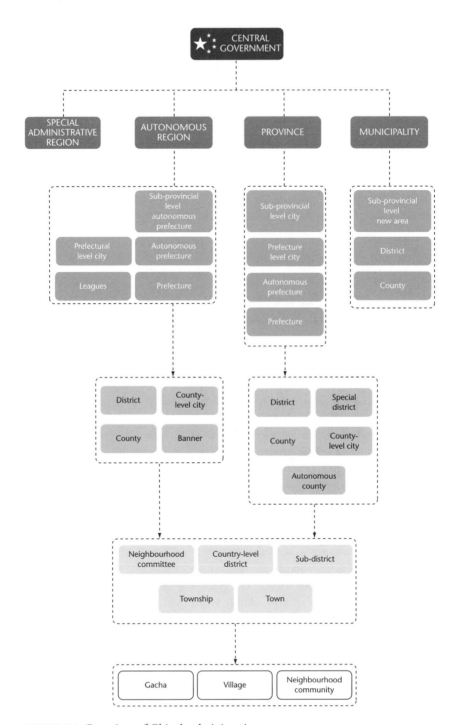

FIGURE 2.2 Overview of China's administrative structure

The State Council Information Office lists the five autonomous regions (ARs) as Guangxi, Inner Mongolia, Ningxia, Tibet and Xinjiang (China Internet Information Centre, 2014). There are also 30 autonomous prefectures, 120 autonomous counties and 1,300 ethnic minority townships. The five ARs have the highest concentrations of ethnic minority groups and have traditionally lagged behind the other provinces in terms of socio-economic development, though both the national and AR governments are taking steps to address the disparities. The economic development and adaptation policies and measures taken by these ARs can have impacts far beyond China's own borders in terms of water use, trade, energy and technology transfer and exchanges of culture and ideas.

The socio-economic, environmental, geographical and administrative differences between rural and urban provinces and the autonomous regions have profound implications for the different vulnerabilities and climate risks faced by each area. This next section explores the socio-economic and environmental

FIGURE 2.3 China's major administrative units – provinces, municipalities and autonomous regions. The designations employed and the presentation of material on this map do not imply the expression of any opinion whatsoever on the part of the authors concerning the legal status of any country, territory, city or area or its authorities, or concerning the delimitation of its frontiers or boundaries

differences between China's regions and how these contribute to their dynamic and variable vulnerabilities. These differences in development trajectories, natural resource distribution and population bases ultimately add to China's adaptation challenge.

China's divergent development contexts

The historical development pathways that a country undertakes create its current development context. The development pathways taken by China's leaders since the founding of the People's Republic of China all contribute to the current, divergent development disparities discussed in this section. Likewise, policies and actions taken today around development, disaster risk reduction, climate adaptation and mitigation will shape future development pathways and China's adaptation outcomes. This section explores the current regional disparities in China's socio-economic development and how these shape evolving regional vulnerabilities and climate risk.

Since the 1980s with the *Open Door Policy* of the Deng Xiaoping era, China's GDP reached CNY56.9 trillion (GBP5.75 trillion) at the end of 2013, having increased by an annual average of 9.2% over the period 1996–2005 and then approximately 10% between 2006–2013 (IMF, 2014). In 2014, China surpassed the United States as the world's largest economy, when measured by purchasing parity power. In a few decades, the country has under gone a dramatic transformation from a largely rural planned economy to a major global economic powerhouse. As a result of socio-economic reform policies, over 600 million Chinese have been lifted out of absolute poverty, defined by the World Bank as being at or below $1.25 a day. Economic forecasts indicate that China is likely to experience continued growth over the next few years.

However, China remains a country of contradictions. Despite its global image as an economic powerhouse, the general level of economic development of China is rather low. In 2013, the annual per capita net income of households in rural China was approximately US$1,459 (based on the then foreign exchange rate), only 11% of the world average level US$13,100 (World Bank, 2014; NBS, 2014). As at 2013, China still had approximately 82.5 million people living below its rural poverty line of CNY2,300 (US$377.2) per year (NBS, 2014). The number of rural people living in poverty decreased by 16.5 million between 2012 and 2013, indicating that economic growth and some of the social programmes promulgated by the government (discussed further in Chapters 7–10) are helping to reduce poverty.

Regional disparities

Despite the great successes and improvement in overall living standards experienced by many Chinese, with such as large population base, ensuring employment opportunities for a growing population is a key concern for the central government. From 2008 to 2012, the number of workers employed in urban areas has steadily increased while employment in rural areas dropped by 6% over the same period (China Labour Bulletin, 2013). China's population is also ageing – in 2013, nearly 202 million people (15% of the 2013 population) were over 60; by 2050, the proportion is predicted to rise to 33% (UNDP China and CASS Institute for Urban and Environmental Studies, 2013; NBS, 2014). Affordable housing, accessible education and medical care, social security, food security and other factors affecting people's living standards remain a critical concern of the government. These are reflected in human development indicator differences between provinces, as shown in Table 2.1.

Within China, there is a huge gap between different regions; economic development has not been evenly felt across all the provinces. In 2000, Jiang Zemin launched the *Go West* strategy to boost growth in the inland regions, but socio-economic development continues to lag in these areas. By 2013, the per capita GDP in China's coastal regions was US$9,512 while the per capita GDP in the western (predominantly autonomous) regions was US$5,187, about 45% less (NBS, 2013). The differences between regions are discussed further below.

The municipalities

China's province-level municipalities of Beijing, Shanghai, Tianjin and Chongqing are home to almost 86.4 million people, though they occupy less than 1.2% of China's land area (NBS, 2012; PRC Ministry of Commerce, 2007a,

TABLE 2.1 Human development data for select provinces, all based on 2012 estimates

Provincial Human Development Indicators

Province	Life expectancy at birth (years)	Adult literacy rate (% ages 15+)	Combined primary, secondary and tertiary school gross enrolment (10,000)	GDP (RMB100 million)
Ningxia	73.4	91.6	29.0	2,565.1
Inner Mongolia	74.4	95.6	75.3	16,832.4
Yunnan	69.5	91.3	695.4	8,893.1
Jilin	76.2	98.6	267.0	10,568.8
Hubei	74.9	94.1	698.2	19,632.3
Guangdong	76.5	97.0	413.1	62,164.0

Source: NBS, 2012.

2007b and 2007c; Tianjin Municipal Government, 2007). Although there is no shortage of heavy industry clustered around the cities, the tertiary sector is stronger here than anywhere else in China, and accounts for 12% of the municipalities' GDP (NBS, 2012). The inhabitants of these municipal cities have an average annual GDP per capita of CNY87,475 (GBP8,835.9) (Beijing), CNY85,373 (GBP8,623.5) (Shanghai), CNY93,173 (GBP9,411.4) (Tianjin) and CNY38,914 (GBP3,930.7) (Chongqing) – more than 2.5 times higher than the national average – and consume the most energy per person (NBS, 2013). Yet, industrial energy and carbon intensity are low, reflecting the industrial mix and relatively scarce local energy resources that encourage efficiency. Chongqing is also technically classed as a province-level municipality, but its unique characteristics – particularly its large rural areas – mean that it has more in common with other provincial regions than the other municipalities.

South and east coastal provinces

China's south and east coast provinces of Shandong, Jiangsu, Zhejiang, Fujian, Guangdong and Hainan have long been at the forefront of China's opening up to international trade and national economic development. The total population of these areas is 374.24 million (NBS, 2013), with more than 61% of the population of living in cities. The population density in the urban areas of these provinces is high, with 25% of China's total population occupying just 7% its land area in cities along the southern coasts. Their large populations and identities as hubs of industrial and economic activity have made them the engines of China's economic growth over the last 30 years. The coastal provinces account for around 50% of China's GDP, and per capita GDP is higher here than in any other region except for the municipalities (see Figure 2.2, in which municipalities are an administrative unit akin to provinces) (Dyck, 2010; NBS, 2012). They consume nearly one-third of China's total energy demand, though the region is not rich in energy resources compared with other areas of the country, with just 4% of China's coal reserves and 11.3% of its oil (NBS, 2013). As a consequence, these provinces have become some the most energy efficient in China. Chapters 7 and 10 provide a more nuanced discussion of Guangdong's diverse vulnerability and climate risk contexts.

The north

To the north are the industrially and agriculturally important provinces of Heilongjiang, Jilin, Liaoning and Inner Mongolia Autonomous Region. These provinces comprise around 21% of China's land area, and the region is bitterly cold during winter. In comparison to the coastal regions, this region is sparsely populated, with just 10% of the national population (NBS, 2013). GDP per capita is higher than the national average at CNY27,000 (GBP2,727.3) per annum, but it is not evenly distributed due to the discrepancies of participation in the important economic sectors of the region. The economies of these provinces are dominated by fossil fuel extraction, heavy industry, farming and livestock production. Those employed in the primary sectors of agriculture and livestock production tend to have significantly lower per capita incomes than those in urban areas or in other economic sectors in these provinces. Approximately 59% of the population lives in cities – the highest level of urbanisation outside the main municipalities. A significant number of herders in grassland areas such as Inner Mongolia continue to depend on grassland-based livestock production for their livelihoods and are primarily responsible for rangeland management. Chapters 6 and 9 discuss more of Inner Mongolia's development context and climate risks.

The region is well supplied with fossil fuels, providing 22% of China's coal reserves (especially in Inner Mongolia), 28% of its oil and 24% of its natural gas, and with iron ore and rare earth metal deposits (NBS, 2013). Heavy industry dominates the economic mix of these provinces, resulting in an energy-intense economy and energy consumption around 28.4% of the national total. All of this is from a lower share of population and highly uneven per capita GDP. While the industrial and fuel extraction booms have certainly led to an increase in wealth for many throughout the urban areas of these provinces, it is not evenly distributed.

For example, the province of Jilin has a total population of about 27.5 million, of which 53% is urban and 47% rural, and covers an area of 187,000 km^2 (NBS, 2013; PRC Ministry of Commerce, 2007d). The province is an old industrial base with both an industrial and agricultural economic structure. In 2010, primary industries were 12%, industry and construction were 52% and services were 36% of GDP, respectively (NBS, 2012). The main industries are automobiles, petrochemicals, food processing, pharmaceuticals and electronics. Moreover, Jilin is also one of the main producers of grain in China, and 78% of its arable land is used to grow grains like maize, soybean and wheat (NBS, 2013). For many years, Jilin has ranked first among China's provinces in terms of per capita grain supply, proportion of grain sold and exports of grains and maize. In 2012, Jilin produced 33.4 billion kg of grain, equivalent to 6% of total national grain output. Average per unit area yields were 7.7 tonnes per hectare, the highest in China. Despite its importance as an agricultural and industrial powerhouse within the country, it continues to lag behind other provinces in terms of socio-economic development. Average per capita incomes in Jilin are around 12% lower than the national average, with its urban areas falling further behind (12%) the national average, while its rural areas have fallen ~8% beyond the national rural average.

China's heartland

China's heartland includes the provinces of Shanxi, Shaanxi, Hebei, Henan, Hubei, Hunan, Chongqing, Jiangxi, Anhui, Chongqing municipality and Ningxia Autonomous Region. It is home to 37% of the nation's population; 48% of which lives in cities (NBS, 2013). Chapters 5 and 8 cover Ningxia's complex social and biophysical vulnerabilities and climate risks. The region includes some of China's fastest developing provinces and has an average per capita GDP of around 89.6% of the national average. Despite this prosperity, provinces like Jiangxi and Anhui retain a strong rural character. Jiangxi, for example, has had a net fiscal budget deficit in recent years and the province is relatively poor. In particular, rural Jiangxi contains large pockets of poverty (ADB, 2013).

China's heartland includes both heavily industrialised areas and some that remain fairly rural, making the socio-developmental disparity evident. The region's industrial sector has the largest share of GDP. It is rich in energy resources, with 57% of China's coal reserves (concentrated mainly in Shanxi province), 20% of its oil, 21% of its gas and over a third of its hydropower output (NBS, 2013). Consequently, coal constitutes the primary energy source for both heavy industry and domestic use – the highest share here of any region in China.

The rural south and west

Guangxi, Guizhou, Yunnan, Sichuan, Gansu and Hainan – China's most rural provinces – can be found in the south-west part of the country. Approximately 18% of China's population lives here, in some of the least developed provinces in the country (NBS, 2013). The region contributes only 10% of national GDP, with agriculture (its primary industry) accounting for 15% of its GDP – compared to 10% for the country as a whole. Per capita GDP figures here are the some of the lowest in China, and only 41% of the population lives in cities. Per capita energy consumption is correspondingly low, though poor industrial energy efficiency pushes up the area's average energy intensity. The region has significant fossil energy reserves – Sichuan has China's second largest natural gas reserves – and the mountainous terrain and numerous large rivers provide tremendous hydropower output (45% of China's total). This region is also a major player in China's *Clean Development Mechanisms*[5] (CDM) market: Yunnan and Sichuan have the most registered CDM projects, and the region as a whole has more than a third of the country's registered projects.

Guizhou, for example, has a total population of 34.84 million, of which 36% was urban and 64% was rural in 2012 (NBS, 2013). In 2008, the per capita GDP of Shanghai was nearly ten times that of Guizhou, and literacy rates in the wealthy coastal areas were almost 15% higher than in the poorest western provinces (UNDP, 2010). Total GDP in 2012 was CNY680.2 billion (GBP68.7 billion) (NBS, 2013). More than 60% of Guizhou's population lives in rural areas, and many ethnic groups are concentrated in remote villages; per capita net income in rural areas is CNY4,753 (GBP480.1), only half of the national average (Guizhou Provincial Bureau of Statistics, 2012; Guizhou Daily, 2013).

Social and economic development in Guizhou province is also relatively low, according to national standards. Smallholder farming still dominates agriculture in the rural areas, though total arable land is low, and many of these farmers are poor. Yields of rice, maize, wheat and potato, and main cash crops such as tobacco and rapeseed, are very low – in part due to the predominance of karst[6] and ecological degradation. Nearly 20% of the total land area (33,000 km²) is affected by rocky desertification (Guizhou Provincial Government, 2009), and total arable land area is low. While smallholder farming still dominates, energy and mining industries are becoming pillars of some local economies. Agro-processing and tourism industries are also growing rapidly.

Located at the upstream of the Yangtze and Pearl rivers, Guizhou is rich in water resources, with the average annual runoff of 106.2 billion m³, rainfall of 1,179 mm, and per capita water resources of 2,800 m³, which is higher than the national level (Zhang *et al.*, 2006; NBS, 2013). However, uneven spatial and temporal distribution of water resources and extensive karst mountains mean that many areas are water-short. Since the karst geology does not hold water and many communities lack large-scale water storage facilities, the province's per capita water supply is only 36% of the national average level (NBS, 2013).

The outer west

The vast western territories of Qinghai, Xinjiang and Tibet (both ARs) make up more than a third of China's land area, but they contain just 2% of its population and contribute just 2% of its GDP (NBS, 2012). All three contain significant populations of ethnic minorities. Yet, with the exception of Tibet (whose per capita GDP is the fourth lowest in China) this region is not as poor as one might expect: per capita GDP in Qinghai and Xinjiang is higher than all of the rural south-western provinces and even some central provinces. Around 40% of the population lives in cities, though at 23%, Tibet has the lowest level of urbanisation in China. Much of the socio-economic development and the central government's keen interest in the region is due to its hydrocarbon reserves (in particular in Xinjiang) – the region contains 19% of China's oil and 24% of its natural gas – and strategic importance, as Xinjiang is also the entry point into China for oil and gas pipelines running from Central Asia (PRC Central Government, 2013; NBS, 2013).

Development processes create disparate vulnerabilities

The regional disparities in per capita incomes, economic mixes and natural resource distribution are partially due to geography. They are also the result of socio-economic processes occurring at different rates throughout the country. Urbanisation, industrialisation, shifts in livelihoods and expectations of greater material wealth are among the many factors improving the lives of China's people; they have also had profound consequences for China's ecosystems. Desertification, soil, air and water pollution threaten the viability of China's continued growth, and regional disparities in environmental problems are large. The interplay between socio-economic, cultural and environmental change processes creates differences in regional vulnerability and disparities between urban populations and vulnerable groups like migrants. This section briefly explores some of these change processes and provides a broad overview of how they contribute to vulnerability for people and regions; other chapters in this volume provide a more detailed overview of vulnerability for particular groups of people and key sectors.

Wealth disparity

Leader of China Deng Xiaoping, who instituted China's economic reforms between 1978 and 1992, is attributed with saying that 'some people and some regions must get rich first.' He believed that economic gains made in some provinces would eventually spread to the others. While standards of living continue to improve, these gains are occurring at a much slower pace than rising wealth disparities. The 2013 *Hurun Wealth Report* (GroupM China 2013) notes that China is now home to approximately 1.05 million individuals with wealth over CNY10 million (GBP1.01 million). This is a staggering figure, but it represents just over 0.7% of the population. The national GINI Index[7] was 0.473 in 2013, another indicator or wealth disparity (NBS, 2014). Economic growth, livelihood shifts and the accompanying rise in living standards have not been universally spread. As noted earlier, there is an increasing wealth disparity between provinces and social groups. This wealth disparity is no longer just between urban and rural populations; the gap between rich and poor can be increasingly seen in the cities.

Urbanisation

Rapid growth and urbanisation have been central to China's poverty reduction in the past 25 years, with the incidence of poverty declining from 85% in 1981 to 27% in 2004. Yet these processes have contributed to growing inequality between rural and urban areas and within urban areas. In 1995, roughly 29% of the population lived in urban centres, and 71% was classified as rural. By 2011, the percentage population defined as rural had dropped to 49% and income inequality between rural and urban areas had grown. Chapter 10, focusing on Guangdong Province, also discusses the socio-economic disparities that are occurring between rural and urban areas even within the same province.

Beyond income inequality between rural and urban areas, development has also created new social vulnerabilities. Urban poverty has become more significant since the 1990s, as economic transition, privatisation of housing and an ageing population have created 'winners and losers'. Large-scale migration of farmers to urban areas has created inequalities in access to housing and social insurance among the urban population. Projections indicate that China's urban population will reach one billion by 2030 if urbanisation rates reach 70% (UNDP China and CASS Institute for Urban and Environmental Studies, 2013). Rapid urbanisation and industrial development have also exacerbated pollution and ecosystem degradation issues; many cities and surrounding peri-urban areas face significant water quality and air pollution issues due to the inability of industrialisation and infrastructure systems (e.g. sewage treatment or solid waste management) to expand quickly enough to meet the needs of burgeoning populations. Rapid growth in cities is also increasing the exposure of people, assets and infrastructure to natural disasters; this, in addition to new social vulnerabilities, is creating new climate risks for rural and urban populations. The projected high percentage of the population living in urban areas by 2030, at the time of writing only 15 years away, will have profound implications for natural resource use, the country's socio-economic development and for its adaptation planning processes and policies.

Livelihoods and changes in the workforce

As economic development has increased, so too has access to education for a greater number of China's population. The number of people who have received a tertiary education has nearly tripled since 2000. However, female illiteracy rates in some provinces like Ningxia are still around 11.3% (NBS, 2012), continuing to place many women at an economic disadvantage compared with their male counterparts and increasing their vulnerability to natural hazards. In recent years, the makeup and livelihoods of the Chinese workforce have also changed considerably. There has been a rapid move from a largely unskilled manufacturing and agriculture-based workforce to a more educated one in many provinces, although the more rural provinces continue to lag behind. Improved access to education has also provided skilled and professional workers for the growing service-orientated industries, such as retail and financial services.

As the workforce is becoming more skilled and educated, the demand for better employment opportunities and higher wages is also rising. China's urban economies based on cheap labour are no longer sustainable, as many factories and industries that were able to keep labour costs low and profits high are no longer able to do so due to increasing wage demands. Shifting demographics and increasing expectations for better employment opportunities will continue to challenge and shape the development of China's economy. Around 75% of China's population is currently of working age (between 16 and 64) (NBS, 2012), and the Chinese government is under increasing pressure to provide jobs and opportunities; 55.2 million Chinese are currently unemployed. In order to improve employment opportunities, it is estimated that the Chinese government must maintain an annual growth rate of at least 8% (Purdy, 2013).

Environmental issues

Another consequence of China's rapid economic growth has been environmental pollution and ecosystem degradation from industry, agriculture and urbanisation, among other development processes. About 27% of China's land area is affected by desertification, and it is currently expanding at a rate of more than 2,640 km^2 per year (PRC Ministry of Land Resources, 2011). Among 500 cities in China, only 1% of them meet the air quality standards of the World Health Organization (Zhang and Crook, 2012). In December 2013, the vice minister of land resources reported that 50 million mu of farmland had medium or serious levels of pollution, mostly in centres of heavy industry – the Yangtze and Pearl River Deltas, the north-east, and parts of Hunan Province (Xinhua, 2013). The World Bank estimates that pollution and environmental degradation cost China roughly 10% of its gross national income on an annual basis and continue to threaten economic development (World Bank, 2013).

Water pollution is another serious issue impacting the availability of quality drinking and agricultural water in both rural and urban areas. Nearly 70% of China's rivers and lakes are too polluted to drink from, fish in, or use for irrigation (Aiyar, 2007). According to the Ministry of Environmental Protection, 39% of major river systems and 57.5% of major lakes were Grade IV or above in 2011, with Grade VI representing the worst water quality rating. Of the 4,929 groundwater monitoring sites in 198 cities, 57.3% were rated as having poor or bad water quality (PRC Ministry of Environmental Protection, 2012). The fourth chapter delves more deeply into the water resource management challenges, including shifting climates that threaten the viability of China's water supplies.

It is in this complex and dynamic development environment that the Chinese government must formulate and implement adaptation and mitigation policies. While the economic well-being of many Chinese has improved significantly since the mid-1990s, economic inequalities remain large between and within provinces. The rural provinces and areas remain socio-economically underdeveloped and still have economies based largely upon their primary sectors (e.g. agriculture, fossil fuel extraction and mining). These sectors and activities can be very vulnerable to natural disasters, as discussed in the chapters in Part II of this book, and the socio-economic and environmental disparities create this vulnerability. Urban areas and heavily urbanised provinces with economies based on a mix of secondary (e.g. manufacturing) and tertiary (e.g. service) sectors are also vulnerable to natural disasters, and disparities in incomes, and access to housing, and to services and education among the workforces in these sectors create the diverse vulnerabilities for different segments of urban populations.

Shifting climate risks

Climate risk is often described as the potential severity of impacts given underlying vulnerability and the probability of occurrence of a severe hazard – either slow-onset, such as sea level rise or drought, or an extreme event like a typhoon or heat wave. China's complex development context, including disparities in socio-economic and environmental conditions, is creating rapidly evolving and differentiated vulnerabilities for different populations and sectors. As discussed previously, China's vast size and diverse topography means that climates are different for various regions. Climate change is altering local climates at different rates. This combination of shifting vulnerabilities and localised climate changes is altering regional climate risks within China.

Significant warming has been observed over China as whole, with annual mean temperature rises between 1951–2009 estimated to be approximately 1.4°C. Warming is more pronounced in the northern areas (north of latitude 34°N) and the Tibetan Plateau, and during the cold season. South-west China and the summer season are not warming as quickly. Daily minimum temperatures are increasing more rapidly than daily maxima.

On a countrywide average, there are no clear annual precipitation trends, but regional shifts are profound. Northern China has experienced a decrease in annual precipitation, while the middle and lower Yangtze River Basin in southern China has experienced an increase, as discussed in Chapters 3 and 4. The shifts in regional precipitation regimes have contributed to droughts and water shortages in the north and heavy flooding throughout the south. The Chinese have termed this phenomenon as 'South Flood and North Drought'.

The nature of extreme events, like heavy rainfall and heat waves, is also changing. Overall warming rates are contributing to more hot days and heat waves throughout China. Record-breaking temperatures increased at a rate of 0.7% per decade between 1961 and 2012, with significant increases since the late 1990s. Conversely, the number of cold snaps has been decreasing. Extreme precipitation events have become more intense and frequent; on average the annual number of rain days has decreased, but more days of heavy rainfall have been observed. No clear trends are yet apparent in typhoon number, severity and landfall rate.

As just discussed and covered in subsequent chapters, climate risks are changing and there are strong regional differences in impacts and for different groups
of people. The four regions of high vulnerability in China include the arid and
semi-arid north-west, the Tibet-Qinghai Plateau, the karst uplands of south-
west China and densely populated coastal zones. Climate impacts on key ecosystems like grasslands or farmlands are likely to serve as significant push factors
encouraging further migration and livelihood shifts, particularly where current
populations are poor or otherwise vulnerable. As will be explored throughout
this book, climate change within China's complex development environment is
increasing disparate climate risks and threatening its food security and water
resources, and it has the potential to disrupt its development gains.

China's adaptation challenge

Population dynamics and differentiated access to services, infrastructure and
socio-political capital, along with accelerated rates of ecological degradation,
combine to make different groups of people and areas of China more vulnerable to suffering harm when a weather event occurs. Extremely rapid rates of
urbanisation, along with significant numbers of unregistered migrants, mean
that vulnerability and capacity disparities are rife between the rural and urban
provinces, within provinces, as well as for certain populations within cities, and
fluctuating greatly. Concentrations of wealth and urban assets along the low-
lying coastal zones or hazard-prone areas are increasing exposure to weather
hazards. Environmental protections, industrial management and access to infrastructure and services have not kept pace with development in many areas,
further exacerbating vulnerability disparities around the country. As vulnerabilities shift, and the frequency and intensity of both slow-onset and extreme
climate events change for China, its climate change risk profiles are also being
altered.

Each of China's provinces, ARs and municipalities has different demographics, socio-economic development pathways, natural resource bases, topography
and climatic conditions, ranging from the frigid north to the tropical south.
Deepening social disparities between rural and urban provinces and areas, within
cities, and between migrants and established populations are challenging issues
for China's policy makers to address; climate change adds another layer of complexity. This means that China's adaptation policies must address the needs and
vulnerabilities of both highly urbanised and underdeveloped rural areas simultaneously. China is one country with many disparate adaptation needs, profiles
and responses. As in many countries around the world, a one-size-fits-all
approach to adaptation processes, policies and actions within a complex development environment is unlikely to deliver the range of adaptation options that
China urgently needs to avoid extensive social, economic and environmental
costs.

This complex context represents China's adaptation challenge. China must come up with policy and action innovations to protect its recent development gains and to address environmental and development challenges in a sustainable way that lead it down flexible, robust and resilient (see Chapter 1) adaptation pathways able to handle an uncertain future. Improper planning and policies that do not account for a combination of economic, political, legal, ecological, technical and development measures may lead to great hardships for the most vulnerable groups and sectors of Chinese society and lock it into development pathways that lead to maladaptation (see Figure 2.4).

Yet, as described in the first and last chapters, there are a number of challenges that policy makers, businesses and communities, among other decision makers, face in developing adaptation policies, plans and strategies in all countries. First and foremost, decision-makers must deal with uncertainty – the future climate, population, economies and societies can never be completely known, nor can the full outcomes of today's decisions, policies and plans be certain until we arrive at that future date. Data and information are often incomplete or lacking and capacities for understanding the information limited, making it not only difficult to understand current vulnerabilities and disaster risks, but challenging to project future vulnerabilities and risks, all in shifting political, cultural, socio-economic and biophysical systems. Scientific capacities to conduct and integrate social vulnerability with biophysical impact assessments may be weak in some contexts, as in China, where strengths lie in engineering and physical sciences, but not the social sciences. The 'wicked' nature of adaptation problems means that integrated, cross-sector and cross-discipline approaches are essential – yet these take time and better communication and coordination that are difficult to implement in some policy contexts. Finally, adaptation policies and choices may conflict with other decision priorities and policies, and lead to trade-offs and unintended consequences. Like many other developing (and developed) countries, the critical question facing China is how to design and implement adaptation policies and mechanisms in the context of an already complex development environment and how to change perceptions of its identity and role in global economic and political spheres. The specific adaptation challenges China faces are discussed further in Chapter 11, as well as an overview of its adaptation planning process and policies to date.

The remaining chapters of this book unpack the vulnerabilities of key sectors. These discussions on vulnerability should be read within the context of China's larger complex and dynamic vulnerability as outlined in this chapter. Sector-specific climate risks are also highlighted in the other chapters. Each chapter offers a brief discussion of policies relevant to reducing vulnerability and managing climate risks for that sector or group of people, but it also notes where such policies are and actions remain deficient. As highlighted in this chapter and Chapter 1, merely designing adaptation policies and actions in an incremental fashion with the aim of reducing vulnerability or risk frequently

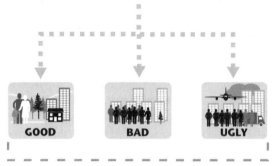

China's Complex and Fluid Development Environment

Governance
- Complex and vast administrative area
- Large, diverse population

Economic Challenges
- Slowing growth
- Rising house prices
- Socio-economic disparity across regions
- Energy security
- Transition from low end manufacturing – export driven economy

Social Challenges
- Demographic change
- Population facing employment challenges
- Growth of inequality
- Limited social security reform
- Limited hukou reform
- Migrant labour

Environmental Challenges
- Limited water resources
- Arable land constraints
- Deteriorating living environment
- Food safety issues
- Widespread air, soil and water pollution

Climate Challenges
- Shifting seasons
- Increasing day and night temperature
- Sea level rise
- Increasing precipitation variability
- Changing extreme events

PRESENT CONTEXT

ADAPTATION CHOICES (Policy and Action):

| Social harmony vs unequal income growth | Sustainable development vs resource exploitation | Long-term planning vs short-term disaster risk reduction | Integrated social and biophysical assessment vs biophysical only | Integrated socioeconomic measures vs engineering and technology only |

GOOD   BAD   UGLY

POTENTIAL FUTURE PATHWAYS

FIGURE 2.4 China's complex development environment influencing adaptation policy and action, and future different pathways

fails to acknowledge the linkages between socio-economic, environmental, cultural, political and climate processes. These challenges are becoming apparent in the Chinese adaptation policy realm, of which the evolution in thinking, policy development and practice are discussed in the final chapter of this book.

Notes

1 Under previous iterations of the IPCC Assessment Reports, vulnerability was viewed as being comprised of exposure to a hazard, sensitivity and adaptive capacity. As 2012, the IPCC has adopted the view that vulnerability and exposure are separate. Vulnerability is the culmination of the sensitivity and adaptive capacity of an individual, group or sector. For instance, an individual might not have much education (sensitivity) but may have a strong network of family and friends that can help in tough situations (adaptive capacity), making this individual more vulnerable in some situations and less in others.

2 The G77 nations are a loose coalition of developing nations within the United Nations. There were originally 77 members – hence the name – although membership to the group had expanded to include 133 member countries as at 2013.

3 The South–North Water Transfer Project is an ambitious project by any standards, originally conceived during the Mao era. It will divert water from south to the water-scarce northern regions, pumping water from the mighty Yangtze River to replenish the Yellow River. Like the Three Gorges Dam, which required the resettlement of more than 1.2 million people with exact numbers of displaced unknown, the project requires the resettlement of many from the Danjiangkou Reservoir area.

4 This excludes the Special Administrative Regions of Macau and Hong Kong.

5 The Clean Development Mechanism (CDM) is one of the 'flexibility mechanisms' defined in the Kyoto Protocol that provides for emissions reduction projects. These flexibility mechanisms are intended to lower the overall costs of achieving emissions targets by enabling countries to achieve emission reductions or to remove carbon from the atmosphere cost-effectively in other countries. The CDM allows industrialised countries to meet part of their emission reduction commitments by funding CDM emission reduction projects in developing countries.

6 Karst topography is a landscape formed from the dissolution of soluble rocks such as limestone, dolomite and gypsum. It is porous and highly uneven, characterised by underground drainage systems with sinkholes, dolines and caves (ESI, 2014). This porosity makes water management extremely difficult; karst systems are highly prone to flooding during wet periods, while surface water can be completely absent during dry periods (Alexander, 2012). This, combined with highly uneven topography, makes karst particularly ill-suited for agriculture.

7 The GINI index measures the extent to which the distribution of income or consumption expenditure among individuals or households within an economy deviates from a perfectly equal distribution. A GINI index of 0 represents perfect equality, while an index of 1 implies perfect inequality.

Bibliography

ADB (Asian Development Bank) (2013) *Jiangxi Pingxiang Integrated Rural–Urban Infrastructure Development*. [Online] Available from: http://adb.org/projects/details?page= details&proj_id=47030-002. [Accessed: 30 October 2014.]

Aiyar, P. (2007) Water woes. *Frontline*. [Online] 24. 16–19 June. Available from: www.frontline.in/static/html/fl2412/stories/20070629000105900.htm. [Accessed: 5 December 2014.]

Alexander, E.C. (2012) *The Impact of Karst on Agriculture: Conduits, Karst, and Contamination – Addressing Ground Water Challenges.* Presented at the 2012 Minnesota Ground Water Association Spring Conference, 24 April 2013. [Online] Available from: www.mgwa.org/meetings/2012_spring/alexander.pdf. [Accessed: 7 December 2014.]

Bhalla, A.S. and Luo, D. (2012) *Poverty and Exclusion of Minorities in China and India.* [Online] Available from: www.palgraveconnect.com/pc/doifinder/10.1057/9781137 283535. [Accessed: 5 December 2014.]

Chen, M. and Goodman, D.S.G. (2012) The China Model: One country, six authors. *Journal of Contemporary China.* 21 (73). pp. 169–185.

China Internet Information Centre (2014) *China Local Overview.* [Online] Available from: www.china.com.cn/aboutchina/zhuanti/09dfgl/node_7067173.htm. [Accessed: 14 November 2014.]

China Labour Bulletin (2013) *Employment in China.* [Online] 22 June. Available from: www.clb.org.hk/en/content/employment-china. [Accessed: 17 November 2014.]

Dyck, S. (2010) *China's Provinces: Digging One Layer Deeper.* Deutsche Bank Research [Online] 25 February. Available from: www.dbresearch.com/PROD/DBR_INTERNET_EN-PROD/PROD0000000000254347.pdf. [Accessed: 2 November 2014.]

ESI (Environmental Science Institute, University of Texas at Austin) (2014) *What is Karst?* [Online] Available from: www.esi.utexas.edu/outreach/caves/pdf/Whatiskarst.pdf. [Accessed: 7 December 2014.]

Faurès, J.M. (1997) Indicator for sustainable water resources development. *Proceedings of the Workshop Organized by the Land and Water Development Division, FAO Agriculture Department and the Research, Extension and Training Division, FAO Sustainable Development Department, 25–26 January 1996.* Food and Agriculture Organization of the United Nations: Rome, Italy.

Ferchen, M. (2013) Whose China Model is it anyway? The contentious search for consensus. *Review of International Political Economy.* 20 (2). pp. 390–420.

Gleick, P.H. (2013) Total renewable freshwater supply by country (2013 update). *The World's Water.* 8. pp. 221–226.

Guizhou Daily (2013) *Guizhou Provincial Government Work Report.* [Online] 20 February. Available from: www.gov.cn/test/2013-02/20/content_2336446.htm. [Accessed: 5 November 2014.]

Guizhou Provincial Bureau of Statistics (2012) *Guizhou Population Development Status Report 2012.* [Online] Available from: www.gzgov.gov.cn/xxgk/zfxxgkpt/zfxxgknb/gzsrmzfzcbm/gzswshjhsyw/437173.shtml. [Accessed: 8 December 2014.]

Guizhou Provincial Government (2009) *Guizhou Province Land Use Planning, 2006–2020.* PRC Ministry of Land Resources. [Online] Available from: www.mlr.gov.cn/tdsc/tdgh/201010/P020101019513276875227.doc. [Accessed: 8 December 2014.]

Guizhou Provincial Government (2011) *The 12th Five-Year Meteorological Development Planning of Guizhou Province.* [Online] Available from: www.kaili.gov.cn/info/17338/185786.htm. [Accessed: 8 December 2014.]

Horesh, N. (2013) In search of the 'China Model': Historic continuity vs. imagined history in Yan Xuetong's thought. *China Report.* 49 (3). pp. 337–355.

GroupM China (2013) *The Chinese Millionaires Wealth Report – Hurun Wealth Report 2013.* [Online] Available from: [Accessed: 22 April 2015.]

ICIS (International Commission on Irrigation and Drainage) (2011) *Regionwise Arable and Permanent Cropped Area of the World.* [Online] Available from: www.icid.org/posters_2012.pdf. [Accessed: 17 November 2014.]

IMF (International Monetary Fund) (2014) *World Economic Outlook: Legacies, Clouds, Uncertainties*. International Monetary Fund: Washington, DC, USA.

Liu, X. and Yin, Z.Y. (2002) Sensitivity of East Asian monsoon climate to the uplift of the Tibetan Plateau. *Paleogeography, Paleoclimatology, Paleoecology*. 183. pp. 223–245.

NBS (National Bureau of Statistics of China) (2012) *China Statistical Yearbook, First Edition*. Statistics Press: Beijing, People's Republic of China.

NBS (National Bureau of Statistics of China) (2013) *China Statistical Yearbook*. Statistics Press: Beijing, People's Republic of China.

NBS (National Bureau of Statistics of China) (2014) *Statistical Communiqué of the People's Republic of China on the 2013 National Economic and Social Development*. National Bureau of Statistics of China. [Online] 24 February. Available from: www.stats.gov.cn/english/PressRelease/201402/t20140224_515103.html. [Accessed: 7 January 2015.]

Population Reference Bureau (2012) *World Population Data Sheet*. [Online] Available from: www.prb.org/pdf12/2012-population-data-sheet_eng.pdf. [Accessed: 17 November 2014.]

PRC Central Government (2013) *People's Republic of China Administrative Divisions*. [Online] Available from: www.gov.cn/test/2005-06/15/content_18253.htm. [Accessed: 2 November 2014.]

PRC Ministry of Commerce (2007a) *Beijing – Survey*. [Online] Available from: http://english.mofcom.gov.cn/aarticle/zt_business/lanmub/200703/20070304508799.html. [Accessed: 28 October 2014.]

PRC Ministry of Commerce (2007b) *Chongqing – Survey*. [Online] Available from: http://english.mofcom.gov.cn/aarticle/zt_business/lanmub/200704/20070404537060.html. [Accessed: 28 October 2014.]

PRC Ministry of Commerce (2007c) *Shanghai – Survey*. [Online] Available from: http://english.mofcom.gov.cn/aarticle/zt_business/lanmub/200704/20070404532924.html. [Accessed: 28 October 2014.]

PRC Ministry of Commerce (2007d) *Jilin – Survey*. [Online] Available from: http://english.mofcom.gov.cn/aarticle/zt_business/lanmub/200703/20070304502281.html. [Accessed: 30 October 2014.]

PRC Ministry of Environmental Protection (2012) *Fresh Water Environment*. [Online] 6 June. Available from: http://jcs.mep.gov.cn/hjzl/zkgb/2012zkgb/201306/t20130606_253418.htm. [Accessed: 3 November 2014.]

PRC Ministry of Land Resources (2011) *Overview of China Land Desertification*. [Online] Available from: www.mlr.gov.cn/tdzt/zdxc/tdr/21tdr/tdbk/201106/t20110613_878377.htm. [Accessed: 3 November 2014.]

Purdy, M. (2013) China's economy, in six charts. *Harvard Business Review*. [Online] 29 November. Available from: http://blogs.hbr.org/2013/11/chinas-economy-in-six-charts/. [Accessed: 5 November 2014.]

Tianjin Municipal Government (2007) *Area and Administrative Divisions*. [Online] Available from: www.tj.gov.cn/english/About_tianjin/Tianjin_Basic_Facts/Area_and_Administrative_Divisions/. [Accessed: 28 October 2014.]

UN (United Nations) (2014) *Population and Vital Statistics Report*. United Nations Department of Economic and Social Affairs, Statistics Division. [Online] Available from: http://unstats.un.org/unsd/Demographic/products/vitstats/Sets/Series_A_2014.pdf. [Accessed: 14 November 2014.]

UN Country Team in China (2004) *Millennium Development Goals: China's Progress. Office of the United Nations Resident Coordinator in China*. [Online] Available from:

http://planipolis.iiep.unesco.org/upload/China/China%20MDG.pdf. [Accessed: 14 November 2014.]

UNDP (United Nations Development Program) (2010) *China and a Sustainable Future: Toward a Low Carbon Economy and Society.* China Translation and Publishing Company: Beijing, People's Republic of China (UNDP China Human Development Report 2009/10).

UNDP China and CASS Institute for Urban and Environmental Studies (2013) *China National Human Development Report 2013. Sustainable and Liveable Cities: Toward Ecological Civilization.* China Translation and Publishing Corporation: Beijing, People's Republic of China.

World Bank (2013) *China 2030: Building a Modern, Harmonious, and Creative Society.* World Bank: Washington, DC, USA.

World Bank (2014) *Data: GDP Per Capita (current US $).* [Online] Available from: http://data.worldbank.org/indicator/NY.GDP.PCAP.CD/countries. [Accessed: 4 November 2014.]

Wu, G., Liu, Y., Wang, T., Wan, R., Liu, X., Li, W., Wang, Z. and Liang, X. (2007) The influence of mechanical and thermal forcing by the Tibetan plateau on Asian climate. *Journal of Hydrometeorology.* 8: pp. 770–789.

Xinhua (2013) Government to invest tens of billions to restore 50 million mu of farmland affected by severe pollution. [Online] 31 December. Available from: www.mlr.gov.cn/xwdt/mtsy/xinhuanet/201312/t20131231_1299035.htm. [Accessed: 3 November 2014.]

Zhang, J., Liu, D. and Shi, H. (2006) Low flow characteristics of Guizhou Province preliminary analysis. *Guizhou Water Power.* 20 (5). p. 8.

Zhang, Q. and Crooks, R. (2012) *Toward an Environmentally Sustainable Future: Country Environmental Analysis of the People's Republic of China.* Asian Development Bank: Manila, Philippines.

PART II
Climate change risks in five key sectors

3

ADAPTING AGAINST DISASTERS IN A CHANGING CLIMATE

Zhou Hongjian, Wang Xi, Wang Changgui, Yuan Yi, Wang Dandan, Xu Yinlong, Pan Jie, Krystal Lair and Anna Barnett

The conditions were perfect in the worst possible way. The earth in the mountainous area of Zhouqu County in Gansu Province was already parched and cracked from ongoing drought and loose from an earthquake two years before.[1] Heavy rain is rare in the dry north-west, but one night in early August 2010, a downpour equivalent to one-fifth of Zhouqu's average annual rainfall fell on the county seat in less than an hour.[2] The brief deluge unleashed flash floods, landslides and a wall of muddy debris five metres deep and 300 metres wide. The mud wall rolled more than five kilometres through four valleys, swept away homes and entombed people in its path. As the debris mounted, it blocked a local river, forming a dammed lake that then broke, flooding most of the local township for nearly three weeks. Roads, water supplies, electricity and communication lines were severed and countless homes destroyed. By the end, more than 1,700 people were dead or missing (Xinhua, 2010).

It was a singular devastating event, but these kinds of disasters are becoming more common as China's climate changes and development increases. Though both geology and pre-existing weather conditions[3] contributed to the large debris flow in Zhouqu, the occurrence of such a rare and extreme period of rain reflects uncertainty not about *whether* global climate change will alter regional patterns of extreme weather in the next decades, but *how*. As the climate changes, extreme weather events in China are becoming more unpredictable in their intensity, as well as where and when they will strike.

In China, a number of weather-related disasters since the early 2000s have taken a heavy human and financial toll as increasing climate variability and change have intersected both population growth and socio-economic development. Disasters may be triggered by slow-onset hazards that persist over an extended period of time or by extreme hazard events. What turns these hazard events into disasters are the pre-existing vulnerability conditions – people and assets sensitive to suffering harm – and, occasionally, pre-existing conditions that resulted from prior disaster events – such as the landslides or mudslides that occurred during heavy rains on slopes already destabilised by the earlier Zhouqu earthquake.

Disaster chains and effects

Heavy casualties and damage (disasters) are triggered either by a single natural hazard – a 'singular disaster' – or through cascading damages to a series of causally-linked systems – 'disaster chains'. Disaster chains are more common and occur when impacts to one system cause secondary and tertiary disasters in other linked systems. An example of a disaster chain includes widespread flooding (primary disaster) that contaminates drinking water supplies (secondary disaster) and leads to an outbreak of waterborne illness like cholera (tertiary disaster). The hazard factors – usually described as vulnerability factors in the international hazards and disasters research community – constitute things like previous land management practices or access to resources by different community members. The combination of exposure, sensitivity and capacity determine a system's underlying hazard factors (see Chapters 1 and 2 for a discussion on vulnerability).

In the flooding and cholera example, a community without knowledge about the need to boil water before consumption or the means to do so during and after a flood is more vulnerable to suffering multiple types of harm. The damage caused by events like the Zhouqu downpour, when superimposed on other stresses and previous hazard damages is magnified by the disaster chain effects – the mudslide, the dammed river, the submerged town – that result.

In September 2010, Typhoon Fanapi passed through Taiwan and weakened into a severe tropical storm before hitting southern China. As it moved down the coast of Guangdong Province, the storm continued to lose energy – but the death toll climbed (Figure 3.1). Fanapi brought heavy rains that triggered mudslides and mountain landslides that left 90 people dead or missing, and flash floods caused a dam failure killing another 28 according to the Guangdong Department of Civil Affairs. Property losses were also heavy.

As is often the case in disaster chains, the secondary events are more damaging, but these have been more difficult to predict and prepare for under China's legacy of a reactionary disaster response system. Although each disaster-related department took emergency response measures, heavy casualties and property loss resulted due to uncertainty about the typhoon's path, heavy rain and each of the other links in the disaster chain. A more holistic disaster risk reduction management system that focuses on identifying and reducing underlying vulnerability factors – like soil erosion or building on steep slopes – would be much more able to prevent disaster chains than the older system.

Extreme weather and slow-onset events are becoming less predictable due to climate change and, when coupled with China's rapid and uneven

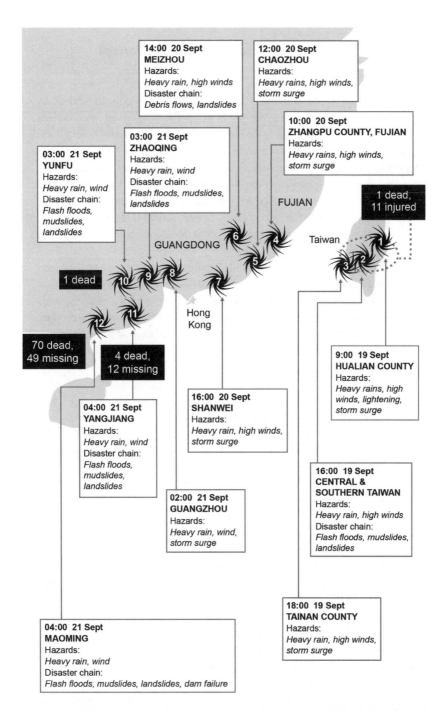

FIGURE 3.1 Disaster chain of Typhoon Fanapi (source: unpublished data from the National Disaster Reduction Center of China database)

Box 3.1 Disaster response for Typhoon Fanapi

Multiple agencies and ministries within China began martialling early warning response and preparations for Typhoon Fanapi prior to landfall. In locations 1–9 of Figure 3.1, a number of actions were taken to help prepare and protect the public. The State Flood Control and Drought Relief Headquarters held an emergency off-site video conference in response to the typhoon. The China Meteorological Commission, the State Oceanic Administration and the Ministry of Water Resources at all levels closely monitored the typhoon, released forecasts on a rolling basis and relocated people in advance from onshore fish farms, ports, berths, school buildings in dangerous conditions, simple sheds, tourist attractions, constructions sites and industrial and mining enterprises.

After a significant number of disaster chains occurred in several locations (9–12 in Figure 3.1) in the early hours of 21 September, the National Disaster Reduction Committee launched a Grade IV emergency response with the typhoon declared a national disaster. At 17:00 on the 23rd, they upgraded it to a Grade III response. The Ministry of Civil Affairs, the Ministry of Finance, the Ministry of Land Resources and the Transport Ministry established a working group.

---

socio-economic growth, are leading to more complex disaster chains, with multiple disasters sometimes occurring in the same area within the same year. These conditions are forcing China to update its ideas and approaches toward disaster management. This includes the need to improve its researchers' ability to analyse and assess disaster chains and their effects that magnify the losses and damages of natural disasters. It will also require policy makers to adopt a more holistic and forward-thinking disaster and climate adaptation response than the current paradigm of reactionary, sector-siloed policy.

This chapter first gives an overview of extreme weather events – the underlying hazards that trigger natural disaster – as well as the changes in the frequency, intensity and distribution of slow-onset shifts in seasons, temperature and precipitation that China is experiencing as a result of the effects of climate variability and change. It then examines China's recent approaches to predicting, mitigating, responding to and reducing the risk of weather-related disasters through practical and policy measures, including an in-depth look at one of China's approaches to disaster risk assessment in a case study. Finally, based on new research, the chapter will examine the remaining challenges China will need to overcome in order to build robust disaster risk reduction strategies and adapt to the impacts of a changing climate.

Emerging trends: disasters in a changing climate

Natural disasters occur when extreme weather or slow-onset shifts overwhelm the natural and human systems. Low adaptive capacity, high exposure (the presence of people, assets and infrastructure in harm's way, such as increasing urban development along coasts prone to typhoons) and sensitivity make some systems more vulnerable to suffering harm when an event occurs. (See Chapter 1 and subsequent chapters for discussion of vulnerability factors, which are termed hazard factors in this chapter, and risk.) Thus, *disaster risk* (the risk of loss or negative outcomes due to a hazard and a system's underlying vulnerability) is determined not only by the magnitude and probability of floods, droughts, landslides, tropical storms and other hazards, but also by the vulnerability of *hazard-bearing bodies* (any system that may suffer harm when a hazard event occurs) such as maize fields or megacities.

In China, rapid development has multiplied the socio-economic assets, livelihoods and numbers of people exposed to natural hazards, leading to widespread vulnerability differentials across communities, sectors and provinces. Climate change will alter the frequency, intensity and predictability of climate hazards. Stronger heat waves, changes in flooding patterns, typhoons and freak cold snaps are just some of the changes that the country is beginning to experience, though there are large regional disparities. Climate change is also likely to cause slow-onset changes like expanding drought or sea level rise that will have profound effects on China's development. Shifts in the nature of extreme and slow-onset weather hazards, in conjunction with China's rapid socio-economic development, and land use and environmental change, are making it difficult to project future climate risk, especially the risk that might result from cascading disaster chains.

Chinese scientists are exploring how an increase in the number of extreme events (partially due to climate change), coupled with China's rapid development over the last 60 years, is leading to changes in loss of life and injuries, as well as economic, asset and livelihood loss and damages due to weather-related disasters. The recent droughts in northern China and the floods in parts of the Yangtze River and north-west regions have contributed to notable losses. The Chinese government is monitoring trends, researching regional adaptive capacity disparities, and developing new disaster risk management strategies that are described later in the chapter.

The following sections examine some of the trends in slow-onset events, disaster chains and singular disasters caused by extreme weather. Because China's environmental and socio-economic vulnerability varies greatly across its vast landscape, the impacts of climate change on these diverse regions are likewise very different, and it is useful to look at both national and regional trends.

Trends in slow-onset events

Over the past five decades, slow-onset meteorological disasters in China have shown a number of worrying trends. Shifts in seasons and extended droughts have been negatively impacting many key sectors, particularly water resource management and agriculture. Environmental degradation, combined with over-exploitation of water resources and drought, is aggravating water shortages in many regions (see Chapter 4); warmer temperatures and irregular precipitation also contribute to the shortages. In northern provinces, farmers are responding to seasonal shifts and warmer temperatures by planting further north, moving sowing and transplanting earlier or selecting seed varieties with longer growing seasons. While these strategies may prove adaptive in the long run, these choices are more sensitive to the occasional cold snap or snowstorm that will still occur over the next 20 or so years from the time of writing. Mechanisms for helping farmers and herders deal with shifting seasons, while still preparing for and recovering from extreme events, is challenging to China's policy makers (see Chapters 5, 8, 9 and 10).

The percentage of China's land area affected by heat and drought has also been increasing. Intensified seasonal droughts coupled with extremely high temperatures, such as the summer droughts along the Yangtze River and the winter and spring droughts in south and south-west China, are becoming more destructive. For example, the middle and lower reaches of the Yangtze River Basin suffered persistent high heat in 2003. Record highs of 45°C were observed in the south-western city of Chongqing in 2006, and the city of Chaoyang in north-east China recorded temperatures as high as 43°C in 2009. Droughts in northern China, which previously occurred mainly in spring, are now extending into the summer as the start of the monsoon is delayed. Extreme drought has been increasing in much of the north, and typically water-abundant south-west provinces (Yunnan, Sichuan and Guizhou) have seen repeated droughts since 2009 (Figure 3.2).

In addition to increased intensity of heat and drought, the land area affected by drought is expanding as well. The *meteorological drought area* (total land area affected by drought caused by weather-related, rather than man-made, factors) has been growing across the country, but it has increased most significantly over the long term in most of China's northern provinces (Figure 3.2). The basins of the Songhua, Liao, Hai and Yellow Rivers experienced a near-unprecedented cluster of droughts from the late 1990s to the early 2000s. However, most southern provinces have not shown substantial changes in meteorological drought area, and some in the south-west have actually seen a decline in the area impacted (PRC National Development and Reform Commission, 2011).

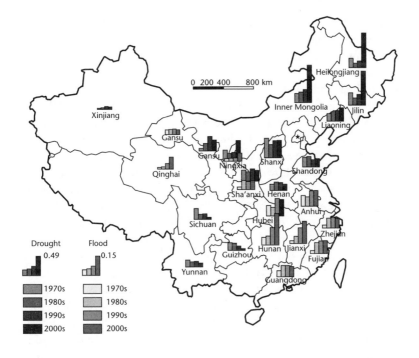

FIGURE 3.2 The proportion of crop areas affected by droughts and floods in each province in 1971–2010 (source: unpublished data from the National Disaster Reduction Center of China database)

Trends in extreme weather events

Extreme weather events such as heavy precipitation are becoming more frequent and more damaging across China. On the national level there have not been significant increases in the intensity and frequency of the heaviest rains since 1951;[4] on the regional level, however, the proportion of annual rainfall that comes from strong events has risen in many areas (Zhai et al., 2007; Min and Qian, 2008; Yang et al., 2008). This is consistent with trends seen in other parts of the world, with many areas experiencing more of their annual precipitation as extreme events with longer periods of drought between heavy rainstorms (IPCC, 2012). While the net effect is little to no change in total annual precipitation, the distributional shifts are having significant impacts on many systems. Evidence shows there have been increasing numbers of rainstorms and floods in the humid south and south-east, as well as in the very dry west and north-west regions of China, though the north has seen a decrease in the number of rainstorm days. (See Chapters 4 and 5 for greater detail on observed trends and projected changes in China's regional precipitation patterns.) The

Second National Assessment Report on Climate Change (PRC National Development and Reform Commission, 2011) found that floods have been on the rise in the middle and lower reaches of the Yangtze River in southern China. The assessment report also noted a decline in light rain days and an increase in stronger rain events nationwide.

Heavy precipitation events, in conjunction with land use changes and development, are altering flood risk around the country. Floods are occurring more frequently in southern China. Heavy rainfall events have increased in the middle and lower reaches of the Yangtze River and also in the south-east and north-west. In northern China, however, the flood situation has generally been improving, despite some increased flooding in recent years. The Huai River, running through the middle of eastern China, creates a dividing line of flood incidence based on extreme events with increasing numbers of rainstorm days to the south – especially in south-eastern river basins such as the Huai, Yangtze and Pearl River basins – and decreasing numbers of rainstorm days to the north (Chen *et al.*, 2010; Zhai *et al.*, 2007). In addition, the frequency of extreme rainfall events in western China has been increasing since the early 1960s (Min and Qian, 2008; Yang *et al.*, 2008). Snowmelt floods are also occurring more frequently in the mountainous, arid areas in north-west China. There have been increasingly frequent geological disasters such as debris flow and landslides triggered by local extreme precipitation events and by rapid land use development and change (Zheng, 2010; Zimmerli and Zhou, 2006; Long *et al.*, 2006).

Corresponding to increased strong rainstorms, the proportion of China's crop area affected by flooding each year has not only increased overall, but has shown more frequent and extreme damage and loss fluctuations (Figure 3.3).

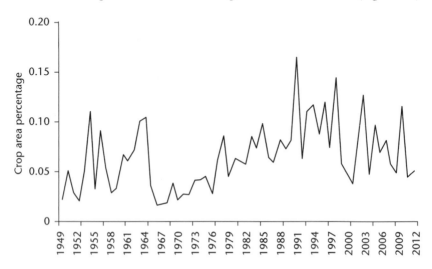

FIGURE 3.3 The percentage of crops affected by floods in China in 1949–2012 (source: NBS, 2009)

In some years, crop loss due to flooding was as high as 15% of China's total annual crop yield. The time between extreme fluctuations also decreased, meaning extensive crop loss due to flooding occurred more frequently with less time for recovery between floods. The average flooded area was 15.7 million hectares from 1991–1999, 1.7 times of that from 1950–1999 and two times of that from 1950–1990.

The middle and lower Yangtze River and areas of north-west China (especially Qinghai province) have experienced the most increases in flood-related crop losses. Though there has been an increase in flooding in the south and south-east of China, there has not been a significant change in the proportion of crops affected in south-east coastal areas, especially in Zhejiang, Fujian and Guangdong provinces.

China also experiences tropical storms and cyclones that cause significant damage. Tropical cyclones are unique extreme weather events that can trigger disaster chains through heavy rainfall, tidal flooding, storm surges and high winds. China's typhoons originate in the western North Pacific (WNP), which generates more tropical cyclones than any other region globally and also affects the distribution of rainfall across the entire East Asian Monsoon region. Many of China's coastal provinces are highly exposed to tropical cyclones. Increasing rates of urbanisation and rural-to-urban migration have led to a concentration of people, assets and infrastructure on China's coasts. Coastal cities like Hong Kong, Macau and Shanghai are particularly vulnerable to suffering harm during tropical cyclones and afterward as disaster chains magnify damages.

There is considerable decadal variation in the frequency, intensity (measured as sustained wind speed), duration and storm tracks of tropical cyclones in the WNP, with some scientists detecting small trends in the past few decades and others not, depending on which storm dataset is used (Lee *et al.*, 2010; Zhang *et al.*, 2009; Yokoi and Takayabu, 2013). According to some studies, the number of storms making landfall in eastern or southern China may have decreased slightly since 2000, but there are no discernible long-term trends in overall number and intensity of cyclones in the WNP (Lee *et al.*, 2010; Chen and Lin, 2013; Zhang *et al.*, 2009). There have been no significant trends in precipitation amount and intensity associated with cyclones as a whole for China, but regional disparities are occurring, with storm rainfall intensity in parts of south-eastern China possibly higher than in the past (Ying and Chen, 2009; NDRC, 2011). It is also difficult to detect trends in landfall location for tropical cyclones in China, with some studies indicating a potential decrease in the number of storms impacting the southern provinces, like Guangdong, but no clear changes along the central coast (Ying *et al.*, 2011). Considerable decadal variability in wind intensity has also been observed, with possible decreases in the number of very intense typhoons making landfall post-1970s (Wang and Ren, 2008).

Information about typhoon losses and damages are also incomplete, making it difficult to assess risk. Since 1983, the Chinese government has undertaken

TABLE 3.1 Major weather-related disasters in China, 2006–2013

Disaster event	Disaster type and mechanism	Impacts
2006 Sichuan and Chongqing *Severe drought*	High-magnitude, single hazard type: • This was the worst drought recorded in ~116-year record. • It was characterised by little rain, high rates evapotranspiration and high temperatures.	Chain effect: extreme drought led to fires, increased agricultural pests and diseases. More than 60 million people were affected to varying degrees, with ~150,000 relocated due to lack of drinking water and more than 300,000 falling ill. The extent of loss and damages has rarely been seen since founding of the People's Republic in 1949.
Early 2008 Southern regions *Severe snow and ice storms, freezing hazards*	High-magnitude, single hazard type: • A cold spell in subtropical southern China hit multiple provinces for weeks and was accompanied by above average precipitation that fell as snow and ice. • It was a 1-in-50-year incident in most areas and a 1-in-100-year event in the worst impacted areas.	Superposition effect: Snow and freezing weather coincided with the Spring Festival (Chinese New Year) travel rush. The very large volume of travellers strained local infrastructure, transportation networks, water and electricity supply and social management that already has to meet the needs of one of the most densely populated regions of China. Subtropical agriculture and forestry dominate the area and are not used to cold. The weather hazard caused these strained systems to collapse. The freeze affected 21 provinces and caused 133 casualties. 1.66 million people were relocated. 11.9 million hectares of crops were affected, with 1.7 million of these a total crop failure. 485,000 houses collapsed and 1.7 million were damaged.
2009–2013 Five southwest provinces *Severe drought*	High-magnitude, single hazard type: • Extremely low precipitation totals were coupled with abnormally warm conditions lasted for several years. • The drought peaked in winter months in most areas.	Chain effect: extreme drought affecting farming, animal husbandry, fish breeding, poultry, service industries and exacerbating environmental degradation. More than 60 million and ~30 million livestock suffered drinking water shortages. Widespread crop losses and damage. 18.2 million people required temporary living assistance.

	Disaster chain	Chain effect
2010 Zhouqu, Gansu province *Large debris flows*	Disaster chain: • The city experienced extremely heavy precipitation (90 mm in 40 minutes) in an arid climate with annual average precipitation of 510 mm. • Precipitation on degraded soils and lack of maintenance in flood infrastructure led to the worst debris flow disaster since 1949.	Chain effect: extreme rainfall triggered flash floods, landslides and debris flow, which dammed a lake. The dammed lake submerged 70% of a county for 20 days. There were more than 1,700 casualties, 300 houses destroyed and many more flooded. Transportation, water and power supplies and communication lines were disrupted across the whole city.
2011 Middle and lower Yangtze River *Drought followed by flood*	Multiple disasters: • Drought struck first, with 105 consecutive days of no rain. Precipitation was half of the normal amount. • The drought was immediately followed by heavy rain that triggered flash floods and debris flows.	Multiple: Two disasters occurred successively and overlapped in space. Droughts exacerbated existing soil erosion and destabilisation, making conditions right for debris flows during heavy rain. 100 people were killed in debris flows. About 40% of counties were hit by flooding that had earlier suffered from drought.
21 July 2012 Beijing *Torrential rainstorm*	Disaster chain: • This was the heaviest rainstorm since 1951. It was a 1-in-500-year rain event on city-wide scale and a 1-in-100-year event in the downtown area. • Rainfall triggered flash flooding.	Chain effect: rainfall triggers flash flooding. The underlying vulnerability of urban hazard-bearing bodies magnifies the effects. 79 people killed, about 10,000 houses destroyed and a large number of public infrastructure works damaged or destroyed. Increased public attention and awareness.
July 2013 Arid and semi-arid regions of northwest China *Extreme rainstorm*	Disaster chain: • Unprecedented precipitation in records since 1951 exceeded 1-in-100-year events. The recorded maximum rainfall is 607.7 mm in Yan Chuan County in Shanxi province (four times the July average) and 894.5 mm in the town of Niang Niang Ba in Gansu province (32% more than total precipitation in first half of year). • Torrential rains on degraded loess soils caused flash floods and mudslides.	Chain effects: Soil erosion and destabilisation, coupled with extreme rainfall, lead to flash floods and debris flows. More than 100 people were killed or unaccounted for at the time of writing, 200,000 houses collapsed. There was significant public infrastructure damage.

Source: Information provided by the National Disaster Reduction Center of China.

systematic collection of casualty and economic loss data; such information is spotty before then, making trend assessment difficult (Zheng, 2010). Despite the shorter tropical cyclone loss and damages record, economic costs associated with such storms have demonstrably increased. Typhoon-induced floods and storm surges, boosted by rising sea levels, are posing an increasing threat to coastal areas. Rapid infrastructure development and urban growth in coastal areas are exposing more people and their assets to tropical cyclones, increasing their vulnerability and risk, as indicated by the economic losses. There are considerable provincial disparities in loss and damage, reflecting the state of disaster resilience in each province.

Because of an increase in economic prosperity and an overstrained infrastructure without requisite incorporation of disaster planning into building codes, development plans or adequate enforcement, parts of China are becoming increasing vulnerable to the effects of severe typhoons. Any intensification of typhoons due to climate change is likely to have a significant impact on China's coasts. Being able to project those changes and adapt accordingly would reduce typhoon impacts; addressing current vulnerabilities and risk can begin building resilience. Climate and weather models can be used to project possible effects on typhoon patterns under different future climate scenarios. The range of potential climate shifts projected by the models can then be used in planning national and local adaptation measures.

The case study below examines research using a regional climate model to project possible changes in typhoon patterns under different emission scenarios. The research was conducted under the Adapting to Climate Change in China I (ACCC I) programme, a four-year, multidisciplinary programme commissioned by the *National Adaptation Strategy* planning committee to study the effects of climate change in various sectors and make practical, science-based recommendations for climate change adaptation policy.

Case study: climate change and tropical cyclone risk – evidence from a regional climate model

Projecting how climate change may alter the strength, location and formation of tropical cyclones is extremely important in helping coastal areas build climate resilience. This case study presents the projections of future tropical cyclone behaviour based on results from a regional climate model (PRECIS) run over the WNP domain. The model is driven by various perturbations of HadCM3, a global climate model, running the medium emission scenario A1B.[5] Each perturbation of HadCM3 produces an ensemble member (QUMP) and allows for investigating a range of possible future climate change.

Tropical cyclones are intense, spinning, large-scale (>1,000 km) storms that form over tropical ocean regions. Storm formation is dependent upon a number of conditions over the open ocean, normally including a minimum sea surface temperature (SST) of 26.5°C. The strength (intensity) of a tropical cyclone depends on warmer SSTs: as temperatures over the ocean rise, evaporation rates increase and fuel the winds of a cyclone, making it stronger.

Climate change-induced temperature shifts on a global and regional basis alter precipitation patterns and oceanic and atmospheric circulation. Together with warming oceans, these changes are expected to affect the frequency, intensity, timing and landfall distribution of typhoons. SST increases of about 0.5°C since the 1950s have been observed in the tropics (Hartmann *et al.*, 2013), and average global SSTs are projected to rise 1–3°C by the end of the twenty-first century (Collins *et al.*, 2013). Regional projections for SST changes vary greatly, with some ocean areas expected to warm more or at faster rates than others (Xie *et al.*, 2010).

Modelling climate impacts on tropical cyclones in the north-west Pacific

Projecting changes in the characteristics of tropical cyclones due the effects of climate change is not an easy task. Tropical cyclones vary from storm to storm, with their characteristics linked to complex atmospheric and ocean phenomena (e.g. the El Niño Oscillation) and temperatures. Projecting changes in these phenomena, while difficult, forms an important area of climate research around tropical cyclones.

In this study, potential changes in tropical cyclone characteristics were estimated from an ensemble suite of climate projections simulated by the PRECIS regional climate model and tracked using a cyclone tracking programme (Hodges, 1994; Hoskins and Hodges, 2002). The programme locates and tracks tropical cyclones using winds and *vorticity* (a measure of wind rotation in a horizontal slice of the atmosphere) data at intervals of six hours.

PRECIS' ability to simulate tropical cyclones was first tested by having it simulate storms over the WNP for 1996–2005, for which there exists good observational data on the number and characteristics of tropical cyclones. Certain tropical cyclone characteristics, such as wind speed thresholds, are not directly modelled by PRECIS (it uses simulated vorticity at a specific height above sea level), so its validity was tested by comparing the number of storms it simulated to the actual number. While the model tends to underestimate the number of tropical cyclones in any given year, overall the model average trend of 22.3 per year is reasonably close to the observed mean of 23.5 per year over 1996–2005, as seen in Figure 3.4.

Once PRECIS' ability in replicating historical tropical cyclones was confirmed, investigators projected how climate change might alter storms. Because of the difficulty and uncertainty in projecting tropical cyclone activities in the very far future (Knutson *et al.*, 2010) only projections for the period 2013–2042 were made. These projections were then tracked across the WNP using the

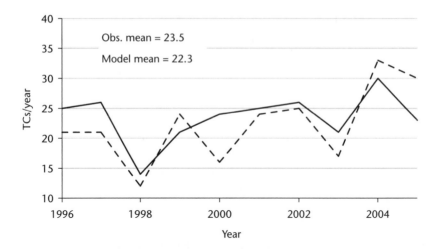

FIGURE 3.4 Number of tropical cyclones generated in the western North Pacific each year between 1996–2005, as simulated by the model (dotted line) and the observational record (solid line)

cyclone tracking programme and compared to observed data (years 1961–1990) of tropical cyclones with a minimum life span of two days that travelled at least 1,000 km. Any changes in number of storms, intensity, frequency, life span, location and precipitation between the past and the future projected storms were noted.

Climate change impacts to tropical cyclones 2013–2042

The ensemble of projections shows that there is some uncertainty about how climate change will alter the characteristics of tropical cyclones over the next 30 years. Though there is an increase in precipitation amounts according to all of the projections, and the genesis and path of storms is likely to change, the types of changes in the frequency, lifetime and strength (intensity) of such storms are not clear. The uncertainty in tropical cyclone changes over the near term found in this study are consistent with other investigations over the WNP (Lee *et al.*, 2010; Yokoi *et al.*, 2012). This uncertainty is partially due to the way climate models simulate land–ocean–atmosphere interactions and our uncertainty of continued and future emission scenarios.

A number of tropical cyclone characteristics might change. Figure 3.5a shows the *genesis density* (location of storm formation and how many tend to form there) from 1961 to 1990 (left) and 2013 to 2042 (right). In the near future, the locations of genesis are expected to remain largely unchanged, but the number forming (density) in each might shift. There are two clear *maxima genesis centres* (clear points were large numbers of storms form) – the South China Sea and the

TABLE 3.2 Projected changes in tropical cyclone characteristics over 2013–2042 when compared with observed storms from 1961–1990. The results are based on multiple members – Q0, Q1, Q8, Q10 and Q12 – of the QUMP ensemble used in the PRECIS regional climate model

	Frequency	Lifetime	Strength	Location (genesis, track)	Precipitation
Q0	No change	Shorter	Stronger	Change	Increase
Q1	Decrease	Shorter	Stronger	Change	Increase
Q8	Increase	Longer	Stronger	Change	Increase
Q10	Decrease	Longer	Weaker	Change	Increase
Q12	Increase	Longer	Weaker	Change	Increase
Ensemble Mean	*No change*	*Longer*	*Stronger*	*Change*	*Increase*

Bismarck Sea – that might shift. The South China Sea centre may move slightly south-east according to the projections, while more cyclones might form in the centre near the Bismarck Sea. Additionally, the cyclogenesis centre that is currently south-east of the Philippines is likely to produce more storms. The two panels in Figure 3.5b show changes in *mean strength* (where tropical cyclones tend to weaken or intensify) over the past (left) and the near-future (right). In comparison with the past, tropical cyclones may become stronger near the coastline area of China and the South China Sea. With regard to *track density* (storm path and where more storms tend to travel), the main paths of the majority of storms is not likely to change much in the future, but they may expand eastward somewhat, as seen in Figure 3.5c. The number of storms following a particular track (density) is expected to remain constant over the South China Sea and the region near the East China Sea, but this may increase south-east of the Philippines. Finally, Figure 3.5d shows tropical cyclone lysis (storm death) over the past (left) and the future (right). More tropical cyclones might dissipate near the South China Sea, as well as the region between 30–40°N and 150–170°E, in the future when compared with the past.

The types of changes projected in the number and characteristics of tropical cyclones in the WNP, while showing some uncertainty, will nonetheless have significant impacts for China due to its current vulnerabilities and the dynamic socio-economic and ecological processes that may exacerbate future vulnerability, particularly in coastal areas. Tropical cyclone formation processes in the WNP influence the development of the East Asia Monsoon System and its rainfall distribution, so any changes to precipitation would have significant implications for the populations of East Asia, impacting everything from food security to energy generation. Tropical cyclones temporarily raise coastal sea levels through storm surges and can inundate wetlands and coastal areas; flooding can be significant when storm surges coincide with high tides, leading to loss of life

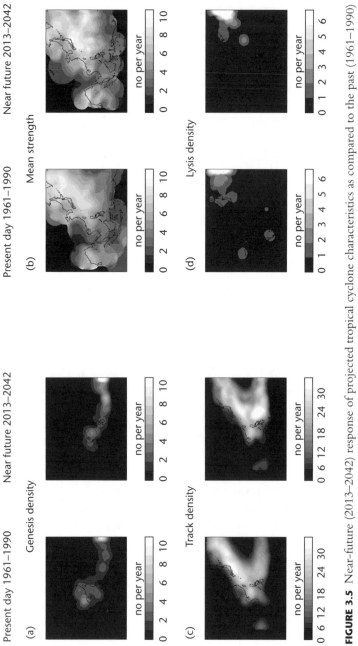

FIGURE 3.5 Near-future (2013–2042) response of projected tropical cyclone characteristics as compared to the past (1961–1990)

and damage to property. Coastal wetlands are currently threatened in many areas of China by pollution, development, natural resource and water use; climate change is one more threat to their continued existence. Yet, they are extremely important as natural protective barriers against storm surges and tidal flooding. Long-term changes in the frequency, intensity, timing and distribution of tropical cyclones may also impact biotic functions (e.g. community structure, extinction rates and biodiversity) in marine communities, particularly near shore.

China's response: policy and practice

China experiences numerous weather-related hazards and suffers significant damages each year (CRED, 2014). As a result, the government is prioritising disaster risk reduction measures, and it has been investing significant time, money and resources in disaster relief response and, more recently, on prevention. However, China's legal and policy frameworks, administrative structures and practical efforts for disaster risk management (DRM) are complex. Mainstreaming DRM into other sectors and development plans remains difficult due to a legacy of reactionary disaster response rather than prevention.

Despite these challenges, China has made a number of recent shifts in disaster risk management, including: a stronger focus on disaster risk reduction, while strengthening disaster response and relief; moves to align legislation and policy on climate change with its DRM policies; better incorporation of science-based adaptation measures into its disaster risk management system; and the recognition of climate adaptation importance on a national level. It has also, for the first time in the history of its socio-economic development plans,[6] made adaptation a national priority as outlined in the *National Adaptation Strategy* (see Chapters 2 and 11), and mandates the various government agencies that deal with disasters in China to begin considering adaptation in their policies and programmes.

This section examines the administrative structures that are responsible for disaster risk management, including the current legal and policy frameworks that address disaster, and briefly examines recent developments and improvements in DRM in China. It also provides a short overview of China's existing administrative structures for addressing disaster management. These structures and legal frameworks form much of the foundation for its adaptation responses. It then discusses how the DRM system in China is responding to the effects of climate change and what China has done to date to integrate adaptation measures as part of its DRM strategy.

Administrative structures

As a disaster unfolds, China deploys relief and disaster response efforts through a number of national mechanisms and stakeholders. These are characterised by a unified central leadership that divides tasks among national ministries and local governments. The National Committee for Disaster Reduction, the State Flood Control and Drought Relief Headquarters, the National Forest Fire Prevention Headquarters, the National Disaster Relief Coordination Office, the Ministry of Civil Affairs and other responsible agencies are led by the State Council[7] and act as coordinating bodies for the organisation of disaster reduction and relief. Other important roles are played by the People's Liberation Army, armed police, militias and public security police, as well as civil society organisations and volunteers. In addition to the coordinating bodies, an amalgamation of various government agencies share responsibility for disaster response and relief as it relates to their core mission. For example, agencies such as the Ministry of Agriculture and the Ministry of Health deal with disasters that impact agriculture and health, respectively. Table 3.3 shows examples of the work of some of government agencies involved in DRM. The agencies listed represent key sectors the central government has prioritised because of their importance to adaptation.

To reduce the impacts of disasters, China has systems in place to respond to emergencies, mobilise communities, spread information, maintain a reserve of relief supplies, and coordinate rescue and relief efforts. However, most of the impacts of extreme weather events are felt most sharply at the local level, and there are wide discrepancies between and within provinces in disaster risk reduction and response implementation and coordination, as discussed in Part III. There is an urgent need to establish regional mechanisms for assessing and responding to disaster chains and to ensure adaptation approaches at the provincial and county levels are fully integrated with the national system.

Disaster-resilient communities

China's smallest units of disaster response, local communities, are on the front lines of natural disasters and climate change. A critical way to reduce losses and narrow regional gaps in vulnerability to natural disasters is to build the capacity of these communities. China has begun some pilot programmes in community-based disaster prevention across the country. The aim of these programmes is to help local communities reduce their disaster risks and fall under the rather lengthy banner of the *National Integrated Disaster Reduction Demonstration Community Activities* (NIDRDCA).

The NIDRDCA is comprised of six national programmes that were rolled out between 2008 and 2012 with the aim of setting up demonstration communities for integrated disaster reduction all over China. Run jointly by the National Committee for Disaster Reduction and the Ministry of Civil Affairs, the programmes drew on international experiences in community-based disaster risk management (CBDRM) and adaptation, but also incorporate local conditions and experiences. Though similar to other CBDRM programmes around

TABLE 3.3 Recent efforts to improve adaptive capacities in China's disaster risk management system by various government agencies

Agency	Recent disaster-related work
Ministry of Civil Affairs	• Improved the *National Emergency Plan on Natural Disasters*. • Organised national integrated disaster risk reduction strategies. • Enacted and facilitated implementation of the *National Disaster Prevention and Mitigation Plan*. • Contributed to the establishment of a geological disaster prevention system across the country. • Further improved regulations on the institutional setup for disaster reduction and relief. • Launched over 1,273 model communities. • Worked with the Ministry of Finance to allocate GPB1.17 billion as a central disaster relief fund.
National Commission for Disaster Reduction	• Enhanced the monitoring and warning mechanism for various types of disasters, especially for extreme weather and climate conditions as part of the climate disaster early monitoring and warning system. • Continued work on the *National Flood Control and Drought Relief Command System*. • Built a risk assessment system for rainstorms, floods and droughts to shore up cities' capacities to withstand extreme weather conditions.
Ministry of Housing and Urban Development	• Published circulars to guide urban flooding prevention and mitigation.
Ministry of Water Resources	• Facilitated non-engineering measures for mountain flash food prevention and control in 2,058 counties. • Facilitated Phase 2 of the *National Flood Control and Drought Relief Command System*. • Conducted flood impact assessment and risk mapping. • Revised flooding and water allocation plan for major river basins.
State Forestry Administration	• Developed the *National Forest Fire Emergency Plan*. • Defined responsibility for hazardous species control among local governments. • Covered 2.65 million km² in 16 provinces with airborne forest fire-fighting for an 87% control rate in 2012.
State Oceanic Administration	• Established a marine disaster reduction system. • Identified maritime risks for major marine projects. • Conducted risk zoning.

continued

TABLE 3.3 Continued

Agency	Recent disaster-related work
Chinese Meteorology Administration	• Helped local governments develop meteorological defence plans by facilitating climate disaster risk identification. • Scaled up climate change assessment in key regions and river basins. • Scaled up technical support for adaptation in featured industries. • Set up a granular forecast service for rainstorms and flooding in major cities.
Ministry of Health	• Issued the *National Health Emergency Response Plan for Natural Disasters*. • Developed health emergency working plans for various disasters. • Published circulars on health emergency response to heat waves and extreme wintry conditions.

Source: PRC State Council, 2008.

the world, China's CBDRM programmes are unique in their focus on exploring the needs of economic migrants as a floating and vulnerable population, along with populations traditionally deemed vulnerable – the elderly, sick, pregnant and poor. That the programmes pay special attention to building the capacity of migrant populations within pilot communities is significant, given their geographic mobility and traditionally low status in Chinese society (despite their large role in the country's economic growth). The focus on migrants marks a growing acceptance, and the need to understand the unique and diverse vulnerabilities, of this population. Chapter 10 discusses more of migrant workers' vulnerabilities and the historical socio-political contexts that have exacerbated their vulnerability to a variety of hazards including and beyond weather disasters.

China's programmes incorporate international principles of mixing 'soft' and 'hard' disaster management approaches, termed in Chinese disaster parlance 'hardware' (such as shelters and storage for relief materials) and 'software' (such as actions to raise risk awareness and strengthen disaster reduction skills). Table 3.4 compares China's evolving CBDRM approach to its historical DRM approaches, as well as elements of international CBDRM approaches it has borrowed and adapted to its specific community contexts.

In order to participate in the programme, applicant communities must meet criteria as outlined in the *Standards for National Integrated Disaster Reduction Demonstration Community*. These criteria are outlined in Table 3.5.

By the end of 2012, a total of 4,116 communities had established community disaster relief organisations and management mechanisms. As part of this, the

TABLE 3.4 Comparison of community-based disaster risk management (CBDRM) models in China to China's historical DRM approach, and elements common to CBDRM implemented in other countries

	China's historical disaster risk management	CBDRM pilots in China	CBDRM abroad
Target	To reduce direct losses caused by disasters, meet the urgent needs of affected areas and help these areas to return to normal conditions.	To reduce direct losses caused by disasters, meet the urgent needs of affected areas and help these areas to return to normal conditions.	To reduce direct losses caused by disasters, meet the urgent needs of affected areas and help these areas to return to normal conditions, or to improve conditions.
Disaster-affected body	Focus on individuals and families.	Establish community-based disaster reduction leadership and execution agencies and focus on the disaster risk and reduction capacity of residents, families and communities.	Focus on individual, family and community capacities for disaster preparedness, and strengthen the organisation of activities.
Participation initiative	Community residents are helpless victims.	Community residents are those leading and executing community disaster risk reduction activities.	Community residents are active participants in community-based disaster reduction and preparedness activities.
Role positioning	Community residents are passive recipients of external assistance.	Community residents create and own participatory disaster risk reduction initiatives.	Through personal involvement, community residents use and further improve their abilities.

continued

TABLE 3.4 Continued

	China's historical disaster risk management	CBDRM pilots in China	CBDRM abroad
Decision-making participation	Disaster management agencies decide the needs and priorities of affected families and communities.	Broad community participation in capacity building and decision making is encouraged.	Members of the community participate in the decision-making process and determine their own priority needs and disaster risk reduction measures.
Disaster risk assessment	External experts assess disaster damage and needs.	Community members are encouraged to participate in the hazard and risk assessment, identification of vulnerable populations (particularly migrant groups), and infrastructure and disaster risk map preparation.	Community members are encouraged to participate in the hazard and risk assessment, identification of vulnerable populations, including accounting for differences in gender, culture and age, as well as the special needs of children.
Responsibility allocation	Disaster management agencies are responsible for providing assistance.	Disaster risk management is everyone's responsibility, and disaster management agencies take a leading role.	Disaster risk management is everyone's responsibility, and disaster management agencies play a supporting role.

Source: Zhou and Zhang, 2013.

TABLE 3.5 Criteria for National Integrated Disaster Reduction communities in China

	A qualified demonstration community should:
Leadership	Establish leadership institutions. Establish agencies for execution. Establish special working groups with clear divisions of labour. Bring together various community groups and leaders. Show particular concern for vulnerable groups (migrants, the sick, pregnant women and the elderly).
Management	Be managed by community members. Have staff who are residents with knowledge of local conditions and future needs. Ensure staff are supervised by other community residents. Ensure staff are subject to a management appraisal system. Ensure residents' rights to take part in and make decisions about major events in their community.
Participation	Ensure community disaster manager, community residents and migrants are all participants in disaster reduction and community building, each with their own clear roles. Have community disaster management agencies plan and organise community disaster reduction activities. Make residents and migrant populations responsible for disaster risk assessment, relocation, guaranteeing relief materials and reporting on disasters.
Planning	Map disaster risks based on integrated assessments. Include assessments of potential disasters (hazard risk analyses) and the populations and housing vulnerable to these disasters (vulnerability analyses). Ensure disaster risk mapping is supported by disaster risk assessment theory.
Approach	Take a long-term approach to disaster reduction. Reduce vulnerability in the long run. Improve the ability of residents to respond to disasters. Establish a secure, disaster-resistant and sustainably developing community. Take into account disaster reduction in the short term. Include organising education and training, building infrastructure, and improving local awareness of and skill in disaster reduction.

Source: NDRC, 2013.

communities are currently conducting, or have already carried out, disaster risk assessments; developing emergency rescue plans; improving disaster reduction education and training; building and improving the infrastructure for disaster prevention and reduction; started improving residents' skills in and awareness of disaster reduction; and encouraging wider participation. As a result, capacities for community-based disaster reduction have improved significantly in some locations, especially in eastern coastal regions, along the Yangtze River and in China's major urban centres, including Beijing and nearby cities, the Yangtze River Delta around Shanghai and the Pearl River Delta in Guangdong (Figure 3.6). Yet, more comprehensive reflections on which approaches are working well (and which ones require modifications) are still required, and initial assessments of the Chinese CBDRM model, like many international CBDRM projects, indicate that it does not yet adequately consider climate change. In subsequent rounds of China's CBDRM programmes, more is work is needed to build public and disaster management agencies' awareness about how climate change might increase the severity of certain disaster risks and to begin taking a view to building long-term resilience.

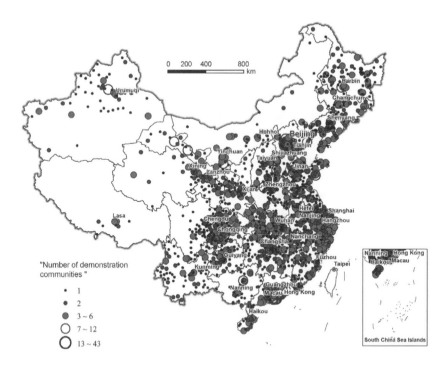

FIGURE 3.6 Distribution of demonstration communities for integrated disaster risk reduction (end of 2012)

Evolution of disaster risk reduction in China – policies and regulations

Until recently, disaster response and relief was managed on a limited per-disaster basis and according to the capacity of the national army. Past strategies focused on post-disaster relief (organising donations, sending money and supplies to affected refugees and local governments, etc.), and disaster response – the government's actions in the immediate aftermath of a disaster. Since the turn of the millennium, however, China has been moving toward facilitating cooperation and communication between relevant government departments and ministries at all levels, transitioning from its traditional 'one law for one event' principle – which entailed passing new legislation to govern the response to each specific major disaster after it occurred – to centralised disaster risk reduction planning that aims to not only respond to disasters in a comprehensive, coordinated and effective fashion, but also to reduce the risk of loss and harm through preventative measures. The evolution in China's recent DRR policies and regulations are outlined in Table 3.6.

Though the development of China's legal framework for disaster risk reduction is still ongoing today, a number of laws and regulations address managing the risks of climate-related disasters have been promulgated as just discussed. These types of policies, laws and activities move China toward a more holistic, cooperative and integrated DRM strategy that could help provide a foundation and learning platform for developing and integrating climate change related policies and activities, if better linkages are made between the two areas.

Adapting disaster risk reduction to the impacts of climate change

As described previously, China's CBDRM and other DRM programmes do not yet adequately account for projected shifts in the frequency and intensity of slow-onset and extreme weather events due to climate change, though they are beginning the process. However, the central government's national planning committees are increasingly emphasising the need to address the rising risk of disaster in a changing climate. The *National Integrated Disaster Prevention and Reduction Plan* (NIDPRP) for 2011–2015 recognises increasing disaster risks from climate change, stating,

> the risk of natural disaster has continued to increase during the period of the *Twelfth Five Year Plan* [2011–2015] in the context of a changing global climate, and much remains to be done in disaster prevention and reduction. Droughts, floods, typhoons, low temperatures, snow and ice, heat waves, dust storms, pests, diseases and other disasters are on the rise, and there is a continued risk of frequent land collapse, landslides, mudslides, flash floods and other disasters.

TABLE 3.6 Evolution of China's disaster risk reduction policies and regulations

Policy	Intent
Disaster Reduction Plan of the People's Republic of China (1998–2010)	First centrally-planned and coordinated legislative action on national DRR guidelines and measures.
Signatory to *Hyogo Framework for Action* (2005–2015)	Ten-year plan of action promulgated by the United Nations International Strategy for Disaster Reduction that provides concepts and guidelines for reducing disaster losses and improving disaster resilience.
Eleventh Five Year Plan (2007)	Requires local governments to begin mainstreaming disaster risk reduction into their social and economic development plans.
National Emergency Response Law (2007)	First national level law on disaster response to natural disasters, accidents, public health emergencies and public security events.
Regulation on Relief of Natural Disasters (2010)	First national level law regulating disaster relief.
Meteorological Defence Plan (2010)	China Meteorological Agency (CMA) and National Development and Reform Commission jointly release plan aiming for 50% reduction in weather-disaster casualties and ratio of ensuing economic losses to GDP.
Twelfth Five Year Plan (2011)	Integrated disaster prevention and reduction tasks are elevated to a separate chapter and priority policy area within national level social and economic development plans.
National Integrated Disaster Prevention and Reduction Plan for 2011–2015 – NIDPRP (2011)	Plan has five priority areas: 1 Strengthen disaster prevention and early warning. 2 More research on disaster chains and interactions between society and disaster risk under climate change. 3 Better inter-agency collaboration and communication, and to increase management efficiency. 4 Increase non-governmental actors (e.g. social organisations and the public). 5 Specific, quantifiable relief objectives.
National Natural Disaster Relief Contingency Plan (2011)	Capacity building efforts are bolstered, particularly around early warning, drought relief and interdepartmental emergency response.

It goes on to stress that 'there are new changes in the spatial and temporal distribution of these natural disasters, the extent of losses, and the intensity and extent of their impact. Disasters are becoming more sudden, more abnormal, and increasingly more difficult to forecast' (PRC State Council, 2011).

Unregulated urban development means that cities' overloaded infrastructure, combined with the stressors of climate change, is struggling to cope with the increasing onslaught of these events.[8] As discussed in Chapter 2, the country's vast rural areas, especially in central and western China, lag socially and economically behind urban centres, and disaster resilience among rural communities is weak. In both urban and rural regions, the risk of secondary disasters caused by natural disasters is high, but the changing climate is driving these risks even higher.

Many of the mechanisms for dealing with these extreme events in China are already in place (as mentioned above); however, they have been formed on the basis of historical climate data, rather than the possible future scenarios under climate change, and therefore do not take into consideration the expected changes in variability and extremity. This means China is inherently underequipped to manage the risk of disasters to come. Nevertheless, as adaptation becomes an increasing priority for the Chinese, the disaster sector is taking steps to incorporate adaptive measures into its disaster risk reduction process.

China is working to upgrade its systems for monitoring and managing disaster risks, bringing them in line with the worldwide trend to gradually standardise its assessments of disaster risk and base them on qualitative and quantitative modelling. The national vision for research and development of technologies for risk assessment, monitoring, early warning and emergency response is detailed in the *National Outlines for Medium and Long-Term Planning for Scientific and Technological Development (2006–2020)*. This strategy is reinforced by the NIDPRP, which specifically requires the establishment of 'a national and regional integrated disaster risk assessment index system and assessment system, study of integrated risk assessment methods for natural disasters and critical hazard conditions, and implementation of an integrated risk assessment pilot and demonstration.'

Different departments of the central government have varying disaster risk reduction management strategies according to their respective functions. The Ministry of Civil Affairs is responsible for disaster risk assessment, for example, while the China Meteorological Administration (CMA), the Ministry of Land and Resources and the State Forestry Administration each produce specialised forecasts and warnings relevant to their sector. Some government departments are also taking the initiative to develop climate adaptation measures under the scope of their particular mandates. For example, in 2009, the CMA promulgated measures for climate feasibility studies as a sector-specific regulation based on the *Law of the People's Republic of China on Meteorological Services*. Land use planning and construction projects are supposed to conduct feasibility studies to assess their suitability for local climate conditions, risk and potential impacts on altering the risks for existing or planned projects. The feasibility studies are now mandated in planning for urban and rural development, major infrastructure projects, major construction projects for regional economic development, and large projects such as for developing solar power.

This regulation is the first in China to explicitly stipulate climate change impact and risk assessment in major construction projects. However, because it ranks low on the legislative hierarchy, it lacks legally binding force or authority over other government departments, and therefore any risk assessment studies, in practice, serve as a reference point for decision-making by local authorities only. It will not be an effective adaptation policy until it has national backing or is adopted as national legislation, though it is a significant step in the right direction.

Authorities in charge of water resources, agriculture and other areas have also conducted considerable research on DRM and early warnings, as have a number of academic research institutions (Zou *et al.*, 2011). One of China's major steps forward has been the increasing use of satellite data and other remote sensing tools to provide a more immediate and complete picture of disaster risks. Having sound scientific backing for any adaptation measures adopted is a priority for China, and studies are currently being rolled out to develop an adaptation-orientated disaster risk assessment and management mechanism, including technical methodology, assessment procedures and technical specifications. Some examples of science-based efforts include a recently-developed meteorological disaster atlas and risk assessments for typhoons, rainstorms and drought, among other major disasters (refer to the case study), as well as comprehensive climate change impact assessment reports for the Yangtze River Basin, East China, Yunnan Province, Boyang Lake and the Three Gorges Dam area. Each of these includes analysis of each area's respective climate change risks and recommended adaptation measures.

Assessments still need to be expanded to understand socio-economic vulnerability and risk, and better integration efforts must be made between these and biophysical impact assessments in order to mainstream adaptation considerations into policy and practice (see also Chapter 1). Furthermore, many of the adaptation measures currently considered focus largely on engineering and infrastructural solutions like reservoirs and flood protection works (see Chapters 4 and 11). If stronger integration of assessment approaches can be achieved, and lessons and experiences from the 'software' options trialled in the CBDRM pilot community programmes incorporated, China may begin considering broader suites of adaptation policies and actions.

Integrating adaptation challenges into disaster risk management

Though China is practised at responding to extreme events with a single cause and direct results, developing disaster risk management strategies – including disaster prediction, risk reduction and relief – that take into account the multiple variables and factors in these more complex disasters is a new research frontier for Chinese scientists. For this reason, it is very important to take into consideration the overall impacts of all elements of a disaster chain when developing measures. In planning and modelling disaster chain events, the fullness of the 'magnifying' effect of disaster chains and the impacts of non-weather-related factors, such as geology, infrastructure and demographic trends, should be prioritised. Mechanisms for improving regional preparedness and response to disaster chains need to be explored, rather than following the current fragmentary system. Better monitoring, iterative vulnerability and forward-looking climate risk assessments, in conjunction with a focus on a participatory understanding of the unique socio-economic, political and environmental conditions in a location, can assist in predicting and preventing or lessening the occurrence of disaster chains. However, better coordination of social and physical disaster science is needed before disaster strategies can move beyond a reactionary state toward building resilience.

Despite the significant progress of the last few years, climate change will bring new challenges for China's disaster management sector, and there is still much to be done to develop an optimally effective and flexible disaster risk reduction system. One of the major weaknesses in the current disaster management system in China is its lack of strong centralised coordination and communication for disaster management as a whole. Officially, the responsibility lies with the State Council, but in practicality it is shared amongst a number of agencies and departments. Each department is tasked with fulfilling disaster reduction objectives as it relates to its central mission but does not necessarily coordinate its objectives with other departments and agencies.

China's legal frameworks, however, have seen improvements in recent years. Perhaps the most significant policy document to date that links disaster risk management and reduction to adaptation is the *National Adaptation Strategy* or NAS. Disaster risk management and reduction are not identified as priority sectors in their own right; however, disaster risk reduction and management are core themes that run through all of the priority sectors.[9] For example, priority tasks for coastal zones and maritime include: strengthening of marine disaster monitoring and early warning; improving the monitoring system for sea level changes and ocean disasters to cover all coastal zones and their associated waters; focusing on integrated monitoring, forecasting and early warning of storm surges, waves, sea ice, red tides, salt tides, coastal erosion and other marine disasters; and building capacity for emergency response services.

In highlighting the vulnerability of the urban coastal cities and provinces to extreme weather events, the NAS designates Shanghai and Guangdong as pilot project regions. Work in Shanghai will focus on addressing losses resulting from extreme weather and climate events, including sea level rise, with a focus integrating climate change into urban planning and development. This also includes a proposed revision of urban protection standards, especially those concerning adaptation infrastructures such as urban flood prevention, drainage, power supply, water and gas services and communications. In addition, existing facilities are to be renovated, and new ones will be built, in accordance with the new standards. Guangdong has been designated as the pilot area for the establishment of urban disaster response systems for typhoons and storm surges. The focus is to strengthen the monitoring, early warning and risk management of urban disasters including development of multi-sector emergency plans, and urban typhoon defence shall be disseminated in schools and communities. Yunnan Province has been designated as the pilot for disaster response systems in rural areas. The initial adaptation focus in this province is to address increased risk of flash floods, landslides and mudslides. Responses will include the development of rural monitoring and early warning systems, disaster response systems and disaster prevention information systems.

The NAS is an important step towards integrating disaster risk reduction and management across key sectors. Adaptation to climate change that is fully integrated with both short-term disaster relief and long-term disaster risk reduction will benefit China and could work toward improving overall socio-economic development goals. The current disaster management system is very familiar with the single-cause disasters that have clear, straightforward effects. However, as the climate changes, unpredictable and complex disaster chains are becoming more common, where one extreme weather or slow-onset event sets off a series of related disasters. To date, disaster risk assessments have not paid enough attention to climate change and are unable to calculate the risks associated with disaster chains. Yet climate disruption could lead to more frequent and challenging disaster events. China urgently needs new approaches to account for the risks of disaster chains, along with integrated response measures to address them. As the impacts of climate change worsen, China's national disaster risk reduction plans should be carefully designed to include response to disaster chain events. More importantly, China's national and provincial plans need to iteratively expand vulnerability and risk assessment, and to work to address underlying vulnerabilities to enhance capacities and resilience to prevent or reduce impacts from happening in the first place.

Notes

1 Zhouqu was one of the areas hardest hit by the Wenchuan earthquake on 12 May 2008. This loosened the surrounding mountains, which are prone to collapse. It would have taken three to five years before the mountains would have returned to their pre-earthquake state.
2 The National Disaster Reduction Center of China recorded on 8 August 2010 that 97 mm of rain fell in 40 minutes in Zhouqu County, an area that normally receives only 400–800 mm per year.
3 Severe droughts in 2010 cracked and shrank the soil, making it more prone to geological disaster.
4 Due to the period of political and governmental upheaval in China during the first half of the twentieth century, detailed meteorological data is only available for 1951 or later.
5 Climate models are run using different scenarios of emissions, population growth, energy choices and land use change to see how the climate might respond. These scenarios allow scientists to test a range of possible climate futures.
6 China's *Five Year Plans* are a set of national mandates that direct the development of the country in the next five-year period, governing all sectors of government and society. The *Twelfth Five Year Plan* included, for the first time, mandates for the development and incorporation of adaptation measures by all relevant government sectors.
7 The State Council is the highest executive organ of state power and administration in China.
8 Beijing has experienced a number of significant flooding events coinciding with intense rain storms and increasingly inadequate drainage systems. Increased building of roads, homes and office infrastructure is reducing the area for rain to infiltrate, routing it instead as floodwater and outpacing upgrades to the drainage system. Rainfall on 21 July 2012 in some districts was the heaviest recorded in the ~60-year record and led to flash floods, approximately 40 deaths and widespread damage (Xu, 2012; *The Economist*, 2012).
9 Priority sectors in the NAS are: infrastructure; agriculture; water resources; human health; coastal zones and maritime waters; tourism and other industries; and forests and ecological systems.

References

Chen, J.H. and Lin, S.J. (2013) Seasonal predictions of tropical cyclones using a 25-km resolution general circulation model. *Journal of Climate*. 26. pp. 380–398.

Chen, Y., Chen, X. and Ren, G. (2010) Variation of extreme precipitation over large river basins in China. *Advances in Climate Change Research*. 2 (2). 108–114.

Collins, M., Knutti, R., Arblaster, J., Dufresne, J.L., Fichefet, T., Friedlingstein, P., Gao, X., Gutowski, W.J., Johns, T., Krinner, G., Shongwe, M., Tebaldi, C., Weaver, A.J. and Wehner, M. (2013) Long-term climate change: Projections, commitments and irreversibility. In: Stocker, T.F., Qin, D., Plattner, G.K., Tignor, M., Allen, S.K., Doschung, J., Nauels, A., Xia, Y., Bex, V. and Midgley, P.M. (eds), *Climate Change 2013: The Physical Science Basis. Contribution of Working Group I to the Fifth Assessment Report of the Intergovernmental Panel on Climate Change*. Cambridge University Press: Cambridge, United Kingdom.

CRED (Centre for Research on the Epidemiology of Disasters) (2014) *EM-DAT: The International Disaster Database*. [Online] Available from: www.emdat.be/database. [Accessed: 24 October 2014.]

Economist, The (2012) Floods in Beijing: Under water and under fire. 24 July. [Online] Available from: www.economist.com/blogs/analects/2012/07/floods-beijing. [Accessed: 18 November 2014.]

Hartmann, D.L., Klein-Tank, A.M.G., Rusticucci, M., Alexander, L.V., Bronnimann, S., Charabi, Y., Dentener, F.J., Dlugokencky, E.J., Easterling, D.R., Kaplan, A., Soden, B.J., Thorne, P.W., Wild, M. and Zhai, P.M. (2013) Observations: Atmosphere and surface. In: Stocker, T.F., Qin, D., Plattner, G.K., Tignor, M., Allen, S.K., Doschung, J., Nauels, A., Xia, Y., Bex, V. and Midgley, P.M. (eds), *The Physical Science Basis. Contribution of Working Group I to the Fifth Assessment Report of the Intergovernmental Panel on Climate Change*. Cambridge University Press: Cambridge, United Kingdom.

Hodges, K.I. (1994) A general method for tracking analysis and its application to meteorological data. *Monthly Weather Review*. 122. pp. 2573–2586.

Hoskins, B.J. and Hodges, K.I. (2002) New perspectives on the northern hemisphere winter storm tracks. *Journal of the Atmospheric Sciences*. 59. pp. 1041–1061.

IPCC (2012) *Managing the Risks of Extreme Events and Disasters to Advance Climate Change Adaptation*. A Special Report of Working Groups I and II of the Intergovernmental Panel on Climate Change [Field, C.B., Barros, V., Stocker, T.F., Qin, D., Dokken, D.J., Ebi, K.L., Mastrandrea, M.D., Mach, K.J., Plattner, G.K., Allen, S.K., Tignor, M. and Midgley, P.M. (eds)]. Cambridge University Press: Cambridge, United Kingdom and New York, New York, USA.

Knutson, T.R., McBride, J.L., Chan, J., Emanuel, K., Holland, G., Landsea, C., Held, I., Kossin, J.P., Srivastava, A.K. and Sugi, M. (2010) Tropical cyclones and climate change. *Nature Geoscience*. 3. pp. 157–163.

Lee, T.S., Lee, W.J., Nakazawa, T., Weyman, J.C., Ying, M. and Tong, T.N. (2010) *Assessments of Impacts of Climate Change on Tropical Cyclone Frequency and Intensity in the Typhoon Committee Region*. Typhoon Committee, Forty-Second Session, 25 to 29 January. Economic and Social Commission for Asia and the Pacific and World Meteorological Organization: Singapore (WRD/TC.42/5.1 Add.3).

Long, H.L., Heilig, G.K., Wang, J., Li, X.B., Luo, M. *et al.* (2006) Land use and soil erosion in the upper reaches of the Yangtze River: Some socio-economic considerations on China's Grain-for-Green Programme. *Land Degradation and Development*. 17. pp. 589–603.

Min, S. and Qian, Y. (2008) Trends in all kinds of precipitation events in China over the past 40 years. *Journal of Sun Yat-Sen University (Natural Sciences)*. 47 (3). pp. 105–111.

NBS (National Bureau of Statistics of China) (2009) *China Compendium of Statistics 1949–2008*. China Statistics Press: Beijing, People's Republic of China.

NDRC (National Disaster Reduction Commission) (2013) *Notice of the National Disaster Reduction Commission General Office on Promulgating the Standard for National Integrated Disaster Reduction Demonstration Community*. PRC Ministry of Civil Affairs. [Online] Available from: http://jzs.mca.gov.cn/article/zjz/zcwj/201309/20130900519336.shtml. [Accessed: 20 October 2014.]

PRC National Development and Reform Commission (2011) *The Second National Assessment Report on Climate Change*. Science Press: Beijing, People's Republic of China.

PRC State Council (2008) *China's Policies and Actions for Addressing Climate Change*. PRC State Council Information Office. [Online] Available from: www.ccchina.gov.cn/WebSite/CCChina/UpFile/File419.pdf. [Accessed: 20 November 2014.]

PRC State Council (2011) State Council on the issuance of the National Comprehensive Disaster Prevention and Mitigation Plan (2011–2015). [Online] Available from:

www.gov.cn/zwgk/2011-12/08/content_2015178.htm. [Accessed: 02 December 2014.] (Guo Ban Fa [2011] No. 55).

Wang, X.L. and Ren, F.M. (2008) Variations in frequency and intensity of landfall tropical cyclones over China during 1951~2004. *Marine Forecasts*. 25. pp. 65–73.

Xie, S.P., Deser, C., Vecchi, G.A., Ma, J., Teng, H. and Wittenberg, A.T. (2010) Global warming pattern formation: Sea surface temperature and rainfall. *Journal of Climate*. 23. pp. 966–986.

Xinhua (2010) Death toll from NW China mudslides rises to 1,435 as authorities ban further searching for the dead. 22 October. [Online] Available from: http://news.xinhuanet.com/english2010/china/2010-08/22/c_13456608.htm. [Accessed: 24 October 2014.]

Xu, N. (2012) Beijing floods: Not enough prevention. 25 July. *China Dialogue*, part of the *Guardian Environmental Network*. [Online] Available from: www.theguardian.com/environment/2012/jul/25/flooding-china?newsfeed=true. [Accessed: 18 November 2014.]

Yang, J., Jiang, Z., Wang, P. *et al.* (2008) Temporal and spatial characteristic of annual extreme precipitation event in China. *Climatic and Environmental Research*. 13 (1). pp. 75–83.

Ying, M. and Chen, B. (2009) Climatic trend of the tropical cyclone's influences on Chinese Mainland as revealed by the wind and precipitation observations. In: *WMO 2nd International Workshop on Tropical Cyclone Landfall Processes (IWTCLP-II)*. World Meteorological Organization: Shanghai, People's Republic of China (WMO/TD-No. 1548).

Ying, M., Yang, Y., Chen, B.D. and Zhang, W. (2011) Climatic variation of tropical cyclones affecting China during the past 50 years. *Science China Earth Sciences*. 54 (8). pp. 1226–1237.

Yokoi, S. and Takayabu, Y. (2013) Attribution of decadal variability in tropical cyclone passage frequency over the western North Pacific: A new approach emphasizing the genesis location of cyclones. *Journal of Climate*. 26. pp. 973–987.

Yokoi, S., Takayabu, Y. and Marukami, H. (2012) Attribution of projected future changes in tropical cyclone passage frequency over the Western North Pacific. *Journal of Climate*. 26. pp. 4096–4111.

Zhai, P., Wang, Z. and Zou, X. (2007) Changes in extreme climate events in major international basins. In: Ren, G. (ed.), *Climate Change and Water Resources in China*. China Meteorological Press: Beijing, People's Republic of China.

Zhang, Q., Wu, L. and Liu, Q. (2009) Tropical cyclone damages in China: 1983–2006. *Bulletin of the American Meteorological Society*. 90. pp. 489–495.

Zheng, D. (2010) Analysis of urgency of agricultural disaster reduction from extreme weather. *Guangming Daily*. 22 March.

Zhou, H. and Zhang, W. (2013) Comparison of community disaster risk management model: Analysis from Chinese Comprehensive Disaster-reduction Demonstration Communities and CBDRM Communities. *Journal of Catastrophology*. 28 (2). pp. 120–126.

Zimmerli, P. and Zhou, J. (2006) *Natural Hazards in China: Ensuring Long-Term Stability*. Swiss Re: Zurich, Switzerland (2/06, 1000 en).

Zou, M., Yuan, Y., Liao, Y. *et al.* (2011) *Integrated Natural Disaster Relief and Security System in China*. Science Press: Beijing, People's Republic of China.

4

A BALANCING ACT

China's water resources and climate change

*Wang Guoqing, Rebecca Nadin and
Sarah Opitz-Stapleton*

Water is salvation and catastrophe in one. It is the lifeblood that keeps China's communities alive, its food growing, its ecosystems flourishing and its commerce flowing. Too much here or too little there, however, and the well-being of the country's 1 billion-plus people is at risk. Managing water resources is a delicate balancing act that the country's administrators have performed for centuries, with their success and failure contributing the rise and fall of many a dynasty.[1]

Water management in China has always been a complex task – the south and mountainous regions of the country are blessed with fairly abundant precipitation and networks of rivers, while the north is arid. However, ever-growing human demands are putting more pressure on the environment. Population growth, rapid urbanisation, land use change, large-scale agriculture, industrialisation and pollution are putting unprecedented strain on the unevenly distributed water resources – so much so that rising demand is now the greatest threat to China's water resources. In 40 years – less than a lifetime – groundwater tables in the northern plains surrounding Beijing have fallen by more than 15 m due to demand, and the rate of their decline continues to accelerate (Foster and Garduño, 2004; Foster *et al.*, 2004; Wang *et al.*, 2006).

The Yellow River, which spans nine northern provinces, has experienced dwindling flows since the 1970s, as have several other major rivers. The first national water census in 2013 reported that 28,000 rivers have disappeared since the 1990s – more than half of those previously listed in the government's database (PRC Ministry of Water Resources, 2013). Over the same few decades, the centre of grain production has shifted to the northern drylands as irrigation systems have expanded in the north and cropland in southern China has been given over to cities. Worsening water shortages threaten this new breadbasket and could also stunt the growth of cities, energy production and a thirsty industrial economy.

As challenging as it is now, balancing the already uneven relationship between demand and water supply could become much more difficult as the climate changes. Human behaviour and climate change have the potential to exacerbate both flood and drought risk throughout the country, particularly in arid regions. Changes in rainfall amounts and timing in certain regions, along with a country-average temperature increase of 1.38°C between 1951 and 2009, are altering river flows and disrupting the recharge rates of crucial groundwater supplies across China. Extreme precipitation events, coupled with rapid changes in land use, are contributing to more frequent major floods, such as those in recent years in the Yangtze and Huai River basins. At the same time, northern and parts of north-east China have registered declines in annual precipitation since the 1970s, leading to droughts. Some areas have been hit by droughts lasting five or more years, inflicting a severe agricultural and economic toll and threatening local food security (He *et al.*, 2011; see also Chapters 3, 5 and 8).

The future is likely to yield further significant and uneven impacts on China's regional water resources, and to alter the frequency and intensity of droughts and floods. It will pose new challenges to water security and traditional water management, including the operation and safety of large-scale water conservancy projects. It will also require different demand management choices (Zhang and Wang, 2007). Without adopting a range of adaptation options, climate change – coupled with demand and environmental degradation – will ensure that water becomes scarcer and will compound related socio-economic and ecological losses.

This chapter looks at the intersection of rising and changing demand with climate change, and their implications for China's water resources. It begins with an overview of China's history of water management and vulnerability, including a discussion of the trends in slow-onset weather conditions and extreme weather events over the past few decades and their impacts on water supply. It then explores China's recent investigations of potential climate change impacts in light of projected demand on water supplies, including a case study on a major water-climate impact assessment of China's regional water resources.[2] Finally, the chapter explores the ways in which the country is building a more robust and resilient system to balance water needs with water supplies through integrated water management approaches and adaptation policies.

China's water resources today

China has a diverse mix of water resources, comprised of approximately ten major river basins (see Figure 4.1), numerous lesser rivers and critical aquifers in the North China Plain and northern China. Four of the most important river basins are the Yangtze, Yellow, Hai and Liao Rivers, which provide water for a

FIGURE 4.1 China's major river systems with select cities. The naming convention in this map uses names commonly used within China for the rivers, with some Western translations (e.g. the Pearl and Yellow Rivers). International names for transboundary rivers are noted in the text

significant proportion of China's population and a variety of uses. The Yangtze, China's largest river, runs from the Tibetan Plateau to Shanghai, covering an area nearly as large as Mexico (1.8 million km²). It provides water to a population of nearly 450 million, including cities such as Shanghai and Chongqing. It serves as a critical waterway for transporting goods and people and, with the installation of the last planned turbines at the Three Gorges Dam, is a key source of hydropower (Gleick, 2011a; Huang and Zheng, 2009).

The Yellow River is the country's second-largest river and one of the few that spans desert and grasslands year-round. The Hai River runs close to China's political and cultural centre, Beijing, while the Liao River is the main artery in the north-east. Other major rivers include the Huai River and the Pearl River, which serves the major population, trade and port cities of Guangzhou and Hong Kong, among others. The Heilongjiang and Lancang Rivers are transnational, with their headwaters in China and flow into several other countries.

The Lancang River, known as the Mekong River outside of China, passes through Vietnam, Cambodia and Laos. It also serves as an important trade conduit to South-East Asia for a few of China's poorer provinces, including Yunnan. The Heilongjiang River is known as the Amur River in Russia, and power projects along its length generate electricity for cities such as Harbin.

According to estimates of *surface water* (found above ground, like rivers, streams, lakes and ponds) and *groundwater* (originating from beneath the ground, such as aquifers or springs) supplies, China has the world's sixth-largest renewable reserves of water (roughly 2,800 km^3/year), but the water available per person is only about 2,151 m^3/year – a quarter of the global average (FAO, 2014; Gleick, 2011b). Surface water is abundant in the south (e.g. the Pearl and Yangtze River basins) and the mountains (Lancang River basin) but much less so in the north and the plains (Yellow River basin and regions north and east of it). Regions with less than 1,000 m^3 of renewable water per person are commonly defined as 'water scarce' (Falkenmark, 1989). Northern China has only 750 m^3 of renewable water per person, less than one-quarter of that available in the south, and one-eleventh of the world average. Yet, it is in the north and the plains, which contains 60% of China's arable land, where much of China's agricultural production takes place, and where large population and industrial centres are located. This region produces roughly half of China's grain and nearly all of its wheat and maize (see Chapters 5 and 8). South China, with 36% of the total landmass, has 84% of the country's surface water.

Groundwater also supplies a significant proportion of water for domestic and agricultural use throughout the country, comprising nearly 49% of the water supply in northern China and roughly 14% in the south (Wang *et al.*, 2006). As with rivers, groundwater is unequally distributed throughout the country (see Figure 4.2). The south and mountainous regions have the greatest share of China's groundwater supply, with smaller aquifers in the north and the plains. Groundwater is increasingly important to the economy. In the parched breadbasket of northern China, it supports much of the region's domestic, industrial and agricultural needs, including up to 70% of the supplies used in irrigation in some areas. This is in part because many surface water sources have become scarce and polluted (Lohmar *et al.*, 2003).

Recent trends in rainfall and temperature

Variations in the timing and amount of precipitation (rain and snow) throughout the country (Figure 4.3) affect river flows from season to season and from year to year. Much of China receives most of its annual precipitation during the East Asian Summer Monsoon (EASM), with southern, south-central and south-eastern parts of the country like the Pearl or Yangtze River basins receiving most of their rain between April and September (Ding and Chan, 2005; He *et al.*, 2008). These areas average 2,000 mm of rainfall per year. The EASM rainy period is shorter in the west and the North and

FIGURE 4.2 Map of major groundwater resources (aquifers) in China (source: adapted from Chen, 1987)

North-East China Plains (the Hai River and parts of the Yellow and Heilongjiang Rivers, for example), with most of the rain falling between June and September. These regions receive just 200–400 mm per year, one-fifth or so of the rain that falls in the wetter parts of China. The rest of the year is much drier (Figure 4.4).

The growing variability of the EASM has led to falls in annual precipitation totals in some parts of the country and increases in precipitation in others. Nationwide precipitation between 1950 and 2010 has not changed significantly, but there are differences between the north-east (decreasing), the north-west (increasing) and the south-east (increasing) (Zhai *et al.*, 2005; Fan *et al.*, 2013). Some of the noted recent trends in precipitation might be partially attributable to climate change, but they are also modulated by natural multi-decadal and multi-century variability (Jiang *et al.*, 2006; Zhao *et al.*, 2012). Only time will reveal the full impact of climate change on top of the natural variability in regional climates.

There is no direct relationship between precipitation, temperature and river flows due to the myriad of human alterations to China's water systems (Wang, Zhang *et al.*, 2013). For example, annual precipitation decreased in the middle reaches of the Yellow River by around 5% between 1980 and 2008, compared with the previous 30 years Yet, overall Yellow River flows decreased by

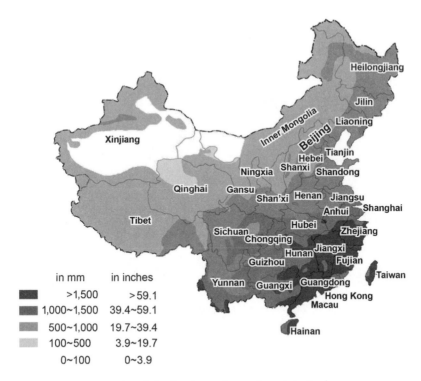

FIGURE 4.3 Uneven regional distributions of annual precipitation[3]

approximately 33% over the same period (Wang *et al.*, 2012). Changes in river flows since the 1950s, with the most noticeable changes occurring since the early 1970s, are predominantly due to increasingly large-scale agricultural diversions and urbanisation, and competition between upstream and down-stream users (Cai and Rosegrant, 2004), with climate shifts in precipitation and temperature making comparatively minor contributions as discussed in the next section.

Extreme precipitation events also play a significant role in modulating river flood responses that affect water quality and destructiveness. The incidences of both flooding and drought in many regions of China cause significant eco-nomic damages and contribute to water shortage and quality issues. Droughts and floods are frequent, often occurring simultaneously within the country in different regions. The Yangtze River basin, for example, has severe floods roughly every ten to 16 years (Jiang *et al.*, 2006). Heavy rains in July 2013 led to severe flooding across 20 provinces in China, which caused landslides and the deaths of hundreds of people. The greatest economic losses, though, are from drought, which can devastate livelihoods in rural areas. A serious drought across five south-west provinces in 2009–2012 affected roughly 7.7 million hectares of farmland and left 24 million people and 15 million

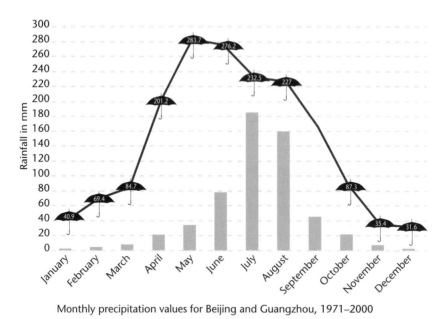

Monthly precipitation values for Beijing and Guangzhou, 1971–2000

▨ Beijing ━ Guangzhou

FIGURE 4.4 Average monthly precipitation totals for two select cities of China that are representative of regional differences in precipitation timing and amount (source: PRC Meteorological Administration, 2012)

livestock struggling to access water. Direct economic losses by late 2010 were estimated at US$3.6 billion (PRC Ministry of Civil Affairs, 2010). Further discussion of flood and drought hazards in China and their impacts can be found in Chapter 3.

A key question is how climate change is likely to exacerbate extreme precipitation events; increase the disparity between dry and wet regions; and alter seasonal patterns for all regions. The subsequent, secondary impacts to water quantity and quality, when combined with changing human demand and alteration of ecosystems and watersheds, will also challenge water management options. Future climate change is likely to increase the incidence of floods and droughts in some of China's regions (IPCC, 2012; Gao *et al.*, 2012; see also Chapter 3). These in turn may exacerbate mudslides, landslides and other geological disasters, triggering disaster chains. Overall, changes to seasonal precipitation patterns, warmer temperatures and the potential for more frequent and intense heavy rainfall (contributing to flooding) and drought will require greater flexibility and different water management strategies, particularly those related to water storage and power-generation reservoirs in large water-conservancy projects like the Three Gorges Dam.

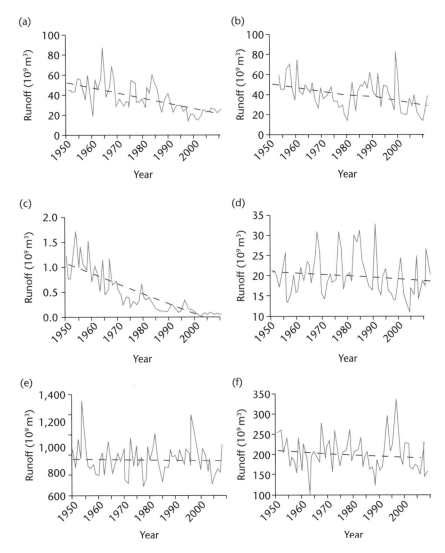

FIGURE 4.5 Trends (dotted line) in annual river flows at points in six of China's major river basins: (a) Huayuankou station on Yellow River, (b) Haerbin station on Heilongjian River, (c) Shixiali station on Hai River, (d) Wujiadu station on Huai River, (e) Datong station on Yangtze River and (f) Wuzhou station on Pearl River. The annual river flows shown here were recorded at single-river gauging stations, but are representative of trends seen in other stations along each river (source: Wang, Yan *et al.*, 2013)

Human demand and recent water resource declines

Demand and other resource pressures, such as declines in water quality due to industrial and agricultural pollution and urban wastewater, have changed river flows throughout the country for centuries. However, it is the rapid acceleration in demand since the 1980s that has caused significant decreases in river flows and the disappearance of many smaller rivers altogether. The World Bank (2007) estimates the cost of water scarcity and pollution at around 2.3% of GDP. The agriculture industry remains China's biggest water user, accounting for roughly 63% of withdrawals, mainly in the north (PRC Ministry of Water Resources, 2008). This share is slowly declining as water conservation policies generate more 'crop per drop' and release water for fast-growing urban and industrial sectors. As combined demand rises, however, so too does the production of wastewater and pollution, making clean water even scarcer.

Changes in river flow directly affect available water supplies, and thus have an important impact on regional socio-economic development and the environment. The declines in China's rivers reflect both human activity and climate shifts, with human activity – rising withdrawals for irrigation, industry and domestic use, and land use change – currently the dominant causes of decreasing flows (Zhang and Wang, 2007; Wang, Zhang *et al.*, 2013; Cai, 2006). In the Hai River in the north-east, one of China's most water-stressed areas, human activities are also the major cause of declining flows. Similar decreases in annual river flows are also seen in the Heilongjiang River in the far north, which feeds domestic and industrial water systems in the city of Harbin. Flows have fallen sharply in the Yellow River over the last 40 years (Figure 4.5a). The Yangtze River has not displayed any statistically significant shifts in flows along the lower reaches between 1950 and 2010 (Figure 4.5e), but flows have decreased slightly in the upper reaches (not shown). Decreases in the upper sections of the Yangtze are primarily due to human withdrawals, and to a lesser degree, reduced summer precipitation (Wang *et al.*, 2012). While human demand is significant on the lower Yangtze, increased precipitation and more frequent rainstorms are currently helping to maintain flows. Trends in Pearl River flows are unclear, with no significant trends in mean annual river discharge recorded. However, annual maximum flows appear to be decreasing and annual minimum flows increasing. The conflicting trends in Pearl River maximum and low flows are more a reflection of significant human alteration (e.g. dams, wetland destruction and urbanisation) of the river system (Chen *et al.*, 2010; Zhang, *et al.*, 2012).

Analysis shows that human demands and withdrawals are responsible in large part for the drop in river flows for most of the river systems in China; recent trends in precipitation and temperature have played only a minor role. Using river flow observation data from 1951 to the mid- to late-1960s in major river basins as a baseline for river flows with minor human activity,[4] several studies

(Wang *et al.*, 2011; Wang *et al.*, 2012; Wang, Zhang *et al.*, 2013) estimated the impact of modern water withdrawal and flood control systems on river flows using two different hydrological models. Most of these modern water engineering systems, such the expansion of extensive irrigation networks and flood control systems, along with population increases and the expansion of agricultural land in China, have occurred since the 1970s. Figure 4.6 shows the relative impact of human demand on the overall reductions in annual river flows for the middle reaches of the Yellow and Hai Rivers, compared to the influence of recent trends in precipitation.

Between 1950 and 2010, there is considerable decadal variation in the amount of precipitation in all river basins in different decades (not shown), with some decades wetter in some regions than in others. Some of the decadal variability is natural and some proportion of it is due to emerging climate change; attributing the degree of variability to natural or climate change causes is difficult at this point due to limited climate records. Whatever the cause, the variability has had some impact on overall flows in most of China's basins. However, analyses demonstrate that most of the falls in river flows in many of China's basins are due to human demand, rather than recent climate trends in precipitation or temperature

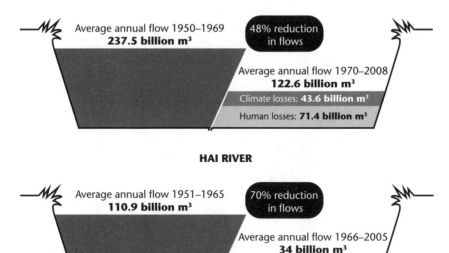

FIGURE 4.6 River flow changes in the Yellow (middle reaches) and Hai Rivers between the baseline period (large bucket) and the recent past (less-full buckets). The proportion of the levels in the buckets is representative of the overall reduction in river flows between the two periods

(Wang *et al.*, 2011; Wang *et al.*, 2012; Wang, Zhang *et al.*, 2013). Human demand is shown to be the main driver of declines in river flows and groundwater tables throughout most of China, especially in the last 30 years.

Groundwater supplies have also shown significant declines in many parts of the country, particularly in arid regions. Overexploitation and pollution are having a negative impact on water availability and quality. Withdrawal rates for domestic, agricultural and industrial water demands are exceeding the recharge rates of many aquifers in China, leading to declines in the water tables. The most important aquifer, in terms of meeting demand, is the Huang-Huai-Hai Plain Aquifer in the North China Plain in the north-east. The aquifer is shallow in some sections (where the water table close to the surface), but groundwater levels have fallen by more than 15 m over the past 40 years, with even greater declines in urban areas of the Hebei Plain (Figure 4.7) (Foster *et al.*, 2004).

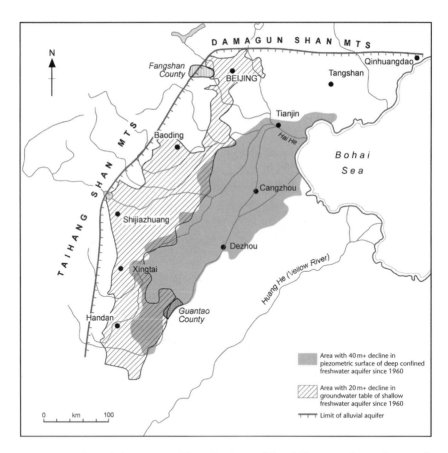

FIGURE 4.7 Cumulative water table reductions of the shallow aquifer in the North China Plain, 1960–2000. The biggest drops in water levels have occurred in and around urban areas (source: Foster and Garduño, 2004)

The value of agricultural production throughout China that could be at risk from unsustainable groundwater use has been estimated at around US$840 million per year in 2003 prices (Foster and Garduño, 2004). Many remaining groundwater sources are becoming polluted with sewage, industrial runoff and agricultural by-products. In a 2011 survey, 57% of urban wells were of 'bad' water quality, and the trend was worsening (Xinhua, 2013). Given that many residents in the Huang-Huai-Hai Plain rely on this source for home use, the pollution could have serious health implications for those people, as well as degrading the overall ecosystem and populations of aquatic species.

At the same time, declines in groundwater tables are increasing rates of land subsidence, with the ground collapsing in extreme cases to form sinkholes. This threatens infrastructure such as buildings and transport networks. Groundwater loss also adds to wetland degradation and the loss of critical habitat for wildlife, as well as increasing soil salinity and loss of cropland. In coastal areas, drops in groundwater tables can have significant impacts. As the levels fall, seawater can be drawn into the soil, causing saltwater intrusion and the fouling of remaining groundwater supplies. Sea level rise, in conjunction with increased demand in coastal areas, is contributing to saltwater intrusion into the Laizhou coastal aquifer and other coastal aquifers (Liu *et al.*, 2001). Some shallow freshwater aquifers in the North-East China Plain that serve cities such as Tianjin overlay salty aquifers, and uncontrolled pumping has allowed saline intrusion into the freshwater aquifer lenses. Groundwater is often viewed as the most stable emergency water source during times of drought or water stress. Increasing demand and the resulting saltwater intrusion, plus sea level rise, heavy pollution and shifts in precipitation and temperature due to climate change, have the potential to seriously threaten the viability of China's groundwater resources, particularly in the arid north (Huang-Huai-Hai) plains. These factors may mean that in the future groundwater might no longer be a reliable resource for arid regions or during times of drought.

In summary, water has become increasingly scarce in China since the 1960s due to declines in river flows and groundwater tables, as well as decreasing quality in remaining sources. Analysis shows that most of the decrease in water resources is due to human demand and activity. The expansion of land for production of grain and other foodstuffs to support China's growing population, plus rapid urbanisation and industrialisation, have increased demand and drawn down supplies. These activities, among others, also contribute to a growing wastewater and pollution problem that exacerbates regional and local water scarcity. Uneven precipitation shifts, such as increasing precipitation in the North and North-East China Plains and decreases in the south, are additional factors in decreasing flows in various rivers around the country. The next section explores the potential vulnerabilities of and risks to China's water resources raised by various projections in human demand and climate change.

Future vulnerability of China's water systems

China has long grappled with regional water security. In the past few decades, its expanding population, rapid growth in urban, farming and industrial demand, and the resultant pollution and ecosystem degradation are making China's water systems more sensitive to both small changes and large shocks. These human activities also reduce the adaptive capacity of China's water resources to support 'ecosystem services', such as providing drinking water, instream flows for aquatic wildlife and fisheries and dilution of the impact of pollution on the surrounding environment. Many of China's water systems are quite vulnerable (likely to suffer harm) to slow-onset shifts in seasonal and annual precipitation and temperature, as well as extreme weather events like heavy rainfall or droughts. Human activities have reduced the capacity of China's water resources to continue to function effectively, especially during a climate event, or to recover or adapt to climate, ecological and social pressures. As these three pressures evolve in the future, the vulnerability of China's water resources will also evolve. As the seasons and the frequency and intensity of precipitation and temperature events shift, the risk profiles of China's various water resources will also change.

Given the serious pressures facing China's water supplies today, the Chinese government has supported numerous studies of the vulnerabilities and risks

---

Box 4.1 Vulnerability and risk

There are many definitions of vulnerability and risk in use, which can be quite confusing. For the purposes of this chapter, and based on the Adapting to Climate Change in China I (ACCC I) programme Hydrology Study, the following definitions of vulnerability and risk are employed.

Water resource vulnerability refers to the degree of harm (impact) that a water system may suffer because of its climate change exposure (changes in rainfall and temperature) and the stresses it faces like pollution, excessive demand and water degradation (factors of sensitivity and level of adaptive capacity). The impacts are measured as declines in the quality of services the water system is able to provide, as well as changes in water flows, timing and amount (structural changes).

Water resource risk refers to the degree of harm a water system might suffer and the likelihood (probability) that it will occur. Risk is a function of the probability of a certain climate hazard occurring, such as how much more likely it is that really wet storms will occur in an area in the future, and the water system's potential future vulnerability. Systems at high risk are unlikely to be able to meet demand in dry or extremely dry years.

facing particular water systems in various regions. It has also begun discussions on various hard and soft adaptation options and planning processes to make the systems more resilient to a range of stressors. China's National Climate Change Programme issued by the State Council in 2007[5] clarified that,

> There are two objectives for development and conservation of water resources in adapting to climate change in China: to promote sustainable development and utilization of water resources; and to enhance adaptive capacity of water resource system to reduce its vulnerability to climate change. How to enhance water resources management, optimize water resources allocation, strengthen infrastructure construction, ensure the anti-flood safety of large rivers, key cities and regions, promote nation-wide water-saving program, guarantee safe drinking water and sound social and economic development, and make a good use of river functions while protecting aquatic ecosystem are the long-term challenges on water resources development and conservation in terms of enhancing climate change adaptation capability.

Climate change may cause a range[6] of regional changes in precipitation and temperature by mid-century when compared with those since the 1980s, depending on the climate model and emission scenario (Gao *et al.*, 2012; see also Chapters 3, 5 and 6). Area-averaged, country-wide warming is expected on the range of ~1.5–2.2°C. Strong regional differences are expected in the warming trends, with the Qinghai–Tibetan Plateau area likely to experience the greatest warming. Much of north and north-east China is likely to undergo modest warming over the near-term. The Yellow and Pearl River basins may potentially warm at a slower rate than the rest of China. Precipitation projections are highly uncertain, with some sets of models and emissions scenarios showing a potential increase in annual precipitation (mostly due to augmented winter) by the 2040s for much of China, except for projected drying in the Yellow and Pearl River basins. Other model and emissions combinations indicate opposite spatial trends during winter months. Most of the models forecast a possible reduction in summer rainfall during the monsoon season. The precipitation projections are too contradictory at this point for widespread application in the construction of water infrastructure, such as reservoirs.

   These projected changes in temperature and precipitation could have a significant impact on river runoff in various basins throughout China. Projections in overall changes in regional water supplies vary, depending on the climate projection and climate model used in the hydrological impact assessment and how far into the future the simulations are run. According to some climate models (HadCM3-PRECIS and MPI-RegCM3), water resources could fall in most regions, particularly in the north-east and upper and middle reaches of the Yellow and Yangtze Rivers. Other climate scenarios (MPI-PRECIS) project contrasting changes in regional water resources, showing reductions in the south and north-west, and potential increases in the Yellow River and parts of the Yangtze River (Figure 4.8).

What lessons can be learnt from the slightly contradictory projections in water resource availability by different climate and hydrologic model combinations? First, it is important to note that due to existing and projected increasing demand patterns, along with the humid climate in southern China and an arid climate in northern China, the current water distribution pattern of abundance in the south and shortage in the north *is not likely to fundamentally change by the 2050s, regardless of conflicting projections in precipitation and temperature due to climate change.*

While under some scenarios, the water shortages in the north might ease somewhat, growing pollution and ecological deterioration will continue to threaten this region's water supplies and contribute to an overall shortage as water becomes unusable. All of the model combinations indicate that variability in the amount and availability of water throughout the year is likely to intensify in the future, with variability in some years approaching 10% of average quantity available throughout the year. The uncertainty (disagreement between models) in water resource availability is most pronounced now (the 2010s) and in the next decade (the 2020s), as seen in Figure 4.8. However, the models begin to converge in projecting an overall decrease in water resources regionally and nationwide in the 2030s, 2040s and 2050s (not shown). National water resources in 2031–2040 may be 1% to 8.4% less than the baseline and are likely to continue to decrease in 2041–2050. Thus it appears that most of the uncertainty about future decreases in China's water supply is around *when* such shifts might happen, rather than if they will happen at all.

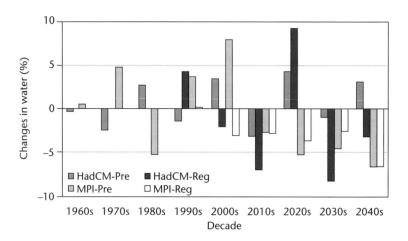

FIGURE 4.8 Projected percentage changes in nationwide (aggregated over all watersheds) water resources according to different climate models

When combined with scenarios of future water demand, population growth and socio-economic development, the shifts in water resource availability due to climate change-induced alterations in temperature and precipitation give some idea of the future vulnerability and climate risk of China's water resources. Again, due to the variations in projected water resource availability under different climate change scenarios, there are different estimates of future vulnerability by the 2050s for China's ten major river basins. The areas in which the river basins are extremely vulnerable either shrink or expand, depending on which climate change scenario is used. Overall, the results suggest that water systems in the Yellow River and Hai River regions of north China are the most vulnerable, while the Pearl and Lancang River basins are relatively stable and of low vulnerability. Regardless of the climate scenario, most of the country's river basins continue to be highly vulnerable. This reflects the findings of Wang *et al.*'s analysis (2012) that most decreases in surface and groundwater supplies are due to human demand. This demand will continue to be the dominant factor in each river's overall vulnerability. As a result, greater climate variability and potential changes in extreme weather events will increase the likelihood of more floods and droughts in many basins, sometimes within the same year.

When it comes to assessing the potential climate risk of future extremely wet or dry years on water resources, certain river basins exhibit an elevated risk. For the Yellow River, which plays a crucial role in maintaining social stability and the rapid economic development in north China, future climate risk is high. All of the climate models suggest that more dry years are likely in the future (2021–2050) when compared with the past (1961–1990). This likelihood of more dry years, coupled with the river's existing extreme vulnerability and projected high-to-extreme future vulnerability, means that the river faces a high risk and is unlikely to be able to meet demand in most dry or extremely dry years. The models also project more wet years in the future, leading to greater flood risks on the Yellow River. Current water management operations and flood and storage control will be challenged by the need to plan for and manage both flood and drought situations, sometimes within the same year. Extended, multi-year droughts may also become more likely in the future.

Climate change-related shifts in precipitation and temperature will also affect the recharge rates of China's groundwater supplies, particularly in shallow aquifer areas such as the north plains. Increasing temperatures contribute to higher rates of evaporation, reducing the amount of water that filters back through the ground into an aquifer and recharges (increases) the water table. The most significant declines in the water table, of 40 m or more, are at points in Hebei Province where the municipalities of Beijing and Tianjin are located, as these municipalities rely heavily on groundwater to meet city demand. Analysis by Wang *et al.* (2012) indicates that a 2°C annual temperature increase by 2041–2050 coupled with (1) a 15% decrease in precipitation would correspond with an additional drop of around 80 cm; (2) no change in precipitation would lead to drops ranging from 0 to ~18 cm; and (3) a 15% increase in precipitation would correspond with or very little change in water tables in the Hebei aquifer. Each of these scenarios was generated under the assumption that no more withdrawals would occur in the future, in order to isolate climate change impacts on the aquifer. However, as it is highly unlikely that the cities will stop using the aquifer at any point in the near future, climate change combined with continued demand could have a devastating impact on water tables (see Figure 4.9).

Case study: measuring China's water resource vulnerability

Hydrologists investigated potential changes in river flows due to various climate projections and socio-economic scenarios for the ten major river basins described earlier as part of the ACCC I programme (Wang *et al.*, 2012). The water resource impact assessment utilised a range of multi-model climate

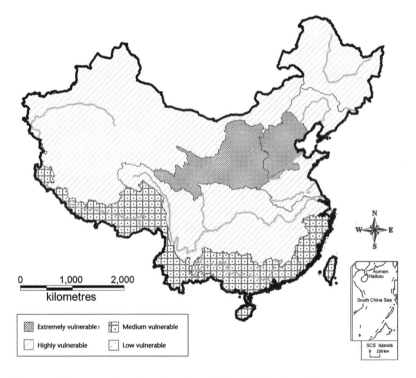

FIGURE 4.9 Current and projected vulnerability of China's surface water resources by the ten major river basins. The figure above displays current vulnerability. The two figures on page 116 represent the range of projected future vulnerability over the period 2041–2050 when compared with today (source: Wang *et al.*, 2012)

continued

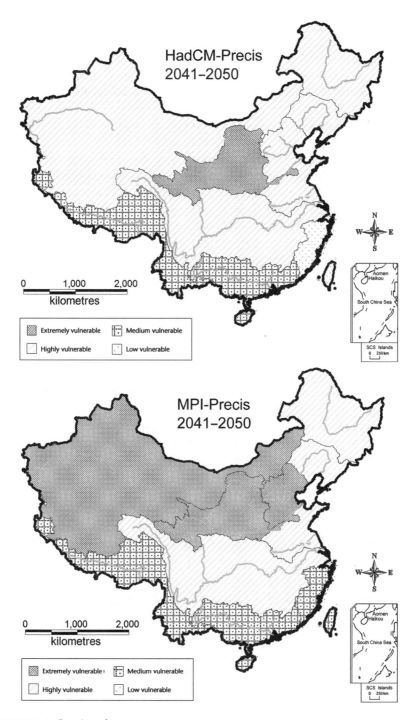

FIGURE 4.9 Continued

projections as inputs to two different hydrology models. The two different hydrology models employed were the variable infiltration capacity (VIC) model and the snowmelt-based water balance model (SWBM). A range of potential future changes in precipitation and temperature, along with future socio-economic and water demand scenarios, were fed into the VIC and SWBM models to evaluate water resource impacts in 216 watersheds (smaller units within the major river basins) in different climate zones of China. The hydrology modelling framework is displayed in Figure 4.10.

Once the potential reductions in river flows were estimated by the hydrological models, Wang *et al.* (2012) determined the vulnerability of the watershed. Watersheds were assigned a vulnerability classification ranging from extremely vulnerable (level V) to not very vulnerable (level I) based on their sensitivity to shifts in precipitation and temperature and their adaptive capacity (determined by human stressors like demand or pollution) to deal with such change. Scenarios of future adaptive capacity were created by estimating future demand and shifts in water management around regulation and storage. The schematic in Figure 4.11 describes how the researchers created a vulnerability index for each of the 216 watersheds, which was used to generate the vulnerability maps in Figure 4.9. Finally, the researchers assessed the risk posed by extreme precipitation events (either extremely wet or extremely dry years) to watersheds by assessing the likelihood of the occurrence of such years in combination with each watershed's vulnerability.

Extremely wet or dry years are immensely challenging in water resource operations, depending on options available to water managers in that watershed. These years have the potential to cause flooding or droughts. If the likelihood of occurrence of extreme precipitation years increases, watersheds with moderate to extreme vulnerability face a greater risk of suffering both floods and droughts. The researchers also conducted the impact assessment for groundwater resources. Identifying watersheds and aquifers with high current and future vulnerability and the potential for increased flood and drought risk allows water managers, communities and policy makers to begin identifying a suite of options for reducing vulnerability and improving the watershed's resilience to future climate risks.

Adaptation planning for China's water resources to meet future challenges

As its economy grows and demand for water increases, China will need to develop robust systems for managing water in an increasingly volatile climate, particularly in the water-scarce north. Although changes in projected runoff remain uncertain for most basins, regional water shortages and flooding remain key issues that are likely only to grow in importance as climate change amplifies existing patterns of shortage and excess. These pressures and uncertainties could

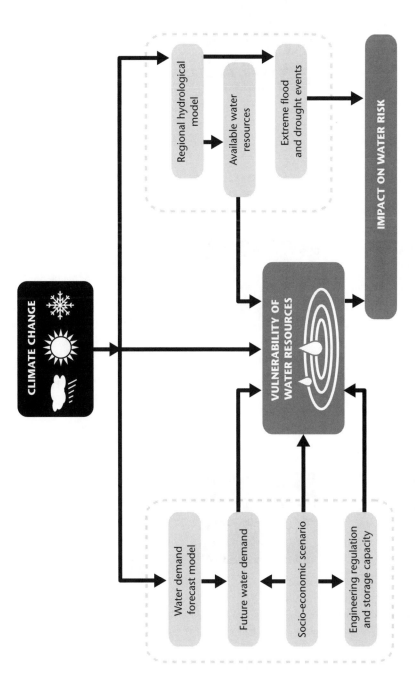

FIGURE 4.10 Hydrology modelling framework used to assess the impact of climate change on water resources

Mean precipitation and
variation coefficient

Mean temperature and
variance

Indicator system
for the
vulnerability
assesment of the
water system

Degree of sensitivity of water
resources to climate change

Impact of climate change on
water resources

Impact of climate change on
extreme floods and droughts

Regional water scarcity rate
under future climate change

Degree of regional water
utilization

Per capita GDP

Per capita water resources
in the future

Water consumption per
RMB10,000 of output value

Regulation and storage capacity
of water projects

FIGURE 4.11 Schematic used to assess watershed vulnerability based on sensitivity to climatic shifts and adaptive capacity, and to determine vulnerability indices

require a new style of adaptive water management, combining use of non-traditional sources such as urban wastewater with better management of existing storage, and much more emphasis on water conservation and reallocation. A mix of *soft management* (policy, financial and institutional approaches for balancing water demand with supply constraints) and *hard management* (infrastructure and land alteration that focuses on manipulating supply to meet demand) options is more likely to build flexibility, robustness, redundancy and safe-failure (elements of resilience) into China's water systems than reliance on infrastructure alone.

Existing policies and water management strategies in China were built and rolled out under the assumption that climate conditions would remain largely as they are, with extreme events like floods and droughts following similar historical frequencies of occurrence and intensity. This assumption of *stationarity* – that historical statistics for a water or climate system will remain the same in the future – is common in traditional, infrastructure-based water resource management strategies around the world (Westra *et al.*, 2010; Lawrence *et al.*, 2013; ISET and CEDSJ, 2011), influencing the planning and construction of reservoirs, flood control and wastewater and storm-water drainage systems, among others. For example, water planners typically construct a reservoir assuming that average annual river flows will always be close to some value and vary by some positive or negative amount, thus determining how much storage capacity a dam should have. However, climate variability and change are shifting both long-term averages and increasing both extreme low and high flows.

Studies since the turn of the millennium have identified the following weaknesses in China's existing water management approaches (Liu *et al.*, 2001; Foster and Garduño, 2004; Wang *et al.*, 2006; World Bank, 2007; Wang *et al.*, 2012):

- Water allocation systems do not promote conservation or efficiency, causing significant water losses due to waste. A lack of appropriate regulation and enforcement around pollution and environmental degradation also renders some water supplies unusable.
- Competition between rural areas and rapidly developing urban areas is creating disparities in water allocation, access and options for management. At the same time, reduced institutional capacity and access to resources (knowledge, funding, etc.) make it difficult for poorer provinces and rural areas to implement and enforce national policies and mesh these with local-level development concerns and priorities.
- Inadequate and ageing infrastructure is unable to create an adequate supply buffer, particularly for carry-over in drought years. Some reservoirs, originally designed for flood control or hydropower in addition to storage, are unsafe and could contribute to flood risk. Furthermore, potential

hydropower resources are largely unexplored and underdeveloped. Focus on existing infrastructure is limiting exploration of alternatives such as rainwater collection, wastewater recycling and seawater desalination.

- There is little awareness or ability among sectors and various government agencies to use available hydro-meteorological information and emerging climate projections. There is also a lack of coordination to access and spread that information. Furthermore, scientists are often unsure of how to communicate their research findings in a policy-relevant manner. Both scientists and decision makers need help to understand and frame problems and policies so they can reach across disciplines.

While the Chinese government acknowledged the concept of climate change in 1994, forward-thinking and long-term planning integrating development needs, ecosystem and watershed protection and climate change implications were not fully integrated into national policy until 2007 under the *National Climate Change Programme* (see Chapter 11). Prior to this, national water policy followed a fragmented approach, with little integration across water themes or government management institutions across scales. A few policies targeted single issues, such as the *Water Law of 1998* (amended in 2002) aimed at streamlining ownership of water resources and licensing of water rights, or the 2008 *Law on the Prevention and Control of Water Pollution*, but these efforts were fragmented.

As climate conditions have begun to shift and social pressures evolve faster than infrastructure can keep up, water planners are increasingly turning to a combination of soft and hard management options to build resilience. In China, the following options for integrated water management (see Table 4.1) are already being considered or employed in combination, or have been suggested by water researchers to address the various stresses and weaknesses mentioned throughout this chapter.

Water policies and management attitudes are shifting from the traditional paradigms of developing water resources to meet growing demand and rigid management. Policy makers are moving toward a stronger focus on conservation, preservation and changing allocation strategies and working to integrate policies, coordination between government entities and implementation and enforcement of policies (Hu, 2007). China is now beginning to take more of an integrated basin management approach through the development of the *National Comprehensive Water Resources Plan* in 2010, which incorporates the objectives of the *Eleventh* and *Twelfth Five Year Plans*, the evolving *National Climate Change Programme* and the *National Strategy of Climate Adaptation* released in 2013. Under the plan, the Ministry of Water Resources is now coordinating with ten other ministries, including the National Development and Reform Commission, the Ministry of Land and Resources, and the Ministry of Environmental Protection to have regular inter-ministerial meetings to ensure cooperation on comprehensive river basin planning. Additionally, the plan proposes a mixture

TABLE 4.1 Integrated soft and hard water management options to improve the current challenging water situation and build more flexibility and resilience against climate change and other future stressors

Soft options		Hard options	
Policy	• Implement and enforce building codes prohibiting construction in high hazard risk areas. • Develop regional and community-specific disaster risk reduction (DRR) and response plans. • Provide incentives and penalties to improve conservation. • Adjust allocation of water resources in-basin in real-time response to current precipitation and flow trends. • Begin considering climate, socio-economic and environmental change in water allocation. • Designate and allow groundwater use only during times of drought, allowing recharge during wet season. • Develop and enforce water quotas for different industries and agriculture. • Establish drought contingency plans. • Develop water rights trading markets to optimise allocation. • Strengthen legal protection, regulation and enforcement of environmental and pollution standards. • Coordinate policy making from the local to the national level that accounts for true water costs and resource sustainability.	Infrastructure	• Build reservoirs, dikes and flood storage for flood control and water buffering for drought. • Modify heights of select levees and coastal defences to protect certain assets and allow a phased retreat. • Improve urban drainage and flood control systems. • Harvest rainwater and recycle grey water. • Utilise inter-basin transfers, such as the *North–South Transfer Project.* • Improve sewage and pollution treatment, including treatment plants and bioretention wetlands. • Promote more water-efficient irrigation and industrial manufacturing methods. • Promote precision application of herbicides, pesticides and fertilisers in agriculture to reduce pollution runoff and waterway contamination. • Explore desalination.

continued

TABLE 4.1 Continued

Soft options		Hard options	
Education, outreach and participation	• Educate the public and government officials at different levels about water pollution and protecting waterways. • Educate about hazards like flooding and drought, and options for preparing for, responding to and recovering from these. • Form multilevel organisations and working groups for coordinating DRR and more resilient recovery. • Conduct public education campaigns via radio, television, social media and other channels to raise awareness about conservation, pollution reduction and DRR awareness. • Hold community-based training courses. • Involve the community in local water resource planning and management.	Land use	• Increase urban green space and open up floodplains. • Plant vegetation and restore natural water bodies and wetlands for flood buffering. • Terrace and replant steep slopes to reduce risk of landslide and river contamination during heavy rain. • Reforest and return non-productive and marginal croplands to forest or native grasslands, especially to slow rates of desertification in arid regions.
Conservation	• Reduce consumption in coastal areas to reduce saltwater intrusion into groundwater. • Explore more drought-tolerant and less water-dependent seeds.		
Insurance	Reduce the impacts of floods and droughts on livelihoods and assets through statutory and voluntary insurance.		

Early warning
- Develop and deploy timely forecasts targeted to specific audiences (emergency responders, agricultural agencies, etc.) to meet their planning and response needs around water and weather hazards.
- Develop multimedia early warning systems to warn the public about water situations and weather hazards.

Better research
- Improve hydro-meteorological monitoring systems and data collection for identifying emerging impacts and changes in watersheds and aquifers, and for early warning purposes.
- Improve monitoring and mapping of hazard-prone areas for updating land use development plans and building codes.
- Improve monitoring and testing of pollution sources, and treatment and clean-up options.
- Develop and maintain a one-stop information system (e.g. river flow data, groundwater depths, meteorological data) where all information can be found. Such a system would assist decision makers and water resource managers who currently must find information from disjointed sources.

of soft and hard measures to promote conservation, water use efficiency and reduction of pollution, including (Cao, 2010; Xinhua, 2011; Jin *et al.*, 2010; Wang and Zheng, 2011; Xue and You, 2010):

- beginning the development of a water market and water trading schemes, with pilot water transfers occurring between some cities (between Dongyang and Yiwu in Zhejiang Province in 2001), and irrigation and industrial transfers in Inner Mongolia Autonomous Region, Ningxia, Liaoning, Gansu and Qingdao;
- implementing watershed protection and ecosystem restoration projects, such as soil remediation, vegetation replanting to reduce soil erosion and a planned pilot project for Boyang Lake in Jaingxi Province to restore sections of the river and establish ecological protection zones for key riverine habitat areas;
- promoting water conservation in both rural and urban areas through educational campaigns around conserving water, improved irrigation and cropping techniques, water allocation controls and metering and consumptive use charges;
- establishing and enforcing limits or 'three red lines of control' for total water consumption, efficiency and allowed pollutant discharge across each province, with decentralised management targets for 2015 down to the municipal level;
- achieving set consumption target levels in agriculture, industry and urban areas through a combination of improvements in technology, fixing leaks, water-saving devices, and better monitoring and enforcement;
- exploring alternative water sources such as rainwater harvesting, grey water treatment and reuse, floodwater utilisation and seawater desalinisation to reduce consumption and increase conservation awareness and watershed protection in order to alleviate the dire water shortages facing many urban areas and some rural communities in the arid north, and even the more water-blessed south;
- implementing large-scale water storage projects and inter-basin transfers, such as the *South–North Water Relocation Project* transferring water from the Pearl River to the Yellow River, in addition to further groundwater exploration (as both floods and droughts are expected to increase in frequency and severity due to climate change, additional storage capacity, including recharging shallow aquifers with flood water, will become increasingly important);
- strengthening institutional capacity and coordination among government ministries and across scales; and
- improving coordination between research institutes and government ministries, which may lead to better communication and tailoring of scientific information to meet policy needs and priorities.

China published its *National Adaptation Strategy* (NAS) in November 2013 (see Chapter 11). Not surprisingly, water resource management is identified as a priority area in which a variety of conservation, ecological restoration and wise-use strategies are being promoted to help the water sector adapt while managing complex demands. Jiangxi has been identified as a demonstration pilot province for enhanced water resource protection and water conservation, with a primary focus on the Poyang Lake region of the province.[7] The Autonomous Region of Xinjiang has also been designated as a demonstration adaptation pilot province, with projects investigating the prevention and control of glacial snowmelt flooding. The NAS represents a significant step towards integrating climate change into water resource management practices. It is anticipated that the lessons learned from the pilot provinces of Jiangxi and Xinjiang will be disseminated to other regions. Priority tasks for water resource management include on a national level are listed in Table 4.2.

In the face of climate, social and ecological pressures, the NAS and other innovations in water, agricultural and disaster risk reduction policies shows China's commitment at a national policy level to the better implementation of more integrated water management approaches, in addition to setting strict limits for water development and use. It is introducing policies and measures related to water efficiency and conservation to curb water waste, in addition to better pollution controls and environmental protection laws to control effluent and contaminant fouling of surface and groundwater supplies. China has also launched overhauls of agricultural irrigation practices, hoping to realise further water savings, but it still has a long way to go in implementing many of the proposed changes and enforcing policies while encouraging more efficient use. Institutional capacity barriers across governance scales, development disparities between rural and urban areas and richer and poorer provinces, a legacy of unmanaged growth and resulting pollution and land use change, in conjunction with increasing climate variability and change, represent the major challenges facing China in shifting its water resource management strategies. Additionally, many existing water management strategies, particularly infrastructure options, were built under the assumption of stationarity; retrofitting and upgrading existing infrastructure, as well as planning for new infrastructure, needs to begin accounting for a greater range of possible drought and flooding extremes influenced by climate change. However, China has made crucial steps toward a more holistic, forward-thinking water resource management policy and has started to see water system resilience as part of the overall process of adapting to climate change.

TABLE 4.2 China's water resource management priorities under the *National Adaptation Strategy*

Actions for better aquatic ecosystem management and protection include	• developing standards to govern the amount of water use in major rivers and lakes to ensure healthy flow and maintain the water table; • increasing water quality and ecosystem monitoring and aqua-ecology protection; • incorporating prevention, protection, monitoring, governance and restoration into comprehensive planning, with specific approaches decided by the local conditions and with measures tailored to specific disasters; • using integrated engineering, biological and agricultural measures; and • establishing a comprehensive prevention system for water and soil erosion in accordance with targets specified in the *Twelfth Five Year Plan* period.
A system for more rational allocation and efficient use of water resources to ensure the safety of urban and rural residents' drinking water must be built by	• devoting greater efforts toward building a water-efficient society, with water storage, distribution and excavation projects designed and built in accordance local conditions and needs; • improving core water resource and irrigation projects, with the construction of the east route and phase I of the middle route of the *South-North Water Relocation Project*, as well as the feasibility study for the west route gaining speed; • implementing a strict water resources management regime which regulates management, water resources project feasibility studies and water access permits to better control the total amount of water use and institute quota-based management; • curbing unplanned urban expansion and development of water-intensive industries; and • exploring unconventional water sources such as flood, seawater, salty and bitter groundwater, recycled water and mine water.
Development of enhanced flood and drought management systems should be promoted by	• accelerating construction of control stations along river tributaries; • hastening construction of major water projects along rivers and their tributaries, with levees reinforced and waterways restored along important rivers; • reshaping urban development and industrial layout, with flood buffer areas deployed in a scientific and rational way; • prohibiting unauthorised reclamation of land and the enclosure of beaches and spillways; • strengthening flood risk management; and • developing flood and drought relief headquarters at all levels with improved emergency mechanisms for more powerful disaster monitoring, prediction, forecasting and early warning.

Notes

1 Anecdotes exist about members of the Xia Dynasty (2100–1600 BC) trying to control flooding on the Yangtze and building canals to channel floodwaters from croplands. Local water governance bodies emerged in parts of north China during the Ming and Qing periods (AD 1368–1922) to address issues of water shortages and challenge bureaucratic water control (Dang et al., 2013).
2 The water resource impact assessment was conducted by researchers from the Nanjing Hydraulic Research Institute, the Research Center for Climate Change and the Ministry of Water Resources with the support of the Adapting to Climate Change in China (ACCC) programme.
3 This figure is adapted from 'The average annual precipitation across Greater China' by Alan Mak, which is licensed under CC BY-SA 3.0. The original image is available from http://en.wikipedia.org/wiki/Geography_of_China#mediaviewer/File:China_average_annual_precipitation_%28en%29.png, and the license can be found at https://creativecommons.org/licenses/by/3.0/us/.
4 The Chinese have been manipulating the hydrology of all of their river systems for centuries for the purpose of irrigation, domestic needs and minor flood control, so it is not possible to estimate what the 'natural' river flows would be without human influence. However, large-scale modern flood control and water resource diversions were not put into place until the 1970s. Thus, in the analysis, Zhao et al. (2012) used the baseline period of flows as 1951 through the 1960s for most rivers to estimate the role of human activity in the observed decreases in river flows from 1970–2010.
5 Taken from *National Climate Change Program.* Available from: www.china.org.cn/english/environment/213624.htm#10, section 3, para 6. [Accessed 13 April 2015.]
6 Each climate model represents the interactions between the land, ocean and atmosphere in slightly different manners based on our current understanding of climate physics and atmospheric and oceanic biogeochemistry. Climate models then produce multiple estimations (projections) of what an area's future climate might be based on different scenarios of greenhouse gas emissions, land use change, and population pressures. For this reason, the projected changes in precipitation and temperature for a region will vary from model to model, and from emission scenario to emission scenario. Because it cannot be known with certainty which land use, energy, population and emission will most accurately reflect future conditions, it is necessary to use multiple projections when investigating potential climate change impacts, and to build resiliency to a variety of futures.
7 Jiangxi is a province included in ACCC II (2014–2017) in which the water resource issues will be investigated in greater detail.

References

Cai, X. (2006) *Water Stress, Water Transfer and Social Equity in Northern China: Implications for Policy Reforms.* UNDP Human Development Report 2006/37, Washington, DC.

Cai, X. and Rosegrant, M.W. (2004) Optional water development strategies for the Yellow River basin: Balancing agricultural and ecological water demands. *Water Resources Research* 40 (8). art. W08S04.

Cao, J. (2010) *The Impact of Climate Change on Water Resources Management and Adaptation Strategies.* Development Research Center. PRC Ministry of Water Resources. [Online] Available from: www.waterinfo.com.cn/xsgz/gndt/Document/55901/55901.html. [Accessed: 28 November 2014.]

Chen, M. (1987) Groundwater resources and development in China. *Environmental Geology and Water Sciences.* 10 (3). pp. 141–147.

Chen, Y.D., Zhang, Q., Xu, C., Lu X. and Zhang S. (2010) Multiscale streamflow variations in the Pearl River basin and possible implications for the water resource management within the Pearl River Delta, China. *Quaternary International*. 226. pp. 44–53.

Dang, X., Webber, M., Chen, D. and Wang, M.Y. (2013) Evolution of water management in Shanxi and Shaanxi Provinces since the Ming and Qing dynasties of China. *Water*. 5 (2). pp. 643–658.

Ding, Y. and Chan, J.C.L. (2005) The East Asian summer monsoon: An overview. *Meteorology and Atmospheric Physics*. 89. pp. 117–142.

Falkenmark, M. (1989) The massive water scarcity threatening Africa: Why isn't it being addressed? *Ambio*. 18 (2). pp. 1112–1118.

Fan, K., Xu, Z. and Tian, B. (2013) Has the intensity of the interannual variability in summer rainfall over South China remarkably increased? *Meteorology and Atmospheric Physics*. 124. pp. 23–32.

FAO (Food and Agricultural Organization of the United Nations) (2014) *Computation of Long-Term Annual Renewable Water Resources by Country (in km³/yr, average): China*. [Online] Aquastat FAO. Available from: www.fao.org/nr/water/aquastat/data/wrs/readPdf.html?f=CHN-WRS_eng.pdf. [Accessed: 18 November 2014.]

Foster, S. and Garduño, H. (2004) *Towards Sustainable Groundwater Resource Use for Irrigated Agriculture on the North China Plain*. Groundwater Management Advisory Team (GW-MATE), World Bank (Case Profile Collection No. 8).

Foster, S., Garduño, H., Evans, R., Olson, D., Tian, Y., Zhang, W. and Han, Z. (2004) Quaternary aquifer of the North China Plain: Assessing and achieving groundwater resource sustainability. *Hydrogeology Journal*. 12. pp. 81–93.

Gao, X., Xu, Y. *et al.* (2012) *Final Report of the ACCC I Project: China Meteorology Administration and National Climate Centre*. ACCC: Beijing, People's Republic of China.

Gleick, P. (2011a) *Three Gorges Dam Project, Yangtze River, China*. Pacific Institute: Oakland, California, USA (Water Brief 3).

Gleick, P. (2011b) China dams. In: Gleick, P.H., Allen, L., Christian-Smith, J., Cohen, M.J., Cooley, H., Heberger, M., Morrison, J., Planiappan, M. and Schulte, P. (eds), *The World's Water: The Biennial Report on Freshwater Resources (Volume 7)*. Island Press: Washington, DC, USA.

He, B., Lü, A., Wu, J., Zhao, L. and Liu, M. (2011) Drought hazard assessment and spatial characteristics analysis in China. *Journal of Geographical Sciences*. 21 (2). pp. 235–249.

He, J., Wu, Z. and Wang, Z. (2008) Climate of China and East Asian Monsoon. In: Fu, C., Jiang, Z., Guan, Z., He, J. and Xu, Z. (eds), *Regional Climate Studies of China*. Springer: Berlin, Germany.

Hu, S. (2007) Hu Siyi on the formation of a 'water-saving society' in the Eleventh Five Year Plan. Ministry of Water Resources. [Online] Available from: www.mwr.gov.cn/zwzc/zcfg/jd/200702/t20070209_26148.html. [Accessed: 28 November 2014.]

Huang, H. and Zheng, Y. (2009) Present situation and future prospect of hydropower in China. *Renewable and Sustainable Energy Reviews*. 13. pp. 1652–1656.

IPCC (2012) *Managing the Risks of Extreme Events and Disasters to Advance Climate Change Adaptation*. A Special Report of Working Groups I and II of the Intergovernmental Panel on Climate Change [Field, C.B., Barros, V., Stocker, T.F., Qin, D., Dokken, D.J., Ebi, K.L., Mastrandrea, M.D., Mach, K.J., Plattner, G.K., Allen, S.K., Tignor, M. and Midgley P.M. (eds)]. Cambridge University Press: Cambridge, United Kingdom and New York, New York, USA.

ISET and CEDSJ (2011) *The Uncomfortable Nexus: Water, Urbanization and Climate Change in Jaipur, India.* Study Report. Institute for Social and Environmental Transition and Centre for Environment and Development Studies, Jaipur: Boulder, Colorado, USA and Jaipur, India.

Jiang, T., Zhang, Q., Zhu, D. and Wu, Y. (2006) Yangtze floods and droughts (China) and teleconnections with ENSO activities (1470–2003). *Quaternary International.* 144. pp. 29–37.

Jin, S., Sheng, Z. and Liu, X. (2010) Basin system complexity and adaptive management. *China Population Resources and Environment.* 7. pp. 60–67.

Lawrence, J., Reisinger, A., Mullan, B. and Jackson, B. (2013) Exploring climate change uncertainties to support adaptive management of changing flood-risk. *Environmental Science and Policy.* 33. pp. 133–142.

Liu, C., Yu, J. and Kendy, E. (2001) Groundwater exploitation and its impact on the environment in the North China Plain. *Water International.* 26 (2). pp. 265–272.

Lohmar, B., Wang, J., Rozelle, S., Huang, J. and Dawe, D. (2003) *China's Agricultural Water Policy Reforms: Increasing Investment, Resolving Conflicts and Revising Incentives.* Market and Trade Economics Division, Economic Research Service, US Department of Agriculture: Washington, DC, USA (Agriculture Information Bulletin Number 782).

PRC Meteorological Administration (2012) China Ground International Switching Station Climate Standard Value – Monthly Value Dataset (1971 to 2000). [Online] Available from: www.cma.gov.cn/2011qxfw/2011qsjgx/. [Accessed: 13 April 2015.]

PRC Ministry of Civil Affairs (2010) *Reports of drought status and control measures.* PRC Ministry of Civil Affairs: Beijing, People's Republic of China.

PRC Ministry of Water Resources (2008) *Annual Report 2007–2008.* [Online] Available from: www.mwr.gov.cn/english/2007-2008.doc. [Accessed: 29 March 2014.]

PRC Ministry of Water Resources (2013) *Bulletin of First National Census for Water.* PRC Ministry of Water Resources: Beijing, People's Republic of China.

Wang, G.Q., Yan, X.L., Zhang, J.Y., Liu, C.S., Jin, J.L. and Bao, Z.X. (2013) Detecting evolution trends in the recorded runoffs from the major rivers in China during 1950–2010. *Journal of Water and Climate Change.* 4 (3). pp. 252–264.

Wang, G.Q., Zhang, J.Y. et al. (2012) *Impact Assessment of Climate Change on Regional Water Resources in China and Adaptation Strategies.* ACCC I National Water Report. Nanjing Hydraulic Research Institute: Nanjing, People's Republic of China.

Wang, G.Q., Zhang, J.Y., Liu, J.F., Jin, J.L. and Liu, C.S. (2011) The sensitivity of runoff to climate change in different climatic regions in China. *Advances in Water Science.* 22 (3). pp. 307–314.

Wang, G.Q., Zhang, J.Y., Pagano, T.C., Lin, J.L. and Liu, C.S. (2013) Identifying contributions of climate change and human activity to changes in runoff using epoch detection and hydrologic simulation. *Journal of Hydrologic Engineering.* 18 (11). pp. 1385–1392.

Wang, J., Huang, J., Blanke, A., Huang, Q. and Rozelle, S. (2006) The development, challenges and management of groundwater in rural China. In: Giordano, M. and Villholth, K.G. (eds), *The Agricultural Groundwater Revolution: Opportunities and Threats to Development.* CABI and IWMI: Wallingford, United Kingdom and Colombo, Sri Lanka.

Wang, W. and Zheng, Y. (2011) Synergies and policy implications of low-carbon development and adaptation to climate change. In: Wang, W., Guang, Z. and Guo, G. (eds), *Annual Report on Actions to Address Climate Change (2011) – Durban's Dilemma and China's Options.* Social Science Academic Press: Beijing, People's Republic of China.

Westra, S., Varley, I., Sharma, A., Hill, P., Jordan, P., Nathan, R. and Ladson, A. (2010) Addressing climatic non-stationarity in the assessment of flood risk. *Australian Journal of Water Resources*. 14 (1). pp. 1–16.

World Bank (2007) *Cost of Pollution in China: Economic Estimates of Physical Damages (Conference edition)*. PRC Environmental Protection Administration and Natural Resources and Environment Management Unit, East Asia and Pacific Region, The World Bank: Washington, DC, USA.

Xinhua (2011) *China's Climate Change Policies and Actions (2011)*. White paper. PRC Central Government. [Online] 22 November. Available from: www.gov.cn/jrzg/2011-11/22/content_2000047.htm. [Accessed: 28 November 2014.]

Xinhua (2013) *Chinese Public Calls for Tackling Water Pollution*. PRC Ministry of Water Resources. [Online] 10 April. Available from: www.mwr.gov.cn/english/news/201304/t20130410_433265.html. [Accessed: 7 July 2014.]

Xue, Y. and You, L. (2010) Water right transfer experiment and the impact on the water resources management policy in China: An overview. *Journal of the Washington Institute of China Studies*. [Online] 5 (3). Available from: www.bpastudies.org/bpastudies/article/view/145/281. [Accessed: 29 November 2014.]

Zhai, P., Zhang, X., Wan, H. and Pan, X. (2005) Trends in total precipitation and frequency of daily precipitation extremes over China. *Journal of Climate*. 18. pp. 1096–1108.

Zhang, J.Y. and Wang, G.Q. (2007) *Impacts of Climate Change on Hydrology and Water Resources*. Science Press: Beijing, People's Republic of China.

Zhang, W., Mu S., Zhang, Y. and Chen M. (2012) Seasonal and interannual variations of flow discharge from Pearl River into sea. *Water Science and Engineering*. 5 (4). pp. 399–409.

Zhao, G.J., Mu, X.M., Hörmann, G., Fohrer, N., Xiong, M., Su, B.D. and Li, X.C. (2012) Spatial patterns and temporal variability of dryness/wetness in the Yangtze River Basin, China. *Quaternary International*. 282. pp. 5–13.

5

FEEDING CHINA

*Li Kuo, Zheng Dawei, Hu Yanan, Ma Jianyong,
Xu Yinlong, Andreas Wilkes, Sarah Opitz-Stapleton,
Krystal Lair and Rebecca Nadin*

Spring already comes two days earlier than it used to. In some parts of China, it arrives an average of four days sooner than it did just three decades ago, in the 1980s. This might seem like a small seasonal shift, but it is one of a host of changes in climate that will have far-reaching consequences for agriculture across the country.

Agriculture is vital to China, supporting the livelihoods of more than 200 million smallholder farmers (Huang *et al.*, 2012) and providing food for the nation. It is also one of the sectors in China most exposed to natural disasters (see Chapter 3). The country's people and economy are on the front line of any changes in weather, and millions experience these effects first-hand, from melting glaciers to longer droughts and spreading deserts. Additionally, while the country's economic growth in recent years has been impressive, rural incomes have risen more slowly than urban incomes, particularly in western and central China (Luo and Sicular, 2013; see also Chapter 2). Uptake and access for many rural people to agricultural insurance or microfinance is still limited (Belete *et al.*, 2007; Wang, M. *et al.*, 2011), and many lack the skills needed to withstand the sometimes dramatic effects of extreme weather and climate change on China's agriculture.

This challenge is intensified by China's need to feed approximately one-seventh of the world's people with just over 10% of its arable land (World Bank, 2014). Even small changes in China's weather can directly alter its agricultural landscape, shift crop zones and affect the types and quantities of food farmers can grow. In recent years, China has experienced many natural disasters, affecting agricultural production (see Chapter 3). Resulting losses in yields or varieties in one part of the country necessarily affects prices, imports, exports and production in other areas. Any climate impacts on agriculture, therefore, significantly impact China's society and economy.

Just how climate change will impact agriculture and animal husbandry is a primary concern for the Chinese government. Sustaining the careful balance necessary to feed a growing population in the face of climatic and other shocks will require careful long-term planning and improvement in China's capacity to adapt to climate change in agriculture. Key to this is investigating the vulnerability of regional agricultural to climate change and developing measures and policies to reduce those vulnerabilities while exploring new opportunities, such as ecological restoration and organic farming opportunities (described below) that build livelihoods and ecological resilience.

Yang Fei is chairman of the Zhongwei Modern Desert Agricultural Company, composed of more than 650 hectares of cropland and greenhouses protected by a ring of date and poplar trees and 'grass grid' sand abatement barriers. In the mixed-use farm, pollution-free groundwater filtered by the desert sands is piped through a trickle-irrigation network to sustain a vast array of organic fruit and vegetables, from aubergines [eggplants] to muskmelons and tomatoes. Alfalfa cultivated in the grass barriers is used to feed cattle, which in turn produce dung to fertilise the date trees. Yang grows what the market demands and reaps a premium for delivering certified-organic produce. As a businessman, Yang's daily focus is on the financial bottom line of his operation. As a resident, however, he is also grateful for the difference in the landscape and lives made by the revegetation push. '[Farming the desert] brings more job opportunities to the local community. Each greenhouse creates two jobs. . . . It brings them good financial benefits,' he says. 'It also changes the desert and the environment. In recent years, we've seen fewer sandstorms in Zhongwei after we planted the forest. Rainwater has become clear and the ecosystem has recovered.'

This chapter provides an overview of China's efforts to date in developing long-term measures to adapt to the effects of climate change in agriculture. The adaptation choices China makes will have broad-scale impacts not only on the viability of the sector and on the livelihoods and business ventures of farmers like Yang Fei, but also far beyond China's borders in terms of its influence on regional and global agricultural markets and international water negotiations (e.g. water management on the Lancang/Mekong River). The chapter first examines the impacts of climate variability and change on agriculture and food security in China, including a case study that examines some of China's recent work in developing biophysical impact assessments for three crops critical to China's food supply – maize, rice and wheat – using climate projections developed under the Adapting to Climate Change in China I (ACCC I) programme.[1] It then goes on to outline some of the measures that the government has been taking to support adaptation in the agriculture sector.

Climate trends and projections for China

Much of China is dominated by the East Asian Monsoon System (EASM). Increasing precipitation variability has led to falls in annual precipitation totals in some parts of the country and increases in others. The nationwide average annual precipitation between 1950 and 2010 has not changed significantly, but there are regional differences between the north-east (decreasing), the north-west (increasing), the south-east (increasing) and parts of the south-west (decreasing) (Zhai et al., 2005; Fan et al., 2013; Zhao et al., 2012). The shifts in precipitation have aggravated incidences of flood and drought throughout the country, with southern floods and northern droughts being particularly severe in the last decade. Northern China has experienced persistent droughts over increasingly larger areas, exacerbating rates of desertification and soil loss (see Chapters 8 and 9) (Song and Zhang, 2003). Drawing conclusions about the causes of trends in precipitation is difficult due to the insufficient record length and few weather stations over vast distances in some provinces, as well as high natural year-to-year and decadal precipitation variability in the Asian monsoon region. Many of the recent trends are due to the natural variability and not climate change (Hijioka et al., 2014; Christensen et al., 2013).

In contrast, southern and south-western areas have been experiencing more extreme precipitation events, contributing to more intense floods, mudslides and significant crop losses (Wu and Zhai, 2013). The south is not immune to drought, however. A widespread drought covered many southern provinces, including Yunnan, Guizhou and Chongqing, from 2009 to 2013, and was accompanied by abnormally warm temperatures; some northern provinces were impacted by it as well. The drought led to severe drinking water shortages in many rural communities, livestock deaths and significant crop losses, with four million hectares of crops lost by August 2013 (Wang and Chen, 2013). While the drought itself cannot be directly attributed to climate change, and indeed seems to have been caused through a confluence of large-scale atmospheric features – such as the development of El Niño and an extremely negative Artic Oscillation (Barriopedro et al., 2012; Feng et al., 2014) – increasing precipitation variability is consistent with climate change projections. In the future, many parts of China are likely to experience an increase in the intensity and frequency of both drought and heavy precipitation, sometimes within the same year (Collins et al., 2013; Hijioka et al., 2014). Persistent, multi-year droughts may become more common, and impact areas not usually accustomed to them. These shifts in extreme events and droughts are also discussed in other chapters of this book, including Chapters 4, 6, 8 and 9.

Most of China has also experienced warming over the past few decades, which has generated a number of impacts on crops and cropping patterns. Mean temperatures, the length of the hot season and daytime and night-time temperatures have generally been increasing. There have been significant regional differences in warming rates, with the largest warming trends occurring in north-east China and Inner Mongolia between 1960 and 2006 (Piao *et al.*, 2010). These trends are expected to continue into the future, with fewer and fewer cold snaps occurring and nights becoming warmer. The south-western areas of China – the Qinghai–Tibetan Plateau – are projected to warm faster than other regions of China and experience greater numbers of heat waves (Christensen *et al.*, 2013; Sui *et al.*, 2014). A more region-specific overview of trends and projections in temperature and precipitation, along with their implications for water resources, are covered in greater detail in Chapters 4, 8, 9 and 10.

Recent climate impacts on agriculture

Climate change is a double-edged sword, bringing changes that both help and hurt farming. Two decades of study on carbon dioxide levels, precipitation, heat, sunshine, extreme events, agricultural vulnerability, and food production suggest that the effects of climate variability and change are different from region to region, intra-annually (season to season) and on a decadal basis. However, the overall observed climate variability impacts on agriculture in China are largely negative (He *et al.*, 2011; Challinor *et al.*, 2010). Detecting the relative impacts of extreme weather, human activities and gradual climate change on agriculture remains difficult due to the historically limited monitoring of the agricultural system – though monitoring networks are being improved. Climate change is likely to shift seasons and increase precipitation variability and the frequency and intensity of extreme events. Current crop losses and damages due to extreme weather or seasonal shifts point to high vulnerability in this sector.

China's growing season traditionally has a very consistent start and end date, based on historical records going back thousands of years in some areas. However, in just a few decades, it has shifted. The spring *phenophase* (the date of the first occurrence of various biological events of spring, such as the first appearance of leaves and flowers and the first activity of different animal species) already comes two days earlier than it used to, and in some parts of China is arriving four days sooner than it did just 30 years ago (Tao *et al.*, 2006).

As China has brought more lands under agricultural production and begun altering cropping practices, crop losses and damage from extreme events have risen. For example, in the North China Plain and the north-east (the primary grain production regions of the country), increasing drought frequency and severity have caused the greatest reduction in *yields* (total weight of the crops produced in a given area, usually measured in tonnes per hectare), followed by damage from hailstorms. The area most severely hit by drought has shifted northwards between 1951 and 2004, from Henan and Shandong toward Beijing and Tianjin (see Chapters 3 and 4). The Beijing–Tianjin region has also seen a steeper rise in hail disasters, with particularly severe hailstorms from the early

1980s to the early 2000s. Liaoning, Jilin and Heilongjiang provinces in north-east China have seen an increase in the percentage of drought-affected farmland increase about 3% per decade on average between 1951 and 2004. Yet, while rainfall has been declining in the North China Plain (see Chapters 3 and 4), extensive groundwater pumping has helped offset precipitation declines and moderated drought impacts on crop yields for those with access to irrigation water. As discussed in Chapter 4, however, reliance on groundwater to moderate drought-crop risk is not sustainable in the long run. Table 5.1 summarises the trends between 1951 and 2004 in the major meteorological disasters (drought, flood, hail and frost) for provinces in north-east China.

Climate shifts in China are also contributing to outbreaks of crop pests, diseases and weeds, and increasing the damage they inflict (Chen and Ma, 2010; Huo et al., 2012; Zhang et al., 2012; Ju et al., 2008). Every year China loses roughly 10% of its potential crop production, worth CNY60 billion (GBP6.01 billion), to these biological disasters. Rising temperatures, in combination with agricultural intensification and shifts in cropping practices, pollution and environmental degradation, have also led to an expansion in the area stricken by crop pests and diseases (Chen et al., 2011; Lu et al., 2010; Wu and Guo, 2005; Rosenzweig et al., 2001). The lifecycles of many pests and diseases have extended in response to more favourable temperature regimes and shifting cropping practices, which has resulted in heavier and more prolonged crop damage. With rising temperatures, these outbreaks are expanding northward and to higher altitudes, and an extended growing season allowing these species to reproduce more generations per year, plus the evolution of pesticide resistance, is leading to greater crop damage. Crops already stressed by drought and heat are more vulnerable to damage and death with an additional pest burden.

Warming and drying associated with climate variability since the 1960s and possibly climate change, together with harmful human activities (damaging land use practices, ecosystem degradation, pollution, etc.), have already caused soil salinisation and desertification in some areas of China (see Chapters 4 and 8). South-west China is particularly prone to landslides and serious soil erosion, resulting in falling soil quality and fertility, and reduced agricultural output (Coxon, 2011; Yin et al., 2011). Warmer temperatures, extended drought and pollution loading are also altering soil microbial composition and health, both of which are key to freeing nutrients from soil for crop uptake, helping soils to hold water, preventing pest microbes and fungi from dominating and leading to further declines in soil quality and fertility (Hueso et al., 2011; Richardson and Simpson, 2011; Bloor and Bardgett, 2012; Kremer, 2012).

Along with increasing competition for overallocated water resources, and increasing soil and water pollution among other factors, temperature rise has contributed to slower growth in agricultural production throughout much of China since the late 1980s (Cai et al., 2008; Cai and Smit, 1996). Models show that by 2030, the Chinese agricultural sector will need to increase agricultural

TABLE 5.1 Meteorological hazards, their trends and impacts for provinces in north-east China

Province	Average annual temperature trend	Average annual precipitation trend	Climate characteristics	Major meteorological disasters	Overall disaster trend	Drought trend	Flood trend	Hail trend	Frost trend
Heilongjiang	Upward	Not obvious	Continental monsoon climate from temperate to cold temperate zone, bitter cold, long and dry winter, warm summer with concentrated precipitation	Drought, flood, hail, frost, coldness, cold wave, snowstorm, lightning	Significantly exacerbated	Significantly exacerbated	Significantly alleviated	Exacerbated	Significantly exacerbated
Jinlin	Upward	Downward	Four distinct seasons, annual and daily temperature difference, rain and heat in the same season, distinct wet and dry seasons	Cold damage, drought, flood, frost	Exacerbated	Significantly exacerbated	Significantly alleviated	Significantly alleviated	Significantly exacerbated

	Trend		Climate	Disaster types					
Liaoning	Upward	Downward	Four distinct seasons, short spring and autumn, rain and heat in the same season, long cold season, abundant sunshine, wet in the east, dry in the west and windy in the plains	Storm, flood, drought, high winds, hail, cold wave, blizzard, cold damage, thunderstorm, tornado, glaze	Slightly alleviated	Slightly exacerbated	Alleviated	Significantly alleviated	Exacerbated
Inner Mongolia	Upward	Downward	Dry and less precipitation, semi-humid climate in the north of Greater Khingan Mountains and semi-arid climate in the west, very arid in western Inner Mongolia	Drought, flood, dust storm, snowstorm, frost, hail, cold damage, cold wave, thunderstorm, dry hot air	Significantly exacerbated	Significantly exacerbated	Slightly exacerbated	Significantly alleviated	Exacerbated
Hebei	Upward	Downward	Temperate semi-humid to semi-arid continental monsoon climate, distinct four seasons, uneven distribution of precipitation	Drought, storm, flood, dust storms, hail, dry hot wind, cold wave and frost, fog, lightning	Alleviated	Significantly alleviated	Significantly alleviated	Exacerbated	Exacerbated

Source: PRC Office of State Flood Control and Drought Relief Headquarters & PRC Ministry of Water Resources, 2008.

output by 1% every three years to make up for losses from increasing extreme events and shifting seasons (Deng *et al.*, 2006; Ju *et al.*, 2005). If proper measures are not taken, the overall capacity of agricultural production – mainly wheat, rice and maize yield – could decline 5–10% in 2030. This impact would intensify after 2050, mainly reflected in a decline in crop yields and quality, more pests and diseases and increased production costs due to reduced water availability and greater application of pesticides, fertilisers and irrigation water.

Not all changes brought by climate change might be harmful, however. In northern China, rising temperatures have extended the growing period and reduced cold-related crop damage, especially in the winter (Pan *et al.*, 2002). In some areas, the boundary of land suitable for farming and *multiple cropping* (planting more than one crop in a year due to a longer growing season) has expanded northward, and farmers are planting southern rice varieties and winter wheat crops further north and west than ever before. Furthermore, the *national cropping index* (the ratio of the total area sown with crops to the total amount of cultivated land in a country each year) is up from 143% in 1985 to 164% in 2001, especially in the Tibetan Plateau and other highland areas (Zhang *et al.*, 2008).

Though rising temperatures have extended the growing season and range of many crops, extreme temperatures can cause significant losses in crops introduced to into new ranges. Between 1990 and 2010, crop losses due to cold spells have occurred less frequently in the north-east and throughout most parts of China, though the unusual cold snap in south-east China in 2008 contributed to widespread rice crop losses in the region. The incidences of cold snaps are decreasing and are expected to continue to decrease in a warming climate (Pan *et al.*, 2013; Christensen *et al.*, 2013). However, they will continue to occur periodically and contribute to significant losses in crops that have adapted to a warmer climate and lost cold tolerance.

Climate variability and change, coupled with changing land-use, cropping patterns, pollution and soil degradation, present serious challenges to China's agricultural viability, with some regions more vulnerable than others. The next section describes the potential climate change impacts on agricultural yield and agricultural risk.

Implications of climate change for agriculture

The main risk to agriculture posed by climate change is crop yield decline. Slow-onset climate change – such as temperature rise, extended droughts, or less rain during the summer monsoon – leads to changes in agricultural production in different regions, which could include an increase *or* decrease in crop yields as well as the range of suitable growing areas. Increases in extreme events like severe storms, floods and heat waves as a result of climate change cause significant crop losses and damages. Both slow, progressive change and shifts in the frequency and intensity of extreme events will impact crop yields.

As discussed in the other chapters, climate change acts synergistically with socio-economic, environmental and political change processes. These include a growing population; increasing demand for meat, dairy and wheat (Fu *et al.*, 2012; Kearney, 2010); degradation and loss of arable land to desertification, soil salinisation, pollution and urbanisation (see Chapters 8 and 9); improvements and shifts in crop types, irrigation and other agricultural practices; increasing water scarcity and declining water quality in some regions (see Chapter 4) and a large rural population abandoning agriculture and migrating to urban areas for different opportunities (Wang, X. *et al.*, 2011; Mullan *et al.*, 2011). Agricultural production conditions will continue to change, pushing up some agricultural costs and investment demand. Internal demand for speciality crops, international trade and shifts in agricultural technologies (irrigation, crop seed manipulation, fertilisers and pesticides) are also shaping the future of agriculture. These processes will impact food security and have profound implications for the future of China's agriculture on the national and regional level (PRC National Development Reform Commission, 2008). They are also part of China's adaptation challenge.

Climate change will act in concert with the aforementioned factors. Some of these effects include changes in vegetation and ecosystem health, as well as livestock and agricultural yields (Deng *et al.*, 2006; Piao *et al.*, 2010; Challinor *et al.*, 2010; Wang *et al.*, 2012). The spatial distribution and crop structure of agricultural production has been shifting in response to temperature changes, manifesting in a longer growing season in some northern provinces and earlier spring planting due to fewer frost days, among other shifts. Drought frequency and duration in the nation's grasslands are expected to increase along with climate warming, resulting in further reductions in soil fertility and primary productivity (see Chapter 6). If continued, desertification and environmental degradation, coupled with warming and increasing precipitation variability, will impact crop production, soil microbial health and pest range and lifecycles. The impact of climate warming on animal husbandry may manifest itself in the increased incidence of certain livestock diseases, livestock vulnerability to temperature variability and extremes and changes to meat quality and flavour at higher temperatures (Gregory, 2010; see also Chapter 9).

The following section outlines a case study on the potential biophysical impacts of climate change to three of China's most important grain crops – maize, wheat and rice – in its breadbasket region, north-east China and the North China Plain. The study draws on the results of the national risk assessment of China's agricultural sector conducted under the auspices of the ACCC I programme. Researchers from the Innovation Research Team 'Climate Change and Utilization of Agro-climatic Resources' of the Chinese Academy of Agricultural Sciences (CAAS) employed a crop yield analysis of historical crops and a crop model incorporating climate projections from the two climate models (PRECIS and RegCM3) used in the programme to determine potential climate change impacts.

Case study: potential climate impacts on China's maize, wheat and rice yields

Crop yield analysis using crop models driven by projected shifts in temperature and precipitation, among other climate projections is the most common means of assessing climate change impacts on agricultural production. Comparisons between historical yield values over a baseline period (1961–1990 in this study) and simulated yields over future periods (2020s and 2050s) allows for an estimate of agricultural climate risk. This section examines the risk to crop yields of maize, wheat and rice, three staple crops in China. It must be highlighted that the analyses here assume that no adaptation actions are taken, though many large-scale initiatives that have been implemented in recent years are summarised in the section on policies and measures below. Also, the analysis is based only on one emission scenario (A1B) run by two climate models (PRECIS and RegCM3).[2] Therefore, uncertainties are high.

The study employed the DSSAT crop model (Jones *et al.*, 2003) to simulate future crop yields, driven by climate projections of future temperature and precipitation from the two climate models. The model's performance was first validated by its ability to reproduce observed annual grain yields for the three different crops over the baseline period of 1961–1990, and bias corrections were made. Using this calibrated model, future projections of annual grain yield over the period of 2011–2050 were made, assuming that future agricultural crop varieties remain unchanged. These grain yields were then compared with the values from the baseline period to assess how much crop yields decreased or increased in particular regions of China. Overall *agricultural climate risk* – the probability of grain yield reduction under different climate change projections – was then assigned to each region and classified by its magnitude of change as one of five risk levels – high, relatively high, moderate, relatively low and low.

Maize

Maize is an important food crop, livestock feed and industrial raw material. It is the third largest crop in China after rice and wheat in terms of the growing area and yield. Maize is mainly grown in agricultural areas with an annual precipitation of 600–1500 mm in the wetter eastern half of the country, in both the northern temperate zone and the warm south (Figure 5.1). Among them, the Huang–Huai–Hai River region (an area spanning from the Qinghai–Tibetan plateau in the west, through parts of Inner Mongolia and Ningxia provinces, to Shandong province in the east – see the map of China's river basins at Figure 4.1, p. 98) is the most concentrated growing area of summer maize, where the sown area and yield ranks first in the country.

In the next 40 years (2011–2050), there are roughly equal chances of national maize yields rising or falling. Both the rate of change and the probability of

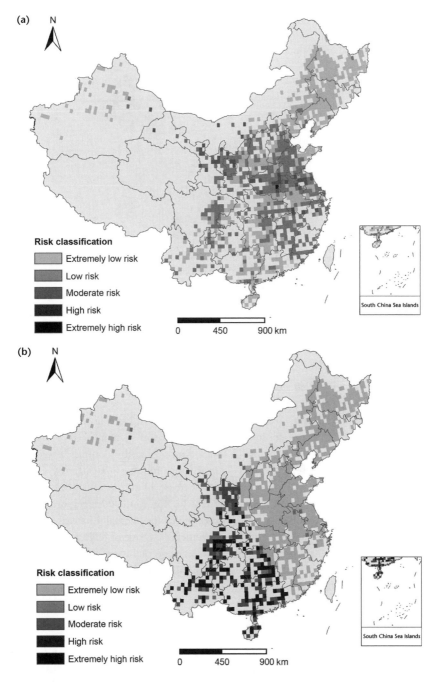

FIGURE 5.1 Distribution of the risk of a reduction in maize yields of (a) <20%, (b) 20–40% and (c) >40% over the period 2011–2050 when compared with 1961–1990 maize yields *continued*

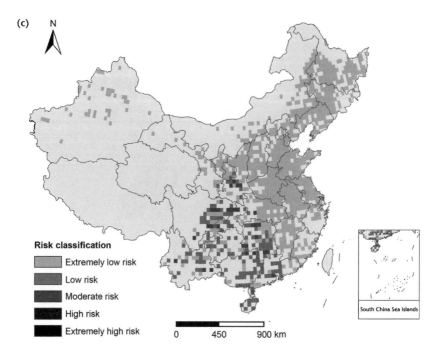

(c)

Risk classification

Extremely low risk
Low risk
Moderate risk
High risk
Extremely high risk

0   450   900 km

South China Sea Islands

FIGURE 5.1 Continued

change increase with each decade in this period (Figure 5.1). The risk of yield reduction varies between regions varies greatly, though the risk of greater losses increases over time in some areas. Higher yields are most likely in parts of north and central China, and the central to north-east regions generally have low to extremely low risk of falling yields. In south-west China, by contrast, there are moderate to high risks that yields will drop by as much as 20–40% by 2050. There is an extremely low risk of a yield decrease of more than 40%, across 83.7% of the total maize planting area (except for the south-west region which exhibits moderate or low risk of this). Maize yields may actually increase in the next 40 years in those areas that had an extremely low risk of falling yields (not shown). The probability of this happening is average or higher in 70.5% of the maize-growing area. It is relatively high or highly probable in areas accounting for 23.9% and 42.6% of the total maize-growing area, respectively.

Wheat

Wheat is second only to rice as a food crop in China and is the most widely cultivated food crop in northern areas. Wheat is grown over much of the same geographic area as maize. Major wheat-producing areas are situated in the region of 20–41°N, covering Henan, Shandong, Hebei, Anhui, Gansu, Xinjiang, Jiangsu, Shaanxi, Sichuan, Shanxi, Inner Mongolia and Hubei. These provinces account for over 80% of the national wheat fields and 90% of the national total output. Wheat growth without irrigation is highly restricted by climatic conditions.

According to the analysis (Figure 5.2), wheat yield risks are limited and are not expected to increase over the period 2011–2050. In most wheat-producing regions, there is a moderate risk that yields will fall slightly, by 20% or less (Figure 5.2a). The risk of any greater yield decrease is extremely low in most areas, though increases in yield are not likely either. In general, the four future decades studied show a consistent probability trend of a slight decrease in wheat yield, with the rate of decrease remaining largely stable in each decade (not accelerating by 2050). The north-east faces moderate risk of a 20–40% wheat yield reduction, and there are small north-eastern areas with high risk of a 20–40% loss (Figure 5.2b). Moderate to high risk of losses above 40% are possible in small north-east areas; only a few grid points show very high risk of serious wheat losses, mostly in north-western Gansu province (Figure 5.2c). There is also the possibility that the wheat yield will drop in some locations due to extreme weather events. The overall national wheat yield is slightly more likely to decrease than increase by 2050.

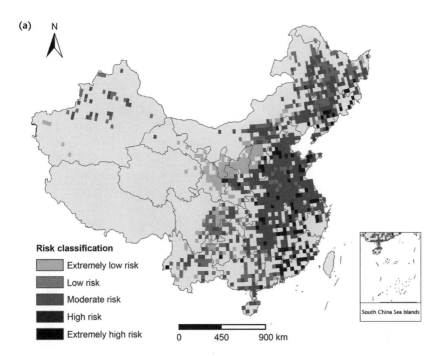

FIGURE 5.2 Distribution of the risk of a reduction in wheat yields of (a) <20%, (b) 20–40% and (c) >40% over the period 2011–2050 when compared with 1961–1990 wheat yields   *continued*

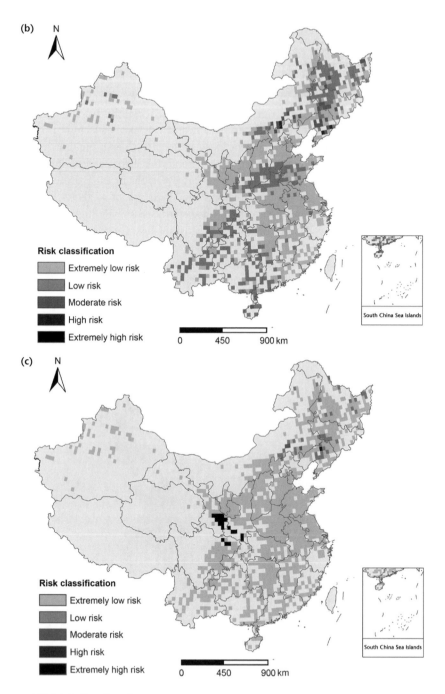

FIGURE 5.2 Continued

Rice

Rice is China's top food crop, and risk analysis suggests that rice yields may be much more strongly affected by climate change than either maize or wheat. Some 35% of the world's rice is grown in China, where rice crops cover a quarter of all cultivated land and make up approximately 44% of national grain production (FAO, 2014). Farmers grow rice throughout China except in Tibet, but 90% of land given over to the crop is in the warm, moist region south of the Huai River and Qin Mountains.

If no adaptation measures are taken, the country's total rice output may see strong declines over the next four decades (2011–2050).[3] Comparing the probability of smaller or greater losses, the most widespread risk under the A1B scenario is one of very large yield drops, of greater than 40% (Figure 5.3c). Large yield losses are a high risk mostly in locations in central and south China. The results show that under the A1B scenario, future precipitation and temperature changes might lead to a significant change in the climatic conditions of the rice-growing area south of the Huai River and Qin Mountains, leading to large volatility in rice yield. On the maps, only 3.1% of the points (Jiangsu and Henan) show an extremely high probability of 20–40% yield reductions (Figure 5.3b).

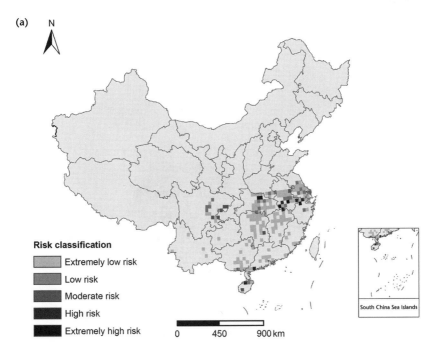

(a) N

Risk classification

Extremely low risk

Low risk

Moderate risk

High risk

Extremely high risk

0   450   900 km

South China Sea Islands

FIGURE 5.3 Distribution of the risk of a reduction in rice yields of (a) <20%, (b) 20–40% and (c) >40% over the period 2011–2050 when compared with 1961–1990 rice yields   *continued*

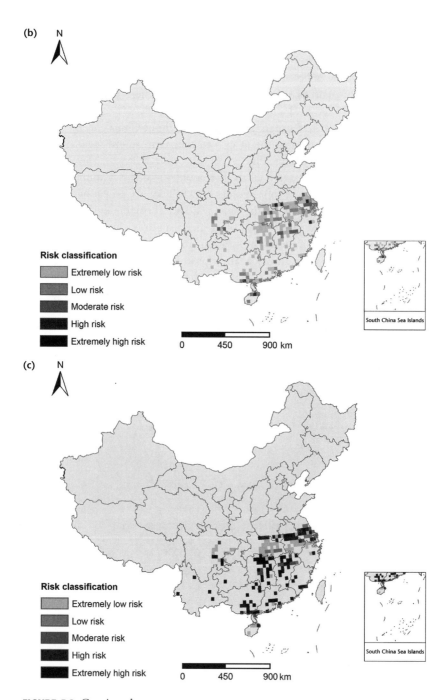

FIGURE 5.3 Continued

However, about 36.6% show extremely high probability of a rice yield reduction over 40%, mainly located in central and southern China. Some 17.8% of the total area shows high probability of a yield decline exceeding 40% (mainly in Jiangsu, Anhui, Hubei, Guangdong and Guangxi), and 6.3% shows a moderate probability (primarily distributed in Jiangxi and Hunan). About 32% of the points demonstrate extremely low risk of yield declines greater than 40% (mainly in Hubei, Sichuan and Jiangsu), and 6.8% face a low probability (primarily in Hubei and Jiangsu) (Figure 5.3c). Very few provinces are likely to experience any rice yield increases (not shown).

This investigation, limited to using climate projections from two climate models, shows that different crop types have varying sensitivities to temperature increases and greater precipitation variability in each province. On a nationwide basis, maize yields are not likely to decline very much, but rice yields may experience a precipitous decline of up to 70% (not shown). Wheat yields also show some climate sensitivities, and most provinces demonstrate a moderate risk of up to a 20% decline in yields over the next four decades, by 2050. The analysis associated with this investigation was limited by the assumption that no adaptation actions will be taken and that water availability for irrigation (groundwater and/or surface water diversions) will remain unchanged. As discussed in Chapter 4, overexploitation of groundwater resources in the North China Plain is leading to precipitous drops in the aquifer water table, which would lead to further reductions in wheat and maize yields across northern China than could be accounted for in this study. The analyses, and their gaps, highlight the importance of holistic adaptation policies and actions in China's complex development environment that account for synergies between water resource management, urbanisation and land use change, pollution and ecological restoration, disaster risk management, and market shifts in food preferences in order to build resilience in its agricultural sector.

Progress in adaptation policies and measures

The preceding analysis considered the potential climate change impacts on crop yield (agricultural climate risk), assuming that production systems remain the same and no adaptation actions are taken. Yet, appropriate adaptation options can greatly reduce the impacts of changing climatic conditions on agricultural production (Tao and Zhang, 2010; Zhang et al., 2013). In addition to individual adaptation actions already being adopted by farmers (Wang et al., 2008), a number of policies and measures have been implemented by the government to support adaptation in the agriculture sector in the past ten to 15 years. Many of these policies and measures were designed with agricultural development goals in mind, but addressing risks related to climate change has been an increasingly important driver of policy innovation. Coordination between various government agencies with different mandates related to different sectors is still weak, as are the resources and ability to implement different policies at some local levels. However, efforts are improving. Initiatives in some four major policy areas are summarised in this section.

Since the 1970s, investments in agricultural research and technological deployments, such as expanding irrigation coverage, have been key drivers of increasing agricultural yields in China. Government investment in agricultural research and development tripled between 1990 and 2010 (Chen and Zhang 2011). In particular, the development of high-yield grain varieties has accounted for almost one-third of incremental production in recent decades (Norse *et al.*, 2014). Public subsidies have promoted widespread adoption of productivity-enhancing techniques and technologies, such as high-yield seeds, chemical fertilisers and agricultural and irrigation equipment (Norse *et al.*, 2014; Huang and Rozelle, 2009). In 2011, government spending on agriculture totalled around US$87 billion, of which inputs subsidies accounted for around 15% (Gale, 2013). Research has shown that improved cultivars and fertilisers have made significant contributions to increasing yields despite greater climate extremes (Zhang *et al.*, 2013; Xiao and Tao, 2014).

Water is another key area of improvement. More water is used for agriculture than for any other use in China, accounting for about 60% of total water use (PRC Ministry of Water Resources, 2012), but efficient water use in irrigated agriculture is relatively rare (Wu, Jin and Zhao, 2010). A considerable proportion of pumped irrigation water is lost to leaks or evaporation. However, large-scale investments in channel-lining, field-levelling and more efficient irrigation systems is beginning to improve water use efficiency. Concerns about water quantity and quality, particularly around decreasing groundwater tables, will have profound impacts on agriculture. Better management of water resources in conjunction with modifying agricultural practices would greatly improve the future outlooks for both of these sectors.

Some steps are being taken to integrate and coordinate water resource management policy with agricultural policy. In 2010, a key policy outlining a national water strategy for the coming decades was announced. This strategy included plans to increase irrigation use efficiency to 60% by 2030 (PRC National Development and Reform Commission, 2012). In 2011, the central government committed to doubling state investment in water infrastructure (e.g. small-scale irrigation facilities) in the next ten years to support climate change adaptation, drought and flood management, and food security (PRC Central Committee and PRC State Council, 2011). Market-based mechanisms have also been introduced to improve the efficiency of irrigation water use (Lohmar *et al.*, 2007). For more about adaptation measures concerning water management in China, see Chapter 4.

The issue of land use is also seeing steps toward improvement. Despite regulations to limit land conversion, arable land has been declining in recent decades due to its conversion to urban and industrial uses. Maintaining a minimum of

120 million hectares of cultivatable land is now a basic national policy (PRC National Development and Reform Commission, 2008), but implementation and enforcement of this policy is spotty. The quality of arable land resources is also a major concern. Improvement of fields with low yield potential, through measures such as land levelling, construction of irrigation facilities and consolidation of fragmented land plots, has been a core agricultural development policy since the late 1990s. Due to the adoption of these measures, from 1985 to 2008 the proportion of low-yield farmland compared to total arable land resources decreased from 50% to 28% (Shi *et al.*, 2010). Significant efforts have also been put into combating desertification (see Chapter 8) and reversing trends in grassland degradation (see Chapters 6 and 9). Soil and water pollution are significant and also contribute to decreases in arable land, though attention is now beginning to be paid to these pollution issues.

With limited land and water resources for agricultural production in the context of a changing climate, recognition of the importance of regional comparative advantage has been a basis for agricultural zonation policies for decades. This forms another area where steps have been taken to adapt agricultural production in the face of climate change. *The Twelfth Five Year Plan for Modern Agriculture* also specifies regional priorities for agricultural development (PRC National Development and Reform Commission, 2012). At the provincial and local levels, agricultural development plans have also been responding to changing climatic suitability, as exemplified by Shaanxi Province's policy to support a northwards shift in apple production within the province (Li, 2010).

Until recently, climate change adaptation has not been explicitly addressed in policies and plans for agriculture or other closely related sectors. Agriculture has, however, been a priority sector in China's climate change strategies and programmes (PRC National Development and Reform Commission, 2007 and 2013). Not surprisingly, agriculture is a priority sector outlined in the *National Adaptation Strategy* (NAS) (PRC National Development and Reform Commission, 2013). Under the NAS, agricultural adaptation actions include further development of agricultural disaster early warning systems, investments in measures to improve productivity and resource efficiency, adjustments in crop cultivation methods, cultivars and spatial distribution of agricultural activities and greater support for agriculture disaster insurance mechanisms. Pilot areas are to be expanded for agricultural disaster insurance, with attempts to explore an agricultural disaster insurance scheme tailored to provincial conditions.

There is a long tradition in China of identifying model villages or pilot provinces to test out policy approaches and plans. The NAS identifies Jilin, Heilongjiang and Inner Mongolia as pilot provinces for carrying out agriculture adaptation projects. In Jilin, the focus is on 'blackland' soil protection and treatment in major grain production areas. Blackland soils are so named due to their dark colour caused by high organic matter content, and are very fertile. Due to soil erosion, soil fertility decline and other problems threatening food production across the blackland in mid-west Jilin province, a pilot and demonstration project is to be implemented to prevent soil erosion and restore soil fertility, and disseminate the best practices in blackland adaptation to climate change.

In Heilongjiang, the planned projects aim to identify and take advantage of climate change benefits, such as the increase in temperature and the longer growing season for crops. Activities that take advantage of shifting temperature regimes include making adjustments to the planting structure and breeding crop varieties tolerant of heat and drought, as well as expanding approaches to increase soil moisture and drought resistance and other agricultural application technologies. The expectation is that experiences obtained through these processes identifying climate change benefits will be further applied toward broader agricultural production and planning in other provinces.

The NAS represents a significant landmark for China's approach to adaptation policy and planning in the agricultural sector. However, the implementation, enforcement and coordination of policies across sectors, departments and governments at different scales (e.g. from the national to the local level) remain significant challenges toward systemic and coherent agricultural resilience.

Barriers to adaptive actions

Due to a lack of unified planning and scientific support, current adaptation actions in the agricultural sector have not been systematically targeted or implemented and do not necessarily support the individual activities being taken by farmers. The autonomous adaptation efforts employed by farmers are in response to recent perceived changes, but they do not typically account for future climate risks. Therefore, farmers may only be building short-term resilience, but without support from the government in the form of adequate, coordinated guiding policies and resources to implement them, are not actually preparing for climate change. To effectively implement adaptation actions and enhance adaptive capacity of the agricultural sector to face climate change, the resource, policy, technology, funding, and institutional barriers listed in Table 5.2 must be overcome.

Conclusion: pressing adaptation needs and recommendations for the future

The potential impacts of climate change on China's crop yields are mixed and regionally dependent. Warmer temperatures may increase wheat yields in northern regions through the expansion of the growing season and allowing for the planting of two crops in a year. At the same time, maize and rice yields might decrease in some areas. Much of the climate risk to various crops also depends on water resource management, and finding ways of helping farmers cope with extreme weather events such as droughts, heat waves and hailstorms. While

TABLE 5.2 Barriers to developing and implementing adaptation policies and actions in Chinese agriculture

---

1 Strategic policy and planning for dealing with climate change and socio-economic implications for agriculture are lacking at local and national levels. Industrial and regional development planning at all levels fail to incorporate agricultural vulnerability assessments.

2 Scientific evidence and bases for adaptation decisions are weak. Current scientific knowledge and monitoring of agricultural and hydro-meteorological conditions is unsatisfactory, hampered by lack of data integration and poor sharing and coordination of research results and data by institutes and government departments. Adaptation decision support systems have yet to be constructed.

3 Existing policies and mechanisms for funding agricultural adaptation schemes are limited.

    Ecological compensation mechanisms for planting and livestock bans, as well as programmes for ecological migration and resettlement and reforestation, are often underfunded at local and provincial scales. Agricultural and livestock insurance programmes need improvement.

    Monitoring and evaluation of current programme spending and accountability is poor, leading to inefficiencies. Budgets for national financing mechanisms are also limited, and there are currently few funding opportunities for international finance mechanisms.

4 Sectoral, regional and national agricultural technological integration is weak, and networks for promoting more efficient technologies and integrated adaptation management are not in place. Technological research, development, adoption and implementation currently lack sufficient policy support and stable funding.

5 International cooperation around agricultural adaptation can be improved, whether it be through better technology transfer, knowledge and capacity building and dissemination or information sharing. China has quite a bit of knowledge and experience it could share, while benefiting from enhanced international cooperation and coordination.

---

agricultural scientists are investigating more drought and heat tolerant crop strains globally and nationally, minimising crop losses due to severe storms remains challenging and will require more than crop engineering approaches. Province-specific agricultural adaptation policies and plans that account for the different climate, land use and water resource challenges specific to each province are needed, and they must be linked with each other and coordinated better with national strategies and policies related to disaster risk reduction, water resource management, climate adaptation and ecological restoration.

The challenges facing China in feeding nearly one-seventh of the world's population are significant, but the lessons emerging from China's experiences can be informative to other countries. When combined with the myriad socio-economic, land use, environmental and water pressures China is facing now and in the future, climate change poses a very real and significant threat to farming in China. Building agricultural resilience to climate change and other socio-economic shocks and shifts will require a range of policies; shifts in local, regional and national cropping practices and natural resource management; better coordination between policy making and implementing bodies at a variety of levels; and stronger integration at the science-policy interface. The NAS is the first step in that direction, but only time will tell if more progress can be made.

Building on the steps it has already taken, China can continue to prepare its farmers and agricultural systems for adapting to climate change. How China does this is of critical importance. China's sheer geophysical scale, as well as its population size, means that anything that impacts on China has the potential for global impact. At present, China can feed its population and, unlike countries like Malaysia, it is not dependent on global food markets to supply staple crops. If China begins importing crops like rice or wheat, this could have serious implications for global supplies. The adaptation choices and decisions China makes with regard to agriculture have important implications for global food prices and commodity markets. China's adaptation pathway choices around holistic agricultural management are important for itself and for the world. If China is able to strengthen climate change adaptation in agriculture, water and ecological restoration and protection, there is the potential to benefit the food security and livelihoods of millions of poor people. China's experience will also bring valuable insights to climate change adaptation in other parts of the world.

Notes

1 See the Introduction for more about the ACCC I programme.
2 Each climate model represents the interactions between the land, ocean and atmosphere in slightly different manners based on our current understanding of climate physics and atmospheric and oceanic biogeochemistry. Climate models then produce multiple estimations (projections) of what an area's future climate might be based on different scenarios of greenhouse gas emissions, land use change, and population pressures. For this reason, the projected changes in precipitation and temperature for a region will vary from model to model, and from emission scenario to emission scenario. Because it cannot be known with certainty which land use, energy, population and emission will most accurately reflect future conditions, it is better to use projections from multiple models and emission scenarios to understand a range a possible climate futures and estimate climate risk than use only one emission scenario and one or two models.
3 It is highly unlikely that no adaptation measures will be taken to mitigate potential yield reductions. The Chinese government is instituting a number of agricultural, water, land and climate adaptation policies and reforms. A number of farmers and communities are beginning to take autonomous adaptation actions and improving farming practices and yield. As such, this study represents a worst case scenario, assuming no actions are taken to reduce risk.

References

Barriopedro, D., Gouveia, C.M., Trigo, R.M. and Wang, L. (2012) The 2009/2010 Drought in China: Possible causes and impacts on vegetation. *Journal of Hydrometeorology*. 13. pp. 1251–1267.

Belete, N., Mahul, O., Barnett, B., Carpenter, R., Cheng, X. *et al.* (2007) *China: Innovations in Agricultural Insurance. Promoting Access to Agricultural Insurance for Small Farmers.* World Bank: Sustainable Development, East Asia & Pacific Region, Finance and Private Sector Development. (68607 v1).

Bloor, J.M.G. and Bardgett, R.D. (2012) Stability of above-ground and below-ground processes to extreme drought in model grassland ecosystems: Interactions with plant species diversity and soil nitrogen availability. *Perspectives in Plant Ecology, Evolution and Systematics*. 14 (3). pp. 193–204.

Cai, C.Z., Liang, Y. and Li, X.L. (2008) China's future food security analysis based on AEZ model forecasts. *Bulletin of Agricultural Science and Technology*. 2. pp. 15–17.

Cai, Y.L. and Smit, B. (1996) China's agricultural vulnerability and adaptation responses in the context of global climate change. *Acta Geographica Sinica*. 5 (3). pp. 202–212.

Challinor, A.J., Simelton, E.S., Fraser, E.D.G., Hemming, D. and Collins, M. (2010) Increased crop failure due to climate change: Assessing adaptation options using models and socio-economic data for wheat in China. *Environmental Research Letters*. 5. e034012.

Chen, K. and Zhang, Y. (2011) *Regional Case Study R2. Agricultural R&D as an Engine of Productivity Growth: China.* UK Foresight Project on Global Food and Farming Futures Regional Case Study. London: Government Office for Science.

Chen, M., Shelton, A. and Ye, G.Y. (2011) Insect-resistant genetically modified rice in China: From research to commercialization. *Annual Review of Entomology*. 56. pp. 81–101.

Chen, Y. and Ma, C. (2010) Progress of the study on climate warming impact on insects. *Acta Ecologica Sinica*. 30 (8). pp. 2159–2172.

Christensen, J.H., Kanikicharla, K.K., Aldrian, E., An, S. I, Cavalcanti, I.F.A., de Castro, M., Dong, W., Goswami, P., Hall, A., Kanyanga, J.K., Kitoh, A., Kossin, J., Lau, N.-C., Renwick, J., Stephenson, D.B., Xie, S.-P., Zhou, T. *et al.* (2013) Climate phenomena and their relevance for future regional climate change. In: Stocker, T.F., Qin, D., Plattner, G.K., Tignor, M., Allen, S.K., Boschung, J., Nauels, A., Xia, Y., Bex V. and Midgley P.M. (eds), *Climate Change 2013: The Physical Science Basis. Contribution of Working Group I to the Fifth Assessment Report of the Intergovernmental Panel on Climate Change.* Cambridge University Press: Cambridge, United Kingdom and New York, New York, USA.

Collins, M., Knutti, R., Arblaster, J., Dufresne, J.L., Fichefet, T., Friedlingstein, P., Gao, X., Gutowski, W.J. Jr, Johns, T., Krinner, G., Shongwe, M., Tebaldi, C., Weaver, A.J., Wehner, M. *et al.* (2013) Long-term climate change projections, commitments and irreversibility. In: Stocker, T.F., Qin, D., Plattner, G.K., Tignor, M., Allen, S.K., Boschung, J., Nauels, A., Xia, Y., Bex V. and Midgley P.M. (eds), *Climate Change 2013: The Physical Science Basis. Contribution of Working Group I to the Fifth Assessment Report of the Intergovernmental Panel on Climate Change.* Cambridge University Press: Cambridge, United Kingdom and New York, New York, USA.

Coxon, C. (2011) Agriculture and karst. In: van Beynen, P. (ed.), *Karst Management.* Springer: New York, New York, USA.

Deng, K., Ju, H., Xiong, W. and Yang, X. (2006) research progress on the impacts of climate change on China's agriculture. *Chinese Agricultural Science Bulletin.* 22 (5). pp. 439–441.

Fan, K., Xu, Z. and Tian, B. (2013) Has the intensity of the interannual variability in summer rainfall over South China remarkably increased? *Meteorology and Atmospheric Physics.* 124. pp. 23–32.

FAO (Food and Agricultural Organization of the United Nations) (2014) *FAOStat v.3.* [Online] Available from: http://faostat3.fao.org/browse/Q/QC/E. [Accessed: 26 November 2014.]

Feng, L., Li, T. and Yu, W. (2014) Cause of severe droughts in Southwest China during 1951–2010. *Climate Dynamics.* 43. pp. 2033–2042.

Fu, W., Gandhi, V.P., Cao, L., Liu, H. and Zhangyue, Z. (2012) Rising consumption of animal products in China and India: National and global implications. *China and World Economy.* 20 (3). pp. 88–106.

Gale, F. (2013) *Growth and Evolution in China's Agricultural Support Policies.* Economic Research Report 153. US Department of Agriculture Economic Research Service.

Gregory, N.G. (2010) How climatic changes could affect meat quality. *Food Research International.* 43. pp. 1866–1873.

He, B., Lü, A., Wu, J., Zhao, L. and Liu, M. (2011) Drought hazard assessment and spatial statistics analysis in China. *Journal of Geographical Sciences.* 21 (2). pp. 235–249.

Hijioka, Y., Lin, E., Pereiera, J.J., Corlett, R.T., Cui, X., Insarov, G., Lasco, R., Lingren, E., Surjan, A. *et al.* (2014) Chapter 24: Asia. In: Barros, V.R., Field, C.B., Dokken, D.J., Mastrandrea, M.D., Mach, K.J., Bilir, T.E., Chatterjee, M., Ebi, K.L., Estrada, Y.O., Genova, R.C., Girma, B., Kissel, E.S., Levy, A.N., MacCracken, S., Mastrandrea, P.R. and White L.L. (eds), *Climate Change 2014: Impacts, Adaptation, and Vulnerability. Part B: Regional Aspects. Contribution of Working Group II to the Fifth Assessment Report of the Intergovernmental Panel on Climate Change.* Cambridge University Press: Cambridge, United Kingdom and New York, New York, USA.

Huang, J. and Rozelle, S. (2009) *Agricultural Development and Nutrition: The Policies Behind China's Success.* Rome: World Food Programme.

Huang, J., Wang, X. and Qiu, H. (2012) *Small-Scale Farmers in China in the Face of Modernisation and Globalisation.* IIED/Hivos: London, United Kingdom and The Hague, Netherlands.

Hueso, S., Hernández, T. and García, C. (2011) Resistance and resilience of the soil microbial biomass to severe drought in semiarid soils: The importance of organic amendments. *Applied Soil Ecology.* 50. pp. 27–36.

Huo, Z.G., Li, M.S., Li, N., Wang, L., Huang, D.P. and Wang, C.Y. (2012) Impacts of seasonal climate warming on crop diseases and pests in China. *Scientia Agricultura Sinica.* 45 (11). pp. 2168–2179.

Jones, J.W., Hoogenboom, G., Porter, C.H., Boote, K.J., Batchelor, W.D., Hunt, L.A., Wilkens, P.W., Singh, U., Gijsman, A.J. and Ritchie, J.T. (2003) The DSSAT cropping system model. *European Journal of Agronomy.* 18. pp. 235–265.

Ju, H., Xiong, W., Ma, S., Yang, X., Ma, C., Ma, Z., Wang, H., Li, Y., Han, X., Hao, Y., Xie, L. and Li, L. (2008) *Climate Change and Food Security in China.* Xueyuan Press: Beijing, People's Republic of China.

Ju, H., Xiong, W., Xu, Y. *et al.* (2005) Impacts of climate change on wheat yield in China. *Acta Agronomica Sinica.* 31 (8). pp. 24–29.

Kearney, J. (2010) Food consumption trends and drivers. *Philosophical Transactions of the Royal Society B.* 365. pp. 2793–2807.

Kremer, B. (2012) Soil microbiology under drought stress. *Acres.* 42 (10). pp. 18–21.

Li, C. (2010) Research on increasing farmers' income from apple cultivation in Shaanxi. *Shanxi Agricultural Science.* 3. pp. 190–192.

Lohmar, B., Lei, B., Huang, Q. and Gao, Z. (2007) Water pricing policies and recent reforms in China: The conflict between conservation and other policy goals. In: Molle, F. and Berkoff, J. (eds), *Irrigation Water Pricing: The Gap Between Theory and Practice.* CABI: Wallingford, United Kingdom.

Lu, Y., Wu, K., Jiang, Y., Xia, B., Li, P., Feng, H., Wyckhuys, K.A.G. and Guo, Y. (2010) Mirid bug outbreaks in multiple crops correlated with wide-scale adoption of Bt cotton in China. *Science.* 328. pp. 1151–1154.

Luo, C. and Sicular, T. (2013) Inequality and poverty in rural China. In: Li, S., Sato, H. and Sicular, T. (eds), *Rising Inequality in China: Challenges to a Harmonious Society.* Cambridge University Press: Cambridge, United Kingdom.

Mullan, K., Grosjean, P. and Kontoleon, A. (2011) Land tenure arrangements and rural–urban migration in China. *World Development.* 39 (1). pp. 123–133.

Norse, D., Lu, Y. and Huang, J. (2014) China's food security: Is it a national, regional or global issue? In: Brown, K. (ed.), *China and the EU in Context.* Palgrave: London, United Kingdom.

Pan, H.S., Zhang, G.H. and Zu, S.H. (2002) Warming impact on the development of rice in Heilongjiang and the countermeasures. *Heilongjiang Journal of Meteorology.* 4. pp. 7–18.

Pan, Z., Wan, B. and Gao, Z. (2013) Asymmetric and heterogeneous frequency of high and low record-breaking temperatures in China as an indication of warming climate becoming more extreme. *Journal of Geophysical Research: Atmospheres.* 118. pp. 6152–6164.

Piao, S., Ciais, P., Huang, Y., Shen, Z., Peng, S., Li, J., Zhou, L., Liu, H., Ma, Y., Ding, Y., Friedlingstein, P., Liu, C., Tan, K., Yu, Y., Zhang, T. and Fang, J. (2010) The impacts of climate change on water resources and agriculture in China. *Nature.* 467. pp. 43–51.

PRC Central Committee and PRC State Council (2011) *Decision from the CPC Central Committee and the State Council on Accelerating Water Conservancy Reform and Development* (The Central Committee and the State Council document no. 1 for 2011).

PRC Ministry of Water Resources (2012) *China Water Resources Bulletin 2011.* China Water and Power Press: Beijing, People's Republic of China.

PRC National Development and Reform Commission (2007) *China's National Climate Change Program.* Science Press: Beijing, People's Republic of China.

PRC National Development and Reform Commission (2008) *Medium and Long Term Plan for China's Food Security.* Science Press: Beijing, People's Republic of China.

PRC National Development and Reform Commission (2012) *China's Policies and Actions for Addressing Climate Change.* Available from: www.ccchina.gov.cn/WebSite/CCChina/UpFile/File1324.pdf. [Accessed: 26 November 2014.]

PRC National Development Reform Commission (2013) *National Climate Change Adaptation Strategy.* Science Press: Beijing, People's Republic of China.

Richardson, A.E. and Simpson, R.J. (2011) Soil microorganisms mediating phosphorus availability: Update on microbial phosphorus. *Plant Physiology.* 156 (3). pp. 989–996.

Rosenzweig, C., Iglesius, A., Yang, X.B., Epstein, P.R. and Chivian, E. (2001) Climate change and extreme weather events: Implications for food production, plant diseases, and pests. *NASA Publications* (Paper 24).

Shi, Q., Wang, H., Chen, F. and Chu, Q. (2010) The spatial-temporal distribution characteristics and yield potential of medium-low yield farmland in China. *China Agricultural Science Bulletin.* 26 (19). pp. 369–373.

Song, L.C. and Zhang, C.J. (2003) Characteristics of changes in precipitation in Northwest China in the 20th century. *Journal of Glaciology and Geocryology.* 25 (2). pp. 143–148.

Sui, Y., Lang, X. and Jiang, D. (2014) Time of emergence of climate signals over China under the RCP4.5 scenario. *Climatic Change.* 125. pp. 265–276.

Tao, F. and Zhang, Z. (2010) Adaptation of maize production to climate change in North China Plain: Quantify the relative contributions of adaptation options. *European Journal of Agronomy.* 33 (2). pp. 103–116.

Tao, F., Yokozawa, M., Xu, Y., Hayashi, Y. and Zhang, Z. (2006) Climate changes and trends in phenology and yields of field crops in China, 1981–2000. *Agricultural and Forest Meteorology.* 138. pp. 82–92.

Wang, J., Mendelsohn, R., Dinar, A. and Huang, J. (2008) *How China's Farmers Adapt to Climate Change.* World Bank Policy Research Working Paper 4758. [Online] Available from: elibrary.worldbank.org/doi/pdf/10.1596/1813-9450-4758. [Accessed: 13 April 2015.]

Wang, L. and Chen, L. (2013) Lingering drought in south China damages agriculture. *Xinhua.* [Online] 7 August. Available from: http://english.peopledaily.com.cn/90882/8356309.html. [Accessed: 12 September 2014.]

Wang, M., Shi, P., Ye, T., Liu, M. and Zhou, M. (2011) Agricultural insurance in China: History, experience and lessons learned. *International Journal of Disaster Risk Science.* 2 (2). pp. 10–22.

Wang, X., Huang, J., Zhang, L. and Rozelle, S. (2011) The rise of migration and the fall of self employment in rural China's labor market. *China Economic Review.* 22. pp. 573–584.

Wang, J., Wang, E. Yang, X., Zhang, F. and Yin, H. (2012) Increased yield potential of wheat-maize cropping system in the North China Plain by climate change adaptation. *Climatic Change.* 113. pp. 825–840.

World Bank (2014) *Data: Arable land (% of Land Area).* [Online] Available from: http://data.worldbank.org/indicator/AG.LND.ARBL.ZS. [Accessed: 25 October 2014.]

Wu, H. and Zhai, P. (2013) Changes in persistent and non-persistent flood season precipitation over South China during 1961–2010. *Acta Meteorologica Sinica.* 27 (6). pp. 788–798.

Wu, K.M. and Guo, Y.Y. (2005) The evolution of cotton pest management practices in China. *Annual Review of Entomology.* 50. pp. 31–52.

Wu, P., Jin, J. and Zhao, X. (2010) Impact of climate change and irrigation technology advancement on agricultural water use in China. *Climate Change.* 100. pp. 797–805.

Xiao, D. and Tao, F. (2014) Contributions of cultivars, management and climate change to winter wheat yield in the North China Plain in the past three decades. *European Journal of Agronomy.* 52. pp. 112–122.

Yin, Z., Zuo, C. and Ma, L. (2011) Soil erosion features by land use and land cover in hilly agricultural watersheds in Central Sichuan Province, China. In: Li, D., Liu, Y. and Chen, Y. (eds), *Computer and Computing Technologies in Agriculture IV.* 4th IFIP TC 12 Conference CCTA 2010, Nanchang, China.

Zhai, P.X., Zhang, X. *et al.* (2005) Trends in total precipitation and frequency of daily precipitation extremes over China. *Journal of Climate.* 18. pp. 1096–1108.

Zhang, L., Huo, Z., Wang, L. *et al.* (2012) Climate change impact on crop pests in China. *Acta Ecologica Sinica.* 31 (6). pp. 1499–1507.

Zhang, Q., Deng, Z.Y. and Zhao, Y.D. (2008) Impact of global climate change on agriculture of Northwest China. *Acta Ecologica Sinica.* 28 (3). pp. 1210–1218.

Zhang, X., Wang, S., Sun, H., Chen, S., Shao, L. and Liu, X. (2013) Contribution of cultivar, fertilizer and weather to yield variation of winter wheat over three decades: A case study in the North China Plain. *European Journal of Agronomy.* 50. pp. 52–59.

Zhao, G.J., Mu, X.M., Hormann, G., Fohrer, N., Xiong, M. and Su, B. (2012) Spatial patterns and temporal variability of dryness/wetness in the Yangtze River Basin, China. *Quaternary International.* 282. pp. 5–13.

6

GRASSLANDS AND LIVESTOCK

Pan Xuebiao, Li Qiuyue, Wang Jing, Chen Chen, Dong Wanlin, Andreas Wilkes, Krystal Lair, Sarah Opitz-Stapleton and Anna Barnett

Grasslands

Grasslands cover a total of 52.5 million km^2, or about 40% of the world's ice-free land area (White *et al.*, 2000). The total biomass of the plant life found in grasslands accounts for about one-third of all land vegetation (Mooney *et al.*, 2001). Grasslands are an important part of the greater terrestrial ecosystem, serving as an important ecological barrier, playing a role in climate regulation, and contributing to global and regional ecosystem balance (Chen and Jiang, 2003; Lu *et al.*, 2009). They provide significant ecosystem services such as biodiversity conservation, regulation of the quantity and quality of water flows, sandstorm abatement and erosion and desertification control; they also serve an important function as a carbon sink (carbon stored in live vegetation), accounting for approximately one-sixth of the total global carbon biomass stock and a quarter of global soil carbon stock (de Fries *et al.*, 1999; Mooney *et al.*, 2001).

In addition to their ecological importance, grasslands make up nearly 70% of all land used for agriculture worldwide (Suttie *et al.*, 2005) and are a key productive resource for hundreds of millions of pastoralists who depend on grasslands for their livelihoods.[1] More than 40% of China's land area is grassland (Zhang, 2000; Chen *et al.*, 2003), from the arid north-west and green meadows in the north and north-east to alpine meadows on the Tibetan Plateau and tropical or subtropical pastures in the south. Sheep, goats, cattle, horses and donkeys are raised on grasslands across China, sustaining the livelihoods of more than 35 million pastoralists (Liu, 2012) and contributing to food security for the whole country.

Yet grasslands are very sensitive to changes in climate. They are complex ecosystems that rely on a balanced interaction between weather, sunlight, soil and water conditions, grazing animals and humans, and they are very sensitive to changes in any one of these factors. Even small changes can have significant effects on grassland *biomass* (the total dry weight of the plant life above and below ground in a specific area) production, species diversity and ecosystem services, all of which directly affect the livestock and the people that depend on them. As China's temperatures continue to increase, and precipitation and weather patterns become more varied and more extreme (see Chapters 3 and 9), grasslands may see far-reaching changes in their size, *condition* (assessed by the proportion of a grassland covered by vegetation, plant diversity or biomass production) and ability to sustain life. For China, grassland–climate change impacts will be significant.

Zhao Taihou is a herdsman raising more than 700 sheep on the grasslands of Siziwang Banner in Inner Mongolia. His livelihood is heavily dependent on the natural world; environmental and climate variability directly impact his family's finances. There is a grazing ban in place on his summer pastures, but he can still collect grass and let his flock graze on his winter pastures. He is happiest when the grass grows well and his sheep have plenty to eat. Zhao's primary concern is inadequate rain in summer and too much snow in winter. So far, he has been able to increase his flock's resilience to extreme weather by installing pens that give his sheep some protection against the elements, but Zhao is likely to have to prepare for other changes to come. 'To adapt to climate change, we have to reduce the number of livestock, but it will mean less income,' he says. 'We could also store more fodder each year. For example, we had 30 tonnes hoarded up for last winter. It would also help if we could dig a well so that we can water the fodder growing in the pastures.'

As with Zhao Taihou, many pastoralists in China depend on grasslands and their associated ecosystem services for their livelihoods and cultural identities (see Chapter 9). Changes in these delicate ecosystems could have devastating effects on a country carefully balancing the sustainability of its food production with the growing demand for food resources from an ever-increasing population. Thus, projecting and adapting to the potential effects of climate change on grasslands is necessary for China's long-term sustainable development and social stability.

This chapter provides an overview of China's grasslands, some of the recent historical trends in their use and development, and the potential effects of climate change on grasslands and livestock production. It also discusses some of the recent research and work done to assess the impacts and risks of climate change to grasslands, using research from the Adapting to Climate Change in China I (ACCC I) programme as a case study. The chapter then summarises relevant policies related to mainstreaming climate adaptation considerations into grassland management and activities – being undertaken spontaneously by herders and promoted by various provincial governments in response to national-level policy guidance – to increase the ecological resilience of grasslands and the livelihoods of herders.

China's grasslands

With an area of more than 3.9 million km² of grassland (Zhang, 2000; Chen *et al.*, 2003), China has the most grassland area per country other than Australia and Russia. An extension of the larger Eurasian Steppe, the majority of these grasslands are in northern and western China, spanning 12 provinces and autonomous regions, in areas with annual precipitation of less than 400 mm (Li, 1999) (Figure 6.1).

With China's varied geography, its grasslands consist of a range of different vegetation types (Figure 6.2). In the northern grasslands, as the precipitation decreases from east to west, vegetation types shift from meadow steppe to typical steppe, desert steppe and steppe desert and then desert. In the grassland regions of Gansu Province and Xinjiang Autonomous Region, variation in vegetation types follows the change in climate along an altitudinal gradient, from mountain desert in the dry and hot lower areas, to mountain steppe and

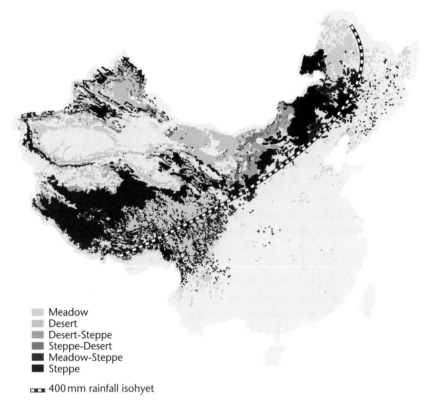

■ Meadow
■ Desert
■ Desert-Steppe
■ Steppe-Desert
■ Meadow-Steppe
■ Steppe

▭▭▭ 400 mm rainfall isohyet

FIGURE 6.1 Distribution of various vegetation types in China, which roughly follows the 400 mm annual precipitation isohyet line (a line of equal or constant rainfall in a given time period; approximate) (source: adapted from Heilig *et al.*, 2000)

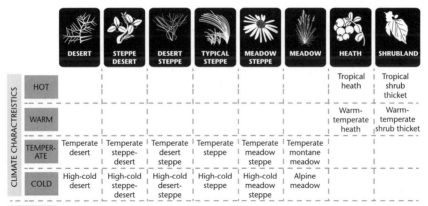

Other types: Montane meadow; Lowland meadow; various marshes; arid sparse shrubland

FIGURE 6.2 The main grassland vegetation types of China. Heath and shrubland are also known as herbosa and shrub herbosa,[2] respectively (source: Liu, 2012)

mountain meadow in the cooler wetter conditions at higher altitudes. Alpine vegetation types are commonly found on the Tibetan Plateau (Piao *et al.*, 2004).

Recent changes in China's grasslands

Grasslands have naturally evolved over millennia under the influence of grazing, initially by wild herbivores and subsequently by domesticated livestock. Different types of grasslands respond differently to grazing. Some types are in best condition, in terms of species diversity and productivity, with little or no grazing, while others are at their best under moderate *grazing intensities* (the proportion of the available aboveground plant material that is consumed over a specific period of time, typically one grazing season). However, even grasslands that thrive under moderate grazing will become *degraded* if grazing is too frequent or intense. After being grazed, even the hardiest grassland needs time for vegetation to recover and regrow and for disturbed soils to recover.

Box 6.1 Degradation

Degradation refers to a severe decline in the condition of a grassland habitat. This is commonly indicated in China by a decrease in plant cover, decreased biomass and the presence of less palatable plants. It is accompanied by physical and chemical changes to the soil including soil fertility decline (particularly in bare areas between vegetation) and erosion of topsoil, which can lead to desertification or other states where it is impossible for the land to return to its original state.

Many grazers such as sheep, cattle and goats find certain grass species more palatable than others due to higher nutritional content. They often preferentially graze these species, reducing their competitive advantage and allowing other less nutritious species to thrive, thereby changing the competitive relationships between plants and the plant community composition overall. As species diversity decreases, vegetation cover declines, soil properties change and the grassland degrades. In extreme cases, the grazed area cannot recover at all, leading to desertification and, sometimes, the complete loss of the grassland habitat.

Historical records indicate that nomadic herders have been grazing China's grasslands since at least 200 BC (Pei and Zhang, 2014). The mobility of herds and herders over large areas of land largely kept the balance of grazing at a reasonable level, allowing enough livestock to sustain the herders while also ensuring that grasslands remained healthy and able to sustain production in the long term. These forms of rotational grazing provided plants with time to recover after grazing, keeping the grasslands in good condition. Cooperation between households and communities was also important in times of natural disasters, such as snowstorms or droughts, to ensure that livestock could move from disaster-stricken areas to locations where grazing conditions were better.

However, political and social changes in the last century have combined with rapid population growth to bring about dramatic changes in the use and management of China's grasslands. China's government began implementing a more structured and centralised system of natural resource management in the 1950s and 1960s, and herding communities were organised into collectives and communes. Land continued to be managed collectively, but livestock belonged to the state, and the commune paid villagers for their labour inputs. After the dissolution of communes in the 1980s, livestock were distributed among households, but grasslands remained collective property. This system encouraged individual livestock owners to overexploit the collectively owned land (Eerdunzhabu, 2001) and contributed to grassland degradation. In the 1990s and 2000s, the state began contracting grassland areas to individual households to begin addressing the situation. The 'family ranch' is now China's typical grassland management unit.

Contracting to individual households was initially believed to give herders stronger incentives to conserve grassland and invest in the protection and restoration of grasslands. However, along with the settling of herders in recent decades, it has also had a number of adverse effects. Contracting specific grassland plots to individual households has limited their ability to use mobility across the landscape as a management tool or a response to natural disasters (Li and Huntsinger, 2011). With sedentarisation, the radius of grazing from homesteads has also decreased, concentrating grazing in particular locations. In some areas, fencing and protection of contracted lands has been accompanied by exploitative use of remaining collective land (Williams, 2002). Social conflict and inequality in access to grassland and water resources have also been reported (Yeh, 2003; Zhao and Long, 2007; Williams, 2002; Yan *et al.*, 2005). However, recognising the potential benefits of cooperation among households (Cao *et al.*, 2011), local governments and communities have not all adopted a policy of contracting to individual households, and almost a third of contracted grasslands have reportedly been contracted to groups or communities (Li, 2007).

Land tenure is not the only driver of grazing management practices. In many pastoral areas, livestock products are the primary source of household income. Increasing needs for cash to finance household expenditures, rising production costs and poor integration with markets have all been cited as drivers of increasing herd size in recent years (Kemp and Michalk, 2011; Squires *et al.*, 2010; Waldron *et al.*, 2007). Grassland conversion for agriculture is also leading to losses, with more than 200 million mu converted to farming since the 1950s. Overgrazing and farmland conversion are the main anthropogenic drivers of grassland degradation, and increasing climate variability and climate change are exacerbating the losses.

Overgrazing and climate variability over the last 50 years have led to severe grassland degradation and losses in the northern grasslands, contributing to soil erosion, sandstorms, imbalances in ecosystem function and desertification. Since the 1970s, 32% of the total northern grassland area has been seriously degraded, and the area lost each year continues to average around 2,460 km^2 (Wei, 2004). Although indicators of degradation and data availability vary by location (Harris, 2010), there is widespread agreement that a significant proportion of China's grasslands are degraded (Akiyama and Karumura, 2007; Han *et al.*, 2008). In some places, vegetation cover and biomass production are reduced or have disappeared entirely, leading to decreased grassland productivity and sometimes to desertification. Soil erosion has been exacerbated, and sandstorms and other disasters have become more frequent (see Chapters 8 and 9). Land degradation has led to a serious decline in the provision of important ecosystem services, constituting a serious threat to the sustainable development of grasslands, especially in northern China.

The impacts of climate change on China's grasslands

The responsibility for degradation and desertification cannot be attributed to herdsmen and grassland managers alone. In addition to significant damage from overgrazing, grasslands have also been increasingly affected by the changes in global climate over the past several decades. The shape and *succession* (replacement of one plant community by another) of grasslands are sensitive to climate conditions such as temperature, precipitation, and the concentration of carbon dioxide (CO_2) in the atmosphere. Slow-onset seasonal shifts in these factors, increasing variability and changes in the frequency and intensity of extreme weather events all impact grassland conditions.

A growing body of research has documented the observed effects of climate change on grasslands in China and simulated potential future trends. The effects are seen largely through grasslands' responses to rising and fluctuating temperatures, increasing carbon dioxide and shifting precipitation patterns, though how and to what extent varies by location. China's grasslands have experienced changes in temperature and precipitation, and the range of various grassland types has been shifting, as have the size and species composition in response to climate shifts. Studies in the Hulunbeier grasslands (Liu *et al.*, 2010) have shown that climate change has increased the area of some vegetation types in some decades and decreased it in others. One explanation for this fluctuation may be that different individual plant species respond differently to changing climatic conditions (Xiao, Wang *et al.*, 1996). Niu (2001) modelled the effects of a 2°C increase in average annual temperature and an increase in annual average precipitation of 20% on grasslands in Inner Mongolia and found that the southern boundary of grasslands would shift northward, reducing grassland area by 30% and causing some particularly sensitive grassland varieties to completely disappear.

Temperature warming trends vary by season and are changing the timing and duration of grassland growth. Studies have also shown that increases in temperature exert more impact on grassland productivity at low altitudes than at high altitudes, but that this effect varies by species (Yang *et al.*, 2002). Analysis of changes in the growing seasons in eastern Inner Mongolia shows that warming trends in spring, summer and autumn have led to the acceleration of the grass growth cycle – grass is becoming greener sooner, but also maturing more quickly and wilting earlier, shortening the growing season at lower latitudes and extending the growing season at higher altitudes (Chen and Li, 2009; Gu *et al.*, 2012; Li and Han, 2013).

Grassland ecosystems are also sensitive to changes in atmospheric CO_2 (Wang and Shi, 2010), but the impact varies by plant community and species (Geeske *et al.*, 2001; Grünzweig and Körner, 2001). Xiao, Chen *et al.* (1996) simulated the *productivity* of the typical steppe in the Xilin River Basin using the CENTURY plant growth model. Theirs and other research suggests that while temperature increases may decrease productivity on a typical steppe, increasing atmospheric CO_2 concentration may partly or even fully offset this effect (Parton *et al.*, 2006). Ultimately, however, future grassland productivity strongly depends on precipitation shifts and grassland management practices that were not accounted for in earlier biophysical impact assessments of CO_2 concentrations.

Grassland productivity each year determines the number of livestock supported, in turn affecting the livelihoods of herders. Because any changes in productivity have significant economic impact, climate change impacts are viewed primarily with an eye to their effects on productivity. Although increasing temperatures may benefit plant growth (Han *et al.*, 2010), changing precipitation patterns also have a strong influence on grassland productivity, as grasslands are especially sensitive to the amount of *available water* (the proportion of all water

Box 6.2 Productivity

Productivity refers to Net Primary Productivity (NPP), the total amount of organic matter available above ground (leaves and stems) and below ground (roots) that a grassland produces over a certain period of time. It is a very basic measure of the amount of food available for grazing livestock, and therefore any changes in productivity have significant economic impact.

in a system that can be used by its vegetation) (Zhou *et al.*, 2002; Lu *et al.*, 2009). When soil moisture falls below a certain level, plants are no longer able to utilise the water still in the soil. Any warming and drying experienced as a result of climate change may decrease productivity (Gao *et al.*, 2009), making grasslands more prone to drought and local desertification (Zhao *et al.*, 2007).

These and other Chinese studies offer important information about potential climate change impacts, but most focus on a particular type of grassland – often known as 'typical steppe' – and on small areas. The scope of research has also been quite limited, mostly emphasising the ecological effects of climatic trends in the past few decades, with little examination of its impacts on livestock or humans.

Researchers are now exploring the potential impacts of climate change on wider regions of China's grasslands, with recent investigations focusing on northern China and Inner Mongolia. China's northern grasslands by area and diversity are largely contained in Inner Mongolia, which has been serving as a pilot province for investigating knowledge gaps and testing the biophysical and socio-economic impacts of policies designed to rehabilitate grasslands and build adaptive capacity. To address these gaps and begin more comprehensive adaptation planning, China commissioned a comprehensive climate change impact assessment for Inner Mongolia's and northern China's grasslands as whole in 2009 via the ACCC I programme. Teams of researchers from the Chinese Academy of Agricultural Sciences (CAAS) and the Institute of Agricultural Resources and Regional Planning (IARRP), a research division within CAAS) investigated the current and potential future impacts of climate change on the productivity of grasslands in these regions. Their research is discussed below.

Case study: the impacts of climate change on grassland productivity[3]

One-quarter of the country's grassland is in Inner Mongolia, the third largest among China's provinces and autonomous regions. The rolling steppes of this region have suffered from climate change and intensive grazing, farming and other human activities. Several studies (Chen, 1999; Wang *et al.*, 1999, 1997) describe ecological disruption and long-term degradation due to overexploitation of Inner Mongolia's natural resources. There has also been significant warming, with the average daily maximum temperature rising up to 0.45°C per decade and the average minimum temperature rising up to 1°C per decade (see Chapter 9), which have reduced aboveground biomass on the Inner Mongolia steppe (Ma, 2007).

Modelling vulnerability

Grassland biophysical impact assessments quantify the likelihood that climate variability and climate change will impact grassland biomass production and the potential losses that would result, in comparison with the historical record. Since the amount of biomass in an area directly influences how many livestock can graze there, assessment of climate change impacts on grassland biomass also provides a strong indication of the risks for livestock production and livestock-dependent livelihoods in that region.

The research described in this case study used the CENTURY ecological plant growth model, driven by both observed and projected climate scenarios, to assess the potential impacts of shifts in precipitation and temperature on grassland productivity. CENTURY is a process-based ecosystem model that includes modules for vegetation productivity, soil organic matter and water movement (Gao *et al.*, 2006), to simulate productivity, estimate optimum and maximum growth temperatures by grassland type and simulate grazing effects (Lv and Zheng, 2006; Yuan *et al.*, 2008).

The teams used CENTURY, driven by climate projections from different combinations of climate models and emissions scenarios, to assess potential changes in biomass production by comparing the model results for a historical baseline period (1961–1990) to projected results for a variety future time periods. To estimate the impacts of climate change on Inner Mongolia's grasslands, the CAAS team used precipitation and temperature projections generated by the PRECIS-HadCM3 climate model, running high (A2) and low (B2) emissions scenarios. For China's northern grasslands, the IARRP team used a different combination of climate models and emissions scenarios, the PRECIS-ECHAM4 and PRECIS-HadCM3 climate models each running the A1B emissions scenario, a medium-emission scenario between A2 and B2, to project changes in temperature and precipitation. The projections of temperature and precipitation from the different model/emission combinations were then fed into the CENTURY plant growth model.

To demonstrate the potential impacts of climate change on these areas, each investigation compared models of the biomass distribution in their respective areas during the baseline period against future projections of biomass distribution in the same area (Chen *et al.*, 2012; Chen *et al.*, 2013). Both teams then estimated current and future grassland vulnerability by creating a biophysical vulnerability index dependent on exposure, sensitivity and adaptive capacity. Exposure (in this case, total grassland area) and adaptive capacity (the change in total grassland area due to additional conservation or preservation measures) were assumed to remain constant in this research. The grassland's sensitivity, a third component of vulnerability, was modelled as the change in biomass distribution in the projections of future time periods relative to the baseline model. Although the indices are simplified and contain unquantifiable uncertainty due to data limitations and model assumptions, they represent one of the first large-scale attempts to estimate regional grassland vulnerability in China.

The relationship between climate and grassland productivity

To start, the IARRP team modelled the average distribution of biomass across Inner Mongolia over the last five decades, based on meteorological data and also using more recently observed biomass data from 45 data collection sites distributed across the region, demonstrating the broad relationship between climate and grassland productivity in Inner Mongolia (Figure 6.3).

Over the last 50 years, Inner Mongolia has been drier and hotter from northeast to south-west, and the production of biomass has followed this pattern, consistent with the findings of Gao *et al.* (2009). The far north-east has the most

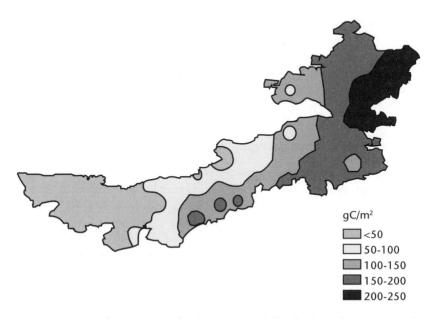

FIGURE 6.3 Map of Inner Mongolia showing spatial distribution of average cumulative aboveground biomass, measured in grams of carbon per square metre, from 1961 to 2010

aboveground biomass, with the highest rainfall (300–400 mm) in the growing season and average annual temperatures of 4–13°C. The western desert, on the other hand, was relatively barren, with less than 200 mm of rain per year and an average annual temperature of 13–15°C.

Inner Mongolia: shifting productivity

The team then compared projected biomass production in several future time periods with the baseline. Figure 6.4 maps the areas of Inner Mongolia where biomass might decrease or increase under the emissions scenarios A2 and B2 for each of different future time periods, respectively. Both emission scenarios were also run over a short historical period, 1991–2010, to allow for model calibration and comparison with observational data to assess the accuracy of the model.

In both scenarios, large portions of the steppe are adversely affected by climate change, especially in the arid west. Impacts in the next two decades are projected to be modest, with most of the region seeing only small shifts from the baseline. During this initial period, the models show more widespread biomass losses under the B2 scenario, and in both the A2 and B2 scenarios the reductions in biomass coincide with higher temperatures. The steep rise in emissions in A2 happens mainly in the later part of the century and leads to larger areas of reduced biomass production, but also to a biomass boom in the north-east. These patterns are related to potential changes in climate: north-eastern locations that become wetter also become greener, while biomass declines as temperatures rise in the west (Figure 6.4). Studies have noted that rising temperature can improve grassland productivity (Bai *et al.*, 2004). However, aboveground biomass on the dry steppe is limited by precipitation. If there is not enough rain, warmer temperatures will not induce growth and may actually dry out the soil, leading to lower biomass levels.

Inner Mongolia: an unstable future

Climate change may also make grassland productivity more unstable and unpredictable. The models show that year-to-year variability in biomass may increase over time, especially in the A2 scenario, which leads to warmer temperatures later in the century and correspondingly greater variations in biomass. Figure 6.5 presents the average cumulative aboveground biomass of the four types of grasslands into which Inner Mongolia can be divided – meadow steppe, typical steppe, desert steppe and steppe desert (in order of wettest to driest) – in different periods under the A2 and B2 emissions scenarios. As climate change intensifies, meadow and typical steppe gain more biomass on average, but variability increases as volatile weather reduces productivity in some years. The fluctuations are greatest, however, in very dry 'steppe desert' areas, which already tend to lose biomass.

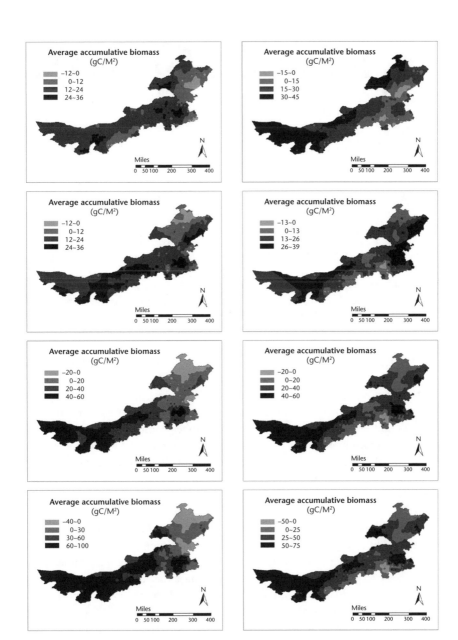

FIGURE 6.4 Modelling the change in average cumulative aboveground biomass relative to the 1961–1990 baseline under A2 and B2 emissions scenarios. Biomass remained the same or increased in lighter areas and decreased in the black areas. A2 emissions scenario (on the left, top to bottom): 1991–2010, 2011–2040, 2041–2070, and 2071–2100. B2 emissions scenario (on the right, top to bottom): 1991–2010, 2011–2040, 2041–2070, and 2071–2100

Period	Scenario	MEADOW STEPPE Biomass gC/m²	Variability %	TYPICAL STEPPE Biomass gC/m²	Variability %	DESERT STEPPE Biomass gC/m²	Variability %	STEPPE DESERT Biomass gC/m²	Variability %
Baseline 1961–1990		218.88	31.6	189.46	44.6	50.62	59.5	35.53	68.9
1991–2010	A2	233.15	30.2	197.26	38.6	55.86	58.6	37.40	73.0
	B2	230.46	42.1	200.28	55.3	49.50	64.4	32.65	71.3
2011–2040	A2	232.66	35.3	193.98	47.7	49.21	65.1	34.37	77.1
	B2	223.69	44.3	198.23	56.1	49.74	58.8	33.96	67.0
2041–2070	A2	255.55	36.9	201.34	53.6	46.43	65.8	32.18	79.3
	B2	235.45	46.3	205.68	60.0	49.42	58.6	33.01	65.8
2071–2100	A2	279.50	40.2	191.42	61.8	41.92	65.8	28.80	82.2
	B2	241.85	49.6	205.22	64.4	40.92	57.8	32.50	64.9

FIGURE 6.5 Mean annual cumulative aboveground biomass and variability,[4] for different types of grassland in Inner Mongolia under climate scenarios A2 and B2 for different decadal epochs when compared with the baseline period. Biomass is expressed as grams of carbon per square metre

Overall, regardless of whether future emissions are more or less intense, biomass could decline in western Inner Mongolia and grow somewhat in the north-east. Over time, the areas with reduced biomass production may spread eastward, which could lead to deserts expanding from the west, affecting the pastures and farms of central and south-east Inner Mongolia. If global greenhouse gas emissions continue to increase quickly, as in the A2 scenario, both the localised biomass gains and the overall losses from climate change will be more dramatic. There remains considerable uncertainty in future grassland response, partially attributable to uncertainty in both the climate and grassland models, emission scenarios and limitations in the observational grassland and meteorological datasets used to calibrate the CENTURY model over the baseline period. Additionally, the models do not capture how potential trends in demand for livestock products, urbanisation, rates of conversion to agricultural land, or future socio-economic or policy pressures among other unknown future trends might impact grassland conditions. Despite model limitations and projection uncertainty, grassland composition, productivity and biomass will continue to evolve and in some locations become degraded in response to shifting climate and anthropogenic causes.

The grasslands of northern China

The results of investigation of potential climate change impacts on grasslands through the whole of northern China closely corroborate those seen in the study limited to Inner Mongolia. Researchers compared future projections for

three overlapping 30-year periods with the 1961–1990 baseline period to determine how biomass is expected change in each of the two climate models under
the more moderate (greenhouse gas emission levels between those of B1 and
A2) A1B scenario.

Researchers used the results of the comparison to construct a vulnerability
index. Figure 6.6 maps the spatial distribution of vulnerability for each of the
three time periods according to two climate models. Lighter areas represent a
decrease in vulnerability, darker areas represent an increase in vulnerability, and
areas halfway in between are relatively stable.

As mentioned at the beginning of the case study, because exposure and adaptive capacity are considered constant, the vulnerability index is directly correlated with the change in biomass under each scenario. This means that the maps,
in effect, also show the expected increase or decrease in biomass in each scenario as well, with darker areas showing a decrease in biomass, lighter areas
showing an increase, and areas in between remaining relatively stable.

One of the scenarios based on the HadCM3 combination (Figure 6.6, top
row) shows a strong reduction in biomass in some areas, especially in Tibet (the
region in the south-west corner of the map). Milder impacts spread gradually
from west to east across Inner Mongolia, the same pattern seen in the other
assessment. Northern China as a whole loses grassland biomass, but productivity
improves in central parts of Tibet and Xinjiang Province, especially in the near
future. A scenario from ECHAM4 (Figure 6.6, bottom row) shows less extreme
degradation, spread relatively evenly through central and western areas. According to this model, the most vulnerable areas are in Tibet, central-western Inner
Mongolia and northern Xinjiang.

Conclusions

Taken together, these studies suggest that grasslands of Tibet and Inner Mongolia are particularly vulnerable to climate change. The highly vulnerable
areas in south-west Tibet are expected to expand, and central and eastern
Inner Mongolia will gradually evolve into more vulnerable areas. With continued climate change, the area experiencing decreased biomass compared to
the baseline may expand over time. It should be remembered, however, that
there are several sources of uncertainty in these large-scale modelling exer-
cises, including uncertainties in climate models, climate scenarios and ecosystem model simulations. Thus, while these results may highlight certain
areas as potentially vulnerable, further research is needed to update the
modelling results as new observational data is collected and climate conditions
continue to change.

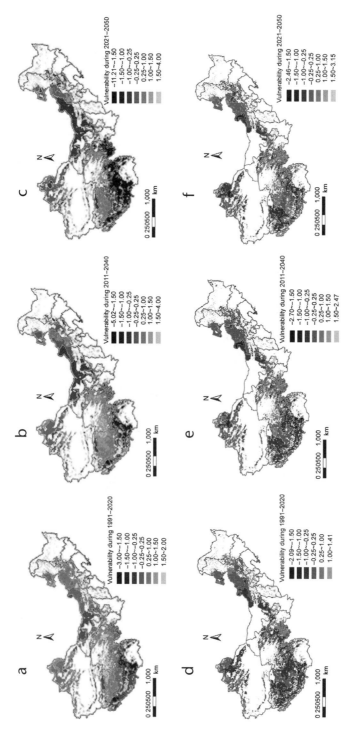

FIGURE 6.6 Grassland biomass changes in northern China, as measured by a vulnerability index. The top row displays results using precipitation and temperature projections from the PRECIS-HadCM3 combination; the bottom row displays results from PRECIS-ECHAM4: (d) 1991–2020, (e) 2011–2040 and (f) 2021–2050

Policies related to grassland management and adaptation

Over the last two decades, the Chinese government has begun to recognise the importance of grasslands in maintaining the ecological security of the country (PRC State Council, 2010). It has passed a number of national-level laws, regulations and plans supporting grassland conservation and sustainable management and the livelihoods of the people living in them as described in Table 6.1 (PRC Ministry of Agriculture, 2007; ADB, 2014). National agricultural development plans for grasslands promote 'steady development' – a balance between agricultural development and environmental conservation (PRC State Council, 2012) – and poverty alleviation as the top national policy priorities for the development and management of pastoral areas (PRC State Council, 2011).

With increasing attention to climate change, and recognising that many policies that promote sustainable grassland management also have potential benefits for adaptation to climate change, China has begun developing interdisciplinary adaptation policies that prioritise good management of its grassland areas. In 2013 the national government published the *National Adaptation Strategy* (NAS), a comprehensive policy developed by multiple national ministries and government

TABLE 6.1 Key Chinese grassland management and development policies and policy documents

Policy	Intent
The Grassland Law of China (1985, amended in 2002)	Legal framework for national and provincial regulations to address degradation and sustainable management. 2002 amendment provides legal basis for grazing ban incentives and compensation.
Several Opinions on Strengthening Grassland Conservation and Construction (2002)	Establishes conservation mechanisms: rotational grazing; seasonal and full grazing bans; livestock shelter, forage and water infrastructure; fencing to protect grasslands. Designates areas as 'basic grassland' that may not be converted to other uses.
Grazing Retirement Program or GRP (piloted 2003, nationwide implementation 2014)	Identifies areas for complete grazing bans, grassland and soil restoration areas, rehabilitating desertified and saline grasslands.
National Grassland Conservation, Construction, and Utilisation Master Plan (2007)	Sets out specific priorities for the GRP and identifies nine major programmes, including the grassland retirement programme, rehabilitation of desertified areas, grassland seed breeding, grassland disaster prevention and disaster reduction, grassland nature reserve construction, settlement and infrastructure investment in nomadic areas and a pastoral area water resources programme.

agencies that identifies guiding principles, priority areas or sectors and pilot provinces for adaptation in response to climate change, and is the most significant piece of adaptation specific policy to date.

The NAS is important for integrating climate change considerations into grassland management as it provides the macro-policy framework for the development of provincial adaptation plans (PAPs), and begins the implementation of actual adaptation actions. Grassland management considerations are covered under two ('Agriculture' and 'Forests and Ecological Systems') of the seven priority sectors included in the NAS. For example, tasks for the Agriculture sector that relate to more sustainable grassland management include: providing clear guidance for the sustainable development of livestock such as the subdivision of pastures into smaller areas; establishing rotational and seasonal grazing, with livestock kept in sheds during winter and spring to ensure a balance between grassland growth and livestock feeding; developing grassland infrastructure which includes pasture upgrading and ecological restoration; and planting fodder to reduce pressure on sensitive areas and grassland husbandry.

Under the priority sector of Forests and Ecological Systems, grassland ecosystem protection has also been identified as a key task. Proposed activities include: restoration and enhancement of grassland capacity through and for water conservation; soil preservation and erosion control through revegetation; capacity-building around grassland fire prevention and control; and grassland rodent and pest monitoring and control. The NAS also states that measures should be taken reduce the risk of livestock consuming poisonous grasses in the natural prairie. In addition, it calls for continued efforts to promote the grassland protection network and improve integrated vegetation coverage, aiming to rehabilitate by 2020 the approximately 55.6% of grassland areas suffering from desertification, salinisation and degradation.

As discussed in Chapter 11, the NAS is a policy framework that provides general direction and guidance to provincial and local decision makers around adaptation-focused planning, policies and actions. It is not, however, a detailed, province-specific plan; provinces such as Inner Mongolia must now begin the task of developing more detailed plans. Inner Mongolia has been identified as the pilot province for a demonstration adaptation project exploring animal husbandry development in 'typical steppe'. The focus of the project will be on degradation and desertification issues as a result of climate warming and drying in the typical steppe in Inner Mongolia. This project aims to restore and protect degraded grasslands through policy, economic and engineering approaches and to better manage the grassland and promote animal husbandry development experiences in a changing climate.

From agricultural policies to adaptation measures and practices

Building on the framework of major national-level policy and legislation, China has been developing a number of regulatory and practical measures at the provincial, regional and local levels in line with its goals of environmental conservation, agricultural development and poverty alleviation. Inner Mongolia in particular has adopted a series of measures to address the ongoing ecological and socio-economic challenges it faces. These measures, which include policy development, infrastructure construction, encouraging the settlement of herdsmen, fencing and rotational grazing, attempts to balance livestock consumption and grass growth and ecological compensation, have led to grassland health improvements in some areas. In 2000, the region enacted the *Provisional Regulations on Livestock-Grass Balance in Inner Mongolia*. After a two-year pilot period, the scope of these activities was gradually expanded to almost all pastoral counties in the province. The policy has also supported exclusion of livestock from degraded grasslands. Monitoring data from the Ministry of Agriculture show that this has had significant benefits for vegetation coverage, grass height, total fresh grass yield and the yield of edible fresh grass (ADB, 2014). For example, since grazing was banned at the northern foot of Yinshan Mountain, grassland degradation has stopped and vegetation cover has increased, reducing soil erosion and sandstorm hazards.

In some agricultural areas near the grasslands, the share of arable land sown to feed and forage crops has even increased. For example, in agricultural areas along the Yellow River near Damao Banner,[5] a dry steppe environment with low carrying capacity, forage crops have been adopted on many farms. During a drought in 2005, local herdsmen partnered with Damao Banner Forest Farm and the Bangdaxing Grass Company to meet feed demand. In Xilingol league, 46,000 ha of fields were irrigated for cultivation of silage maize in 2007. Forage crops, such as leguminous grasses, feed corn, millet and green oats, have also been intercropped with other crops such as potato, which reduces wind erosion (Zhao, 2002). After storing enough forage for their own livestock, famers often sell the remainder to nearby pastoral areas, better ensuring sufficient feed supplies in the face of winter or spring disasters and earning extra income. Another emerging business trend is the formation of cattle cooperatives, where families band together to share resources and climate and market risks, which are quickly developing in China. It is largely because of cooperatives that the income of many herders remained stable during the severe drought that hit central and eastern Inner Mongolia in 2009.

With higher economic returns, herders have more incentive to work toward grassland conservation and are better able to invest in climate resilience. Adoption of improved and climate-resilient management practices does require some investment. While access to credit remains an issue for many herders, loans are increasingly available to livestock companies, cooperatives and other market actors from financial institutions such as the Agricultural Bank of China. Government grants are also available for livestock cooperatives and companies to develop their operations. Several of the government programmes aimed at grassland conservation provide financial support to individual households in the form of partial subsidies for purchase of inputs, like seed or equipment, or basic infrastructure. Some of the most important items of infrastructure in northern China are winter warming sheds to protect livestock from cold, such as the one shown in Figure 6.7. In a warm shed, livestock lose less weight than if they are unprotected in winter, increasing animal survival and body weight.

Yet, the success of various measures is mixed locally, in part due to the severity of existing damage and implementation challenges. Inner Mongolia's social, economic and ecological challenges, and its response to these challenges, are profiled in Chapter 9. The types of strategies being employed may have some merit in aiding grassland management and pastoralists' adaptive capacity, though the future implications are not fully understood and require further research.

Although grazing restrictions are ecologically beneficial, and an increasing area of grassland is earmarked for environmental conservation, such practices have implications for herders' livelihoods and agricultural practices. Reduced forage area makes pastoralists more reliant on purchasing fodder, and grassland managers and pastoralists alike are exploring the ecological and economic implications of growing fodder. Many pastoral areas are surrounded by rich

FIGURE 6.7 Barn in Old Barag Banner, Inner Mongolia. The left-hand section is for grass storage, and on the right is a heated barn that shelters livestock from wind (photo credit: Pan Xuebiao)

farmland with small populations. Except for a few places affected by serious soil erosion and desertification, all of these agricultural zones are important producers of commodity grains. Crops are energy-rich, so crop by-products are generally no longer used as household fuel but rather are processed into livestock feed. While increased growing of crops for animal feed may reduce pressure on some sensitive grassland areas and prove adaptive for droughts and blizzards, it might also lead to the complete conversion and loss of grassland in some areas.

Although much has been done over the last several decades to improve the condition of the grasslands and the lives of herders and, in more recent years, to adapt to the effects of increasing climate variability, environmental degradation and, ultimately, of climate change, China still faces some challenges. The types of adaptive actions undertaken by pastoralists on a planned or autonomous basis, and the complex national-level policies with spotty modification, implementation and coordination at the provincial to local levels, will need to be monitored and evaluated more thoroughly in order to anticipate and respond to shifting socio-economic, ecological and climate conditions.

Grassland management challenges facing China

In addition to a legacy of poor grassland management that has left many grassland areas degraded and, in some areas, desertified, new model simulations confirm that China's northern grasslands will be under greater stress from climate change in the next few decades, as discussed in the case study. Two key lessons from recent experiences with grassland conservation in northern China are that the conservation of natural resources must be balanced with creation of opportunities for income generation, and that changing grassland management practices requires supportive investments in improved livestock management, animal health, marketing and other livelihood options, including off-farm income sources. Compared to the historical practice of heavy grazing, the resilience of grasslands to climate change can be improved by reducing grazing intensity. Smaller numbers of livestock can only deliver increased income if livestock productivity is increased, livestock products are sold to more remunerative markets and alternative income generation opportunities supported. Also, with rapid growth in demand for livestock products in China, especially in urban areas, new forms of market linkages between herders, companies and urban consumers have developed. By increasing the economic returns for livestock production in grassland areas, these linkages also strengthen herders' ability to adapt to climate change, but they may ultimately increase pressure on grasslands.

However, imposition of grazing bans in degraded areas does not provide herders with incentives for sustainably managing remaining grasslands. In 2011, the central government initiated the *Grassland Ecology Conservation Subsidy and Rewards Mechanism*, which makes reward payments to herders who maintain a balance between livestock numbers and forage availability. A total of CNY13.4 billion (GBP1.35 billion) will be invested in this scheme each year (ADB, 2014). Although these policies and schemes are generally beneficial for grassland condition and thus promote ecosystem resilience to climate variability and climate change, implementation has been beset by a number of issues. These issues include opportunity costs, insufficient subsidies to offset herders' investment costs and the additional cost of livestock management imposed by grazing restrictions (ADB, 2014). In particular, restrictions on grazing have increased dependence on feed sources other than grasslands, but with limited potential in many grassland areas for forage or feed cultivation. This can lead to increased feed costs, which in turn increases production costs for herders (Zhang, 2011; Bao, 2006; Li, 2006). In drought years, the price of feed can increase dramatically, so feed-dependent production systems may make herders more vulnerable to the effects of climate change (Wang, 2013). Complementary efforts to improve livestock management and productivity and to support the development of alternative livelihoods are needed (ADB, 2014).

Although these government programmes and other changes may have benefits for conservation of grassland resources and livestock and livelihood development, their specific implications for herders' ability to adapt to climate change and climate variability has not been systematically assessed. Not all technical measures that improve grassland or livestock will increase the resilience of pastoralist households to climate risks (as discussed further in Chapter 9), and while adoption of some practices may be complementary with other practices, there may also be trade-offs, with implications for herders' adaptive capacities. To date there has been very little assessment of the implications of different policies, programmes and technical measures for the resilience of pastoralists' households to climate change in China. The next generation of research will have to therefore integrate a variety of natural and social science disciplines to better understand the impacts of climate change and options for adaptation in grassland areas of China.

Notes

1 UN FAO suggests that there are 100–200 million pastoralists worldwide, but this is most likely an underestimate considering that India reportedly has more than 100 million pastoralists (McGahey *et al.*, 2014) and that the rural population in China's 264 pastoral and agro-pastoral counties is at least 35 million people (Liu, 2012).
2 Herbosa refers to a predominance of leafy, herbaceous species and is found in the east and south-east of China. A distinctive separation between herbosa types and other grassland types is clear, with herbosa primarily found in areas that generally receive more than 400 mm of precipitation per year while grasslands exist in areas that receive less than 400 mm, on average.
3 Because of the importance of Inner Mongolia's grasslands, the international research programme Adapting to Climate Change in China I (ACCC I, 2009–2013) commissioned two teams of researchers to conduct biophysical vulnerability assessments.

One team, from the Chinese Academy of Agricultural Sciences (CAAS), focused specifically on climate change's impacts on Inner Mongolia, while the other team, from the CAAS Institute of Agricultural Resources and Regional Planning (IARRP), studied the impacts on China's northern grasslands as a whole.

4 Here, variability is defined as the average difference between a certain year and the long-term average, divided by the long-term average.

5 In Inner Mongolia, prefectures are known as leagues and counties are called banners.

References

ADB (Asian Development Bank) (2014) *Strengthening Carbon Financing for Grassland Management in the People's Republic of China: Incentive Mechanisms and Implications*. Asian Development Bank: Manila, Philippines.

Akiyama, T. and Kawamura, K. (2007) Grassland degradation in China: Methods of monitoring, management and restoration. *Grassland Science*. 53 (1). pp. 1–17.

Bai, Y., Han, X., Wu, J., Chen, Z. and Li, L. (2004) Ecosystem stability and compensatory effects in the Inner Mongolia grassland. *Nature*. 431 (9). pp. 181–184.

Bao, L. (2006) Research summary on grassland retirement program policy investigations in China. *Issues in Agricultural Economy*. (8). pp. 62–65.

Cao, J.J., Xiong, Y.C., Sun, J., Xiong, W.F. and Du, G.Z. (2011) Differential benefits of multi-and single-household grassland management patterns in the Qinghai-Tibetan Plateau of China. *Human Ecology*. 39 (2). pp. 217–227.

Chen, C., Wang, J., Pan, X. and Wei, Y. (2013) Simulation study regarding the impact of climate change on grass productivity in Inner Mongolia. *Acta Agrestia Sinica*. 21 (5). pp. 850–860.

Chen, C., Wang, J., Pan, X., Wei, Y. and Feng, L. (2012) Validation and adaptability evaluation of grass ecosystem model CENTURY in Inner Mongolia. *Acta Agrestia Sinica*. 20 (6). pp. 1011–1019.

Chen, X. and Li, J. (2009) The relationship between *L. chinensis* phenology and meteorological factors in Inner Mongolia steppe. *Acta Ecologica Sinica*. 29 (10). pp. 5280–5290.

Chen, Z. (1999) 20-year research progress and prospects for grassland ecosystem. *Chinese Journal of Grassland*. 3. pp. 1–10, 27.

Chen, Z. and Jiang, F. (2003) Grassland degradation governance. *Natural Disaster Reduction in China*. 3. pp. 45–46.

Chen, Z., Wang, S. and Wang, Y. (2003) Update progress on grassland ecosystem research in Inner Mongolia steppe. *Chinese Bulletin of Botany*. 20 (4). pp. 423–429.

de Fries, R.S., Field, C. B, Fung, I., Collatz, G.J. and Bounoua, L. (1999) Combining satellite data and biogeochemical models to estimate global effects of human-induced land cover change on carbon emissions and primary productivity. *Global Biogeochemical Cycles*. 13. pp. 803–815.

Eerdunzhabu (2001) Ecological environment and institutional arrangements. *Journal of Inner Mongolia Normal University*. 30 (2). pp. 3–6.

Gao, C., Yang, G., Wang, J. and Zhang, X. (2006) CENTURY model's application in farmland ecosystem and its parameters' determination. *System Sciences and Comprehensive Studies in Agriculture*. 22. pp. 50–52.

Gao, H., Pan, X. and Fu, Y. (2009) Impact of climate change on climate productive potential in Central Inner Mongolia grassland. *Chinese Journal of Agrometeorology*. 30 (3). pp. 277–282.

Geeske, J., Chapin, F.S., Chiariello, N.R., Thayer, S.S. and Field, C.B. (2001) Species-specific responses of plant communities to altered carbon and nutrient availability. *Global Change Biology*. 7. pp. 435–450.

Grünzweig, J.M. and Körner, C. (2001) Growth, water and nitrogen relation in grassland model ecosystems of the semi-arid Negev of Israel exposed to elevated CO_2. *Oecologia*. 128. pp. 251–262.

Gu, R., Li, S., Zhao, H., Li, C., Song, W., Meng, J. and Wang, Y. (2012) Response of Hu-lun Lake watershed runoff to climate change. *Chinese Journal of Ecology*. 31 (6). pp. 1517–1524.

Han, F., Niu, J., Liu, P., Na, R., Zhang, Y. and Wang, H. (2010) Impact of climate change on forage potential climatic productivity in desert steppe in Inner Mongolia. *Chinese Journal of Grassland*. 5. pp. 57–65.

Han, J.G., Zhang, Y.J., Wang, C.J., Bai, W.M., Wang, Y.R., Han, G.D. and Li, L.H. (2008) Rangeland degradation and restoration management in China. *The Rangeland Journal*. 30 (2). pp. 233–239.

Harris, R.B. (2010) Rangeland degradation on the Qinghai-Tibetan plateau: A review of the evidence of its magnitude and causes. *Journal of Arid Environments*. 74 (1). pp. 1–12.

Heilig, G.K., Fischer, G. and van Velthuizen, H. (2000) Can China feed itself? An analysis of China's food prospects with special reference to water resources. *International Journal of Sustainable Development and World Ecology*. 7. pp. 153–172.

Kemp, D. and Michalk, D. (eds) (2011) *Development of Sustainable Livestock Systems on Grasslands in North-Western China*. Australian Centre for International Agricultural Research: Canberra, Australia (ACIAR Proceedings No. 134).

Li, B. (1999) Grassland degradation in Northern China and countermeasures. In: *Collected Works of Li Bo*. Science Press: Beijing, People's Republic of China.

Li, W. and Huntsinger, L. (2011) China's grassland contract policy and its impacts on herder ability to benefit in Inner Mongolia: Tragic feedbacks. *Ecology and Society*. 16 (2). p. 1.

Li, X. (2006) Empirical research on the effect of Grassland Retirement Program on farmers' benefits in Inner Mongolia. *Agricultural Technology and Economy*. 3. pp. 63–68.

Li, X. and Han, G. (2013) Response of dominant pasture of Eastern Inner Mongolia grassland during growing season to meteorological factors change. *Chinese Journal of Ecology*. 32 (4). pp. 987–992.

Li, X.L. (2007) A review of China's institutional arrangements for rangeland management. In: Li, X.L., Wilkes, A. and Yan, Z.L. (eds), *Rangeland Co-management: Proceedings of an International Workshop Held in Diqing, Yunnan China, 13–15 May 2006*. China Agricultural Science and Technology Press: Beijing, People's Republic of China.

Liu, J. (2012) *Small Grass, Large Sector*. Guizhou People's Press: Guiyang, People's Republic of China.

Liu, J., Chen, Y. and Chen, Y. (2010) Response of wetland landscape pattern of Hulunbuir grassland to climate change. *Journal of Arid Land Resources and Environment*. 24 (11). pp. 73–78.

Lu, C., Xie, G., Cheng, S., Ma, B. and Feng, Y. (2009) Rangeland resources utilization of China: Conflict and coordination between product function and ecological function. *Journal of Natural Resources*. 24 (10). pp. 1685–1696.

Lv, X. and Zheng, D. (2006) Impacts of global change on the Alpine meadow ecosystem in the source region of the Yangtze river. *Resources and Environment in the Yangtze Basin*. 15 (5). pp. 603–607.

Ma, R. (2007) Climate change of Inner Mongolia grassland in recent 50 years and its impact on grassland productivity. Unpublished thesis (Masters), Graduate School of Chinese Academy of Agricultural Sciences.

McGahey, D., Davies, J. and Hagelberg, N. (2014) *Pastoralism and the Green Economy: A Natural Nexus?* United Nations Environment Programme and International Union for Conservation of Nature: Nairobi, Kenya.

Mooney, H.A., Roy, J. and Saugier, B. (eds) (2001) *Terrestrial Global Productivity*. Academic Press: San Diego, California, USA.

Niu, J. (2001) Prediction studies on impact of climate change on distribution and productivity of Inner Mongolia grassland. *Acta Agrestia Sinica*. 9 (4). pp. 277–282.

Parton, W.J., Scurlock, J.M.O., Ojima, D.S., Schimel, D.S., Hall, D.O. and Scopegram Group Members (2006) Impact of climate change on grassland production and soil carbon worldwide. *Global Change Biology*. 1 (1). pp. 13–22.

Pei, Q. and Zhang, D.D. (2014) Long-term relationship between climate change and nomadic migration in historical China. *Ecology and Society*. 19 (2). p. 68.

Piao, S., Fang, J., He, J. and Xiao, Y. (2004) Spatial distribution of grassland biomass in China. *Acta Phytoecologica Sinica*. 28 (4). pp. 491–498.

PRC Ministry of Agriculture (2007) *National Grassland Conservation, Construction and Utilization Masterplan*. PRC Ministry of Agriculture: Beijing, People's Republic of China.

PRC State Council (2010) *National Main Functional Zonation Plan*. PRC State Council: Beijing, People's Republic of China. (Guofa [2010] No. 46).

PRC State Council (2011) *Several Opinions of the State Council On Promoting Good and Rapid Development in Pastoral Areas*. PRC State Council: Beijing, People's Republic of China. (Guofa [2011] No. 17).

PRC State Council (2012) *National Modern Agriculture Development Plan (2011–2015)*. PRC State Council: Beijing, People's Republic of China. (Guofa [2012] No. 4).

Squires, V., Hua, L., Li, G. and Zhang, D. (2010) Exploring the options in North-West China's pastoral lands. In: Squires, V., Hua, L., Michalk, D., Zhang, D. and Li, G. (eds), *Towards Sustainable Use of Rangelands in Northwest China*. Springer: New York, New York, USA.

Suttie, J.M., Reynolds, S.G. and Batello, C. (eds) (2005) *Grasslands of the World*. Food and Agriculture Organization of the United Nations: Rome, Italy.

Waldron, S., Brown, C., Longworth, J. and Zhang, C. (2007) *China's Livestock Revolution: Agribusiness and Policy Developments in the Sheep Meat Industry*. CABI: Wallingford, United Kingdom.

Wang, S., Li, Y. and Chen, Z. (1999) Research on suitable grazing rate of pastures-livestock system in Inner Mongolia typical grassland. *Acta Prataculturae Sinica*. 7 (3). pp. 192–197.

Wang, W., Liu, Z., Hao, D. and Liang, C. (1997) The dynamic respond of degenerative steppe vegetation into grazing prohibited in the Inner Mongolia. *Climactic and Environmental Research*. 2 (3). pp. 236–240.

Wang, X. (2013) Grassland drought in the context of institutional change: Effects of herder settlement, grassland fragmentation and pastoral marketization. *China Agricultural University Journal Social Sciences Edition*. 30 (1). pp. 18–30.

Wang, Y. and Shi, J. (2010) Analysis of characteristics of atmospheric CO_2 concentration during growing season in typical grassland. *Chinese Agricultural Science Bulletin*. 26 (13). pp. 363–365.

Wei, Y. (2004) Research on pasture growth and development and pastures-livestock balance model of China's typical grassland. Unpublished thesis (Masters), China Agricultural University.

White, R., Murray, S. and Rohweder, M. (2000) *Pilot Analysis of Global Ecosystems Grassland Ecosystems*. World Resources Institute: Washington, DC, USA.

Williams, D.M. (2002) *Beyond Great Walls: Environment, Identity and Development on the Chinese Grasslands of Inner Mongolia*. Stanford University Press: Stanford, California, USA.

Xiao, X., Chen, D., Peng, Y., Cui, X. and Ojima, D.S. (1996) Observation and modeling of plant biomass of meadow steppe in Tumugi, Xingan League, Inner Mongolia, China. *Vegetatio*. 127 (2). pp. 191–201.

Xiao, X., Wang, Y. and Chen, Z. (1996) Typical steppe primary productivity and dynamics of soil organic matter and its response to climate change in Xilin River Basin of Inner Mongolia. *Botany Gazette*. 38 (1). pp. 45–52.

Yan, Z.L., Wu, N., Yeshi, D. and Ru, J. (2005) A review of rangeland privatization and its implications in the Tibetan Plateau, China. *Nomadic Peoples*. 9 (1/2). pp. 31–51.

Yang, Y., Wang, Z., Yasuo, S., Tang, C. and Shizuo, S. (2002) Effects of global warming on productivity and soil moisture in Taihang Mountain: A transplant study. *Chinese Journal of Applied Ecology*. 13 (6). pp. 667–671.

Yeh, E. (2003) Tibetan range wars: Spatial politics and authority on the grasslands of Amdo. *Development and Change*. 34 (3). pp. 499–523.

Yuan, F., Han, X., Ge, J. and Wu, J. (2008) Net primary productivity of *Leymus chinensis* steppe in Xilin River basin of Inner Mongolia and its responses to global climate change. *Chinese Journal of Applied Ecology*. 19 (10). pp. 2168–2176.

Zhang, Q. (2011) The effect of grazing prohibition and enclosure in Ningxia's grasslands shows that it is necessary to improve ecological compensation mechanisms. *China Animal Husbandry Bulletin*. 4. pp. 77–78.

Zhang, X. (2000) Eco-economic function of grassland and its paradigm. *Science and Technology Review*. 8. pp. 3–7, 65.

Zhao, C.Z. and Long, R.J. (2007) The impact of property rights on overgrazing of grasslands: A case study in Hongshiwo, Sunan County, Gansu Province. In: Li, X.L., Wilkes, A. and Yan, Z.L. (eds), *Rangeland Co-management: Proceedings of an International Workshop Held in Diqing, Yunnan China, 13–15 May 2006*. China Agricultural Science and Technology Press: Beijing, People's Republic of China.

Zhao, H., Wang, G. and Wei, X. (2007) Research on GIS-supported Regional Prediction Model for Yield of Native Grass. *Acta Prataculturae Sinica*. 16 (4). pp. 100–106.

Zhao, J. (2002) Research on conservation tillage model under wind erosion and desertification control in agriculture pasture ecotone, north foot of the Yinshan Mountain. Unpublished dissertation (doctoral), China Agricultural University.

Zhou, G., Wang, Y. and Wang, S. (2002) Responses of grassland ecosystems to precipitation and land use along the Northeast China Transect. *Journal of Vegetation Science*. 13 (3). pp. 361–368.

7

HUMAN HEALTH, WELL-BEING AND CLIMATE CHANGE IN CHINA

Ma Wenjun, Lin Hualiang, Liu Tao, Xiao Jianpeng, Luo Yuan, Huang Cunrui, Liu Qiyong, Cordia Chu, Zeng Weilin, Hu Mengjue, Gao Xuejie, Jessica M. Keralis, Esther Onyango, Sarah Opitz-Stapleton and Rebecca Nadin

Cai Songwu works for the Guangdong Centre for Disease Control and Prevention, studying disease outbreaks. In the past, communication between Cai and other officials about outbreaks was slow, hampering their ability to anticipate and respond. Since 2005, districts and counties across the province have been able to connect to a real-time online monitoring system. 'With real-time data, we are able to understand the breeding speed, growth and decline of vectors and pest density,' he says. This kind of monitoring is becoming increasingly important as climate change alters the environmental conditions – temperatures, humidity, rainfall and carbon dioxide concentrations – that allow different kinds and numbers of pests to survive and thrive. 'In the future, regions previously without vector organisms might become more suitable for vectors to breed, and this is likely to give rise to infectious diseases.'

The links between climate variability, seasons, human behaviour and health have been areas of concern for researchers and public health officials globally, as described by Cai Songwu; climate change must now be factored into health programmes. Shifts in the frequency and intensity of heat waves, increasing incidences of floods and droughts, and sea level rise are just some of the many examples of a visibly changing climate. Death, injuries and illness due to extreme weather and slow-onset events have unfolded at unprecedented scales in the turn of the millennium; these have finally begun to attract attention to the critical challenge the impacts climate change poses to human health (Field *et al.*, 2014; Huang, C. *et al.*, 2011; Parry *et al.*, 2007). Vector-borne and zoonotic disease transmission rates are also likely to be altered by climate change and are being investigated by research organisations.

The Fifth Assessment Report from the United Nations Intergovernmental Panel on Climate Change (IPCC) states with *very high confidence* that the health of human populations is sensitive to shifts in weather patterns and other aspects of climate change.[1] For example, in many parts of the world, including China, heat waves and other extreme temperature events have led to increased morbidity and mortality. Climate change, in conjunction with rapid urbanisation and development, is altering the distribution of infectious diseases. Climate shifts are contributing to livelihood losses and food insecurity due to reductions in agricultural productivity associated with floods, droughts and storms. These can in turn increase risk of malnutrition or illness from contaminated food and water (WHO, 2010; Kan *et al.*, 2012). If the climatic changes continue as projected, the health of a large number of populations, particularly those who are poor and vulnerable, will be at risk and their existing problems will be exacerbated (Field *et al.*, 2014). Current research suggests that climate change will primarily exacerbate existing health problems, although unanticipated health consequences cannot be excluded.

Compared to sectors like agriculture, forestry, ecology and water resources, climate change related health impacts have received little attention from decision makers. The need for many countries to develop response strategies to protect health continues to go unnoticed. Until recently, health impacts were not assessed or well-quantified, nor have the findings been communicated effectively beyond the scientific community. This lack of information may have contributed to the perception in China that the burden of ill health from climate change is minimal and will continue to be so. There exists a gap in understandable information that clearly explains the potential health effects of climate change, as well as what can be done to reduce climate change-health risks.

This chapter looks at the range and magnitude of climate change impacts on human health in China. The chapter opens with a brief overview of trends in climate change and health in China, drawing from an extensive literature review of the contemporary work of Chinese researchers. The chapter then presents a case study on Guangdong Province, drawing from two separate investigations conducted by the Guangdong Provincial Institute of Public Health (GD IPH) and the Guangdong Provincial Centre for Disease Control (GD CDC), with support from Griffith University (Australia). Guangdong is one of the most populated and urbanised provinces in China and has the largest GDP. Despite this, extreme regional imbalances in economic development, a large population of economic migrants and rural/urban disparities result in low per capita economic indicators. The province's location on China's south-eastern coast leaves it highly exposed to tropical cyclones, storm surges and tidal flooding, all of which will be exacerbated by sea level rise. Its climate is hot and humid, with an average annual temperature of 23°C − perfect conditions for vector-borne diseases. Further detailed information on Guangdong's current and future vulnerability and climate risks beyond those posed to health are presented in Chapter 10. The combination of these factors makes the province of great research interest in terms of climate impacts on human health, and research and climate resilience activities and policies conducted within it can provide lessons to the rest of China. The chapter concludes with current policy responses in China at the national and provincial levels and outlines some of the existing challenges in building a response.

An overview of trends in climate change and health in China

Climate change is not only a major environmental and socio-economic issue, but also an important public health issue (McMichael *et al.*, 2006; Ma, 2012). Annual mean temperatures in China have increased by 0.5–0.8°C over the past century and this warming trend is expected to continue into the next century, with related increases in negative health impacts. China, and Asia in general, are likely to experience more frequent and intense extreme events (Field *et al.*, 2014). Climate change impacts may lead to drought-related food and water shortage, increased flooding, sea level rise and shrinking mountain glaciers, leading to changes in water availability in many Chinese rivers, as discussed in Chapter 4. Climate change may also negatively impact total rice yields (see Chapters 5 and 8). These impacts will have negative effects on people's livelihoods and health: for example, competition for resources could lead to conflicts and deaths; reduction in crop yields are likely to contribute to localised food insecurity and malnutrition; an increase in flooding and shifts in water quality and quantity may lead to an increase in water-borne diseases; increases in temperatures will exacerbate climate-sensitive diseases; and more frequent heat waves will lead to an increase in heat-related deaths and decreases in labour productivity.

China can expect climate impacts to vary from region to region as discussed in previous chapters, and so, accordingly, will the health implications. In the north-east, rising temperatures, floods, droughts and frequent cold spells are the major health threats. In north China, the most important health-climate factors are increasing temperatures and droughts, while in the north-west, drought is the major climate threat to health. In eastern China, heat waves, intensified precipitation and frequent floods threaten human lives and increase the risk of water-borne diseases. In central China, the primary threat comes from heat waves, and precipitation shifts are expanding the scope and duration of schistosomiasis (a parasitic infection whose lifecycle also requires a certain species of freshwater snail). In the south, heavy rains associated with severe typhoons and standing water from frequent storm surges and sea level rise are likely to further the spread of dengue fever and malaria, while in the south-west, alternating droughts and heavy rains could trigger landslides in mountainous areas, posing great dangers to health.

The following incidents reflect some of the emergent health risks in China due to global warming: some are new and unusual, which have caught people unprepared, while others are existing problems that could be exacerbated by the more intense and extreme events projected in the future.

In Tibet – the so-called 'rooftop of the world', with an average altitude of more than 4,000 m – mosquito species not previously recorded have established populations with warming temperatures and the construction of the Qingzang Railroad, increasing trade and tourism (Liu, Q. *et al.*, 2013; Li *et al.*, 2010). Different species of mosquitoes depend on particular temperature, humidity and rainfall conditions for propagation and survival. As climate regimes shift, and trade, agriculture and transportation facilitate the transfer of zoonotic hosts (e.g. rats and birds) and disease vectors (e.g. ticks, mosquitoes), different types of diseases are emerging in locations in which residents are unaccustomed to them (Moore *et al.*, 2012). Low standards of living, lack of awareness about prevention measures (such as the elimination of standing pots of water in and around a home) and certain agricultural practices and trade, in combination with shifting climates, are allowing disease vectors to move into new areas or re-establish themselves in locations from which they were once extirpated (Reiter, 2001).

The residents of Lhasa City in the Tibet Autonomous Region (TAR) of China reported large numbers of mosquitoes and bites, beginning in 2009, during a particularly hot summer of record daytime temperatures reaching 30.4°C – average daytime summer temperature are around 22.5°C. While the *Anopheles* mosquito and other mosquito species have long caused diseases like malaria and encephalitis throughout various parts of Tibet, research on mosquito-borne disease was limited in the area due to the low reported incidence of illness and no official record keeping prior to 2009 (Li *et al.*, 2010; Huang, F. *et al.*, 2011; Liu, Q. *et al.*, 2013). Better disease monitoring, coupled with the unusual number of people seeking treatment, lead to the discovery that a species new to the area – *Culex pipiens* – had reached the city (Liu, Q. *et al.*, 2013). These *Culex* mosquitoes are now established in the region and may be responsible for transmitting diseases such as West Nile virus and filarial worms. Much of the local population was woefully unprepared, as there was limited experience of living with large numbers of mosquitoes. From the beginning of 2009 to the end of 2012, approximately 85.3% of local respondents reported being bitten by mosquitoes; almost one in 20 (4.5%) had to go to hospital for treatment for complications. In the future, with further warming and an acceleration of trade, tourism, transportation and population growth, it is expected that outbreaks and epidemics of diseases such as Japanese encephalitis and malaria, amongst others, will be more frequent.[2] The population of Lhasa and more remote regions of Tibet, due to their limited prior exposure and low capacity for managing vector-borne diseases and other health issues, may be at greater risk.

China is also no stranger to heat waves, and records of such events go back more than 300 years. For example, in July 1743 about 11,000 people reportedly died in Beijing when the capital sweltered in an 11-day heat wave, according to an account of the incident in a nineteenth-century medical journal (Levick,

1859). The difference now is that these heat wave events, whilst once isolated occurrences, are becoming hotter and more frequent. In August 2006, the Qijiang area of Chongqing was exposed to extreme high temperatures of 44.5°C. In 2010, a severe heat wave affected many areas across the northern hemisphere, including parts of north-east China. In 2013, southern China experienced a severe heat wave with exceptionally high temperatures not seen in the past 60 years. Multiple regions experienced sustained temperatures of over 40°C (Zhejiang, Chongqing, Shanghai and Hunan). Hangzhou experienced 56 consecutive days over 40°C. These sustained high temperatures, in areas with normally high humidity, had severe negative impacts on health and affected millions of lives, particularly the elderly, those with chronic diseases and outdoor workers. Many people suffered from heatstroke and heat stress.

The potential impacts of climate shifts and change on health are emerging policy and research topics in China. With its rapid development and large, yet diverse, populations with differentiated adaptive capacities and abilities to handle health impacts, assessing health–climate vulnerabilities is crucial. Some recent research efforts to understand current health risks and extrapolate future ones include studies by teams of researchers in Guangdong province under the auspices of the Adapting to Climate Change in China I (ACCC I) programme. The case study summarises the findings of the two investigations.

Case study: climate change health impact assessments in Guangdong province

Guangdong Province (Figure 7.1) lies on the south-east coast of China in the East Asian monsoon region. The province covers 177,900 km^2 of land, has a population of 104 million and China's third largest river, the Pearl River, runs through it. Despite having the largest GDP of any Chinese province, Guangdong is low in per capita economic indicators due to the large population base. The province also has extreme regional imbalances in economic development. The Pearl River Delta, covering 30.4% of the total land in the province, contributes the greatest share of the overall GDP – 79.4% in 2008 – with the rest of the province accounting for roughly 20% of GDP (OECD, 2010). The wealth distribution closely mirrors the distribution of urban, peri-urban and rural areas in the province (Figure 7.1). Paradoxically, due to the dense population and high concentration of assets, the Pearl River Delta also suffers greater economic losses from climate disasters. Yet, the underdeveloped rural and peri-urban areas are even more vulnerable to extreme weather events and less able to adapt to climate change. The vulnerability and adaptive capacity of Guangdong's citizens is variable, depending on socio-economic conditions.

One of the major challenges is that Guangdong's core development plans do not yet include any measures to address the health impacts of climate change. Public awareness of climate health risks, such as those associated with the heat

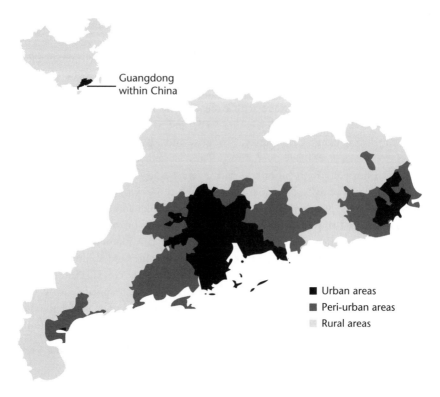

Guangdong
within China

■ Urban areas
■ Peri-urban areas
▢ Rural areas

FIGURE 7.1 Guangdong Province in China

waves that the province regularly suffers, remains low among certain demographics (Zeng, Ma *et al.*, 2012; Xu *et al.*, 2012). Ability to access and understand early warnings about heat waves or take protective measures follow a sharp educational and economic divide (Liu, T. *et al.*, 2013). For instance, in the investigation by the GD IPH, GD CDC and Griffith University, researchers found that of the respondents aware of various protective measures for reducing heat stress, less than half used air conditioners, with more utility in urban areas versus rural areas at 75% and 28%, respectively; usage was dependent on income, age and labour activity (e.g. not practical for outdoor workers) (Zeng, Ma *et al.*, 2012; Xu *et al.*, 2012; Liu, T. *et al.*, 2013). Though the province has been hit hard by heat waves in the last few years and awareness among the general public of heat risk and appropriate actions remains low, the provincial government is beginning to take policy and action steps to protect public health. The authorities have, for example, changed labour regulations to ensure that construction teams and other outdoor workers can escape the heat, though enforcement is challenging.

Temperatures are expected to continue to rise in Guangdong, with more frequent incidences of heat waves. Extreme events and slow-onset shifts in temperature and precipitation seasons will alter the incidence of vector-borne and zoonotic diseases, although limited research exists on the latter in Guangdong. The coastal areas in particular are prone to tropical cyclones, heavy rainfall, floods, storm surges and haze. Since the mid-1990s, the average annual death toll from these hazards was approximately 100 deaths (Du *et al.*, 2012). Rapid development, environmental degradation and limited incorporation of disaster risk considerations into infrastructure planning and codes, among other factors, contribute to climate-related morbidity and mortality impacts on Guangdong's residents (these are also discussed in greater detail in Chapter 10). More efforts are needed to improve health risk awareness and establish early warning communication channels to residents with different socio-economic backgrounds, along with identifying mechanisms to help individuals and households cope and adapt.

Temperature variation and mortality

According to data covering 1960–2007, the annual temperature in Guangdong has risen by an average of 0.21°C per decade, close to the national average (Guangdong Climate Change Assessment Team, 2007). Heat waves are becoming more frequent and severe (Huang *et al.*, 2008). The number of heat wave days was the lowest in the 1970s, with less than ten days annually; from 1998 onwards, however, the number increases substantially, up to more than 20 days annually on average (Huang *et al.*, 2008). The number of very hot days per year has risen in most of Guangdong's prefectures over the past 35 years (Figure 7.2). Urban areas, such as Guangzhou, have experienced more significant increases in the number of hot days, due to added urban heat island effects (Figure 7.3).

Temperature variation affects health in a variety of ways. For example, highs and lows can cause death in those with circulatory and respiratory diseases, while seasonal temperature changes are a major factor determining the seasonal variation of some diseases. In Guangzhou, Guangdong's biggest city with a population of 14 million, statistics on daily mean temperature and mortality between 2006 and 2010 reveal a U-shaped relationship. This means that deaths occur with both heat waves and cold spells – mortality is lower when the daily mean temperature stays between 14.5°C and 29.5°C, and higher at temperatures greater than 29.5°C or lower than 14.5°C (Figure 7.4) (Ma, 2012; Yan *et al.*, 2011; Zeng, Li *et al.*, 2012). Consecutive days of high temperatures further increase the risk of heat-related deaths and incidences of heat stress and stroke.

Many deaths can also be attributed to unusually hot summer nights that offer no respite from harmful temperatures. This phenomenon is measured by the diurnal temperature range (DTR), which is the difference between the maximum and the minimum temperatures on the same day. The DTR is narrowing with climate change (Luo, Zhang *et al.*, 2013). In Guangzhou, a high

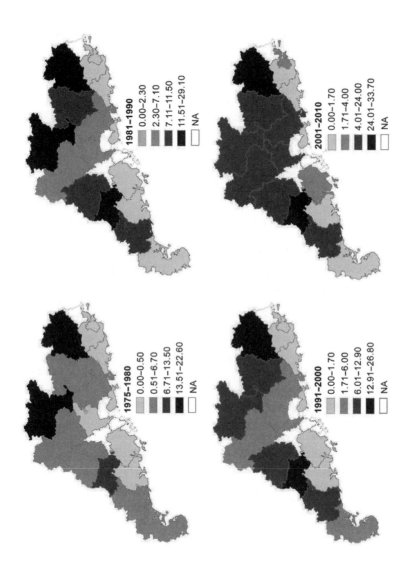

FIGURE 7.2 Heat wave duration (total number of heat wave days per year) in different prefectures of Guangdong, 1975–2010. A heat wave was defined as three or more consecutive days with daily maximum temperature ≥35°C

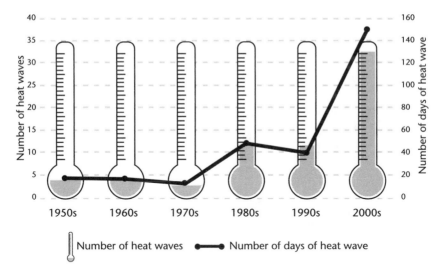

FIGURE 7.3 Heat waves Guangzhou, 1951–2010. Includes the number of heat wave events per year and the total days each year that were part of heat waves

DTR has the greatest impact on mortality on the same day, while the impacts of a lower DTR may be seen two to three days later. With the mean DTR as the benchmark, a low DTR (1.7°C) results in a 64% increase in the accumulated risk of total deaths and a 50% increase in mortality from cardiovascular disease. A high DTR (14.5°C) has a more modest impact, increasing total deaths by 23% and cardiovascular deaths by 22%. The results suggest that if warming continues, the DTR will decrease and death risks will rise.

In an investigation of county-level vulnerability to heat, using geographical and epidemiological data, GD IPH and GD CDC found a gradual increase in heat stress vulnerability going from south to north, with the southern coast and economically developed areas being less vulnerable while the underdeveloped inland areas are more vulnerable (Figure 7.5). For this study, daily health data were obtained from China's central database for disease control and prevention, and meteorological data collected from the Guangdong Meteorological Centre.[3] The research team assessed the vulnerability to climate change and future health risks from climate change in different regions in Guangdong Province. It helped to fill the research gap at the regional level by assessing climate vulnerability and risks in the health sector and developing policy guidance.[4]

Trends emerging from the study show that poorer areas are not able to adapt as well to climate change and are more vulnerable to heat waves. The epidemiological survey also revealed that some groups are more vulnerable to risk of death or stroke from heat waves. These groups were identified as: residents with cardiovascular disease; elderly populations; people engaged in outdoor activities

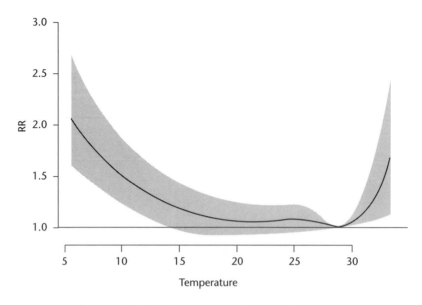

FIGURE 7.4 Relative risk of death (RR) as a function of daily mean temperature (°C) in Guangzhou, 2006–2010

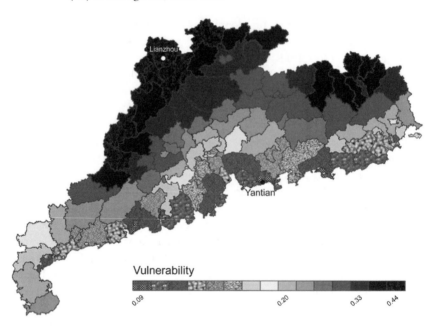

FIGURE 7.5 Map of vulnerability to heat waves in 124 counties in Guangdong Province

such as agriculture, forestry, animal husbandry and fishery; populations with a lower socio-economic status; and rural populations.

A separate investigation by the Guangdong Centre for Disease Control on the impacts of heat waves on mortality in two cities, Guangzhou and Zhuhai, and two rural townships, Nanxiong and Taishan, corroborated the findings of the provincial-level heat vulnerability assessment (Figure 7.6). Guangzhou and Zhuhai are large metropolises on the Pearl River Delta, the heart of Guangdong's economy, while Nanxiong and Taishan are each home to several hundred thousand people in northern and southern Guangdong, respectively. Heat waves were found to increase mortality risk by about 8%, with greater risks in the rural areas, which are less socio-economically developed, have low penetration of air conditioning and have poor access to health services. The study also identified females, elderly people aged 75 or above, and people with respiratory diseases as highly vulnerable groups for priority protection during heat waves. Incidentally, the same study found that the risk of drowning among rural residents, particularly among the younger populations (age 0–14), increases during heat waves and hot months as people seek relief in rivers and lakes (Ma, Xu et al., 2010).

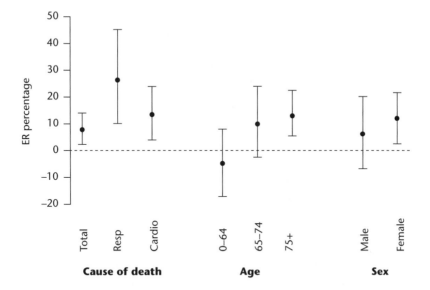

FIGURE 7.6 Impacts of heat waves on mortality in four cities in Guangdong Province by age, gender and disease. ER% indicates the percentage increase in mortality risk. Dots show mean values across the four cities, and error bars show the 95% confidence interval

Health risk assessment of future change in temperature

While there is now considerable research on evaluating current heat vulnerability and risk in Guangdong, studies are only beginning to emerge that estimate future health risks under a changing climate. The study by GD CDC also investigated potential future climate heat and vector-borne disease risk on a provincial scale. They utilised the approach recommended by the World Health Organization (Blössner and de Onis, 2005) to predict excess mortality caused by high temperatures under different future climate projections (estimated by one climate model running three different emission scenarios), by comparing future temperature-related death rates with those over the period 1981–2000.

The GD CDC used the climate model BCC_CSM1.0[5] running three different emission scenarios (A2 – high, A1B – medium and B2 – low) to project different rates and amounts of temperature increase over 2031–2050, 2051–2070 and 2071–2090. Results from all three scenarios used in the study show that deaths caused by low temperatures decrease slightly, mostly among men and the elderly. On the other hand, deaths from high temperatures increase substantially as temperatures increase with increasing emissions, primarily among women and the elderly.

Meteorological factors and vector-borne diseases

Vector-borne diseases worldwide have been on the rise with climate warming in recent years. The GD CDC also investigated the effects of temperature and precipitation on dengue fever, malaria, and hand, foot and mouth disease (not included) in the province.

Dengue fever

Dengue is a viral fever caused by infection with the dengue virus. The virus is transmitted by two species of mosquito, *Aedes albopictus* and *Aedes aegypti*. Temperature rise can affect mosquito breeding and speed up the insects' growth. The distribution of the vector mosquitoes has also shifted with climate change, according to some studies, and dengue fever has spread to higher latitudes and altitudes (Wu, J.Y. *et al.*, 2010). Guangdong's climate is favourable for the virus, but thanks to integrated prevention and control measures – such as treatment, education and eradication of mosquito breeding sites – there have not been any large outbreaks recently (Lu *et al.*, 2009). However, dengue is likely to remain a continued threat to the Guangdong Province as the density of *Aedes* is expected to increase with warming.

A study of records by the GD CDC research team of monthly dengue fever cases from 2005–2011 shows a striking seasonal pattern, with most cases reported between August and October (Figure 7.7). Dengue fever cases are

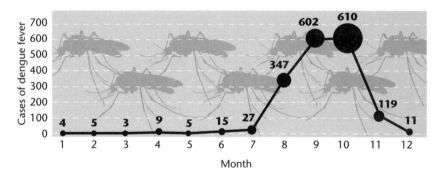

FIGURE 7.7 Cases of dengue fever each month in Guangdong, 2005–2011

positively correlated with warmer temperatures and the wet season. This suggests that climate warming and precipitation changes may add to the risk of dengue fever in Guangdong.

Malaria

Malaria is a parasitic disease spread by the bite of infected female *Anopheles* mosquitoes. Both the *Anopheles* mosquito and the malaria parasite are very sensitive to changes in climate, specifically changes in temperature, precipitation and humidity. Research shows that mosquitoes have shifted to higher altitude areas following changes in temperature associated with climate change and human activity. Malaria epidemics have also been recorded following periods of high rainfall activity.

Guangdong experienced a long epidemic of malaria in 1980–2004, and data from this period show that malaria cases peak around July to September, and then bottom out from December to March. The peak in malaria cases lags behind the temperature peak by one month and the precipitation peak by two months (Figure 7.8), corresponding with the length of time between hatching and adulthood and the emergence of a large enough population to infect many people (Luo, Zhang *et al.*, 2012).

Current Chinese research findings into the impacts of climate change and human health

Compared to other sectors such as water and agriculture, a limited number of studies covering only a small number of cities have been conducted on the impacts of climate change on health in China. In general, these studies find that the most direct impact on health is likely to be through temperature shifts. Studies suggest that both high and cold temperatures increase mortality risks. Heat waves that arrive early in the summer have a greater impact on mortality,

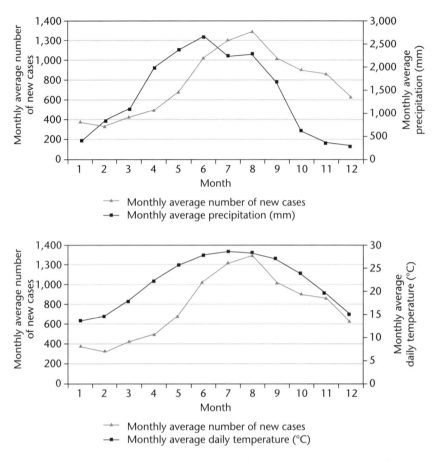

FIGURE 7.8 Number of new cases of malaria each month in Guangdong as related to precipitation and temperature, 1980–2004

and the mortality risk increases as heat waves last longer (Zeng, Li *et al.*, 2012). High temperatures with rapid onset and short duration most strongly affect residents with cardiovascular disease (Yan *et al.*, 2011), while cold temperatures with slow onset and long duration are worst for those with respiratory diseases (Zeng, Li *et al.*, 2012; Yan *et al.*, 2011; Wu *et al.*, 2013; Xie *et al.*, 2013). These impacts will be particularly evident in urban environments where buildings and roads concentrate heat (the urban heat island effect) and where heat and cold are strongly related to morbidity and mortality. Specific groups will also be more vulnerable to these impacts. For example, mortality has been shown to be higher in those aged 60 and older, and in infants.

Extreme weather events, such as typhoons, floods and droughts, also have a significant impact on health, elevating the risk of deaths and injury (Luo, Ma *et al.*, 2012). Other sensitive groups include China's economic migrant and low-income populations (Luo, Ma *et al.*, 2012). Due to high transiency, dangerous working environments and poor living and dietary conditions, migrant workers are prone to a higher rate of infectious diseases and greater susceptibility to climate-related illness and injury from extreme weather events. Their vulnerability is also increased, as most are ineligible for urban medical insurance under the hukou system (see Box 7.1) (Luo, Zhao *et al.*, 2013). Furthermore, if they are recent migrants to an area, they are not as likely to be aware of the area's climate hazards or know what public resources they can access to prepare for or recover from an event.

Other studies point to higher disease risks from climate change. A number of meteorological factors, including increasing precipitation, more hours of sunshine, more rainy days and rises in mean temperature, will increase the activity and geographic distribution of disease-causing microorganisms such as bacteria and viruses. These factors, in addition to population growth, ecosystem degradation, trade and transportation, are facilitating the rapid spread and transmission of disease. Vector-borne diseases are also spreading to higher altitudes and latitudes due to warming and human behaviour (Wu, J.Y. *et al.*, 2010; Lu *et al.*, 2009; Edelman, 2005; Luo, Zhang *et al.*, 2012; Wu, Y. *et al.*, 2010; Kang *et al.*, 2012; Ma, E. *et al.*, 2010; Guarino *et al.*, 2013). As seen in Tibet in 2009, disease carriers such as mosquitoes can spread farther afield with warming. This raises the likelihood of transmission of infectious diseases such as dengue fever, malaria, schistosomiasis (bilharzia) and intestinal diseases.

In terms of future impacts, Chinese researchers have found that as the temperature rises, there will be a worsening of the impacts identified above. An increase in heat-related deaths is projected. Transmission risk of infectious diseases such as dengue fever, malaria, infectious intestinal diseases and schistosomiasis will rise, while deaths related to cold weather will decline (Zhou *et al.*, 2008; Wu, J.Y. *et al.*, 2010; Lu *et al.*, 2009; Edelman, 2005; Luo, Zhang *et al.*, 2012). The losses in health caused by heat waves, floods and droughts are expected to grow exponentially with climate shifts (Sun *et al.*, 2002; Ding *et al.*, 2007; Kan, 2011).

The overall research literature on climate, weather and health in China is subject to many limitations, not least because there are only a few studies, which cover only a small number of cities and focus on the impacts of future climate change on health. Most of these studies are short-term and focus overly on certain research areas at the expense of other critical research areas. For example, the association between temperature and mortality in particular has been investigated extensively, and numerous studies have shown that ambient temperature has short-term effects on overall mortality; however, the impact of climate change on injury, those with chronic conditions, mental health impacts or overall labour productivity have been neglected. More research evidence is also needed on the effect on other climate-sensitive diseases such as schistosomiasis and Japanese encephalitis. In addition, the methods and approaches are not consistent among studies, and therefore the results of different studies cannot be integrated and used to inform policy decisions. Moreover, most of these studies are limited to analyses of indicators such as residents' mortality and chronic and infectious diseases, and do not include vulnerability and adaptation assessment, which is critical for planning (Kan, 2011). Future research studies need to include past, current and future impacts of climate change on health as well as an assessment of groups that may be particularly vulnerable to these impacts. Focus should shift from a reliance on impact indicators of mortality and disease rates, to a broader picture of risk and measures of coping with this risk in order to effectively inform policy decisions.

Current government policy response

As discussed in the previous section, there are a number of health-related impacts associated with climate change. Consequently, the Chinese government is seeking to address some of these research constraints and is looking to explore development of polices and institutional arrangements to respond to the health impacts of climate change. China is a vast country with a diverse and complex climate, different regional economic characteristics and different socio-economic development levels. Strategies must therefore be targeted and region-specific.

Policy and regulatory efforts at the national level

As climate change intensifies, China is putting greater emphasis on improving its adaptive capacity at the national level. In 2007, China launched the *National Climate Change Assessment Report*, which specified a series of actions important for human health, including accelerating the construction of water infrastructure, improving forecasts of meteorological disasters that can trigger disease, providing weather forecasts tailored for medical services, and implementing heatstroke prevention programmes. In order to strengthen the legal system, China has also adopted a series of related laws and regulations, such as the *Meteorology Law of China*, the *National Meteorological Disaster Emergency Plan*, the *Notice on Further Improving Heatstroke Prevention and Cooling at Workplaces in Summer*, the *Decision on Actively Responding to Climate Change* and the *National Climate Change Programme (2011–2020)*.

One of the most important climate change adaptation and health related policy documents is China's *National Adaptation Strategy* (NAS), which identifies guiding principles, priority sectors and pilot provinces for adaptation responses to climate change. Human health is identified as a priority sector and core tasks for health sector outlined include: monitoring and assessing the impacts of climate change on human health including the health of vulnerable and sensitive populations; developing and establishing human health-related weather monitoring and early warning network and public information systems; and strengthening the capacity of epidemic prevention systems, including vector-borne disease prevention and control systems. Other priority tasks include raising awareness for public health protection and emergency response to climate change and extreme events, including the provision of special information services for vulnerable groups sensitive to extreme weather. Reinforcement of emergency response systems, including the redoubling of health emergency responses emergency planning to deal with heatstroke, freezing rain and snow, haze and other extreme weather and climate events, are also planned.

Moving towards enhancing adaptive capacity in the field of human health and well-being

The prioritisation of health in the NAS is an extremely positive move. However, in order to effectively implement it, it is crucial to perform large-scale, long-term comprehensive studies on climate change impacts on health. Such studies are currently lacking. In addition, enhancing China's human health adaptive capacity means reforms and new approaches are needed. The country's overall health system is in the midst of reform and, as part of the process, the central government is trying to increase funding for health services, improve responses to public health emergencies and recognise the role of community and grass-roots institutions in public health. However, it is the reforms to the overall social safety-net system that are the most critical to reduce the nation's vulnerability, but also the most challenging to implement.

The social safety-net system

While China is moving towards more robust policies for adaptation in agriculture, forestry and water resources, there has been less attention given to climate change adaptation work on social and economic institutions, including social support systems. Climate change presents an enormous challenge for China's entire social safety net, especially pensions and social assistance, as part of its overall adaptation challenge as discussed in Chapter 2. Populations most vulnerable to climate change, like migrants, who are in greater need of protection from these mechanisms, are often excluded and unable to benefit from them. The large-scale migration of the young and middle-aged labour force from rural areas to cities leaves those left behind – the elderly, women and children and the migrants themselves – vulnerable. Migrants are often unable to access health services when they move to cities. Access to health clinics in some rural areas remains limited for those populations left behind, and the quality of care can be variable.

Reforms to the social safety net system to enable vulnerable populations easier access to social assistance is urgently required. Without adequate social assistance systems, the impacts on people's physical and psychological health can be severe due to the direct livelihood, property and well-being losses triggered by extreme weather and slow-onset events. Only by integrating climate change awareness and adaptation into the social support system will it be possible to protect people's health and well-being from the impacts of climate disasters. An effective social assistance system can reduce the impact of climate change and natural disasters on people's health and livelihoods, and improve the adaptive capacity among the public. Tables 7.1 and 7.2 show the relationships between climate change adaptation, disaster management and social assistance.

Box 7.1 *Hukou*

China adopted a birthplace registration system – called *hukou* – in 1958. The system determines what benefits a person can access. Rural-to-urban migrants are unable to access health and social services outside their registered place of birth. This makes migrants particularly vulnerable to suffering harm from socio-economic stresses and weather hazards, and less able to adapt to changing conditions.

TABLE 7.1 Improving adaptive capacity through social assistance and social security

	Methods for social security and social assistance	*Benefits in climate change adaptation and disaster response*
Protective measures	• Social welfare services • Social donations (cash/in-kind) • Social pension scheme	Protection and assistance to vulnerable groups who are least capable of adapting to climate change
Preventive measures	• Social transfer payment • Diversification of livelihoods • Weather index insurance for crops • Social insurance	Prevention of potential losses for the population prone to the impact of climate change
Promotional measures	• Social transfer payment • Loans • Property transfer • Increased availability of public resources	Promotion of diversification of livelihood sources, and encouragement to seize new opportunities from climate change

Source: Luo, Zhao *et al.*, 2013.

TABLE 7.2 Benefits and challenges of social assistance

Social assistance measures	Benefits to risk management and climate change adaptation	Existing issues and challenges
Cash payment	• Targets groups most impacted by climate change • Increases the adaptation capacity through risk tolerance and investment behaviour • More flexibility	• Requires transfer payments to be able to assist a large number of people • Takes longer time to show effect • Target groups to be identified scientifically
Weather index insurance	• Fast compensation • Avoids 'reverse selection' (those who needs it the most not being covered) and moral risk • Mobilises more funds for climate change adaptation capacity building • Closely linked with the trends of climate change • Encourages people to take more adaptive measures	• Difficult to assist marginalised farmers • Poor people may be reluctant to pay or cannot afford the insurance premium
Employment incentive project	• Encourages the provision of more non-agricultural job opportunities	• Potential impact on agricultural production
Transfer of assets	• Targets at the population impacted by climate change • Ensures their livelihoods	• Deciding how to ensure assets are in line with local needs • Funding methods
Pension project	• Targets at the ageing population impacted by climate change • Ensure their livelihoods	• Fund use efficiency

Source: Luo, Zhao *et al.*, 2013.

Social assistance

The social assistance system has become an important supplement to the national medical insurance and agricultural insurance systems. However, limited work has been done so far to integrate climate change factors into social programmes. At present, social assistance – material assistance provided to meet basic needs and ensure a minimum standard of living – is available to victims of natural disasters, those who cannot work and low-income citizens. Subsistence allowance lies at the core of the social assistance system. Social assistance covers a minimum subsistence allowance, disaster relief, medical aid, assistance to rural destitute households, the 'five guarantees' (the childless and infirm elderly are guaranteed food, clothing, medical care, housing and burial expenses), unemployment assistance, education assistance and legal aid. In more developed rural areas, the subsistence allowance programme has been successful, but it still lags behind in poverty-stricken urban areas and remote rural areas.

China's current (2014) pension insurance system is as complex and fragmented as the social insurance system. Funds for various groups are funded and administered differently, and there are large disparities between populations. For example, urban migrant workers, despite being eligible to participate in the urban pension insurance system, are often excluded due to the high payment threshold and inability to transfer their contributions from one area to another. Compared to the urban pension insurance system, the new rural old-age insurance system is facing even more serious problems: a growing percentage of the young rural population is migrating to urban areas, leaving behind middle-aged women, children and the elderly. Many elderly rural farmers cannot collect a pension because neither they (having no fixed income) nor their families can afford to contribute to the pension scheme. In addition, current laws allow local authorities to suspend implementation of the pension programmes in locations where basic provisioning of food and clothing is problematic, which effectively excludes farmers in poverty-stricken areas from participating in the old-age insurance (Gao, 2003). Thus, the new pension insurance system in China fails to meet the overall needs for its development strategy in the response to climate change. In disadvantaged areas with poor natural endowment, little resources, low economic level and few job opportunities, those most in need of pension insurance to secure their old age are not covered by the current system. This increases their vulnerability to suffering harm post-weather hazards and less able to recover, increasing some rural populations' climate risk.

While on paper the social assistance system could improve many populations' climate resilience, there are disparities in coverage between urban and rural areas, and between eastern and western regions. Unemployment benefits and housing assistance, to which urban residents are entitled, are not available to rural residents, while many other assistance projects exist in name only. Economically disadvantaged groups mainly live in the less-developed central and western regions, particularly in ethnic minority areas, old revolutionary bases and border areas. Local governments often determine the size of population entitled to social assistance in their jurisdiction based on their own financial constraints, resulting in very low levels of assistance in these areas. Furthermore, non-governmental organisations (NGOs) in China are not well developed, and social organisations have a negligible role in providing social assistance.

In order to respond to the challenges of climate change, the government is starting to examine how social assistance can be targeted to assist farmers and improve conditions in poor areas to achieve regional balance. This will require looking at the threshold and assistance standard for each category of social assistance and making eligibility assessments based on the basic needs of rural residents, level of regional economic development, price and consumption, and financial affordability. Landless farmers and migrant workers should be included in the social assistance system to achieve full coverage. The social disaster relief system also needs to be strengthened by standardising procedures and improving training for personnel. In less-developed areas, a rural social medical aid system should be put in place, with emphasis on poverty alleviation through developing the economy and improving medical aid by addressing poor-quality health facilities and lack of doctors and medicine in resource-poor areas.

The funding and implementation mechanisms for social assistance also need reform if it is to ensure the health and well-being of society's most vulnerable groups. At present, projects with direct investment from the central government include relief funds, medical aid funds and transfer payments for the five guarantees. Provincial and local government also provide funds for households entitled to five guarantees, destitute families, subsistence allowance and temporary assistance.

Compared to poorer urban areas, rural social assistance receives less allocation from the central government; in particular, the rural subsistence allowance, at the heart of the social assistance system, is still completely reliant on local governments. The central government needs to play a more active role in minimising the disparities among regions to effectively achieve horizontal equity. Finally, government management of the rural social assistance programme also needs to be improved. A sound social assistance management system and implementation mechanism is urgently required, which features government leadership, administration of the civil affairs department, interdepartmental collaboration and social participation. Legislation efforts also need to be enhanced to establish appropriate policies and regulations in a timely manner while improving the social assistance system, so that the assistance work has a legal basis and standardised procedures.

Medical care and access to health-care insurance

At the time of writing (2014), the central government is examining both medical-care responses to treat injury and illness associated with climate change and access to health insurance for vulnerable groups. The health-care system in some regions is ill-equipped to deal with climate-related hazards like extreme heat, particularly in rapidly urbanising areas. The capacity of staff and medical facilities to treat patients varies around the country. As with disaster relief responses, and emphasised in the NAS, there is recognition that developing closer cooperation between medical service providers and other government departments such as meteorological, civil affairs and water conservancy departments, to provide timely information about weather conditions and related health risks and mobilise emergency medical response, is essential.

China's medical insurance system includes (as at 2014) basic medical insurance for urban employees and urban residents and new rural cooperative medical insurance (Gu, 2008). In urban areas, subscribers must make regular contributions in order to receive benefits from the pool, but many are unable to afford the contributions and do not receive benefits (Wang, 2007). Health-care costs are increasing, and the insurance system is struggling to expand coverage. Providing medical support for migrant populations in urban areas is also a major issue, as these groups are currently excluded from the system. There are also gaps in the existing rural cooperative medical system (NRCMS) in protecting the rural poor population. Farmers have to bear most medical expenses, as reimbursement rates are low (Cheng, 2008). Inconsistency in policy among different areas creates barriers to accessing the NRCMS compensation fund for rural residents who migrate (Zhang, 2009). There is a gender gap in access to health services as well, with rural women and girls being the most marginalised (Wang, 2010).

The medical insurance system needs to be reformed to narrow the gap, and thus eliminate disparities, between urban and rural insurance. For example, one approach could be for existing health resources in rural areas to be redistributed according to current population needs to better fit the regional health planning requirements. More funding is urgently required to expand the health insurance coverage in rural areas and to improve health-care services in township clinics. Management and operation of the rural cooperative medical system also needs improvement. Participation should be compulsory to achieve full coverage among farmers, with contributions calculated according to income (Cheng, 2008). Government spending should be increased to exempt the destitute population from contribution, and to raise the cap of contribution.

Further developing policy: understanding where and who is vulnerable at regional and local levels

A key part of developing robust climate adaptation policy is identifying groups and regions most vulnerable to the climate change impacts, as this allows policy makers to adequately plan for the potential impact of climate change on population health and assist those who will be most affected. China is a vast country with considerable differences among the regions in terms of economic development, level of urbanisation, land cover and hydro-meteorological conditions, as discussed in the other chapters of this book. Each city or region has priority needs in terms of adaptation, and requires specific adaptive measures targeting different challenges (see also Chapters 1 and 2). While centralised planning and preparation is critical, each city and region needs to develop its own climate change adaptation strategies tailored to its particular challenges in order to protect the health and safety of local populations.

As discussed in Chapters 2 and 3, China is rapidly urbanising, which means more areas are becoming densely populated, thus concentrating more people, assets and infrastructure in disaster-prone areas. China's coastline and its populations are vulnerable to health issues linked to frequent typhoons and seasonal droughts and floods. In these areas, it is critical to strengthen early warning systems for typhoons along the coast, and for rainstorms and flash floods in the mountains. In central coastal areas such as Shanghai, urban areas will experience increases in temperature and precipitation, see worsening droughts and floods and grapple with uncertainties. Adaptation in this region will also need to focus on capacity building against extreme meteorological disasters, particularly drought, flood, heat wave, low temperature and snow; setting up a sound urban health-care system; and improving disease surveillance and the public health service system, with special focus on vector-borne diseases such as schistosomiasis. Table 7.3 contains an overview of specific measures that can be taken in urban areas to improve capacity to address the health-related impacts of climate change.

Some experience has been gained from pilot projects in certain areas and can be extended to other regions. Chongqing (Three Gorges area) has been identified in the national strategy as a pilot and demonstration adaptation project for vector-borne disease prevention and control system, emergency response to heat waves and human health monitoring and early warning, including development of health education and risk communication systems to address heat waves and extreme weather conditions. The Shanghai urban infrastructure resilience-building project was launched to cope with impacts on urban development from increasing heat island effects, extreme precipitation, sea level rise and environmental degradation. The project aims to build up adaptive capacity by improving urban protection standards, observation, early warning and emergency response of extreme weather events, and research on adaptation strategies and countermeasures (Luo, Zhao *et al.*, 2013). Building overall resilience could help in reducing the direct morbidity and mortality health effects of disasters, and a number of risk reduction demonstration projects are underway in different provinces.

Conclusion

Compared with agriculture, forestry, ecology and water resources, the impact of climate change on health has attracted less attention in China. A review of the literature reveals that research on the impacts of climate change on health and adaptation in China is still in its infancy. Summing up the trends in climate change and health, the evidence makes clear five important points:

1   temperature increases will have the most impact on health, both directly (through increased mortality, heat stress and mental health impacts) and indirectly (through food insecurity and reduced labour productivity in China, though the latter is poorly researched);

TABLE 7.3 Impacts of climate change on human health and corresponding adaptation measures

Adaptation measures	Heat waves	Extreme weather events	Infectious diseases	Smog	Ultraviolet radiation
Communications	Help the public understand the hazards and take protective measures	Warn of impending natural disasters Inform the public on protective measures and preparing relief supplies	Help the public understand the hazards, symptoms and preventive measures	Educate the public about measures to be taken individually	Help the public understand the hazards and preventive and remedial measures
Detection	Screen at-risk populations Establish targeted programmes and an early warning system	Early warning system	Early warning and feedback systems	Early warning and response systems	Early warning system
Urban planning	Plant trees to reduce the heat island effect	Reduce water and soil erosion and floods	Eliminate breeding environments of harmful bacteria	Increase green space and parks	Increase green space and parks
Infrastructure	Public drinking water and cooling facilities	Public shelters and dams	Public health facilities and laboratories	Public transport system	Shading facilities
Technological	Roof heat isolation and related technologies	Better construction standards		Alternative energy sources	UV protection substances
Medical	Adjust working hours Increase hospital staffing and beds	Include rapid medical response in disaster prevention planning	Develop new vaccines and drugs	Increase hospital staffing and beds	Increase medical capacity to treat UV radiation–related conditions

Source: Luo, Zhao et al., 2013.

2   with temperature and precipitation shifts, there will be higher disease risks;
3   changes in other extreme events like flooding or drought will have direct (e.g. drowning deaths) and indirect (e.g. illness due to poor quality water during drought) health impacts;
4   research on health impacts related to decreases in water quality and quantity due to the intersection of pollution, environmental degradation and climate change is extremely limited; and
5   China can expect health impacts to vary from region to region.

The chapter presented a case study to illustrate in detail the assessment of risks and vulnerability to climate change across different regions in Guangdong Province, followed by an analysis of the health risks of future climate change. Under future climate change scenarios, it was projected that the impact on people's health will be more significant, with higher vulnerability in economically underdeveloped areas. However, public awareness of these health risks and adaptive capacity to cope with climate change remain low. Despite the recent prioritisation of the health sector in the *National Adaptation Strategy*, national and provincial level impact and vulnerability assessments on health are needed. Research findings must be translated into region-specific actions and policies. Each province should identify its major climate and health risks, vulnerable areas and vulnerable groups through multidisciplinary and multi-sector cooperation and research. This kind of assessment will determine appropriate plans and resource allocation to formulate and implement effective adaptation policies and measures in China.

Climate change will disproportionately impact the health of populations without access to health and social services, and traditionally vulnerable populations like the elderly, children and the poor. Successful adaptation strategies will be those that involve local communities in assisting vulnerable populations and strengthening services and disaster early warning. Further exploring the best ways to reach vulnerable groups will be an important step in preventing illness and health problems as the climate changes in China. Given the sheer size of China and the diverse climate risks facing different provinces, the challenge is to how develop effective adaptation policies and plans that can reduce the negative health impacts from climate change.

Notes

1   IPCC AR5, WGII, Chapter 11.
2   Vector-borne and zoonotic disease transmission is not only due to changes in climate. Population growth, ecosystem degradation, agriculture and livestock practices, trade, tourism and transportation are moving illnesses around at much faster rates than they could shift through changes in climate alone. The shifts in climate make it much easier for new diseases to establish in a location or for old diseases, previously eradicated, to reappear. Malaria used to be common as far north as Norway, Canada and Russia.

The mosquitoes that cause it still live in those places, but transmission rates are low because of better control and living standards. How human behaviour and climate change will act together to facilitate the emergence or re-emergences of diseases is a critical research topic.

3 The data used in this study include daily mortality, infectious diseases and meteorological data. Daily mortality data cover non-accidental deaths (NAD), respiratory disease (RD) mortality, circulatory disease mortality and cerebrovascular disease (CBD) mortality. Daily infectious diseases data cover malaria, dengue fever (DF) and hand, foot and mouth disease (HFMD). Daily meteorological data include maximum temperature, mean temperature, minimum temperature, hours of sunshine, relative humidity (RH), average wind speed, average precipitation, average pressure, as well as average monthly mean temperature, monthly maximum temperature, monthly minimum temperature, monthly mean precipitation and monthly RH. The A2, A1B and B2 scenarios are chosen to study future climate change.

4 With funds from ACCC I, the Institute of Public Health at the Guangdong Provincial Centre for Disease Control and Prevention sought to help policy makers develop more comprehensive strategies to address climate change and reduce health risks. A multidisciplinary research team studied the health impacts of climate change in Guangdong and considered the implications for national and provincial adaptation policy.

5 Beijing Climate Center Climate System Model (BCC_CSM1.0) is the first generation, coupled climate model developed at the Beijing Climate Center (BCC), China Meteorological Administration.

References

Blössner, M. and de Onis, M. (2005) *Malnutrition: Quantifying the Health Impact at National and Local Levels*. World Health Organization: Geneva, Switzerland (WHO Environmental Burden of Disease Series, No. 12).

Cheng, C.H. (2008) Fairness of the demand side of the new rural cooperative medical system. PhD thesis. Shandong University: Shandong, People's Republic of China.

Ding, Y., Ren, G., Shi, G., Gong, P., Zheng, X., Zhai, P., Zhang, D., Zhao, Z., Wang, S., Wang, H., Luo, Y., Chen, D., Gao, X. and Dai, X. (2007) China's National Assessment Report on climate change (I): Climate change in China and the future trend. *Advances in Climate Change Research*. 3 (Suppl.). pp. 1–5.

Du, Y., Liu, J., Zhao, X., Zeng, Y., Chen, X., Liu, B., Fang, C., Li, X., Tang, L., Li, C., Hu, Y., He, J., Ai, H., Duan, H., Zheng, J., Wang, B., Wu, X. and Zheng, D. (2012) *Final Report on Climate Disaster Risk Assessment and Adaptation Strategies for Guangdong*. Guangdong Climate Center.

Edelman, R. (2005) Dengue and dengue vaccines. *Journal of Infectious Diseases*. 191 (5). pp. 650–653.

Field, C., Barros, V., Mach, K., Mastrandrea, M. *et al.* (2014) Technical summary. In: Barros, V.R., Field, C.B., Dokken, D.J., Mastrandrea, M.D., Mach, K.J., Bilir, T.E., Chatterjee, M., Ebi, K.L., Estrada, Y.O., Genova, R.C., Girma, B., Kissel, E.S., Levy, A.N., MacCracken, S., Mastrandrea, P.R. and White L.L. (eds), *Climate Change 2014: Impacts, Adaptation, and Vulnerability*. Contribution of Working Group II to the Fifth Assessment Report of the Intergovernmental Panel on Climate Change. Cambridge University Press: Cambridge, United Kingdom and New York, New York, USA.

Gao, H.R. (2003) Economic and social reasons for difficulty in implementing China's rural social old-age insurance scheme. *Journal Jilin Normal University (Edition of Humanities and Social Sciences)*. 3. pp. 71–72.

Gu, X. (2008) Incrementalism road towards universal health care coverage. *Dongyue Tribune*. 1. pp. 6–11.

Guangdong Climate Change Assessment Team (2007) Assessment report on climate change in Guangdong (selection). *Guangdong Meteorology*. 29 (3). pp. 1–6.

Guarino, A., Quigley, E.M.M. and Walker, W.A. (eds) (2013) *Probiotic Bacteria and Their Effect on Human Health and Well-Being*. Karger: Basel, Germany.

Huang, C., Vaneckova, P., Wang, X., FitzGerald, G., Guo, Y. and Tong, S. (2011) Constraints and barriers to public health adaptation to climate change: A review of the literature. *American Journal of Preventive Medicine*. 40. pp. 183–190.

Huang, F., Zhou, S., Zhang, S., Wang, H. and Tang, L. (2011) Temporal correlation analysis between malaria and meteorological factors in Motuo County, Tibet. *Malaria Journal*. 10. pp. 54–61.

Huang, Z.Z., Zhang, J.H., Shi, X.J., He, J. and Hua, C.H. (2008) Global warming and climate changes in Guangdong. *Tropical Geography*. 28 (4). pp. 302–305.

Kan, H. (2011) Climate change and human health in China. *Environmental Health Perspectives*. 119 (2). p. A60.

Kan, H., Chen, R. and Tong, S. (2012) Ambient air pollution, climate change, and population health in China. *Environment International*. 42. pp. 10–19.

Kang, M., Ma, W.J., Lin, J.Y., Sun, L.M., Deng, A.P. and Zhang, Y.H. (2012) Short-term effects of weather on the incidence of hand, foot and mouth disease in Guangzhou city. *Chinese Journal of Epidemiology*. 33 (2). pp. 244–245.

Levick, J.J. (1859) ART. II. Remarks on sunstroke. *American Journal of the Medical Sciences*. 73 (1). p. 40.

Li, W.J., Wang, J.L., Li, M.H., Fu, S.H., Wang, H.Y., Wang, Z.Y., Jiang, S.Y., Wang, X.W., Guo, P., Zhao, S.C., Shi, Y., Lu, N.N., Nasci, R.S., Tang, Q. and Liang, G.D. (2010) Mosquitoes and mosquito-borne arboviruses in the Qinghai–Tibet Plateau – focused on the Qinghai Area, China. *American Journal of Tropical Medicine and Hygiene*. 82 (4). pp. 705–711.

Liu, Q., Liu, X., Cirendunzhu, Woodward, A., Li Bai, P., Shaowei Sang, B., Fangjun Wan, D., Zhou, L., Guo, Y., Wu, H., Li, G., Lu, L., Wang, J., Dawa, Chu, C. and Xiaoruodeng (2013) Mosquitoes established in Lhasa City, Tibet, China. *Parasites and Vectors*. 6 (1). p. 224.

Liu, T., Xu, Y.J., Zhang, Y.H., Yan, Q.H., Song, X.L. Xie, H.Y., Luo, Y., Rutherford, S., Chu, C., Lin, H.L. and Ma, W.J. (2013) Associations between risk perception, spontaneous adaptation behavior to heat waves and heatstroke in Guangdong province, China. *BMC Public Health*. 13. p. 913.

Lu, L., Lin, H., Tian, L., Yang, W., Sun, J. and Liu, Q. (2009) Time series analysis of dengue fever and weather in Guangzhou, China. *BMC Public Health*. 9. p. 395.

Luo, Y., Ma, W.J., Liu, T. and Xiao, J.P. (2012) Effects of extreme climatic events on human health. *South China Journal of Preventive Medicine*. 38 (2). pp. 75–77.

Luo, Y., Zhang, Y., Liu, T., Rutherford, S., Xu, Y., Xu, X., Wu, W., Xiao, J., Zeng, W., Chu, C. and Ma, W. (2013) Lagged effect of diurnal temperature range on mortality in a subtropical megacity of China. *PloS One*. 8 (2). p. e55280.

Luo, Y., Zhang, Y.H., Pei, F.Q., Liu, T., Zeng, W.L. *et al.* (2012) Time-series analysis on the malaria mortality affected by meteorological factors in Guangdong Province. *Chinese Journal of Preventive Medicine*. 46 (10). pp. 892–897.

Luo, Y., Zhao, H., Hu, B., Yu, H., Zheng, X., Tao, R., Gu, X., Zhu, F. and Xie, J. (2013) *Study of the Climate Change Adaptation Mechanism Based on Social Vulnerability Analysis* (ACCC I Technical Report).

Ma, E., Lam, T., Wong, C. and Chuang, S. (2010) Is hand, foot and mouth disease associated with meteorological parameters? *Epidemiology and Infection*. 138 (12). p. 1779.

Ma, W., Xu, Y. and Xu, X. (2010) Is drowning a serious public health problem in Guangdong Province, People's Republic of China? Results from a retrospective population-based survey, 2004–2005. *International Journal of Injury Control and Safety Promotion*. 17 (2). pp. 103–110.

Ma, W.J. (2012) Strengthen the research on climate change and health to define the health risks. *Chinese Journal of Preventive Medicine*. 46 (10). pp. 876–878.

McMichael, A.J., Woodruff, R.E. and Hales, S. (2006) Climate change and human health: Present and future risks. *Lancet*. 367 (9513). pp. 859–869.

Moore, S.M., Monaghan, A., Griffith, K.S., Apangu, T., Mead, P.S. and Eisen, R.S. (2012) Improvement of disease prediction and modeling through the use of meteorological ensembles: Human plague in Uganda. *PLoS ONE*. 7 (9). e44431.

OECD (2010) *OECD Territorial Reviews: Guangdong, China 2010*. OECD Publishing.

Parry, M.L., Canziani, O.F., Palutikof, J.P. *et al.* (2007) Technical Summary. In: Parry, M.L., Canziani, O.F., Palutikof, J.P., van der Linden, P.J. and Hanson, C.E. (eds), *Climate Change 2007: Impacts, Adaptation and Vulnerability*. Contribution of Working Group II to the Fourth Assessment Report of the Intergovernmental Panel on Climate Change. Cambridge University Press: Cambridge, United Kingdom.

Reiter, P. (2001) Climate change and mosquito-borne disease. *Environmental Health Perspectives*. 109 (1). pp. 141–161.

Sun, C.Q., Gao, F. and Qu, J.S. (2002) Latest knowledge on global climate change. *Chinese Journal of Nature*. 24 (2). pp. 114–122.

Wang, S.J. (2010) Empirical research on new rural cooperative medical care and health fairness in Qinghai. *Qinghai Social Sciences*. 5. pp. 83–88.

Wang, Y.Z. (2007) China's basic medical insurance system research. Dissertation. Fudan University: Shanghai, People's Republic of China.

WHO (World Health Organization) (2010) *Climate Change Adaptation to Protect Human Health: China Project Profile*. [Online] Available from: www.who.int/globalchange/ projects/adaptation/en/index3.html. [Accessed: 29 June 2014.]

Wu, J.Y., Lun, Z.R., James, A.A. and Chen, X.G. (2010) Dengue fever in mainland China. *American Journal of Tropical Medicine and Hygiene*. 83 (3). pp. 664–671.

Wu, W., Xiao, Y., Li, G., Zeng, W., Lin, H. and Rutherford, S. (2013) Temperature–mortality relationship in four subtropical Chinese cities: A time-series study using a distributed lag non-linear model. *Science of the Total Environment*. 449. pp. 355–362.

Wu, Y., Yeo, A., Phoon, M.C., Tan, E.L., Poh, C.L., Quak, S.H. and Chow, V.T.K. (2010) The largest outbreak of hand; foot and mouth disease in Singapore in 2008: the role of enterovirus 71 and coxsackievirus A strains. *International Journal of Infectious Diseases*. 14 (12). pp. e1076–e1081.

Xie, H., Yao, Z., Zhang, Y., Xu, Y., Xu, X., Liu, T., Lin, H., Lao, X., Rutherford, S., Chu, C., Huang, C., Baum, S. and Ma, W. (2013) Short-term effects of the 2008 cold spell on mortality in three subtropical cities in Guangdong Province, China. *Environmental Health Perspectives*. 121 (2). pp. 210–216.

Xu, Y.J., Liu, T., Song, X.L., Yan, Q.H., Xie, H.Y. and Zhou, S.E. (2012) Investigation on the perception of risk level of heat wave and its related factors in Guangdong province. *Chinese Journal of Preventive Medicine*. 46 (7). pp. 613–618.

Yan, Q.H., Zhang, Y.H., Ma, W.J., Xu, Y.J., Xu, X.J., Cai, Q.M., Pan, B. and Zeng, S.Q. (2011) Association between temperature and daily mortality in Guangzhou, 2006–2009: A time-series study. *Chinese Journal of Epidemiology*. 32 (1). pp. 9–12.

Zeng, W.L., Li, G.C., Xiao, Y.Z., Xu, Y.J., Xu, X.J. Liu, T., Luo, Y., Xiao, J.P. and Ma, W.J. (2012) The impact of temperature on cardiovascular disease deaths in 4 cities, China: A time-series study. *Chinese Journal of Epidemiology*. 33 (10). pp. 1032–1036.

Zeng, W.L., Ma, W.J., Zhang, Y.H., Liu, T., Luo, Y. *et al.* (2012) Modification effect of latitude on relationship between high temperature and mortality risk among elderly: A meta-analysis. *Journal of Environment and Health*. 29 (7). pp. 639–642.

Zhang, Y.H. (2009) China's rural cooperative medical system. PhD thesis. Northwest A&F University: Xianyang, People's Republic of China.

Zhou, X.N., Yang, G.J., Yang, K., Wang, X.H., Hong, Q.B., Sun, L.P., Malone, J.B., Kristensen, T.K., Bergquist, N.R. and Utzinger, J. (2008) Potential impact of climate change on schistosomiasis transmission in China. *American Journal of Tropical Medicine and Hygiene*. 78 (2). pp. 188–194.

PART III

Social vulnerability and climate risks in three provinces

8

NINGXIA

Zheng Yan, Meng Huixin, Zhang Xiaoyu, Zhu Furong, Wang Zhanjun, Fang Shuxing, Sarah Opitz-Stapleton, Pan Jiahua, Ma Zhongyu, Fan Jianmin, Shi Shangbai, Fan Jianrong, Xie Xinlu, Rebecca Nadin and Samantha Kierath

This chapter highlights Ningxia Province, with a largely agriculture-based economy that is undergoing both planned (policy-driven) and autonomous (individual- and household-level) transitions. Environmental degradation, overexploitation of water resources and agricultural intensification make the province's ecosystems particularly vulnerable to harm during droughts and other weather hazards, in turn increasing the vulnerability of the populations that depend upon the land and its ecosystem services to support their livelihoods. Ningxia is one of the most arid regions of China, experiencing serious water resource shortages due to lack of supply availability, inefficient use of water supplies and high demand, with high evapotranspiration rates (Xu *et al.*, 2013). The province's average annual per capita water availability is 687 m³, less than one-third of the national average at an amount categorised as 'severe water shortage' according to World Bank standards (Qiu *et al.*, 2012; see also Chapter 4). Fragile soils, land use changes and multi-year droughts have intensified desertification rates, with degraded areas now accounting for around 44% of provincial land area (Qiu *et al.*, 2012). The types of challenges that Ningxia faces exemplify some aspects of China's larger adaptation challenge.

Families in Ningxia that rely on agriculture and livestock raising for their living, like Ma Changjun's, cannot afford to waste a drop of water. His family and those living in Yanchi in Ningxia make their living by growing maize and breeding sheep, and through temporary migration to find work in other places. Many families in rural communities in central and northern parts of the province (Figure 8.1) rely on cisterns to meet drinking water needs, and they ration and recycle water from bathing to wash clothes and water their vegetables and sheep. Despite this, there is not enough water in some years,

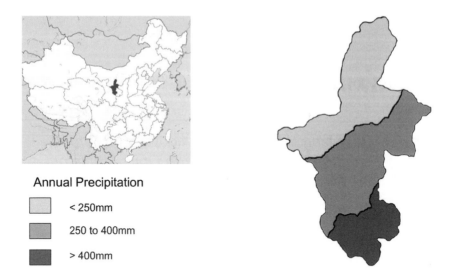

Annual Precipitation

< 250mm

250 to 400mm

> 400mm

FIGURE 8.1 Agro-ecosystem zones of Ningxia as demarcated by annual average precipitation isohyets (lines of equal or constant rainfall in a given time period)

Ma says in a 2012 interview. Drought, declines in rainfall over the past two decades and overgrazing that damages the land are stressing these families' abilities to survive.

The types of issues facing Ningxia's families – land use and water resource management, transitioning socio-economic conditions, pollution issues and migration – are emblematic of the types of issues facing families in other provinces in China, particularly rural families. Many rural provinces, including Ningxia, have greater proportions of ethnic groups who have different cultures, traditional livelihoods and relationships with the land – in effect marking multiple Chinas. These identities and socio-cultural values are shifting in response to wider environmental, policy and economic pressures, as discussed in Chapter 2. Climate change is an additional pressure placed upon the inhabitants of Ningxia, and altering their climate risks.

Ningxia: shifting livelihoods and environmental degradation

Ningxia Hui Autonomous Region is located close to China's northern breadbasket, but a dearth of water resources prevents it from contributing significantly to overall grain production (~0.6% of national totals in 2010; Ningxia Provincial Bureau of Statistics, 2011) in spite of fertile loess soil deposits in the central region. The province lags behind most of the rest of China in terms of socio-economic development, and poverty levels are quite high; the total population is 6,470,000 (3,191,651 in rural areas and 3,278,349 in urban cities), and per capita incomes are only 81% of the national average (National Bureau of Statistics of China, 2013).

Ningxia is the only provincial Hui Autonomous Region in China, with 20.8% of the total Hui population across China living in the province. The Hui people have different culture, lifestyle and religious traditions (Islamic) than the dominant (two-thirds majority) Han population. Hui people make up 34.8% of the total population of the province, with more than 1 million Hui people living in central and southern Ningxia. These areas constitute several impoverished areas in China and are being supported by key national and provincial anti-poverty projects. Socio-economic and cultural change processes, in combination with continued environmental degradation and contradictory policies for encouraging economic development (e.g. large-scale development and investment projects in ecologically sensitive areas) versus protecting the environment (e.g. programmes for ecological resettlement and fallowing farmland for reforestation), are creating complex vulnerability contexts for Ningxia's peoples. These shifts make those engaged in agriculture or animal husbandry more susceptible to harm when exposed to the climate hazards, such as drought, that are becoming more variable and intense in Ningxia.

Livelihoods, ecosystem health and services

The livelihoods of, and crop varieties planted by, Ningxia's farmers are shaped by access to water resources, uneven precipitation, high climate variability and mixed soil conditions. The Yellow River is the lifeblood and economic lifeline of Ningxia, accounting for more than 90% of the province's water supply.[1] Groundwater also constitutes an important water supply. Agricultural water demand dominates total water consumption, accounting for nearly 93% of usage (Ningxia Provincial Bureau of Statistics, 2010b). Its agricultural area is effectively divided into three agro-ecosystems by the precipitation and ecosystem differentials that determine the suitability of different crop and animal husbandry mixes (see Figure 8.1): the mountainous southern regions, the semi-arid middle area and the arid north.

The mountainous southern region with thin yet fertile, highly erodible loess soils, has an average annual rainfall of 400 mm or greater. Potatoes are the dominant crop, with silkworms, cattle, pigs and sheep the principal livestock (Li et al., 2013). In the semi-arid middle area, the products are corn and spring wheat mixed with some sheep and cattle husbandry. Precipitation averages between 250–400 mm a year and irrigation is limited through this region, reducing the crop yields as agriculture is primarily rain fed. Wolfberry, wine grapes and other speciality crops are now being promoted in this area (Li, J. et al., 2008). In the northern arid area where precipitation is less than 250 mm a year, water diverted from the Yellow River supports widespread agriculture. This region produces roughly 74% of the province's total grain yield on 29% of its total arable land (Li, Y. *et al.*, 2008). Soil salinisation and decreasing soil fertility due to centuries of extensive irrigation now impacts about 40% of this area (Merkle, 2003).

Water shortages, recurrent droughts, and soil erosion and desertification due to agricultural and livestock intensification on marginal lands create economically tenuous situations for rural households. Groundwater shortages due to excessive demand and overextraction (see Chapter 4) have a significant impact on domestic and industrial supplies, with an average of 80% of domestic (60% industrial) supply sourced from groundwater in Ningxia (Lohmar *et al.*, 2003). In the remote mountainous areas, water cellars constitute the main water storage of local residents and supply both domestic and livestock needs, as groundwater supplies are too saline for most uses. Drinking water supplies in rural areas are frequently contaminated with fluorine, arsenic and high levels of bacteria (Li, J. *et al.*, 2008). During years of extreme drought, residents in the mountains must often resort to consuming unsafe groundwater, migrating for work or borrowing to subsidise the purchase of drinking water.

The three agro-ecosystem zones of Ningxia translate into spatially diverse livelihood options between farmers of each zone. The northern area's agriculture, fed by Yellow River irrigation, supports diversified livelihood options – rice, wheat, and fruits and vegetables that command higher commodity prices, such as grapes and greenhouse vegetables. The incomes from commodity cash crops account for more than half of net income per capita for farmers in the northern area. Moreover, as this area is closer to cities with more convenient means of transportation, seasonal migration to urban areas and access to urban markets have improved livelihoods while presenting new economic opportunities for rural residents in the northern region that are not available to farmers in the central or south. For example, a joint venture between residents in the peri-urban area of Yinchuan and those in the surrounding rural areas allows both groups to rent land for growing vegetables and accessing Yellow River irrigation water, giving the peri-urban residents respite from urban pollution and allowing the rural residents greater market access. Through this venture, the rural farmers involved are able to transport and sell their vegetables in Hong Kong, where they can fetch a much higher price than in local markets.

In the central arid belt and southern mountainous areas, the chances of obtaining similar lucrative profits are very slim. In central and southern regions relying on rain-fed agriculture or diversions from the Yellow River Diversion Project, only one-third of revenue can be derived from agriculture (the main crops including corn and potatoes) and animal husbandry. Wheat yields are extremely low in such arid environments. Due to perennial drought, soil erosion (affecting nearly 80% of the arable land) and continued environmental degradation (Merkle, 2003), migrating elsewhere to work has become the main source of livelihood of many families in central and southern areas since the 1980s. Households cannot solely derive their incomes through planting traditional crop types or livestock raising; migration has become an important source of income within overall livelihood mixes as depicted in Figure 8.2. According to 2010 data from a rural social survey (see the case study), 38% of the total labour force (farmers) in the Guyuan area were working as migrant workers, and the proportion was as high as 52% in some remote mountainous areas, such as Jingyuan County (Pan *et al.*, 2010).

Drought and occasional flooding in the smaller mountain watersheds, caused by erratic precipitation, currently represent the most significant weather-related

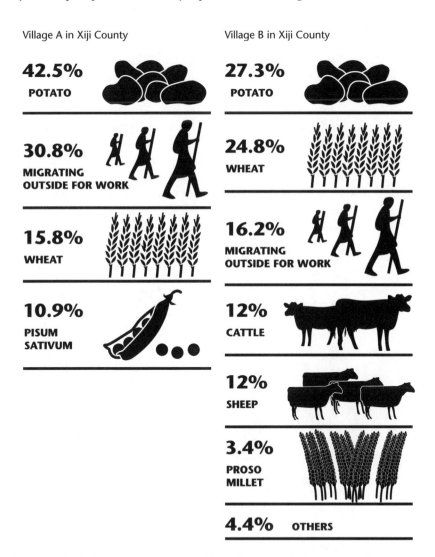

Village A in Xiji County

42.5%
POTATO

30.8%
MIGRATING
OUTSIDE FOR WORK

15.8%
WHEAT

10.9%
PISUM
SATIVUM

Village B in Xiji County

27.3%
POTATO

24.8%
WHEAT

16.2%
MIGRATING
OUTSIDE FOR WORK

12%
CATTLE

12%
SHEEP

3.4%
PROSO
MILLET

4.4%   OTHERS

FIGURE 8.2 Livelihood mixes in two villages in Xiji County, Ningxia (source: Pan *et al.*, 2010)

hazards in Ningxia. Weather hazards impacting agriculture currently affect the majority of Ningxia's population and contribute to endemic poverty (Li *et al.*, 2013). From 1992 to 2008, weather-related hazards negatively impacted between half and two-thirds of Ningxia's population engaged in agriculture in 12 out of the 16 years (Figure 8.3). Between 1960 and 2010, the province has experienced gradual warming, with average annual temperatures increasing by 2.9°C over the whole period and the most pronounced increases occurring in the last decade. Seasonally, the winter months (December through February) have shown the greatest warming. Annual precipitation trends are difficult to detect. However, modest decreases do appear in the summer and autumn seasons over the whole province, with pronounced spring and summer decreases from 1981 to 2010 in the central and southern regions (Li *et al.*, 2013). Droughts – particularly the severe drought that lasted from 2004 to 2006 – caused significant economic losses, reduced crop yields in the central region and led to drinking water shortages. Farmers in the northern region were less affected by the drought, as they were able to access water from the Yellow River.

Desertification and environmental degradation also contribute to crop loss in Ningxia, although the government is taking steps to improve the situation. Ningxia is one of the provinces participating in China's *Green Great Wall* reforestation programme, which has been working to combat desertification since 1978. This programme aims to slow soil erosion and prevent agricultural and

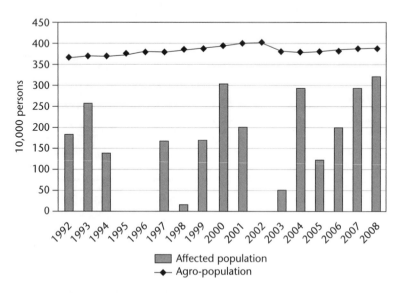

FIGURE 8.3 Total population (bars) impacted on a yearly basis by weather hazards out of the total population engaged in agriculture (line) in the recent past (source: Ningxia Provincial Bureau of Statistics, 2010b)

livestock mismanagement in Ningxia and neighbouring provinces (see Chapter 9) by restricting grazing and agriculture on marginal lands with compensation to the farmers and herders, as well as through the widespread planting of trees, shrubs and grasses (Mitchell *et al.*, 1998). The programme has proven successful in restoring ecosystems in some previously degraded locations, but the overall rate of desertification continues to accelerate due to land use intensification and increasing precipitation variability. The socio–cultural and economic costs and benefits of these policies, as typified through the ecological resettlement programmes promulgated in Ningxia, are mixed. These issues are explored in the following case study[2] and the rest of the chapter.

Case study: farmers' social vulnerability and climate risk in Ningxia province

Ningxia's people and their livelihoods are vulnerable to harm due to a variety of stressors, particularly those related to climate variability, ongoing ecological degradation and reduction of water resources. As a rural province, Ningxia lags behind many other provinces in terms of socio–economic development (ADB, 2004). Public health care and education remain limited in many areas. Many individuals suffer chronic health issues, including endemic echinococcosis (a parasitic infection), that reduce work productivity, increase childhood and elderly morbidity and mortality and make the ill more susceptible to contracting

---

Box 8.1 Participatory vulnerability and capacity assessments in Ningxia

Under the auspices of the Adapting to Climate Change in China I (ACCC I) programme, researchers from CASS and Ningxia research institutes conducted participatory vulnerability assessments in rural Ningxia communities. The purpose of the assessments was to understand the relationships and interactions between socio-economic, environmental and climate change processes, based on the 'sustainable livelihood approach' (Chambers and Conway, 1992). The teams conducted surveys, interviews and transect walks with more than 300 farmers from 15 villages across seven counties that span the agro-ecological zones of the province. Qualitative and quantitative data were obtained from meetings with local officials, focus group discussions with villagers, a survey questionnaire and visits to rural households. Vulnerability indicators were identified via literature review, expert evaluation and statistical analysis of the collected data. A VARC index was created at the county-level and visualised on a map, shown at Figure 8.6 (Zheng *et al.*, 2013).

other diseases (Yang *et al.*, 2008). Life expectancy is lower than the Chinese median (National Bureau of Statistics of China, 2013). In comparison with urbanised regions with relatively sound public health systems and health services, indices of health and life expectancy of the population are relatively low in rural areas – the Engle coefficient[3] in the urban areas was 36.2%, compared to 39.3% in rural areas in 2012.

These and other social, cultural and environmental factors are combining to make Ningxia's farmers more vulnerable to harm from current climate variability (e.g. droughts and temperature fluctuations) and change. Researchers from the Chinese Academy of Social Science (CASS) and Ningxia research institutes investigated the complex interplay of social factors with policies that typify China's adaptation challenge (see Chapter 2) that combine to shape farmers' climate risk and their vulnerability to a variety of stressors. These are described below.

Socio-economic disparities

In some remote mountainous areas, fertility rates remain relatively high, compared to the national average of one child per family (Ningxia Provincial Bureau of Statistics, 2011). Hui families tend to be larger than those of other ethnic groups.[4] To reduce population pressures in the poorer areas, a policy promoting 'fewer births, rapid prosperity and poverty alleviation' was instituted in Ningxia in 2003, with Guyuan City as the pilot area. This policy represents a departure from the original birth control policy of fines for unscheduled births, transitioning to one of encouraging fewer births through monetary incentives. For example, for a family with three children, a one-time sum of CNY5,000 (GBP505.05) will be given for no further births; and CNY8,000 (GBP808.08) will be awarded if the three children are all girls. Due to its positive results, this policy has been included in the *Twelfth Five Year Plan*.

Years of schooling and the quality of education in rural areas of Ningxia lag behind the urban areas. The *Eleventh Five Year Plan* sought to address the education gaps in Ningxia and succeeded in increasing the average length of schooling from six and a half years in 2005 to eight years in 2010, which is similar to the national average (Zhang, J. *et al.*, 2012). Literacy levels still remain low, particularly among women, although improvements are seen in younger cohorts. A survey of working-age people (ages 16–59) of rural households in central and southern Ningxia found that approximately 34% of the population are illiterate to semi-literate, with roughly 8.5% having an education beyond secondary (high school) levels (Zhang, J. *et al.*, 2012). In addition to cultural barriers, women and elderly interviewed as part of the social vulnerability assessment conducted by the research team reiterated that access to transportation networks and the quality of the school also determined whether or not children would attend. In remote villages, parents do not send their children to school because of the distance.

The research included interviews with women from poor rural areas to elicit gendered perspectives on vulnerability and capacity differentials. There are sharp disparities between the rural Hui and Han populations in terms of length of education, household assets and wealth, though both groups have household incomes significantly lower than the national average. Hui women tend to be less educated than Han women, as are Hui men compared with Han men, and thus have a more difficult time finding employment outside the farm. Many of the women interviewed were completely or nearly illiterate, indicating that they had not attended school at all or had only had a few years of primary school (Zheng *et al.*, 2012). Cultural expectations around the role of women among Hui and other rural groups limit educational attainment and financial self-sufficiency for women. For example, one young woman from Gansu Province, who married a man in a remote mountain village in Xiji County, reported being unaccustomed to the strict cultural standards upon her arrival to the area. She had liked going to the city for work prior to marriage, but village elders and her new in-laws forbade it.

Due to low levels of education, coupled with the traditional ideas of the older generation, many young women are confined at home throughout the year. Women in particular bear the brunt of educational and economic vulnerability, making them less able to access and understand early hazard warnings or other sources of information and to protect and plan for themselves and their families before, during and after various weather hazards. In families practising female confinement, economic migration by women is lost as a coping mechanism (refer to Zhang [1999] for a discussion on female migration and economic empowerment in China) to offset livelihood losses due to drought or ongoing environmental degradation. Women with lower social status have lower livelihood capacities that translate into lower quality of life for their children and less resiliency in the face of hazards. These factors, among others, translate into a mean income gap of 21% between the two ethnic groups (Gustafsson and Ding, 2012), and thus higher economic vulnerability for both rural and urban Hui.

Cultural practices create different sets of economic burdens and opportunities for both groups. Hui culture attaches great importance to weddings and funerals; expenditures on these are far greater than among rural Han households. Wedding and funeral costs can quickly plunge a Hui household into debt, reducing their economic adaptive capacity when faced with climate variability and change (Zheng *et al.*, 2012). These findings are consistent with vulnerability research elsewhere, which has found that certain cultural practices can translate into greater economic vulnerability for families under rapidly shifting social and ecological conditions (Parker and Kozel, 2007; Gray and Mueller, 2012; Bhattamishra and Barrett, 2010).

Social capital, cultural practices and traditional ecological knowledge

In spite of socio-economic shifts and environmental migration programmes (discussed later in this chapter), social capital and cultural ties within ethnic groups remain strong. The Hui have strong traditions of mutual assistance for historical and cultural reasons. Even after migrating to urban areas for work or being resettled, migrants tend to gather together into communities and form communication networks, like Doha village in Hongsipu District in northern Ningxia, which spontaneously formed without formal government planning. The strong sense of mutual cooperation boosts the social capital of Hui groups and allows them to provide assistance to one another during times of stress.

Cultural traditions and livelihoods in rural Ningxia are based on agriculture or animal husbandry. These are highly dependent on traditional knowledge, expertise and skills around agro-meteorological knowledge and technologies (e.g. construction of greenhouses, recognition of crop pests and methods of controlling them or ascertaining the possibility of weather shifts and rain). According to the investigation, farmers rely on two channels of knowledge transfers: traditional agricultural knowledge and experience, and use of public (government) information sources for meteorological, agriculture and livestock information. Farmer groups noted that public services provided by the government are of great use, and they hope to obtain more effective support, such as help with choosing crop varieties, as well as pest and disease control technology. Interestingly, farmer groups of different ages maintain quite different views on traditional knowledge and experience. Older farmers can judge whether it is more arid or comparatively rainy for a certain year by relying on their long-accumulated experience, and then decide farming time and crop varieties; they therefore rely less on conventional information sources such as television and mobile phones (many poor families do not have TV sets). However, traditional knowledge transfer between generations appears to be breaking down, with numerous young people interviewed expressing disinterest in learning from their elders or having the same levels of experience. A young farmer born in the 1980s, who alternates between farming and migrating to a city for work, said, 'I will go out sooner or later [leaving farming and earning his living in the city]; relying on farming cannot feed me, and what's more, I am not good at farming.'

Migration is also altering gender divisions of labour in rural families, and it will alter attitudes toward women in the long run. The more educated young men tend to migrate away from the countryside, leaving women, middle-aged men and the elderly as the dominant demographics. In Zhangjiawa village, a gendered division of labour is evident in various aspects of agricultural production (see Figure 8.4). Men are mainly responsible for planting and insecticide spraying, while women and men work together in planting, seed sowing, and

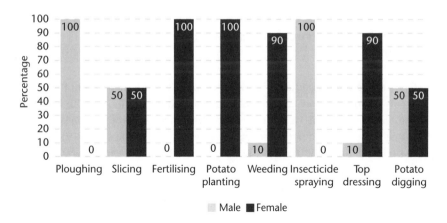

FIGURE 8.4 Division of labour in Zhangjiawa village, typical of gender divisions seen in other villages (source: Pan *et al.*, 2010)

harvesting. Women handle much of the day-to-day physical farm labour, such as weeding, fertilising and top-dressing. To compensate for the lack of agricultural livelihoods, males from many families migrate out to work after the planting season in early May and do not return until the harvest season in October. Unlike unmarried young people, who often go to Yinchuan or another province for long-term work, these male labourers with family members to support are mainly engaged in short-term work in towns nearby and adjacent villages, so as not to affect the farming activities of the family.

Access to infrastructure and communication networks

Access to infrastructure and services such as transportation and communication networks lags behind the rest of the country (FAO, 2012). In a 2010 survey of over 2,300 administrative villages in Ningxia, only 58% of the villages had access to running water (Ningxia Provincial Bureau of Statistics, 2011). Significant efforts have been made to improve transportation networks and vehicle ownership for commuting to access services and employment opportunities, with vehicle ownership having reached 98% in the surveyed village and in-home telephone connectivity amounting to 100%. Roads are key to villages in the hilly and mountainous southern and central regions of the province. Some very remote outlying villages have yet to realise access to running water, vehicle ownership and communications and transportation networks. Water cellars and rainwater cisterns remain the primary source for domestic supply in the mountains, with groundwater supplies being saline, although some families still resort to digging wells. Transportation and communication networks in these more remote areas are also tenuous and tend to be easily disrupted and damaged during extreme weather events. When these lifelines are disrupted, whole

---

Box 8.2 Infrastructure improvements in remote Ningxia

One very remote mountain village visited by the researchers did not have access to roads before 2008; the road only led to the foot of the town before and remained 12 km away from the village. According to villagers, women ready to give birth were carried down to the hospital by hand until the mid-1990s. Now, the sick and women in labour are transported via tractors that can navigate the new road. There is also now a primary school in the village. However, the teachers report that there are few students and that the students are gradually decreasing in number.

---

villages can be isolated from outside sources of information and are difficult to reach, limiting the timeliness of disaster relief delivery and aid and the ability to recover.

Information, particularly weather forecasts and access to early warning systems, is problematic in the more remote mountainous villages. Most of the villages receive weather forecasts via TV and radio broadcast, though the signal from the Ningxia TV network is often weak. As a result, many rely on meteorological information released by the neighbouring Gansu TV and Shaanxi TV networks, but these forecasts are more specific to those provinces and do not provide adequate warning of heavy rain events or other weather hazards that will impact various regions of Ningxia. Many farmers also wish for greater access to weather and seasonal forecasts for agricultural planning and production purposes. Many young and middle-aged farmers have mobile phones – there are roughly 185 mobile phones per 100 households, though coverage is lower in remote areas (Ningxia Provincial Bureau of Statistics, 2010a), and many do not subscribe to the *Meteorological Short Message Service*. Respondents to the survey indicated that the subscription cost of CNY2 (GBP0.20) per month is too expensive for them.

Institutional shifts: migration and resettlement programmes

Migration to urban or township areas on a seasonal to multi-year basis remains an important economic coping mechanism for many rural households within the province. Poverty levels are endemic in many of the more remote areas of the province. Due to continued ecological degradation, the central government has begun instituting policies limiting agricultural activities in sensitive areas, in addition to promoting reforestation and compensation to farmers for loss of land (Zhang *et al.*, 2008). Soil erosion and lack of water resources and drought, particularly in the mountainous and central regions of the province, are rendering some areas of land completely unsuitable for continued agriculture. As a result, the Ningxia provincial government instituted a relocation and ecological resettlement programme (Zhang, J. *et al.*, 2012). Since the programme's inception in 1983, over 785,800 people have been relocated in a planned manner. Other families have opted to migrate on their own. The original purpose of the resettlement programme was to improve the living and development conditions of people living on marginal lands and to reduce their poverty. Families and whole communities in the poor rural areas of southern Ningxia were relocated to newly reclaimed, irrigated areas in the north. During the first phase of the programme (1983 to 2000), the government focused primarily on resettlement through the integration of the *National 8–7 Poverty Reduction Plan* with the *Ninth Five Year Plan* (Merkle, 2003). The second phase (2001 to 2010) combined the aims of poverty reduction with national policies on reforestation by allowing marginal farmlands to return to forest.

The third phase of the programme, launched during the *Twelfth Five Year Plan*, will resettle around 350,000 people in the central and southern regions according to multiple objectives: the development of planned towns with access to better infrastructure and services; poverty reduction and slowing the need for economic migration by ensuring that planned communities are large enough to support industrial and service sectors, and providing the necessary labour force; and the incorporation of disaster risk reduction and climate change impacts into land use and city development plans. Of all of the objectives, reducing seasonal economic migration through improving local economic development and concentrating urban services in planned areas are currently the principal priorities (Meng, 2013). These measures recognise migration and urbanisation trends already occurring, as well as the ability to use these to promote ecological protection and restoration while building climate resilience (Zheng *et al.*, 2013).

A number of the villagers living in resettled communities surveyed by Zheng *et al.* (2013) as part of the research indicated that their living conditions have improved, as had their ability to plant different types of cash crops using irrigation to earn a better income. According to the villagers,

> [we] lived relying upon the weather and could only grow wheat, potatoes, millet and other grains; the crops brought in no money year round and only sustained life. Now, because of the irrigation channels, we can grow wolfberry and go outside for work, with our household income amounting to CNY10,000 (GBP1,010.10). In previous days, we dug wells for water; we now have running water in each household.

The villagers explained that their access to infrastructure was also greatly improved. Better roads were enabling easier access to school, and more reliable electricity and domestic and irrigation water improving their lives (see Figure 8.5). Overall, the programmes appear to have improved access to services,

FIGURE 8.5 An ecological resettlement village, with improved infrastructure in terms of a hand well for domestic water consumption and an irrigation system diverting water from the Yellow River Diversion Project (photo credit: Zheng Yan)

infrastructure and markets, yet the benefits of the programmes are unevenly distributed, and not all villages are relocated to areas with sufficient access to water (Sjögersten *et al.*, 2013).

There are problems with the resettlement programmes, however. While the government pays about two-thirds of the cost of resettlement, families are expected to cover the remaining third. The poverty of many families often prohibits them from participating in such schemes, as the costs of purchasing new living quarters and agricultural lands are often beyond their means. One resident from a village in Xiji County, which is included in the relocation planning for the *Twelfth Five Year* period, said,

> We can afford if we're asked to pay CNY5,000 (GBP505.05), but CNY10,000 (GBP1,010.10) will put us in trouble. If CNY30,000 (GBP3,030.30) is required for relocation, we're likely not to move. Nearly half of the villagers won't move because they don't have so much money.

During interviews, a local official from Yuanzhou District, who is responsible for the resettlement project at the village level said, 'For some poor families, even CNY1,000 (GBP101.01) is beyond their capacity. If they ask for a loan, they're not likely to pay back the interest and will be caught in a vicious cycle.'

Since the government only provides agricultural production loans after farmers jump through significant bureaucratic hoops, many families are forced to borrow private high-interest loans for the purpose of relocation. Migrants in some early resettlement areas in the central and northern parts of the province are still repaying their original loans. In a migrant village in Haiyuan County, a 50-year-old middle-aged farmer told the research team that it took eight years after relocation to finish paying back his loans. Lack of economic capacity hinders migrant groups' adaptation to new production and living environments and can further indebt the family. Furthermore, resettlement can negatively impact community and family fabric, while placing significant pressures on cultural traditions and identities (Duan and McDonald, 2004). While these resettlement programmes may lead to greater future economic security and better access to infrastructure and services for families, at the same time enabling reforestation and ecological restoration of marginal lands, the short-term costs and cultural pressures can be significant for families.

Financial capital

Disaster relief and social security programmes do exist in Ningxia, but their success in shifting livelihood strategies and reducing long-term poverty has been mixed. Recurrent weather hazards, deteriorating ecological conditions and local fiscal deficits mean that government poverty alleviation and disaster relief funds are insufficient. Some of the families interviewed expressed that while Xiji

County granted food aid and relief funds during times of drought, such as the severe drought of 1993–1995, the food rations covered the caloric needs of only one-half to two-thirds of family members per household. Remaining family members were asked to migrate in order for the families to survive the famine. Only 10% of farmer income sources are composed of government subsidies, relief, subsistence allowances and ecological transfer payments (Ningxia Provincial Bureau of Statistics, 2010a). Compared with urban residents, the social assurance programmes for Chinese farmers are relatively weak, and only since 2009 have farmers been included under the unified national policy support system. The policy provides a yearly pension for those over the age of 60 and includes farmers in a national health insurance programme where each participant pays a yearly medical insurance premium of CNY30 (GBP3.03) for comprehensive serious disease coverage and reimburses up to 80% of incurred medical expenses. The new rural old-age insurance is considered a safety net in farmers' old age. Elderly villagers surveyed in the central and southern areas are mostly satisfied with this new policy. However, in northern regions, such as Hongsipu District, a planned relocation city, many migrants complain that such subsidies make no difference because their current cost of living (post-relocation) is higher than it was when they lived in the mountains.

Aggregate vulnerability

An integrated vulnerability and capacity assessment of multiple villages in the three agro-ecological zones of Ningxia allowed researchers to combine the factors discussed previously into a county-level aggregate vulnerability index (Zhu *et al.*, 2013). The combination of low rates of education, gender disparity, access to infrastructure and social assistance programmes make Ningxia's farmers more vulnerable to harm during extreme events (e.g. heavy rain or hailstorms) and slow-onset events like droughts (see Chapter 5).

The findings reveal that vulnerability has high spatial variation, reflecting linkages between ecological conditions and socio-economic indicators. Vulnerability progressively increases from the northern counties to the central and southern, with the highest vulnerability occurring in Xiji, Haiyuan, Yuanzhou and Tongxin counties (Figure 8.6). The lag in socio-economic development, differentiated access to infrastructure and services, and widespread ecological degradation in areas with fragile soils lead to higher vulnerability in the southern and central regions. The northern regions of the province have more diversified livelihood sources and less soil erosion, contributing to lower overall vulnerability. Cultural preferences for larger families among the ethnic minorities and an excess of labour as more land becomes agriculturally unproductive due to degradation are also contributing to poverty traps in the south-central regions.

As the climate continues to change, and the social vulnerability of Ningxia's farmers evolves, so too will their climate risk. The research team combined the

■■ 5 (high vulnerability)   ▩ 4   ▨ 3   ▢ 2   ☐ 1(low)

FIGURE 8.6 Ningxia county-level vulnerability map (source: Zheng *et al.*, 2013)

findings of the social vulnerability assessment with climate projections to generate scenarios of future climate risk on a provincial level.

Future climate risks

The research team, using multiple climate models (PRECIS-HadCM, RegCM-HadCM, PRECIS-ECHAM4, RegCM-ECHAM4) each running the three emission scenarios (A2 – high, B1 – low and A1B – medium), found that there is likely to be a steady rise in maximum and minimum annual average temperature and a potential slight decrease in overall mean annual precipitation in Ningxia over the next 30 years (Figure 8.7). Projections indicate the potential for annual

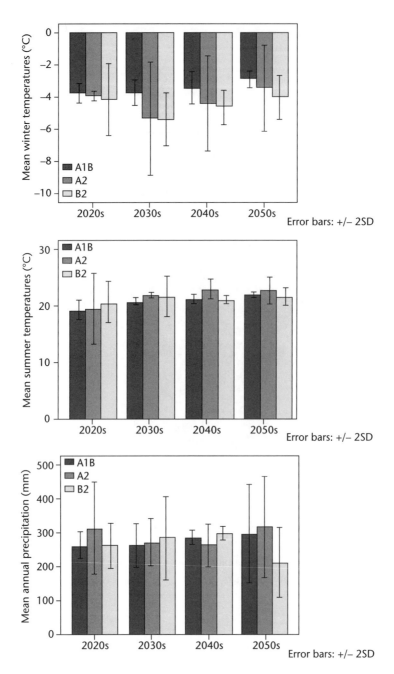

FIGURE 8.7 Seasonal temperature and annual precipitation projections for three different emission scenarios (A1B, A2 and B2). Historical area-average winter
temperatures were −8.5°C, with historical summer temperatures averaging from 20.5°C across the province (source: Zhang, X.Y. *et al.*, 2012)

maximum temperatures to increase between 0.29 to 0.62°C per decade to 2050, and for minimum annual temperatures to increase by 0.37 to 0.69°C per decade over the same period.

The projections are less certain for precipitation with one emission scenario indicating potential increases (A1B) by the 2050s and others demonstrating possible decreases (A2 and B2). Precipitation shifts are the most difficult for climate models to capture, particularly in boundary regions such as Ningxia, which is on the northernmost edge of the East Asia Monsoon System and experiences considerable spatial and temporal variability. There was overall model agreement, however, that most of the precipitation decreases are likely to occur in the summer and autumn seasons, with potential slight increases in wintertime precipitation. The projected precipitation shifts until 2050 are consistent with the recently observed trends. In spite of model disagreement around precipitation, projections indicate that climate change is likely to lead to greater precipitation variability, with shifts in the frequency and intensity of drought and heavy rain events.

The scenarios of future temperature and precipitation change, when combined with the social vulnerability assessment, led to regional differences in climate change risk for sub-regions of Ningxia. Three weather hazards (temperature increases, annual precipitation declines and droughts) which currently cause significant risk for Ningxia's farmers, and one impact influenced by climate change (reductions in Yellow River flows), were identified as contributing to the greatest potential future climate risks for the province.

Decreases in Yellow River flows are not solely attributable to climate change-induced shifts in temperature, precipitation and evapotranspiration; they are also due to burgeoning demand, pollution and ecosystem degradation, as discussed in Chapter 4. As with current vulnerability, the scenarios of future climate risk have high spatial variability, as seen in Figure 8.8. Decreases in Yellow River flows are not applicable to the southern region of the province, as the river does not currently reach the counties in that region and they do not

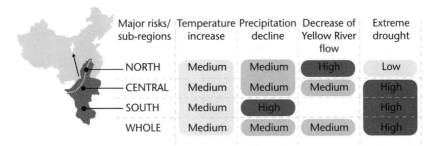

FIGURE 8.8 Spatially disaggregated climate change risk by region for particular hazards and climate change related impacts in Ningxia (source: Zhang, X.Y. *et al.*, 2012)

withdraw any water from it. Future drought risk in the northern region is low, as long as decreases in Yellow River flows are not occurring concurrently. As long as this region can continue to rely upon the Yellow River for irrigation and industrial and urban needs, future drought risk is likely to remain lower for the north when compared with the other two regions. Risk to water resources, and to the irrigated croplands of the north, are high if drought coincides with decreased Yellow River flows.

The future climate risks these four hazards are likely to cause also vary by sector. A few of the impacts may be beneficial to some, such as warmer annual temperatures and warmer winter temperatures potentially lengthening the growing season and improving the productivity of certain crops like winter wheat (Table 8.1). Overall, the negative impacts are likely to outweigh beneficial impacts for crop yields in parts of the province. The assumptions of future climate risk are predicated upon scenarios of future vulnerability and capacity unchanged from the present; improvements in socio-economic and environmental conditions will lead to different risk profiles, while worsening conditions would lead to greater risks for Ningxia's farmers. Farmers in southern and some central counties face the highest risks associated with precipitation declines and extreme drought due to their current poor access to irrigation water from the Yellow River, lower socio-economic status and the environmental degradation in these areas. Farmers in the northern counties face fewer risks associated with extreme drought and precipitation declines as long as they can continue to rely upon irrigation flows from the Yellow River. Declines in its flows and competition with urban areas over water supplies would seriously reduce this current adaptive capacity measure and lead to high climate risks for this region.

Climate change impacts on Ningxia farmers' livelihoods and well-being

The case study highlighted that the various regions of Ningxia face different social vulnerabilities due to socio-economic disparities, gender and cultural division, and other factors. The types of challenges Ningxia faces typify some aspects of China's larger adaptation challenge within a complex development environment, as discussed in Chapter 2.

Increasing aridity will have the greatest impact on agriculturally based livelihoods and the ecosystems upon which they depend, particularly in the rain-fed cropping regions of central and southern Ningxia. These regions, which already experience large socio-economic disparities, are likely to experience decreased incomes from farming and raising livestock, and larger uncertainty in income mixes. Ningxia's crops are already vulnerable to fluctuations in temperature and precipitation (Simelton *et al.*, 2009; see also Chapter 5). Crop failure and output instability, particularly of maize and potatoes, may contribute to localised food security issues and reduce Ningxia's ability to be entirely food self-sufficient

TABLE 8.1 Potential future climate risks for key sectors in Ningxia

Sectors	Major risks
Agriculture	• Temperature increases: longer growing period conducive to increased agricultural productivity, particularly of winter wheat. Agricultural increases may be offset by increased insect pest occurrence. • Decreased annual precipitation and increased variability: greater uncertainty in livestock production and reduced crop yields and grassland productivity, especially in rain-fed areas. • Increased intensity and frequency of extreme events: livelihood uncertainty and poverty increase, as well as shifting disease and pest burdens among animals and plants. • Yellow River flow shifts: less water for irrigation and reduction in irrigated crop area.
Water resources	• Temperature increases: reduced water quality and greater evapotranspiration, potentially leading to higher compensating demand by agriculture and industry. • Decreased annual precipitation and increased variability: increased pressure on water resources and decreased water for ecosystem needs; less recharge of groundwater tables. • Increased intensity and frequency of extreme events: greater need for both flood prevention and water storage as drought buffering, particularly in small river basins in the south of Ningxia. • Yellow River flow shifts: water shortages due to increased demand and lower supplies; less water to be allocated to central Ningxia.
Desertification	• Temperature increases: increased loss of vegetation, soil erosion and salination. • Decreased annual precipitation and increased variability: ecological restoration and reforestation programmes threatened, along with wider ecosystem health and management implications. • Increased intensity and frequency of extreme events: increased soil erosion during both drought and flood, exacerbating water quality and quantity issues. • Yellow River flow shifts: less water and greater desertification of central Ningxia over the mid- to long term.
Socio-economic development	• Drinking water quality and quantity issues in the central and southern regions; higher water costs. • Less water for agricultural and livestock production and related industries, leading to greater income insecurity and price fluctuations. • Social stability issues as more households migrate under the relocation schemes or on a voluntary basis, placing greater pressures on labour markets and urban services. • Natural resource pressures in migrant-receiving areas (e.g. Hongsipu), placing greater demands on local water resources and ecosystem services, concentrations of pollution streams and environmental degradation. • Extreme climate events: greater incidence of morbidity and mortality and asset losses without adequate disaster risk reduction and resilience planning processes.

Source: Zhang, X.Y. *et al.*, 2012.

(not importing food) in some future years. During times of recent drought, Li *et al.* (2013) found that households in the central and mountain regions had to purchase drinking water, the costs of which often amounted to 30% or more of the annual household income. Drinking water shortages, desertification and grassland degradation rates may be exacerbated by the combination of warmer temperatures, drought and pressures exerted by increasingly desperate farmers. Warming temperatures are already contributing to higher wildfire risks and species shifts in the mountainous regions. These changes are likely to continue.

Farmers may have to spend more of their income on purchasing water and, in irrigated areas, power for pumping irrigation supplies during drought years. Policy makers have introduced water tariffs on Yellow River diversions as part of national water management reforms, the results of which have been mixed for actually reducing demand (Wang *et al.*, 2005). It is likely that water management reforms will lead to further increases in water tariffs as part of a package of incentives to increase agricultural water-use efficiency. These measures can place additional economic burdens on families, especially those living in the irrigated northern regions that have historically been sheltered from the worst economic impacts of droughts. More families may turn to migration to alleviate agricultural losses (Zhou *et al.*, 2012), placing further stress on urban job markets and leading to further urbanisation problems and social resource conflicts. Increased rates of migration may also create water resource conflicts between urban areas and farmers (Desakota Study Team, 2008). Climate change is likely to exacerbate many of the current socio-economic disparities and environmental degradation issues that contribute to farmers' current vulnerability and capacity contexts. These contexts are changing rapidly, lending some difficulty to determining the full nature, severity and type of future risk faced by Ningxia's population. Future climate risks will be determined by the interaction of rapidly evolving socio-cultural, economic, institutional and policy shifts occurring within Ningxia, as well as on national and international levels.

Based on observations of the factors currently contributing to the vulnerability and capacity of farmers, as well as economic and land use development trends that are not yet systematically figuring into policy, the general objectives given in Table 8.2 can build overall resilience to climate change and other types of shocks facing Ningxia's population. More specific recommendations for planned adaptation strategies, embedded within a wider and more comprehensive adaptation planning process mainstreamed into various policies, will have to be developed through a series of dialogues with multiple stakeholders, from farmers to national-level policy makers.

Opportunities and challenges in adaptation planning

Ningxia has not yet fully developed a climate change adaptation plan but it is starting to mainstream climate change concerns into its socio-economic five-year

TABLE 8.2 General recommendations for improving Ningxia farmers' climate resilience based on findings of the vulnerability assessments in 2010

Adaptation areas	Objectives
Water security	• Seek better balance between demand and supply and promote greater use efficiency, particularly in agriculture. • Reduce income disparity and uncertainty by improving reliability and safety of supplies. • Explore different Yellow River allocation schemes based upon socio-economic development needs and demographic inequalities. • Improve both flood control and drought relief measures in the central and southern regions of Ningxia.
Food security	• Provide assistance and incentives for improving agricultural technologies and promoting more weather hazard resilient crops. • Improve access to hazard early warning and seasonal forecast information for farmers. • Employ the latest scientific knowledge on soil conservation, chemical application, pest management and crop production area.
Ecosystem restoration	• Support reforestation and restoration of marginal and degraded lands, with the secondary objective of reducing desertification area. • Increase forest and grassland coverage, and promoting increased biodiversity. • Implement revegetation efforts to improve soil quality and water retention. • Put greater environmental protections in place and enforce air, water and soil pollution standards for agriculture, industry, mining and urban areas. • Improve waste and wastewater management in urban and peri-urban areas.
Disaster risk reduction	• Strengthen early warning mechanisms, including public awareness campaigns and forecasting ability and coverage. • Improve the emergency rescue capabilities of first responders. • Improve disaster relief and social and agricultural subsidies and insurance schemes to lessen hazard risk. • Incorporate a long-term, multi-hazard perspective into disaster recovery projects in order to build resilience.
Reducing poverty	• Support livelihood diversification and access to services and infrastructure in the central and southern regions to reduce poverty and overall vulnerability. • Continue to support ecological restoration programmes to slow the deterioration of local ecosystems and ecosystem services. • Continue to monitor and adjust ecological resettlement programmes based on evaluations of socio-economic, cultural and environmental conditions, as well as projections of future climate risk. • Conduct assessments of the potential impacts of migration, urbanisation, industry and mining upon overall climate risk and resilience, and for particular regions and groups within Ningxia.

development plans. The province is beginning to make some strides in climate change mitigation and adaptation related to agriculture, through establishing a climate adaptation working group led and coordinated by the Ningxia Development and Reform Commission (in 2009) and setting mitigation and adaptation goals through the *Ningxia Climate Change Programme* instituted in 2009. The programme highlighted the objectives of improving agricultural infrastructure; adjusting cropping systems and varietal selection to reduce disaster risks; optimising water allocation through engineering, biological and agronomic practices to increase water utilisation rates and efficiency; strengthening management of natural forest and nature reserves; desertification and sandstorm control; and ecological migration.

Ningxia's *Twelfth Five Year Plan* highlights the following priorities for climate change adaptation: strengthen capacity building for adaptation; integrated assessments of climate change impacts on socio-economic development; optimise water resource allocation; shift crop varieties and planting timing for more drought and heat tolerant crops, while promoting soil and water conservation in agriculture; continue to implement *Grain for Green*, a grazing prohibition and desertification control programme; and, based on water resources, implement ecological migration. The plan also focuses on agricultural disaster risk reduction by establishing a system for the prevention, reduction and management of disasters to address extreme climate events and increase agricultural resilience. It will also set up agricultural pest and animal disease prevention systems and use cloud seeding to increase rainfall. Other measures include establishing plans for disaster preparedness and materials reserves for disaster relief, including flood, forest- and grassland-fire prevention materials reserves.

Policies addressing migration

Human migration is a complex, multi-causal phenomenon. Migration is often a proactive risk diversification strategy for households facing environmental stressors amidst a range of other risks (Berkes *et al.*, 2003; Hussein and Nelson, 1998). While environmental change is just one of many interrelated factors that influence an individual's decision to relocate (Black *et al.*, 2008), it is clear from the literature that environmental factors can have a multiplier effect on other migration drivers such as poverty, limited state support to communities, lack of economic opportunities, effectiveness of decision-making processes and the extent of social cohesion within and surrounding vulnerable groups (Warner *et al.*, 2009). Climate change is not a significant driver of global human migration flows, but may play an increasingly important role in the future.

China's 2013 *National Adaptation Strategy* (NAS) frames ecological migration as a priority with set targets and designates Ningxia as a pilot area for what China terms 'ecological migration'. Ecological migration programmes will be used to reduce population pressure on sensitive and degraded ecosystems and to introduce new, adaptive livelihood approaches and practices in areas that are ecologically vulnerable to climate change. China frames large-scale ecological migration as both an economic development and an adaptation measure, as evidenced by its inclusion in the NAS. Its aim for ecological migration is to link poverty alleviation to ecological protection.

Ningxia has a history of migration programmes, going back to the 1980s when the primary focus of relocation was on economic development. Although the concept of ecological migration did not enter policy discourses at that time, economic migration policies effectively helped to alleviate population pressures on degraded and vulnerable ecological areas. Populations relocated under the early programmes had better access to ecosystem services and natural resources than in depleted locations, and were able to move faster out of poverty than their counterparts who were left behind. During the *Twelfth Five Year* period, 350,000 people will be relocated; of these 259,500 people from 58,700 households are considered ecological migrants, while 86,500 from 20,100 households are considered labour migrants.

Research on the current implementation of ecological migration has identified several issues for further study (Nadin, 2013). For example, some resettlement planning efforts lacked foresight and integrated implementation; current migration areas in Ningxia were established a while ago for the purposes of medium- and long-term migration development and, as a consequence, lack flexibility and did not account for climate change. In addition, the planning objectives of some areas have little scientific basis or reasoning and are not consistent. However, researchers have found that ecological migration planning in Ningxia does explicitly recognise multi-causality and complex needs driving environmental migration, and it gives consideration to organisational leadership, relocation methods, settlement patterns, land adjustment, financial integration, project construction, industrial cultivation and social development.

Current migration planning efforts are working to incorporate 'scientific decision-making', which embodies setting clear objectives and tasks such as site selection, migrant housing, livelihood provision through industrial development, farmland irrigation and water conservancy, infrastructure construction, and social factors such as public welfare provision. The provincial government is drawing on past experience and lessons learned for current and future programmes: identifying which factors determined whether past relocations were successful or unsuccessful; designing land tenure and water rights for long-term poverty alleviation; establishing financing arrangements between central and local governments, and with the migrants themselves. Migration sites are now being selected to ensure the long-term viability of the area and maximise potential for effective adaptation; further monitoring studies are needed to assess the successes and weaknesses of current efforts.

Summary

Ningxia faces a number of challenges to developing adaptation planning processes and building resilience to climate change. Gaps in socio-economic development between the northern and the central and southern regions of the province continue to widen, increasing development and poverty alleviation pressures. Industrialisation and urbanisation offer different economic opportunities to Ningxia's farming populations but are sometimes in conflict with efforts to improve ecosystem health and services. Coal mining and shale gas production are expanding in Ningxia and, while creating jobs, are also exacerbating air and water pollution and soil erosion, and are leading to social conflicts over resources and land rights. Though a decision-making coordination agency for climate change adaptation has been established, policy-maker priorities continue to be centred around mitigation (emission reduction) and low-carbon development. Furthermore, understanding of the linkages between poverty, migration and climate variability and change remains low. Due to the lack of specialised adaptation funding mechanisms, existing policies targeting areas such as ecological resettlement rely upon national and provincial-level poverty alleviation and infrastructure construction funds. As discussed previously, families that participate in the ecological resettlement programmes are expected to pay a portion of the resettlement costs but can often ill-afford them and incur large debts. The *Ningxia Climate Change Programme* fails to consider the synergies between these and how the development goals around low-carbon development, energy conservation, emission reduction and urbanisation can either enhance or exacerbate longer-term resilience.

The majority of projects and programmes in Ningxia are designed with poverty alleviation or ecological protection in mind, but they often fail to account for both ongoing processes (migration, urbanisation, and construction and investment projects in the southern and central areas) and long-term change processes, such as climate change or the planned water diversion from the Yangtze River to northern China, and the implications these will have for the province. While farmers have been observing shifts in the climates of each of Ningxia's three agro-ecosystems, public awareness of climate change remains low.

Notes

1 Agricultural diversions in Ningxia must compete with Beijing, which is diverting Yangtze River water through the South–North Diversion project.
2 The Chinese Academy of Social Sciences (CASS) and researchers from institutes within Ningxia Province conducted assessments of farmers' social vulnerability for the Adapting to Climate Change in China I (ACCC I) programme.
3 Engel's coefficient is a standard of living statistic, measured as the proportion of income spent on food in relation to total income. The higher the percentage, the more income that must be spent on food, leaving less income for other necessary expenditures and leading to a lower standard of living.

4 Ningxia's status as an autonomous region grants ethnic minorities, such as the Hui, certain privileges such as exemption from the one-child policy. However, birth rates among all ethnic groups, including the Han, remain high in the more remote, rural locations, potentially due to limited access to health and family planning services as well as traditions.

References

ADB (Asian Development Bank) (2004) *Poverty Profile of the People's Republic of China.* Asian Development Bank: Manila, Philippines.

Berkes, F., Colding, J. and Folke, C. (2003) *Navigating Social-Ecological Systems: Building Resilience for Complexity and Change.* Cambridge University Press: Cambridge, United Kingdom.

Bhattamishra, R. and Barrett, C.B. (2010) Community-based risk management arrangements: A review. *World Development.* 38 (7). pp. 923–932.

Black, R., Kniveton, D., Skeldon, R., Coppard, D., Murata, A. and Scmidt-Verkerk, K. (2008) *Demographics and Climate Change: Future Trends and their Policy Implications for Migration.* Development Research Centre on Migration, Globalisation and Poverty: Brighton, United Kingdom (Working Paper, No. T27).

Chambers, R. and Conway, G. (1992) *Sustainable Rural Livelihoods: Practical Concepts for the 21st Century.* Institute of Development Studies: Brighton, United Kingdom (IDS Discussion Paper 296).

Desakota Study Team (2008) *Re-imagining the Rural–Urban Continuum: Understanding the Role Ecosystem Services Play in the Livelihoods of the Poor in Desakota Regions Undergoing Rapid Change.* Institute for Social and Environmental Transition – Nepal: Kathmandu, Nepal.

Duan, Y. and McDonald, B. (2004) *Involuntary Resettlement as an Opportunity for Development: The Application of 'Resettlement with Development' in the People's Republic of China.* School of International Development, Melbourne University: Melbourne, Australia (Working Paper No. 14).

FAO (Food and Agriculture Organization of the United Nations) (2012) *Information Services in Rural China: An Updated Case Study.* FAO Regional Office for Asia and the Pacific: Bangkok, Thailand.

Gray, C. and Mueller, V. (2012) Drought and population mobility in rural Ethiopia. *World Development.* 40 (1). pp. 134–145.

Gustafsson, B. and Ding, S. (2012) *Assessing Ethnic Disparities in Income and Poverty in China: The Case of Han and Hui in Ningxia.* Paper presented at the 4th World Conference on Remedies to Racial and Ethnic Economic Inequality, Minnesota, USA.

Hussein, K. and Nelson, J. (1998) *Livelihood Diversification.* Institute of Development Studies: Brighton, United Kingdom (IDS Working Paper).

Li, J., Zheng, G., Liu, H., Wang, L., Tang, Z., Shi, H., Guo, W. and Wang, H. (2008) *Situation Analysis of Ningxia Province.* China Climate Change Partnership Framework – Enhanced strategies for climate-proofed and environmentally sound agricultural production in the Yellow River Basin (C-PESAP).

Li, Y., Conway, D., Wu, Y., Gao, Q., Rothausen, S., Wei, X., Ju, H. and Erda, L. (2013) Rural livelihoods and climate variability in Ningxia, northwest China. *Climatic Change.* 119. pp. 891–904.

Li, Y., Wu, Y., Erda, L., Gao, Q., Shifeng, Ju, H., Conway, D., Zhang, J., Wang, T., Jia, Y., Preston, F. and Avis, K. (2008) *Impacts of Climate Change on Chinese Agriculture*

– *Phase II. Climate and Livelihoods in Rural Ningxia: Final Report.* ED02264 Issue 2. AEA Group: United Kingdom.

Lohmar, B., Wang, J., Rozelle, S., Huang, J. and Dawe, D. (2003) *China's Agricultural Water Policy Reforms: Increasing Investment, Resolving Conflicts, and Revising Incentives.* US Department of Agriculture: Washington, DC, USA (Agriculture Information Bulletin No. 782).

Meng, H. (2013) Coordination between spontaneous migration and planned migration: Case of Ningxia labor migrants. *Thinking.* 5. pp. 95–99.

Merkle, R. (2003) Ningxia's third road to rural development: Resettlement schemes as a last means to poverty reduction? *Journal of Peasant Studies.* 30. pp. 160–191.

Mitchell, D.J., Fullen, M.A., Trueman, I.C. and Fearnehough, W. (1998) Sustainability of reclaimed desertified land in Ningxia, China. *Journal of Arid Environments.* 39. pp. 239–251.

Nadin, R. (2013) Final report of Adapting to Climate Change in China, Phase I (unpublished). Adapting to Climate Change in China Programme (ACCC I).

National Bureau of Statistics of China (2013) *China Statistical Year Book 2013.* [Online] Available from: www.stats.gov.cn/tjsj/ndsj/2013/indexeh.htm. [Accessed: 25 November 2014.]

Ningxia Provincial Bureau of Statistics (2010a) *Ningxia Social Survey Data 2010.* China Statistics Press: Beijing, People's Republic of China.

Ningxia Provincial Bureau of Statistics (2010b) *Ningxia Statistical Yearbook 2010.* China Statistics Press: Beijing, People's Republic of China.

Ningxia Provincial Bureau of Statistics (2011) *Ningxia Statistical Yearbook 2011.* China Statistics Press: Beijing, People's Republic of China.

Pan, J. Shi, S., Zheng, Y., Meng, H., Wang, J. *et al.* (2010) Social vulnerability survey results for Ningxia. IUE-CASS and NX Economic Research Development Centre. Unpublished raw data.

Parker, B. and Kozel, V. (2007) Understanding poverty and vulnerability in India's Uttar Pradesh and Bihar: A Q-squared approach. *World Development.* 35 (2). pp. 296–311.

Qiu, X., Liu, Z., Wang, Z., Tang, Z. and Shi, H. (2012) Climate change impacts on Ninxgia desertification and adaptation measures. In: Ma, Z.Y. (ed.), *A Study of Strategic Solutions to Global Climate Change in Ningxia.* Ningxia Sunshine Press: Ninxgia, People's Republic of China.

Simelton, E., Fraser, E.D.G., Termansen, M., Forster, P.M. and Dougill, A.J. (2009) Typologies of crop-drought vulnerability: An empirical analysis of the socio-economic factors that influence the sensitivity and resilience to drought of three major food crops in China (1961–2001). *Environmental Science and Policy.* 12. pp. 438–452.

Sjögersten, S., Atkin, C., Clarke, M.L., Mooney, S.J., Wu, B. and West, H.M. (2013) Responses to climate change and farming policies by rural communities in northern China: A report on field observation and farmers' perception in dryland north Shaanxi and Ningxia. *Land Use Policy.* 32. pp. 125–133.

Wang, J., Xu, Z., Huang, J. and Rozelle, S. (2005) Incentives in water management reform: Assessing the effect on water use, production, and poverty in the Yellow River Basin. *Environment and Development Economics.* 10. pp. 769–799.

Warner, K., Ehrhart, C., de Sherbinin, A., Adamo, S.B. and Onn, T.C. (2009) *In Search of Shelter: Mapping the Effects of Climate Change on Human Migration and Displacement.* A policy paper prepared for the 2009 Climate Negotiations. United Nations University, CARE and CIESIN-Columbia University: Bonn, Germany.

Xu, X., Huang, G., Sun, C., Pereira, L.S., Ramos, T.B., Huang, Q. and Hao, Y. (2013) Assessing the effects of water table depth on water use, soil salinity and wheat yield: Searching for a target depth for irrigated areas in the upper Yellow River basin. *Agricultural Water Management*. 125. pp. 46–60.

Yang, Y.R., Craig, P.S., Sun, T., Vuitton, D.A., Giradoux, P., Jones, M.K., Williams, G.M. and McManus, D.P. (2008) Echinococcosis in Ningxia Hui Autonomous Region in northwest China. *Transactions of the Royal Society of Tropical Medicine and Hygiene*. 102. pp. 319–328.

Zhang, J., Huang, X., Tan, Y., Wang, T., Ren, T., Li, S., Ji, H., Liu, C., Yang, J., Ma, N., Yang, B., Cheng, Z. and Zhang, L. (2012) Adapting to climate change: Ecological migration in Ningxia. In Ma, Z.Y. (ed.), *A Study of Strategic Solutions to Global Climate Change in Ningxia*. Ningxia Sunshine Press: Ningxia, People's Republic of China.

Zhang, L., Tu, Q. and Mol, P.J. (2008) Paying for Environmental Services: The sloping land conversion program in Ningxia Autonomous Region of China. *China and World Economy*. 16. pp. 66–82.

Zhang, X.Y., Guo, D. B, Li, H. Y, Zhang, W. P, Yuan, H. Y, Wang, J., Duan, X. F, Zhang, X. Y, Liu, J., Zhang, L., Wei, J. G, Ma, G. F, Han, Y. J, Cao, N. and Ma, N. (2012) Climate change impacts on agriculture and adaptive measures in Ningxia. In: Ma, Z.Y. (ed.), *A Study of Strategic Solutions to Global Climate Change in Ningxia*. Ningxia Sunshine Press: Ningxia, People's Republic of China.

Zheng, Y., Meng, H. and Pan, J. (2012) *Ningxia Field Research Debriefing Report*. Chinese Academy of Social Sciences: Beijing, People's Republic of China.

Zheng, Y., Pan, J. and Zhang, X. (2013) Relocation as a policy response to climate change vulnerability: The arid region of northern China. In: *ISSC and UNESCO, World Social Science Report 2013, Changing Global Environments*. OECD Publishing and UNESCO Publishing: Paris, France.

Zhou, H., Zhang, W., Sun, Y. and Yuan, Y. (2012) Policy options to support climate-induced migration: Insights from disaster relief in China. *Mitigation and Adaptation Strategies for Global Change*. 19 (4). pp. 375–389.

Zhu, F., Fan, J. and Ma, Z. (2013) *ACCC I Final Report: Ningxia*. Center for Economic Research, Ningxia Hui Autonomous Region Development and Reform Commission.

9

CLIMATE CHANGE AND INNER MONGOLIA

*Hang Shuanzhu, Shan Ping, Bao Lu, Ao Renqi,
Wang Jianwu, Zheng Yan, Wei Yurong, Du Fenglian,
Su Hao, Wang Mingjiu, Zhu Zhongyuan, Zhou Liguang,
Sarah Opitz-Stapleton, Rebecca Nadin and
Samantha Kierath*

On the pastures around Xilinhot, grass is life. It is the foundation for long-standing communities of herders who eke out their livings in the punishing conditions of the plains of Inner Mongolia. Extreme winters are the norm here, but now pastoralists must contend with longer periods of drought. Zhamu-surong has seen that change for himself. He was born and raised on the grass-lands and lived through the decade-long absence of plentiful rains. Less rain means less grass, and thus little fodder for his livestock. 'We have a serious fodder shortage. Compared with snowstorms, droughts are a bigger threat for us, as our hands are really tied during droughts,' he said. 'When there is little grass we only keep a small number of livestock over the winter and slaughter the rest for sale. It very much depends on the weather.'

China is a vast country composed of diverse cultures. Its peoples' livelihoods and traditions shape and have been shaped by a variety of landscapes and eco-systems. The north of China is particularly arid, comprised primarily of grassland steppes. Inner Mongolia Autonomous Region, China's third-largest province, spans much of northern China and lies on the border with Mongolia and Russia. The pastoral areas of Inner Mongolia are mostly located in the Greater Khingan Range and the Inner Mongolia Plateau in the west and are made up of highlands, grassland and sand lands. The western half of Inner Mongolia over-laps the vast Gobi Desert, and a crook of the Yellow River crosses through the south-west. Even though the Han population is now dominant (79%), the customs and traditions of the ethnic Mongol population (17.1%) and those of groups such as the Hui, Duar and Orogen peoples have shaped the landscape for millennia (Inner Mongolian Statistical Bureau, 2013). Many of the population traditionally engaged in nomadic pastoral lifestyles that emphasised simple living and an intimate awareness of the climate and ecology of the harsh grassland steppe. Ethnic Mongol communities can still be found practising their traditional nomadic way of life, following herds of goats, sheep or cattle across the open steppe (Hang *et al.*, 2012).

Economic, social, environmental and climate change processes are dramatically altering the lifestyles, livelihoods and traditions of the peoples of Inner Mongolia. The livestock industry of Inner Mongolia is China's largest, producing meat, dairy, cashmere and other animal products for domestic and international markets. However, much of the region's recent economic boom – Inner Mongolia has seen an average annual GDP growth of 18.7% from 2000 to 2009 – has been driven by energy extraction and industry (He, 2011). The expansion of industries has increased economic development and led to improvements in infrastructure and services. At the same time, these mining practices, conducted with little environmental regulation and minimal oversight, have contributed to the widespread destruction of fragile grassland ecosystems, increased demand on the area's meagre water resources, and exacerbated pollution and the gradual loss of nomadic lifestyles.

Addressing the challenges facing the peoples of Inner Mongolia around resource and economic development, and their implications for economic, ecological and climate well-being, is critical. The grassland ecosystems and the herding communities that rely upon them are very sensitive to climate and environmental change (Dong *et al.*, 2011; Yin *et al.*, 2011; Zhang, 2011; Wang and Zhang, 2012). Climate and socio-economic change have imposed risks on traditional pastoral livelihood systems. Land degradation and drought, wildfires, and increasing climate variability have contributed to productivity decreases in grassland production and livestock, as well as biodiversity loss and increasing desertification (FAO, 2009). The socio-economic, environmental and climate consequences of mining operations are juxtaposed against the desires for grassland protection.

Inner Mongolia contains nearly one-quarter of the world's coal reserves, as well as substantial deposits of rare earth metals critical in the manufacturing of the world's electronics such as cell phones and computers (Dai *et al.*, 2008; Dai *et al.*, 2006; Kexi, 2005). The coal reserves of Inner Mongolia help to support economic development throughout China and provide electricity to many urban and industrial centres. At the same time, however, the exploitation of such resources is contributing to rapid grassland degradation, mining pollution and stress on water resources within Inner Mongolia. Within China, the use of coal in power generation is contributing to severe air and water pollution and negative health impacts (Chan and Yao, 2008; Stanway and Birsel, 2014). Coal emissions contribute to the Asian brown cloud which, in addition to altering the Asian monsoon system and climate systems across the Pacific, is exacerbating global climate change (Wang *et al.*, 2014; Lau *et al.*, 2005). In short, the socio-economic and environmental change processes that are occurring within Inner Mongolia have much larger geographic repercussions; meanwhile, the local populations and grassland ecosystems have to deal with the localised impacts.

Despite the challenges pastoralists face due to the intimate connection between their livelihoods, culture and the elements, they are taking action to adapt. Zhamusurong's household has joined forces with others in the area to form a cooperative. They pooled some of their land and resources to build protective infrastructure and plant fodder. 'We are building more infrastructure for livestock and creating more fodder plant fields, which are irrigated and thus can produce feed to sustain animals through winter, when it is extremely dry,' he said. 'This is how we offset the impact of natural disasters.' Zhamusurong hopes the organisation can grow to make its members more resistant to changes in the environment around them. 'Nobody knows how the climate, the grasslands and the market price will change in the future . . . [but] herders can only carry on their lives when there is grass.'

As discussed in Chapter 1, some goals of adaptation planning processes are to be able to develop policies and actions that help communities, improve livelihoods and help preserve or restore ecosystems. This chapter focuses upon the herder populations of Inner Mongolia and the socio-economic, environmental and climate change pressures facing the grassland ecosystems upon which their livelihoods and culture depend, and how these pressures influence their vulnerability, adaptive capacity and climate risks. This chapter is different from Chapter 6 in that it predominantly focuses upon the social vulnerability of pastoralists. In contrast, Chapter 6 focused on the projected climate change impacts to grassland productivity using biophysical impact assessment approaches.

The research in this chapter highlights one of the first studies within China to integrate regional-scale climate projections with participatory assessment research on social vulnerability and adaptation planning at the pastoralist household level (Du *et al.*, 2012). The work of the study connected local knowledge, perceptions and insights from nomadic populations, as well as those of recently-settled communities, to academic and policy maker views of climate change. The importance of this study in China's adaptation journey should not be underestimated, as it offers a bridge between the traditional academic research that characterises many of China's adaptation assessments (also typical in many other countries' adaptation programmes) and herders' knowledge and observations of their vulnerabilities, risks and views of a changing climate. The research examines factors affecting people's and ecosystems' vulnerability, potential climate impacts in light of observed and projected changes and steps taken and needed to improve adaptation policy in Inner Mongolia.

Inner Mongolia: overview of current climate hazards, trends and future climate risks

The natural grassland area of Inner Mongolia covers some 71.9 million hectares, or approximately 83% of the total pasture area of the province. Administratively, the central government designates Inner Mongolia as an autonomous administrative region because of its ethnic Mongol population. The region is divided into prefectures (also called leagues; see Figure 9.1), then counties (banners), and finally cities (hots) or villages (gachas). Most counties are classified as pastoral areas, with some semi-pastoral or agricultural areas in the east and south of the province where the land is less arid and farming is more common (Figure 9.2). Around 3.5 million people live in pastoral counties, and 4.4 million people in semi-pastoral counties (Hang *et al.*, 2012).

The Mongol populations traditionally engaged in a nomadic herding lifestyle well suited to the fragile grassland ecosystems they inhabited. For centuries, they

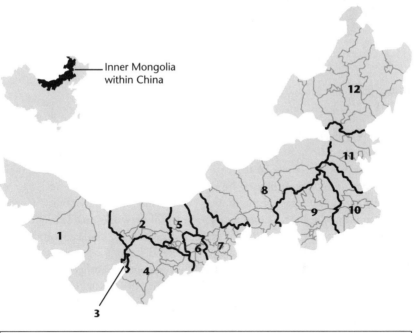

Prefectures:		
1 Alxa League	5 Baotou	9 Chifeng
2 Bayannur	6 Hohhot	10 Tongliao
3 Wuhai	7 Ulanqab	11 Hinggan League
4 Erdos	8 Xilingol League	12 Hulunbeier

FIGURE 9.1 Prefectures of Inner Mongolia Autonomous Region

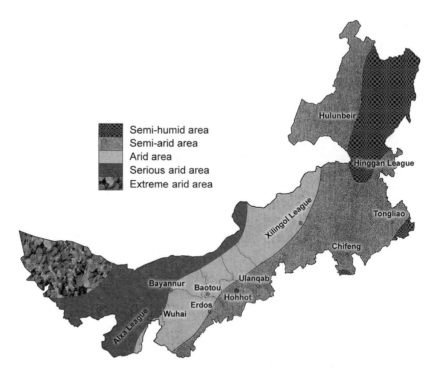

Semi-humid area
Semi-arid area
Arid area
Serious arid area
Extreme arid area

Hulunbeir

Hinggan League

Xilingol League

Tongliao

Chifeng

Bayannur   Baotou   Ulanqab
            Hohhot
        Erdos
Wuhai

Alxa League

FIGURE 9.2 Inner Mongolia climate zones (source: Hang *et al.*, 2012)

moved their herds of horses, sheep, goats, camels and oxen through communally held pastures in search of grass and water for the livestock. Multiple herd
relocations over the course of the year reduced overgrazing and the subsequent
soil erosion which contributes to desertification, and allowed recharge of
groundwater and surface water resources (Wang *et al.*, 2013a). Mobility, flexible
use of communally held pasture and strong social networks enabled herders to
move to better locations and pool resources to survive the climate hazards, such
as drought, severe winter snowstorms ('white disasters') or winter droughts
('black disasters'), that have plagued the Inner Mongolian steppes for centuries
(Fernández-Giménez and Le Febre, 2006). During the 1700s (Qing Dynasty),
large numbers of Han Chinese began moving into what is now Inner Mongolia
to pursue agricultural opportunities. The gradual expansion of the Han population, with different concepts of land tenure and property boundaries, was not
conducive to the nomadic lifestyles of the Mongol and other ethnic populations
and led to conflict.

Development policies under economic reforms instituted in 1978 encouraged greater settlement of the nomadic populations. Agricultural expansion, in
combination with growing sedentary herds, shifts to higher-impact livestock
such as cattle and fixed property boundaries, have contributed to widespread

environmental degradation and grassland destruction (Hang *et al.*, 2012; Zhang *et al.*, 1997; Zhao *et al.*, 2002). Subsequent economic and environmental policies were promulgated to address the increasing rates of grassland loss, desertification and shifts in herder livelihoods, with mixed results (Yu, 2003). This combination of socio-economic, policy and environmental change processes makes the herder populations, and other populations who rely on agriculture as their primary source of income, particularly vulnerable to suffering harm due to increasing climate variability and ultimately climate change.

The combination of human activity and climate variability are creating feedback loops causing grassland degradation and desertification (Wang *et al.*, 2006; see also Chapter 6). For decades, the grasslands have been retreating and are being replaced by sand dunes spreading from the Gobi Desert and local desertification areas. Overgrazing, mining and other intensive human activities that leave the plains bare and unprotected from the scouring winds drive grassland degradation. Falling water tables due to human demand and climate shifts (see Chapter 4) and climate variability and change are exacerbating the degradation processes. Beijing has countered the expanding deserts aggressively. The 'Great Green Wall', the world's largest reforestation effort, is being planted along the southern border of Inner Mongolia to slow sand migration into the agricultural provinces of Ningxia, Shanxi and others, and to reduce the number of sandstorms impacting Beijing (Sun and Fang, 2001; Veste *et al.*, 2007). Some of the government programmes are controversial. Since the 1980s, resettlement programmes have relocated most of Inner Mongolia's nomadic populations onto fixed pastures or into towns. These programmes were instituted to restore the grasslands and facilitate economic development among the herders. Yet, their success in mitigating desertification and slowing grassland degradation is difficult to gauge, and the policies have had a dramatic impact on nomadic traditions, cultures and livelihoods (Wang *et al.*, 2013a, 2013b; Fernández-Giménez, 2000). As will be shown in a case study later in this chapter, these policies have had mixed socio-economic and environmental impacts on herders and grasslands, in some instances increasing both human and biophysical vulnerability.

The arid nature and highly variable climate of the province strongly influence grassland health and the livelihoods of the herder populations. Precipitation is distributed unevenly throughout the province, increasing from west (<250 mm per annum) to east (>500 mm); it experiences four distinct seasons. Changes in precipitation and temperature since the 1960s, some due to natural decadal climate variability and some attributable to climate change, have been leading to greater climate risks and pressures on the grassland ecosystems and the herders (also discussed in Chapters 4 and 6). Both slow-onset changes (temperature increases and overall decreases in precipitation during the grass-growing season of April to September) and increases in extreme weather events (the

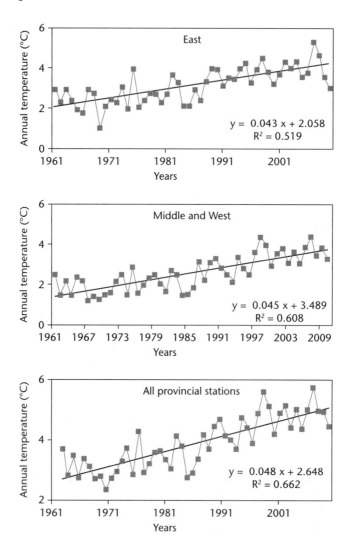

FIGURE 9.3 Trends in annual mean temperature (above) and average precipitation in various regions of Inner Mongolia between 1960–2010. Station data for the large province is sparse, with only 24 stations recording for the whole period. Trends are significant at the 95th percentile for R^2 values of 0.061 or higher. No statistically significant trends are seen in overall annual precipitation (page 249) (source: Wei, 2012)

occurrence of drought has been increasing in spatial scope, severity and frequency, with an increasing proportion of spring and summer rainfall occurring in concentrated, heavy rainfall events) are challenging grassland management and livelihoods. The following climate shifts over the past few decades (Figure 9.3), in combination with changing socio-economic, ecological and

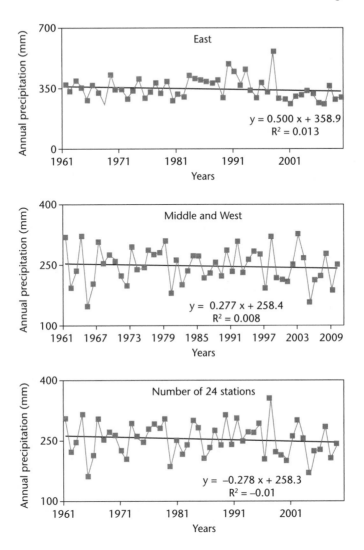

FIGURE 9.3 Continued

policy processes (vulnerabilities), have led to some of the impacts that have been observed throughout Inner Mongolia (Table 9.1).

Out of all of the climate-related hazards Inner Mongolia has historically experienced, and will continue to experience in the future, drought presents the greatest risk to pastoral and agricultural livelihoods and to grassland ecosystems. Analysis reveals that severe drought used to occur on average two years out of ten, although there was considerable variability in the historical record with multi-year droughts occurring (Xue, 1996). In the past two decades, the severity and frequency of drought has been increasing and

TABLE 9.1 Weather and climate risks in Inner Mongolia since the 1960s

Hazard	Rates of change	Impacts
Temperature rise	• Annual mean temperature increase by 4°C from 1961 to 2009, with areas of Inner Mongolia warming at different rates. • Warming trends were most pronounced in winter and spring. • Minimum temperatures increased faster than maximum temperatures. • Extreme hot days during summer have increased ~2–5 days per year; extreme cold days in winter have decreased.	• Higher evapotranspiration and greater stress on water supply, with human demand remaining the primary stressor (see Chapter 4). • Exacerbation of drought conditions and acceleration of grassland degradation. • Reduced snowpack recharging groundwater supply. • Decreased livestock mortality due to snowstorms and fewer winter cold events; increased livestock disease rates in summer.
Precipitation change	• There has been significant decadal and interannual variation. There are no statistically significant trends in annual precipitation from 1961 to 2009, though some regions show a slight downward trend.	• Decreasing flood risk in river basin areas in the past decade, due to increased drought. • Lowering of groundwater tables and loss of surface water supplies.
Extreme events	• Incidents of drought are increasing in all seasons; years of consecutive drought are becoming very problematic. • Winter droughts, or 'black disasters', have significant decadal variation. There is no apparent trend. • Heavy rainfall events and snowfall, or 'white disasters', show no trend but large variability. • Windstorms are becoming less frequent, but events are becoming more intense (stronger winds). Windstorms still spawn intense sandstorms.	• Loss of forage for livestock; widespread livestock starvation and death. • Culling of herds to curb economic losses. • Desertification and soil salination. • Rodent infestation. • Decreased livestock productivity and livestock derivative (e.g. cashmere and wool) quality. • Health issues, destroyed property and livestock harm from sandstorms.

multi-year droughts, such as the one that lasted from 1999–2002, have been harming herders' livelihoods and exacerbating grassland loss and desertification. Some of the recent variability in drought occurrence is due to shifts in the El Niño Southern Oscillation and other large-scale climate oscillations (Gao *et al.*, 2013) though studies suggest that climate change is also contributing to the temperature rises and drought increase seen in the Inner Mongolian and Mongolian steppe (Wei, 2012).

The seasonal timing of drought affects livestock management in different manners. Spring droughts inhibit grass growth and regeneration after winter dormancy, and can lead to early crop failure during seed planting and germination phases. Summer and autumn droughts, especially if consecutive, deplete herders' stores of hay and livestock feed and contribute to financial difficulty if persistent, as farmers must purchase feed at a premium. Winter droughts, especially during cold snaps, are known as 'black disasters' and typically result in widespread livestock starvation and death. Overgrazing during drought periods contributes to further grassland degradation; soil salination and erosion, also exacerbated during drought, enhance the spread of the desert and fuel sandstorms.

A series of projections using different climate models each running three emission scenarios (A2 – high, A1B – medium and B2 – low) (Angerer *et al.*, 2008) and the Chinese Academy of Agricultural Sciences indicate that temperatures are likely to rise across most of Inner Mongolia by the 2050s. Annual precipitation might also slightly increase, due to the potential for increases in winter precipitation. At the same time, extreme precipitation events and variability (e.g. drought) are likely to become more frequent. Due to the projected temperature increases, grassland boundaries (warm steppe) may increase. The overall carrying capacity of the grasslands is not expected to increase, however, due continued decreasing trends in water resources. Under these changing climate conditions, Inner Mongolian herders could face more intense and frequent droughts, blizzards and spring sandstorms – all while dealing with rapid socio-economic, cultural and environmental change.

The actual nature and severity of the impacts (climate risk) that herders experience after a weather hazard are dependent upon their underlying vulnerability and capacity. Socio-economic, cultural and environmental factors, among others, combine to make pastoralists more or less vulnerable to suffering harm. The next section explores some of the vulnerability and capacity contexts within Xilingol League, an area that typifies experiences across Inner Mongolia as a whole, through a case study conducted under the Adapting to Climate Change in China I (ACCC I) programme.

Case study: herders' climate vulnerability and risk in Xilingol League, Inner Mongolia

CASS and researchers from Inner Mongolia University, Inner Mongolia Agricultural University and the Inner Mongolia Academy of Social Science formed three teams to investigate the impacts of climate-related hazards on herders in a typical region of Inner Mongolia from 2011 to 2012 under ACCC I. The team sought to examine the ecological, economic and socio-cultural factors contributing to herder vulnerability and risk. Through participatory research, including group interviews, questionnaires and household surveys, the research teams consulted more than 120 pastoral families to understand perceptions of climate variability and change and their impacts on livestock production, grassland health and their lives. The team also interviewed decision makers at various jurisdictions, from the village to the provincial level, and local researchers.

Xilingol League was selected as the case study location because this region is typical of the province as a whole, as it represents a variety of ethnic groups and steppe environments and encompasses approximately 17% (~202,000 km²) of the province. In 2010, the total population of the league was approximately 1,045,000, including 205,200 herders (Hang *et al.*, 2012). Xilingol is presently inhabited by 23 ethnic minorities, including Mongol (29.6%), Hui, Tibetan, Korean and Daur, plus a sizeable Han Chinese population. Participatory case studies were conducted in Duolun County in Xilinhot, and Siziwang Banner, Abaga Banner and Keshiketeng Banner in Wulanchabu, each covering different steppe environments (Figure 9.4). Duolun represents a moderately dry 'typical steppe' environment and Siziwang a semi-arid desert steppe; both of these are Han Chinese-dominated settler villages engaged in farming and grazing. Abaga and Keshiketeng are Mongolian-based gacha villages. The former is typical steppe with herding in the traditional nomadic mode, and the latter is a natural meadow rich in water and grass, where settled pasturing is dominant.

The climate in Xilingol League is windy, drought-prone and extreme, averaging −20°C in January and 21°C in July, similar to the average climate throughout Inner Mongolia. Precipitation is uneven, largely concentrated in June to August and decreasing gradually from south-east to north-west; the annual mean is 295 mm. The league has experienced similar shifts in temperature, increasing drought and precipitation variability, and fewer but more intense sandstorms as seen throughout Inner Mongolia.

Herders' vulnerability and capacity contexts

The research conducted in Xilingol League investigated multiple factors contributing to herders' vulnerability and capacity to cope with, adapt to and shift strategies in an increasingly variable and changing climate. It focused on several

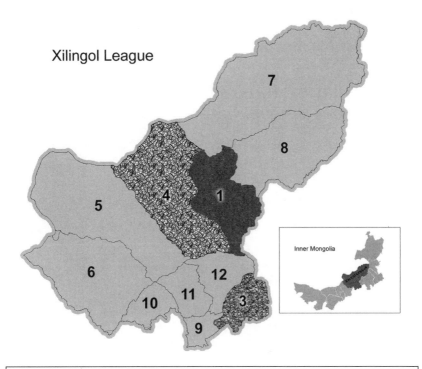

Counties:
1 Xilinhot City   7 East Ujimqin Banner
2 Erenhot City   8 West Ujimqin Banner
3 Duolun County   9 Taibus Banner
4 Abaga Banner   10 Bordered Yellow Banner
5 Sonid Left Banner   11 Plain and Bordered White Banner
6 Sonid Right Banner   12 Plain Blue Banner

FIGURE 9.4 Xilingol League and its counties. The study was conducted in counties
1, 3 and 4

factors in Table 9.2, drawn from natural hazards and social vulnerability research
traditions, which have been identified in the literature as contributing to overall
vulnerability and capacity (Chambers and Conway, 1992; Adger *et al.*, 2004;
Aguilar *et al.*, 2009) and that are relevant to the context facing pastoralists in
Inner Mongolia (Sayre *et al.*, 2013; Zhen *et al.*, 2010). The research team
created a vulnerability index on a county-level based on sensitivity, hazard exposure and capacity indices based on indicators in Table 9.2 for the herding
populations.

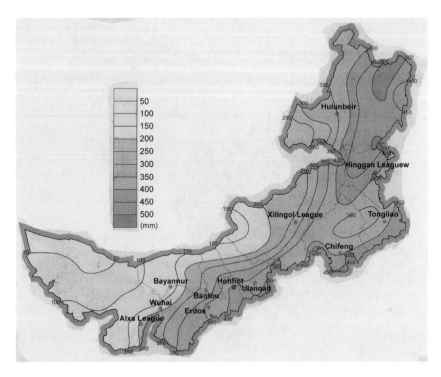

FIGURE 9.5 Annual precipitation distribution in Inner Mongolia. Xilingol League (source: Wei, 2012)

Ecosystem health, services and climate change processes

Overgrazing, grassland degradation and declining water resources due to over-exploitation are increasing the sensitivity of herders' livelihoods to increasing climate variability and change. Interviews with pastoral populations encompassing a broad range of age groups indicated that they are acutely aware of changes, and how these are impacting their livestock management strategies and grassland health. Interviewees are noting worrying ecosystem shifts, particularly losses of plant and animal species. For example, one elderly woman said that there were over 60 kinds of herbs in an acre of grass when she was young, but only a dozen now. These observances are consistent with observations of ecosystem and climate shifts in neighbouring Mongolia (Marin, 2010).

The two main rivers in the area are the Lightening River, part of the Luan River Basin, and the Xilin River. Along with groundwater, these serve as vital water resources for domestic, agricultural and livestock use. However, drinking water access for people and livestock is becoming increasingly difficult due to lower water tables in wells across the league. Herders reported that shallow wells near ranches used to supply sufficient water for domestic and animal

TABLE 9.2 Factors contributing to herders' social vulnerability and adaptive capacity

Factor	Indicators
Socio-cultural factors	• Social and economic capital • Gender roles • Access and attitudes toward education • Traditional ecological knowledge
Socio-economic change	• Loss of community reciprocity and risk sharing • Labour shortages • Increasing livestock production costs • Resource competition with other households and industries
Physical infrastructure	• Access to roads and transportation • Electricity • Reliable water sources • Communications (mobile phones, TVs, etc.)
Ecosystem health and services	• Grassland health (see Chapter 6) • Forage and water supply quality and quantity • Livestock health
Institutional processes	• Grassland management policies • Herder settlement policies and compensation • Disaster risk reduction and climate adaptation policies

consumption; however, they must now access water from deep wells often located far from their living arrangements during the more frequent drought periods. The burden for procuring water disproportionately falls upon women, as it is traditionally their responsibility to fetch water. Women belonging to settled pastoral and agricultural households lose a lot of time to fetching water at distant wells.

While the incidents of severe snowstorms, or 'white disasters', during the winter appear to have decreased since the late 1990s, increasing variability in all seasons is challenging livestock management and herder livelihoods. White disasters resulted in pasture icing, as well as livestock starvation and death from cold exposure. Herders traditionally constructed stalls to protect livestock during the winter and stored as much forage as possible. These measures have sometimes proven inadequate; in 2009–2010, for example, a severe white disaster wiped out nearly 20% of the national livestock herds and impacted 28% of neighbouring Mongolia's population (Fernández-Giménez et al., 2012). These conditions are shifting. A 40-year-old herdsman from Siziwang Banner described snow cover as thick as 20 cm in his childhood (in the 1970s) and explained that herders had to reserve forage and food for winter to cope with potential road blockages by snow. Deep snow like that of their remembered pasts is now rarely seen; winter droughts, or 'black disasters', are more common.

Black disasters, or drought in any season, result in severe economic losses for herders, as they must often purchase hay and supplemental livestock feed. If drought occurs during the winter, farmers may be unable to reach their live-stock to feed them, and the lack of snow as drinking water for the animals can contribute to widespread herd losses. Prolonged droughts and the resulting overgrazing contribute to continued grassland desertification and can trigger culling of herds or selling of livestock for low prices in order to minimise loss. Herders also noted that disease incidence in livestock, possibly due to the animals' malnourishment and stress conditions, increases during drought periods, as do incidents of insect infestation. For instance, continuous high temperatures and scant rainfall during the summer of 2010 created favourable conditions for locusts, triggering an infestation that caused widespread grass destruction and loss of fodder for livestock. In short, weather conditions, particularly precipitation amounts and timing, play a considerable role in herders' livelihoods and livestock morbidity and mortality (Wang *et al.*, 2011).

Physical infrastructure access

Shelter quality and construction are the first line of defence for herders to protect themselves and their livestock from inclement weather events. Herders have built feed storage warehouses to prepare for snowstorms, among other types of livestock infrastructure protection measures. Wells enable grazing on dry steppes, and winter shelters significantly increase the survival rate of young animals. These measures have greatly improved herders' resilience against natural disasters (Wang and Zhang, 2012). However, many traditional nomadic herders still live in remote areas and have limited access to building materials for maintenance and construction improvements. Many of these homes were built in the 1970s and are now dilapidated. In deteriorating housing conditions, it is difficult for people and livestock to withstand extreme weather events, especially cold snaps, and rates of hypothermia and illness due to cold can be high.

Infrastructure has improved greatly since the early 2000s for locations within and near cities, and along mining transects, with contributions from both the national and provincial governments (FAO, 2012). Access to transportation and communication networks, as well as reliable electricity, remains spotty for more rural settlements and nomadic populations. It is currently uneconomical to con-struct and maintain high-quality, fixed infrastructure like roads or meteorologi-cal monitoring stations to serve such vast and sparsely populated lands. In a typical Mongolian gacha, herders are scattered and live 5–10 km apart, and rely primarily on solar and wind energy for power. Families in many gachas have received government subsidies for wind power generation projects, but power supply instability remains an issue. Households rely upon trucks and carts for daily transportation needs and for fetching water, with motorcycles used for personal transportation. Many families still maintain the habit of horseback riding as the preferred mode of transportation, because horses are faster and less prone to breakdowns on the bumpy grasslands.

Herders rely primarily on satellite phones, and each household has at least one mobile phone or a landline (dependent on proximity to an urban area/ banner) for communication with the outside world. Despite their high cost, the phones play an important role in disaster warning and relief, especially without formal early warning systems due to the lack of meteorological monitoring stations in these remote locations. Particularly in the event of droughts and snow-storms, gachas closer to the banner and with convenient transportation and communications have higher adaptive capacity for accessing resources and outside assistance in a timely manner, while more remote gachas can only rely on mutual aid and assistance between families and communities.

Socio-economic change processes

Institutional shifts since the 1950s favouring settlement and individual property rights, higher stocking rates on smaller land areas and increasing population pressures due to in-migration of non-Mongolian people have had marked impacts on traditional community-based and household economies, while contributing to grassland degradation (see Chapter 6 and Kemp et al., 2011). The policies contributing to the institutional shifts were crafted with the goal of encouraging economic development and meat production, but have exacerbated grassland degradation and traditional herders' modes of dealing with risk. Historically, the nomadic pastoral system was a grassland/livestock dual-contract system within the community, guaranteeing movement of livestock and herders and access to water resources (Li and Huntsinger, 2011; Jun Li et al., 2007; Zhang et al., 2013). The community-based business 'hot' model encouraged reciprocity and mutual assistance in production and during weather hazards, to minimise the economic losses any single family might suffer during and after these extreme events. Policies encouraging settlement have begun to displace the hot model, emphasising a market-based economy of each family on its own. Because of this, individuals and families have experienced shifts in customary divisions of labour and are forced to assume more livestock production risk. Isolated and settled families are more vulnerable to suffering economic and livestock losses during hazards and other shocks (Wang and Zhang, 2012).

These socio-economic change processes are also contributing to labour short-ages and demographic shifts among the active herders. In the more remote communities, fewer herders are practising their trade and young people are migrating to urban areas for other employment opportunities. Wulan Tuga Gacha, for example, has neither migrant workers nor new households moving into the area, and the existing workforce is ageing, with the average age of herdsmen ranging from 35 to 40. Increasing labour shortages are breaking down the traditional divisions of labour in which children trained and assisted their parents in herding.

Given the slow economic improvement in many of the remote pastoral areas, and continued grassland degradation, the children of herdsmen indicated during the interviews that they preferred to leave for study or work elsewhere. A small number of herdsmen interviewed want to abandon the high-intensity work but feel that they have neither the skills nor the ability to adapt to economic activities beyond livestock production. These parents tend to pin all their hopes on their children in making a better living in urban areas. When asked if they hoped that their children would choose to go into livestock production, almost all herdsmen replied negatively, 'unless that's what they wish'. Many of the older generation consider stewardship of the grasslands to be their responsibility, but they do not see their children continuing their traditions or ways of life. Few herders may be left when climate change impacts become more significant in the future.

The rise of other economic activities, such as industrial and mining operations, is also creating pressures for herders, particularly around competition for water resources. Urbanisation, industrial and mining development activities are depleting water resources in the steppes. As some surface water and well resources have dried up, herders have had to find new sources of water or dig new wells, pushing up the proportion of livestock costs attributed to water. Livestock and livestock product derivatives are the principal, and sometimes the only, source of income for many pastoral families, with associated costs accounting for the majority of expenditures. Nearly 50% of the income is immediately reinvested into production, with the remaining portion used for living expenses; little is left for savings. In Gacha G of Keshiketeng Banner, where herders are settled, fodder purchases account for 75% of production expenses. In Gacha Y of Abaga Banner, also settled, expenditures on feed, stalls and water consume over 40% of total income.

This imbalance of income to expenditure, and the prevalence of and need for private lending, leave herders little capacity for dealing with climate variability and change, and other shocks such as market shifts (Wang and Zhang, 2012). Of the 30 households surveyed in Gacha G, 25 households borrow money, ranging from CNY10,000 to 150,000 (GBP1,010.10 to 15,151.52) to purchase forage, with an average household debt of CNY38,500 (GPB3,888.89). According to herdsmen in Gacha Y, it costs CNY100,000 (GBP10,101.01) to drill a 100 m-deep well, and CNY100 to 200 (GBP10.10 to 20.20) to fetch water (covering vehicle depreciation costs, fuel charges, maintenance charges and water expenses), adding up to an annual cost of CNY25,000 to 35,000 (GBP2,525.25 to 3,535.35) or more, simply for water. High expenditures in livestock production and domestic needs force most herders (90%) to turn to loans. Luckier households can apply for a new loan after paying back the previous loans, while poor families need guarantees or rely on private lending.

Institutional processes

In an effort to improve economic growth in Inner Mongolia while slowing grassland degradation, the central government has instituted a number of policies and programmes to settle nomads, beginning in the 1980s. Published studies are divided as to whether these policies have exacerbated or decreased herders' vulnerability to a variety of stressors, including climate variability and change. Some analysts contend that settlement reduces stress on the prairies and increases grass yield and herders' income, notably in pastoral areas with small pasture area, large herds and dense populations (Ma and Zhang, 2013; Su et al., 2012). Other researchers have demonstrated that settlement contracts have led to overgrazing in concentrated areas and weaken the resilience of herders who had previously used migration to avoid ecological and weather disasters (Li and Zhang, 2009; Li and Huntsinger, 2011; Wang and Zhang, 2012). With household-based pasture contracting, rather than *hot* contracting, the size of each household's pasture area is constrained and using another's pasture is considered a contractual infringement. As the type and size of designated pasture varies for each household, the grazing capacity also varies and contributes to income gaps between households. Households with poor pasture or small allotments are particularly vulnerable to weather hazards and pests, and they are often plunged into debt and poverty because they can no longer move their herds to unaffected areas (Su et al., 2012).

The case study research conducted among herders in Inner Mongolia found that both sedentary and nomadic lifestyles have capacities and vulnerabilities (Wang, 2005, 2013; Su et al., 2012). For example, in Wulan Tuga Gacha, where nomads still practise traditional mobile seasonal grazing, the grassland is ecologically healthier than in neighbouring areas. Herdsmen believe that seasonal grazing is conducive to the conservation and sustainable use of pastures. If this pattern is abandoned, the pasture conditions are likely to worsen. However, these herdsmen also find it particularly hard to fetch water and constantly move throughout the year to follow the herd. Settlements require that several conditions be met, namely, water sources or wells near the houses, long-term housing for residences and nearby pasture for livestock production. Even with these conditions in place, successive droughts may cause water depletion and desertification of the steppe, and windstorms may damage houses. Moreover, pastures with wells support sedentary grazing over a longer time span, so if all households have wells, increasing herd sizes will put greater stress on the grasses.

From the perspective of disaster reduction, both the nomadic and sedentary lifestyles have their limitations. For example, fencing (in settled areas) can solve the problem of insufficient forage during snow, but is less effective in coping with drought and ecological disasters (such as pests); on the other hand, the nomadic model is often powerless in the event of large-scale disasters and heavy snowstorms. Many prairie communities are caught in an apparent dilemma between conserving grasslands for the future and improving livelihoods through more grazing. Decision makers in Inner Mongolia face a similar dilemma when they consider adaptation options in the context of climate change.

Socio-cultural processes

Socio-cultural factors, such as traditional gender roles and values, play a significant role in both individual and group vulnerability and capacity in dealing with a variety of challenges. Such factors will both enable and constrain the options a person or group perceives as available to them when dealing with weather hazards and, ultimately, climate change. Traditional ecological knowledge used to sync livelihoods and lifestyles with the patterns and rhythms of the ecosystems within which a group lives may be threatened by external pressures, such as the mining and climate variability seen in Inner Mongolia, and internal pressures, such as cultural shifts in preferences for different types of material wealth and livelihood expectations. Changes to the socio-cultural fabric of pastoralists in Inner Mongolia, as described below, are altering their vulnerability and capacity to handle climate and ecological changes.

Traditional ecological knowledge and coping mechanisms

Traditional Mongolian nomadic culture is built around adaptive practices to cope with the high uncertainty in the steppe environment (Ao, 2003; Wang, 2005; Wang, 2013). The Mongolian nation has a historical nomadic tradition of adaptation to the environment and a changeable climate; it cultivates a deep affection for the grassland and eco-cultural ideas of simplicity. Mongol herdsmen have much traditional meteorological knowledge and many weather proverbs, for example, 'look south-east early and north-west late to forecast the weather'; 'do not travel when there is early sunglow, and travel farther when sunset comes out'; 'the cloud circle around the sun is accompanied by sandstorm on the prairie'; and 'south wind and north-west morning rainbow is a sign of rain, while a halo indicates that the weather will deteriorate.' In the form of cultural knowledge like this, Mongolian ideas about grassland protection are passed down from generation to generation. As herders age and new generations seek livelihoods elsewhere, this knowledge and culture of protecting the grasslands may be lost, making subsequent generations of herders more vulnerable to the vagaries of an increasingly changing climate.

The traditional ecological knowledge and associated lifestyle differences between Mongol pastoralists and Han Chinese agriculturalists is also apparent in their adaptive strategies and coping mechanisms for dealing with climate variability and change. Living a nomadic lifestyle, herders pay more attention to grassland sustainability, rather than temporary material wealth, and in the harvest year, prefer consumption and entertainment (Nadamu Fair is usually held in the

FIGURE 9.6 A researcher from Inner Mongolia Academy of Social Sciences interviews a 90-year-old Mongol woman (photo credit: Meng Huixin)

harvest year) to saving cash. As discussed previously, risk during times of weather hazards was mitigated by moving herds and relying upon a community-based pastoral contract and reciprocity system for spreading losses. In contrast, the Han Chinese herders are more influenced by agricultural culture emphasising settlement and set property boundaries, which require different strategies for weather and climate risk mitigation, such as saving and planning according to crop cycles, to cope with such hazards.

Family and gender roles

Researchers uncovered during the exchanges that traditional patriarchal ideas have been in transition, and most herdsmen hold a tolerant and open attitude to the options of the next generation. In an interview with a family in Gacha Y, when asked whether they would have preferred a boy to their ten-month-old girl, the parents answered that girls are as good as boys, as they can study, work and support parents. Boys, after they grow up, might stay with their parents and take care of them when they grow old, but this also means that parents will have to give him a large ranch, meaning that the average pasture size and income per capita of the household may show a downward trend in the long run.

Education and social capital

Pastoral households generally put great emphasis on education. After Xilingol League began to merge schools in 2004, children went to the banner for schooling. Because of communication inconvenience, parents have to accompany the children in rented apartments, incurring an additional cost of over CNY6,000 (GBP606.06) per year. Some of the herders are reduced to poverty by the education of their children, selling all their livestock and working on pastures for other families in order to pay for university. Many families believe that investing in education will pay off for family welfare in the long run by enabling their children to take jobs in urban areas or in sectors outside of livestock production. Anecdotal evidence during the course of the interviews revealed that such investment can improve a family's overall social and economic capital.

Families with smaller debt burdens, higher education, or family members working outside the area are generally more affluent and fall into the middle and upper class in gachas. For example, a 70-year-old Mongol couple interviewed still operated their own ranch and were very proud that, without formal school education themselves, they had raised two sons and one daughter who have become 'useful persons for the country', working in urban banks and government agencies. With their children's help, the old couple had mobile phones with a total bill of over CNY100 (GBP10.10) per month. Although they were older, they had over 100 contacts on their phones, which they regarded as social capital. This enhanced social and economic capital enabled them to solve many issues by phone, including the purchase of winter fodder, daily purchases, drilling subsidies and medical treatment. Such examples, seen in other households as well, demonstrate the permeation of urbanisation processes and modern consumerism into these remote locations, and attitudinal shifts toward the accumulation of material wealth.

Overall vulnerability and capacity profiles – implications for climate change

The various processes and factors described in the case study combine to produce herders' overall vulnerability to suffering harm as a result of a particular hazard or enhancing their capacity to cope with and shift strategies as conditions change. Both nomadic and sedentary styles of livestock production have their particular strengths and weaknesses for dealing with extreme events and slow-onset shifts in climate. Vulnerability to drought in particular varies between communities in relation to shifts in grassland health, market forces, livestock production practices and institutional policies. Climate zones (semi-humid to extremely arid) play a strong role in the spatial distribution of drought risk due to exposure, with sensitivity and capacity moderated by socio-economic, environmental and policy processes (Du *et al.*, 2012; Zhou *et al.*, 2014).

Local and provincial government, community groups, and individual herdsmen in Inner Mongolia have taken both active and passive measures to cope with climatic variability and environmental change, and achieved some success in various situations. Resourceful herders have a variety of strategies they employ on an individual/household level, contingent upon settlement status and opportunities and constraints, but these autonomous adaptation efforts have not been widely organised by policy makers. Herders' and farmers' activities are reactive, made in response to the hazards and changing conditions they are experiencing; these actions do not anticipate climate change impacts at any future time scale (Wang, 2013; Ao and Wen, 2013). Additionally, these approaches are not unified or organised, with limited coordination amongst policy makers in promulgating planned disaster risk reduction and adaptation policies and strategies and in using these to encourage or bolster the autonomous measures taken by herders. Few of the stakeholders, policy makers included, are anticipating potential climate and socio-economic change impacts over the mid- (next 10–20 years) or long-term (beyond 20 years) in their planning or activities. This is understandable on the part of both settled and nomadic herders, whose autonomous adaptation actions are focused primarily on coping with the next few seasons or a year or two in the future at most and are limited by the constraints they currently face. Local- and provincial-level policy makers rarely focus beyond the next five-year planning cycle. Accordingly, capacity for adaptation and resilience planning and action is still relatively weak. The need for reducing current vulnerability and risks through addressing underlying socio-economic, cultural and ecological challenges is not well understood or adequately valued by some, nor streamlined across different sector plans and policies.

Progress, challenges and future options for adaptation policy

Vulnerability and capacity are dynamic as they shift with changing socio-economic, cultural, environmental and climate processes. They contribute to China's adaptation policy challenge within a complex development environment. The types of shifts seen in the vulnerability and capacity of various herder and agricultural groups in Xilingol League are typical of the change processes occurring throughout Inner Mongolia. Compared to other provinces, Inner Mongolia has a number of advantages that could lead to more robust adaptation planning, including a strong economy, increasing social and economic development and rapidly improving road, power and communications facilities. It is also facing a number of institutional, socio-cultural and ecological changes that challenge the development of anticipatory adaptation planning processes. Yet, these challenges also represent opportunities for building resilience to a variety of stressors and shocks beyond climate variability and change.

Progress so far

The province has already identified healthy grasslands as a crucial resource for climate resilience and sustainable development. In addition to its importance for livestock production, the steppe serves important ecological functions, including functioning as a barrier between the desert to the north-west and the farmland and cities to the south-east of Inner Mongolia. The provincial government has prioritised strengthening the protection and restoration of grasslands, and rolled out a number of policies, which also support climate adaptation (Hang *et al.*, 2012):

- *Implementation Rules for the Regulations of Inner Mongolia on Grassland Management (2006)*
- *Circular of the People's Government of Inner Mongolia Autonomous Region on Further Strengthening the Grassland Supervision and Management (2007)*
- *Administrative Measures on Grassland Wild Plant Collection and Acquisition in Inner Mongolia Autonomous Region (2009)*
- *Basic Regulations of Inner Mongolia on Grassland Management (2011)*

In order to bolster the implementation of the grassland restoration policies, the provincial government has provided increased funding for investing in grassland restoration projects, the creation of nature reserves, and paying herders to refrain from grazing livestock in sensitive areas. Long-term and short-term restorative grazing bans have been introduced in some areas, and rotational grazing systems are being implemented in order to slow overall deterioration. Herders above the age of 60 are entitled to an additional subsidy on top of the subsidy for not being able to graze, in order to provide extra income to those with fewer remaining working years. Other measures around shifting livestock management strategies, such as moving lambing times and reducing livestock, have been suggested and demonstrated on a limited basis of improving herders' incomes and reducing grassland pressures (Michalk and Kemp, 2008).

The construction of grassland ecological observation and a meteorological service system has been accelerated, allowing for increased monitoring and real-time observation of grassland conditions. Such measures have assisted the tailoring and design of ecological protection and restoration projects, including the Beijing and Tianjin sandstorm source control efforts, and sandy desert governance and protection efforts. This has slowed deterioration in some areas and led to the improvement of some key treatment areas (Gao, 2009).

Challenges ahead

In spite of the progress made in slowing the rates of grassland degradation and desertification in some areas of the province and in overall provincial economic growth, many challenges remain in building resilience to hazards and events over the short-term (next five years) and robust adaptation planning for the future. Slow economic development, lack of access to basic physical infrastructure and services, conflicts between policies and traditional herder lifestyles and customary resource management practices, and competition over water resources continue to plague underdeveloped rural areas. Emphasis on a market-based economy has encouraged some herders to intensify animal husbandry practices on small plots of land, exacerbating ecological losses. While policies to protect grasslands are primarily centred around pastoral and agricultural practice, rapid industrial development and mining constitute severe threats to water resources and grassland ecosystems and are not yet adequately addressed by policy and regulation. Mining, predominantly large-scale, open-pit coal mining and rare earth metal extraction, and manufacturing – mainly of energy and chemical products – now account for more than half of Inner Mongolia's economy. Yet, the water, air and soil pollution from these industries and urban areas undermine grassland management and restoration efforts.

These processes are also intensifying the vulnerability of grassland communities to climate hazards and change. With accelerated urbanisation and industrialisation, the income gap between pastoral and urban areas is widening. Steppe society is also ageing fast (Su *et al.*, 2012; Ao *et al.*, 2013; Wang, 2013). A basic system of social security has started to take shape, but there are many gaps in infrastructure and social services, and the rise in living standards for pastoral communities generally lags behind that in farming and urban areas.

Traditional grassland culture is also suffering. Governments at all levels have invested in settling herdsmen and fencing pastures, intending to improve production, living conditions and capacity to respond to climate change. But these policies and practices fundamentally change traditional production methods and living conditions. In many areas, herdsmen have been forced to abandon a nomadic mode of production that may be more resilient to climate change and natural disasters than intensive, sedentary livestock production (Naess, 2013). This also means the loss of valuable cultural heritage and diversity, as well as traditional ecological knowledge.

Widespread adaptation planning processes, and the integration of these within development and ecological management programmes, have yet to occur within Inner Mongolia. Efforts to date are focused more on the initials stages of such processes (see Chapter 6). In June 2008, Inner Mongolia set up a provincial climate change leading group in which 26 provincial departments are represented, in accordance with national government requirements, and released the *Inner Mongolia Autonomous Region Implementation Plan on Climate Change* (2010), with the priority action areas as set out in Table 9.3.

The first policy advisory report under this programme focused upon adaptation needs in the steppe during the *Twelfth Five Year Plan* period (2011 to 2015) and included recommendations such as the expansion of agricultural and

TABLE 9.3 *Inner Mongolia Autonomous Region Implementation Plan on Climate Change* priority action areas

Priority action area	Activities
Ecosystem conservation	• Ecological conservation finance and compensation mechanisms • Forest tenure reform • Ecological migration and grazing prohibitions in vulnerable areas • Ecological health monitoring • Implementing key conservation projects (e.g. afforestation, soil conservation, grassland retirement programmes and anti-desertification measures)
Water resource management	• More efficient irrigation infrastructure and techniques • Setting industrial water quotas • Reducing urban water use and reusing water • Water rights transfers • Cloud seeding to encourage rainfall • Better management of groundwater resources
Increase grassland resilience	• Grazing prohibitions • Increasing fodder area and irrigation • Using crop silage for fodder • Warming sheds • Controlling stocking rates and breeding for hardier livestock
Increase agricultural resilience	• More water-efficient irrigation • Improving soil conservation, tillage and composting practices • Adjusting crop varieties for more drought and/or pest tolerant species • Shifting cropping zones as warmer temperatures spread north • Timely agro-meteorology services with seasonal forecasts and early warning
Disaster risk reduction	• Improving network of meteorological stations for better monitoring and event prediction • Early warning systems for herders, farmers and urban residents • Better disaster risk reduction planning and response coordination

livestock insurance schemes and ecological subsidies for grazing bans. These initial adaptation planning efforts have not incorporated the perspectives and knowledge of pastoralists and agriculturalists, thus potentially missing or under-estimating both the benefits and repercussions of various programmes to date. The programmes also fail to account for mining and rare earth metal extraction within the province, nor do they consider the impacts these activities are having on the social fabric of communities, water resources, urbanisation rates and grassland ecosystems. As discussed in Chapter 6, China's *National Adaptation Strategy* (2013) identifies Inner Mongolia as the pilot province for a demonstration adaptation project on animal husbandry development in 'typical steppe'.

The project aims to restore and protect degraded grasslands through policy, economic and engineering approaches and to better manage the grassland and to promote animal husbandry development experiences in a changing climate. It is likely to begin addressing some of the previous research and policy limitations.

Limited research attention to date has been given to decision-making processes at different scales – from the household level to the local government (micro) or national government level (macro). Studies of the long-term behaviours of pastoralists and agriculturalists in Inner Mongolia in response to perceived socio-economic, environmental, policy and cultural change processes remain limited. The perceptions of the herders interviewed in the case study, as well as those of provincial-level decision makers, represent a novel development in climate adaptation research in China. As the regional climate begins to shift, placing an additional degree of uncertainty upon development choices and pathways, it will become all the more important for policy makers and researchers to monitor dynamic vulnerability and capacity contexts, and adjust adaptation planning processes to account for these.

Yet, as mentioned in earlier chapters, part of China's development and adaptation challenge lies in meeting the diverse needs, and supporting and building upon the many capacities, of its diverse population, and doing so on local scales where climate impacts are most acutely felt. As discussed in this chapter and in Chapter 6, the herders of Inner Mongolia are taking action within the policy frameworks piloted in the province. Herders are now banding together again to manage grasslands along the mandated household divisions to avoid further degradation, and efforts are being made to engage communities in determining what areas need to be fallowed and what can be used to grow fodder. Investment in infrastructure and training is becoming more important as conditions fluctuate and weather disasters inflict greater tolls. All of these herder efforts, in conjunction with national and provincial policies, are laying the groundwork to help them build resilience to climate change.

References

Adger, W.N., Brooks, N., Bentham, G., Agnew, M. and Eriksen, S. (2004) *New Indicators of Vulnerability and Adaptive Capacity*. Tyndall Centre for Climate Change Research (Technical Report 7).

Aguilar, M.Y., Pacheco, T.R., Tobar, J.M. and Quiñónez, J.C. (2009) Vulnerability and adaptation to climate change of rural inhabitants in the central coastal plain of El Salvador. *Climate Resilience*. 40. pp. 187–198.

Angerer, J., Han, G., Fujisaki, I. and Havstad, K. (2008) Climate change and ecosystems of Asia with emphasis on Inner Mongolia and Mongolia. *Rangelands*. 30 (3). pp. 46–51.

Ao, R.(2003) Heritage and innovation on the grassland grazing system. *Journal of Inner Mongolia Finance College*. 3. pp. 36–40.

Ao, R. and Wen, M. (2013) *Social Vulnerability and Change of Natural Resources Using Case from an Inner Mongolia Village.* 2012 CASS Sociology Forum on Climate Change and Social Vulnerability. Yinchuan, Ningxia, 15 July 2013.

Ao, R., Wen, M., Tian, Y. and Meng, S. (2013) *Studies on Climate Change, Production Change, and Social Vulnerability: Case Studies of Abaga Banner and Gacha Y in XilinGol League in the Inner Mongolia Typical Steppe.* Inner Mongolia Academy of Social Sciences (ACCC I Technical Report).

Chambers, R. and Conway, G. (1992) *Sustainable Rural Livelihoods: Practical Concepts for the 21st Century.* IDS Discussion Paper 296. Institute of Development Studies: Brighton, United Kingdom.

Chan, C.K. and Yao, X. (2008) Air pollution in mega cities in China. *Atmospheric Environment.* 42 (1). pp. 1–42.

Dai, S., Li, D., Chou, C.L., Zhao, L., Zhang, Y., Ren, D., Ma, Y. and Sun, Y. (2008) Mineralogy and geochemistry of boehmite-rich coals: New insights from the Haer-wusu Surface Mine, Jungar Coalfield, Inner Mongolia, China. *International Journal of Coal Geology.* 74 (3/4). pp. 185–202.

Dai, S., Ren, D. and Li, S. (2006) Discovery of the superlarge gallium ore deposit in Jungar, Inner Mongolia, North China. *Chinese Science Bulletin.* 51 (8). pp. 2243–2252.

Dong, S., Wen, L., Liu, S., Zhang, X., Lassoie, J.P., Yi, S., Li, X., Li, J. and Li, Y. (2011) Vulnerability of worldwide pastoralism to global changes and interdisciplinary strategies for sustainable pastoralism. *Ecology and Society.* 16 (2). p. 10.

Du, F., Zhou, L., Yang, L., En, H., Ba, T., Meng, H., Yang, Z. and Dong, J. (2012) *Adaptation to Climate Change in China and the Adaptive Policies Evaluation: Evidence from Inner Mongolia.* School of Economics and Management, Inner Mongolia University (ACCC I Technical Report).

FAO (Food and Agricultural Organization of the United Nations) (2009) *Review of Evidence on Drylands Pastoral Systems and Climate Change: Implications and Opportunities for Mitigation and Adaptation.* Land and Water Discussion Paper 8. Food and Agricultural Organization of the United Nations: Rome, Italy.

FAO (Food and Agriculture Organization of the United Nations) (2012) *Information Services in Rural China: An Updated Case Study.* FAO Regional Office for Asia and the Pacific: Bangkok, Thailand.

Fernández-Gémenez, M.E. (2000) The role of Mongolian nomadic pastoralists' ecological knowledge in rangeland management. *Ecological Applications.* 10. pp. 1318–1326.

Fernández-Gémenez, M.E. and Le Febre, S. (2006) Mobility in pastoral systems: Dynamic flux or downward trend? *International Journal of Sustainable Development and World Ecology.* 13 (5). pp. 341–362.

Fernández-Giménez, M.E., Batkhishig, B. and Batbuyan, B. (2012) Cross-boundary and cross-level dynamics increase vulnerability to severe winter disasters (dzud) in Mongolia. *Global Environmental Change.* 22. pp. 836–851.

Gao, J., Shi, Z., Xu, L., Yang, X., Jia, Z., Lü, S., Feng, C. and Shang, J. (2013) Precipitation variability in Hulunbuir, northeastern China since 1829 AD reconstructed from tree-rings and its linkage with remote oceans. *Journal of Arid Environments.* 95. pp. 14–21.

Gao, X. (2009) *Overall Deterioration Slowed Down and Key Treatment Areas Improved in Inner Mongolia Ecological Conservation.* Inner Mongolia Forestry, no. 10.

Hang, S., Shan, P., Bao, L. *et al.* (2012) *Research Report on Strategic Adaptation Planning on Inner Mongolia: Grassland Husbandry and Water Resources.* Inner Mongolia Development Research Centre (ACCC I Technical Report).

He, Y. (2011) Inner Mongolia registers a per capita GDP of almost US$7,000, catching up with many coastal provinces including Guangdong. *China Business News*. [Online] 20 August. Available from: www.ce.cn/cysc/newmain/yc/jsxw/201108/20/t201108 20_21024700.shtml. [Accessed: 11 June 2014.]

Inner Mongolian Statistical Bureau (2013) *Inner Mongolian Statistical Yearbook 2013*. China Statistics Press: Beijing, People's Republic of China.

Jun Li, W., Ali, S.H. and Zhang, Q. (2007) Property rights and grassland degradation: A study of the Xilingol Pasture, Inner Mongolia, China. *Journal of Environmental Management*. 85. pp. 461–470.

Kemp, D.R., Brown, C., Han, G., Michalk, D., Nan, Z., Wu, J. and Xu, Z. (2011) Chinese grasslands: Problems, dilemmas and finding solutions, pp. 12–24. In Kemp D.R. and Michalk D.L. (eds.), *Development of Sustainable Livestock Systems on Grasslands in North-Western China*. ACIAR Proceedings No. 134. Australian Centre for International Agricultural Research: Canberra, Australia.

Kexi, P. (2005) *The Depth Distribution of Chinese Coal Resource*. School of Social Development and Public Policy, Fudan University. Available from: https://gcep.stanford.edu/pdfs/wR5MezrJ2SJ6NfFl5sb5Jg/10_china_pankexi.pdf. [Accessed: 25 November 2014.]

Lau, K.M., Kim, K.M. and Hsu, N.C. (2005) Observational evidence of effects of absorbing aerosols on seasonal-to-interannual anomalies of the Asian monsoon. *CLIVAR Exchanges*. 10 (3). pp. 7–9.

Li, W. and Zhang, Q. (2009) *Dilemmas on the Grassland: Understanding of Utilizing and Management on the Arid and Semi-arid Pasture*. Economic Science Press: Beijing, People's Republic of China.

Li, W.J. and Huntsinger, L. (2011) China's grassland contract policy and its impacts on herder ability to benefit in Inner Mongolia: Tragic feedbacks. *Ecology and Society*. 16 (2). pp. 1–14.

Ma, L. and Zhang, Y. (2013) A study on the sustainable development model and countermeasures of pastoral areas in China. *Chinese Journal of Grassland*. 35 (2). pp. 104–109.

Marin, A. (2010) Riders under storms: Contributions of nomadic herders' observations to analysing climate change in Mongolia. *Global Environmental Change*. 20. pp. 162–176.

Michalk, D.L. and Kemp, D.R. (2008) Re-designing livestock strategies to reduce stocking rates and improve incomes on western China's grasslands, pp. 140–151. In: *Development of Sustainable Livestock Systems on Grasslands in North-Western China: Proceedings of the Combined International Grassland Congress and International Rangeland Conference*. Hohhot, Inner Mongolia. ACIAR: Canberra, Australia.

Naess, M.W. (2013) Climate change, risk management and the end of nomadic pastoralism, *International Journal of Sustainable Development and World Ecology*. 20 (2). pp. 123–133.

Sayre, N.F., McAllister, R.J., Bestelmeyer, B.T., Moritz, M. and Turner, M.D. (2013) Earth stewardship of rangelands: Coping with ecological, economic, and political marginality. *Ecology and Environment*. 11 (7). pp. 348–354.

Stanway, D. and Birsel, R. (2014) Beijing says one third of its pollution comes from outside the city. *Reuters*. [Online] 16 April. Available from: www.reuters.com/article/2014/04/16/us-china-pollution-beijing-idUSBREA3F07C20140416. [Accessed: 16 April 2014.]

Su, H., Shang, B., Wu, R. and Ai, J. (2012) *Climate Change and Herdsmen's Livelihoods*. Inner Mongolia Academy of Social Sciences (ACCC I Technical Report).

Sun, B. and Fang, T. (2001) Desertification in China and its control. In: Breckle, S.W., Veste, M. and Wucherer, W. (eds), *Sustainable Land Use in Deserts*. Springer: Berlin, Germany.

Veste, M., Gao, J., Sun, B. and Breckle, S.W. (2007) The Great Green Wall: Combating desertification in China. *Geographische Rundschau International Ed.* 2 (3). pp. 14–20.

Wang, J. (2013) *Climate Change Vulnerability Assessment of Herdsmen Livelihood, Case in Y Gacha of Inner Mongolia* (ACCC I Technical Report).

Wang, J., Brown, D.G. and Agrawal, A. (2013a) Sustainable governance of the Mongolian grasslands: Comparing ecological and social-institutional changes in the context of climate change in Mongolia and Inner Mongolia, China. pp. 423–444. In: Chen, J., Wan, S., Henebry, G., Qi, J., Gutman, G., Sun, G. and Kappas, M. (eds), *Dryland Ecosystems in East Asia: State, Changes, and Future*. HEP-De Gruyter: Beijing, People's Republic of China and Berlin, Germany.

Wang, J., Brown, D.G. and Agrawal, A. (2013b) Climate adaptation, local institutions, and rural livelihoods: A comparative study of herder communities in Mongolia and Inner Mongolia, China. *Global Environmental Change*. 23. pp. 1673–1683.

Wang, X. (2005) Management absence: A case study of the management of a semi-farming and semi-pasturing area. *Journal of Huazhong Normal University (Humanities and Social Sciences)*. 44 (6). pp. 19–28.

Wang, X., Chen, F. and Dong, Z. (2006) The relative role of climatic and human factors in desertification in semiarid China. *Global Environmental Change*. 16. pp. 48–57.

Wang, X.Y. and Zhang, Q. (2012) Climate variability, change of land use and vulnerability in pastoral society: A case from Inner Mongolia. *Nomadic Peoples*. 16 (1). pp. 48–57.

Wang, Y., Wang, M., Zhang, R., Ghan, S.J., Lin, Y., Hu, J., Pan, B., Levy, M., Jiang, J.H. and Molina, M.J. (2014) Assessing the effects of anthropogenic aerosols on Pacific storm track using a multiscale global climate model. *Proceedings of the National Academy of Sciences of the U.S.* [Online] Available from: www.pnas.org/content/early/2014/04/09/1403364111. [Accessed: 5 May 2014.]

Wang, Z., Jiao, S., Han, G., Zhao, M., Willms, W.D., Hao, X. and Havstad, K.M. (2011) Impact of stocking rate and rainfall on sheep performance in a desert steppe. *Rangeland Ecology and Management*. 64 (3). pp. 249–256.

Wei, Y. (2012) *Climate Change Impact Assessment and Adaptive Measures*. Inner Mongolia Ecology and Agricultural Meteorological Research Centre (ACCC I Technical Report).

Xue, Y. (1996) The impact of desertification in the Mongolian and the Inner Mongolian grassland on the regional climate. *Journal of Climate*. 9 (9). pp. 2173–2189.

Yin, Y., Hou, X. and Yun, X. (2011) Advances in the climate change influencing grassland ecosystem in Inner Mongolia. *Pratacultural Science*. 28 (06). pp. 1132–1139.

Yu, Y. (2003) Analysis of the policy factors causing desertification in Inner Mongolia since the founding of the National Republic of China. *Journal of Inner Mongolia Normal University (Philosophy and Social Science)*. 32. pp. 79–83.

Zhang, C., Li, W. and Fan, M. (2013) Adaptation of herders to droughts and privatization of rangeland-use rights in the arid Alxa Left Banner of Inner Mongolia. *Journal of Environmental Management*. 126. pp. 182–190.

Zhang, L., Fang, X., Ren, G. and Suo, X. (1997) Environmental changes in north China framing-grazing transitional zone. *Earth Science Frontiers*. 4. pp. 127–136.

Zhang, Q. (2011) Herders' social vulnerability to climate change: A case of desert grassland in Inner Mongolia. *Sociological Studies*. 6. pp. 171–195.

Zhao, H., Zhao, X., Zhang, T. and Zhou, R. (2002) Boundary line on agro-pasture zigzag zone in north China and its problems on eco-environment. *Journal of Desert Research*. 22. pp. 740–747.

Zhen, L., Ochirbat, B., Lv, Y., Wei, Y.J., Liu, X.L., Chen, J.Q., Yao, Z.J. and Li, F. (2010) Comparing patterns of ecosystem service consumption and perceptions of range management between ethnic herders in Inner Mongolia and Mongolia. *Environmental Research Letters*. 5. p. 015001.

Zhou, L.G., Du, F.L., Zhang, X.F. and Zhang, C.H. (2014) The vulnerability assessment of grassland livestock industry to drought: A case study in pasture of Xilingol, Inner Mongolia. *Chinese Journal of Ecology*. 1. pp. 259–268.

10

GUANGDONG

Du Yaodong, Zeng Yunmin, Ma Wenjun,
Chen Xiaohong, Wu Xioxuan, Ai Hui, He Jian,
Liu Jinhuan, Sarah Opitz-Stapleton, Rebecca Nadin
and Samantha Kierath

There is a saying in the natural hazards and disasters research field that hazards happen and disasters are created. Socio-economic, political and environmental processes act in concert to make different groups of people more or less susceptible to harm when exposed to a hazard (Wisner *et al.*, 2003). Guangdong Province, along the coast of southern China in the Pearl River Delta, is highly exposed to a variety of weather-related hazards, frequently experiencing tropical cyclones, heavy rainfall events and heat waves. Its rural counties have agrarian-based economies in which poverty is endemic, and residents do not enjoy the same levels of access to services as do their urban counterparts. Meanwhile, the urban areas have experienced a surge of economic growth and have concentrated buildings and assets in low-lying coastal areas.

During China's economic reforms of 1978, Guangdong was one of the first areas opened to foreign investment and trade as a 'special economic zone'. Manufacturing and export industries thrived under the pilot programme, and Guangdong has become a cornerstone of the national economy, producing more income than any other province for over two decades. From 1979 to 2009, its annual GDP growth averaged 13.6%, while its population has swelled by two-thirds since 1990 to 104.3 million (Du, 2013; GDASS, 2011). The main industries include manufacturing (e.g. electronics, chemicals, biopharmaceuticals, automobiles and light manufacturing), construction, farming and fishing. Guangdong plays a leading role in the socio-economic development of China as a whole. Its GDP (GBP540 billion in 2011) accounts for 11.2% of the national GDP and was ranked the highest in the nation for 22 consecutive years in 2010 (Lu, 2012; Li & Fung Research Centre, 2012).

With its agglomeration of coastal cities and wealth, Guangdong is also highly exposed to weather hazards and climate change (Du, 1997; GDCC, 2013).

Rapid economic development and transformation, coupled with regional imbalances in such processes, have exacerbated the vulnerability of provincial socio-economic systems. Systems for preparing for, responding to and recovering from climatic threats remain inadequate, and economic disparities make the situation more precarious, especially for large populations of highly vulnerable groups, such as migrants, elderly people and children.

This chapter explores the disparities in vulnerability and risk profiles between rural and urban areas of the province to current climate hazards, with a discussion on migrants. As touched upon in Chapters 1 and 2, differential access to economic opportunities, education and other factors combine to make an individual or group of people more prone to harm (vulnerable) when exposed to a hazard like a typhoon. Access to economic opportunities can also be a strong enticement for migrating and seeking better options. The economic boom in Guangdong's urban areas has attracted large numbers of migrants to the cities from its rural areas and from neighbouring provinces, and these migrants have helped to sustain the province's impressive economic development through their labour. However, upon reaching the cities, many migrants still do not have access to quality housing or government-provided social services, making them more vulnerable than established urban residents to heat waves, flooding and other extreme events. While migrants may no longer face the risk of crop losses or extreme drinking water shortages due to droughts like they did in their rural communities, they often trade one set of vulnerability conditions for another to which they are unaccustomed, as discussed later in this chapter. These dynamic and mixed development contexts, in combination with shifts in the frequency and intensity of weather hazards, make the rural areas and migrant populations of the province more vulnerable to suffering harm during current weather hazards and may make them more vulnerable to climate change in the future.

The Guangdong coast and the Pearl River Delta concentrate tens of millions of people, provincial and national essential economic assets, and strategic facilities such as harbours and nuclear power plants – all of them now facing sea level rise, potentially more intense typhoons, and other aspects of a changing climate. The rapid economic growth, massive population movement and subsequent urbanisation have taken a toll on the province's ecosystems and further contribute to spatially differentiated vulnerability between the rural and urban areas. Pollution and ecological degradation have compromised the ability of many of the province's coastal ecosystems, in which many of the cities are located, to buffer the forces of typhoons and high tides. Pollution and degradation in rural areas is contributing to drinking water shortages and agricultural declines, as mentioned later in the chapter.

Remaining wetlands and efforts to restore these areas are becoming increasingly important in disaster risk reduction and climate adaptation efforts. After Typhoon Hagupit pounded Guangdong in 2008, the strength of healthy ecosystems compared to man-made infrastructure was clear to Tian Guanghong. 'Typhoon Hagupit caused great damage to Zhuhai. One-third of the granite seawall was smashed to pieces. But the Oi'ao Nature Reserve was not affected at all because of the mangroves,' Tian, the reserve's education officer says. The reserve is a 650-hectare expanse of mangrove forest established in 1999 to counter the destructive effects of an invasive saltmarsh grass introduced from South America. The grass prevented indigenous mangroves from taking root until the authorities started planting a fast-growing variety of mangrove found in Bangladesh. It is hoped that native species will return to the area and help protect the coastline. 'Concrete barriers can only resist a typhoon to a certain degree. And they cannot have other beneficial effects on the environment,' she says. 'But mangroves can not only resist typhoons; they also purify the seawater, among other things.' As climate change induces more extreme weather events such as typhoons, mangroves can help shield local communities and fishing boats from the worst of the storms' winds and waves. They also have longer-term benefits.

Guangdong is taking a number of steps toward ecological restoration and disaster risk reduction, such as the establishment of the Oi'ao Nature Reserve, that may lay the foundation for future disaster risk management policy and action in the province's complex development environment. Addressing the ongoing environmental pollution and degradation problems while meeting diverse development needs – from the poor migrant labourers to wealthy industries in urban areas to the poor farmers in its rural hinterlands – is critical for the province in terms of developing resilience to a variety of future stressors.

Guangdong's current complex development environment, and policy choices around future development, disaster risk reduction, environmental protections, and climate adaptation and mitigation will shape its future. The chapter discusses the potential changes in climate, socio-economic and development processes that could exacerbate or decrease Guangdong's future vulnerability and climate risk. It draws on case study research conducted by research teams from the Guangdong Climate Centre, the Guangdong Social Science Academy and the Guangdong Centre for Disease Control for the Adapting to Climate Change in China I (ACCC I) programme, and it discusses some of the recommendations for adaptation options and policies that arose from that work.

Guangdong – disparities in development and vulnerability

Much of Guangdong's current and historical economic significance to China and in global trade routes is due to its geography. Because of its location in the Pearl River Delta, with an extensive coastline along the South China Sea, access to safe harbour and major shipping lanes, Guangdong has served as a major port and centre of international trade since the 1500s. Its waters contain abundant marine resources, including petroleum, natural gas and fish. Due to its warm subtropical to tropical climate, the province is also a critical agricultural producer of fruit, flowers and vegetables that are transported to the north in the winter, and it is a source of warm-ocean fish.

Socio-economic disparities

As a hub of economic activity, Guangdong attracts a large number of people from rural areas within the province, as well as from rural and urban areas of neighbouring provinces (Figure 10.1). The economic reforms of the late 1970s increased migration to and urbanisation rates within Guangdong, making it one of the three pre-eminent economic development urban agglomeration regions within China, which also include the Yangtze River Delta and the Beijing-Tianjin-Hebei conurbations (Chen and Greene, 2012). As of 2011, the three agglomerations constituted approximately 15% of China's population and contribute nearly 35% of the GDP, although they make up only 8% of the national's land area (Wang and Liyun, 2013). The Pearl River Delta economic zone centres around Hong Kong, Guangzhou and Shenzhen, with Macau on the west bank of the estuary.

Guangdong's economy has quadrupled in the past decade and has attracted extensive foreign investment, with more billionaires than any other Chinese

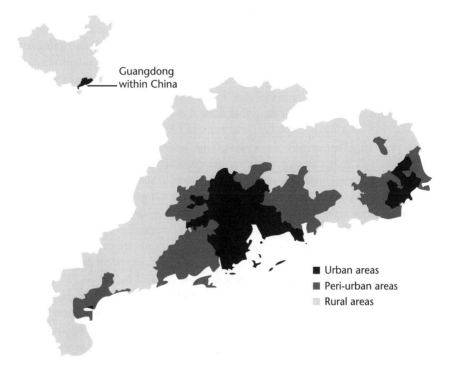

FIGURE 10.1 Rural-to-urban continuum in Guangdong Province

province (Du, 2011). However, the region still struggles with inequality and poverty, which is reflected in differential access to infrastructure and services like water supply, transportation networks, health care and information within cities and between rural and urban areas. Guangdong has 50 counties in its mountainous areas – mainly in the east, west and north of the province – which account for two-thirds of the province by area and 41% of its population, but only 20% of provincial GDP. The economy of the mountains is predominantly based on agriculture, growing much more slowly than in the urban areas, and poverty is endemic (GDASS, 2011). In 2010, rural household per capita incomes averaged CNY8,000 (GBP808.1), just a third of average urban dwellers' per capita income (Li & Fung Research Centre, 2012). Many rural residents remain in poverty due to a complex mix of socio-economic and environmental factors, including limited farmland and scattered farming operations; difficulty in bringing agricultural products to market due to inadequate infrastructure; higher government spending on urban areas; declining soil fertility; pollution; and water shortages (Li, 2007; Liao and Wei, 2012; Emran and Hou, 2013). Rural–urban and inland–coastal inequalities are quite large (Liu, 2006; Zhang and Donaldson, 2010), with transitions to a more market-based economy slowly altering traditional agricultural customs and institutions.

Poor soils, environmental pollution and too-small plots of land continue to plague many of the households and communities in more remote areas of the province. Pollution and environmental degradation are particularly critical in many of Guangdong's rural areas, due to economic reform policies, outdated farm and manufacturing equipment employed in family business enterprises and the increasing use of fertilisers, pesticides and herbicides for agricultural intensification (Li, 2007). Non-farm sectors have been growing, but this is contributing to greater income inequality between those in agriculture and non-farm sectors (Fan and Zhang, 2004). Development of and access to infrastructure, such as transportation and communications networks and electricity use, is occurring at a much slower rate than in urban areas (Fan and Zhang, 2004). Educational attainment levels remain lower as well (Halbrendt *et al.*, 1994).

The types of socio-economic, cultural and environmental change processes that shape vulnerabilities in Ningxia (see Chapter 8) and Inner Mongolia (see Chapter 9) are also evident in the rural areas of Guangdong. Though numerous policies and actions have been implemented at multiple levels of government, poverty reduction and redressing imbalances in access to services and infrastructure between rural and urban residents remains difficult for China (Yao *et al.*, 2004; Ding *et al.*, 2007). As a result, the rural inhabitants of Guangdong also share many of the same vulnerabilities as inhabitants of predominantly rural provinces, but these differences are frequently underestimated or overlooked in aggregate, provincial-level assessments or inter-province comparisons and investigations. The fruit, rice and vegetable farmers of rural Guangdong face many of the climate risks faced by the farmers in Ningxia (see Chapter 8), although they are not as accustomed to cold snaps. These rarely occur, but when they do – such as the January–February 2008 winter storm – they can have devastating financial and health consequences for farming communities and plant varieties adapted to a subtropical climate.

Economic migrants to urban areas are also not enjoying the same growth rates in wealth and are disproportionately vulnerable to harm during and after the frequent weather hazards that plague the province. Inequality between migrants and established city residents can also be substantial, partially due to the *hukou* system[1] (Sicular *et al.*, 2006; Kanbur and Zhang, 2004). Individuals who have migrated without the necessary permits and are thus unregistered find it difficult to access official services such as health care, education or housing, and they are frequently employed in service or construction industries without formal labour protections (Solinger, 1993; Guang, 2005; Wei, 2007). Women migrants in particular can face appalling labour conditions and sexual exploitation in export-orientated industries like textiles and electronics. Many migrants frequently lack contracts and are unable to access social or health insurance in Guangdong (Oxfam, 2004; Zhang, 1999).

Because this floating population, some of which may migrate for a few seasons or for decades, lacks land tenure and the ability to purchase property in their adopted location, they are often forced to rent properties in the marginal areas of the cities, such as in floodplains, which are more exposed to weather hazards. They have little recourse for protecting and relocating their assets before a hazard occurs, and can face significant financial losses. Many recent migrants are unfamiliar with the types of climate risks they might face in a city (e.g. severe flooding in a particular district) and may thus be more likely to suffer injury or asset losses than long-time residents. Additionally, a major influx of migrants during the 1980s post-economic reforms are now ageing and face difficulty in trying to access health and social services. These factors, in addition to the added stressors of urban and peri-urban pollution, declining water resources, inadequate access to sanitation and other environmental change processes, increase unregistered migrants' vulnerability before, during and after weather hazards.

Ecological changes

Large urban populations and growth rates are also having significant impacts on ecosystems within the province. Even though annual precipitation amounts have remained largely the same between 1961 and 2008, pollution and total runoff into the Pearl River have increased due to human-induced vegetation coverage loss, soil erosion and narrowing of the floodplain due to development, as well as larger seasonal precipitation variability (Du *et al.*, 2012). In the Pearl River Delta, water quality is a serious issue. Guangdong is on the downstream end of the Pearl River, so pollution anywhere along the river affects water quality and safety in the province. Along the coast, surface and groundwater pollution from rapid industrialisation, manufacturing and the inability of sewage and storm-water infrastructure to keep pace with urbanisation has not been effectively controlled (Azzam *et al.*, 2014). Other water quality and safety problems are related to increased pollution and sedimentation runoff during rainfall as vegetation is cleared and soil eroded by human activity (Chen *et al.*, 2007; Chen *et al.*, 2012). The severe drought that persisted from 2002 to 2004 caused a concentration of pollutants in water resources and led to severe drinking water shortages for more than 7.2 million people – equivalent to the urban-core population of Hong Kong. All of these inland pollution sources drain into the Pearl River and run off into the sea, causing significant nutrient-loading in coastal waters that triggers eutrophication and algal blooms and kills marine life (e.g. fish) (Fan *et al.*, 2010; Wong *et al.*, 2009). Fishing industries are impacted, and such blooms can disrupt shipping routes by damaging ship motors.

Guangdong's coasts have also been losing their natural storm barriers, the mangrove forests and coral reefs. Half of Guangdong's mangroves disappeared between the 1950s and the 1990s – either cut down or killed by pollution – and some reefs have started to bleach and die as a result of warming ocean temperatures and ocean acidification caused by carbon dioxide emissions (Du, 2007). Historically, mangroves and coral reefs slowed coastal erosion, particularly during high tides and storm surges. Loss of these ecosystems allows wave intrusion further inland, threatening infrastructure and water supply and exacerbating pollution by allowing tidal and storm surge flood waters to spread pollutants over a wider area. Coastal water supplies are additionally threatened by saltwater intrusion from rising seas, loss of coastal wetlands and tides penetrating further inland, as well as overdraft of water resources in the dry season (Figure 10.2). Salination is threatening domestic and industrial water supplies for the urban and peri-urban areas of Guangdong, as well as shifting species distributions within the river and impacting pollution mixing.

Current climate hazards, trends and associated impacts

Guangdong has a humid, subtropical to tropical (extreme south) climate and is prone to weather hazards. The majority of annual precipitation occurs during the wet season (April to September) and is associated with the East Asian Monsoon and tropical cyclones. Precipitation is significantly less in the dry season, although average monthly humidity remains high (greater than 65%). Seasonality impacts the types of hazards Guangdong experiences, with tropical cyclones and heat waves occurring during the wet season and drought, with occasional freak cold snaps during the dry season. Guangdong has a highly variable climate and faces a diverse set of weather-related hazards that present different risks to the rural, urban, migrant and official resident populations. Its farmers and construction workers increasingly suffer downpours, floods and even

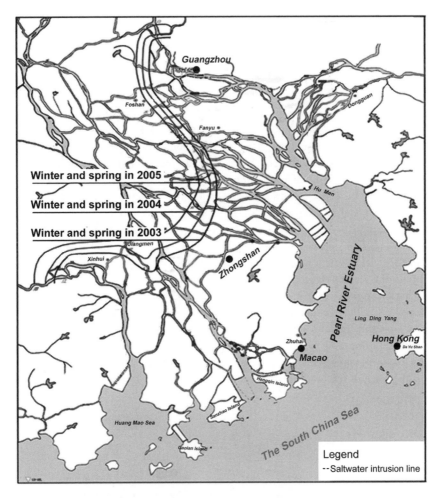

FIGURE 10.2 Saline intrusion boundaries into the Pearl River Delta, where salt concentrations exceed the 250 mg/l water quality standard for drinking water established by China. Saltwater intrusions have been penetrating farther inland with time and impacting water quality (source: Du *et al.*, 2012)

blizzards, interspersed with dry spells. Sea level rise is threatening infrastructure and increasing wave damage during storms. The underdeveloped areas of Guangdong are even less prepared for coping with current weather hazards or other types of natural or technological shocks. These types of hazards are likely to continue to threaten Guangdong in the future.

Tropical cyclones

Average annual losses due to weather hazards already equal 1.5% of provincial GDP (GDCC, 2011). Meteorological hazards constitute more than 80% of annual disasters according to statistical analysis of almost 30 serious natural hazards affecting Guangdong (Du *et al.*, 2012). Of these, tropical cyclones and typhoons cause the most damage. A total of 217 tropical cyclones, with 116 of these designated as typhoons, made landfall in Guangdong over the period 1951–2008. While the total number of tropical cyclones appears to have decreased slightly or shown no change, the number of storms strengthening to typhoon status is showing a slight increasing trend post-1990 (see the case study in Chapter 3). These results are consistent with observed trends in tropical cyclogenesis and landfall across the Indochina peninsula over the same period (Chen and Lin, 2013; Yokoi and Takayabu, 2013). Spatially, the low-lying coastal areas are most at risk of suffering severe impacts due to typhoons and their associated storm surges, flooding and high winds, given their direct exposure to the sea and flat topography (Figure 10.3).

Tropical cyclones can generate significant heavy, localised rainfall, contributing to flooding, widespread damage, loss of assets (see Chapter 3) and health problems through the spread of sewage as urban drainage networks are overwhelmed. The low-lying coastal areas can also experience significant flooding due to storm surge which, if coinciding with high tide, can cause inundation far up the Pearl River and inland around areas that have lost their mangrove and

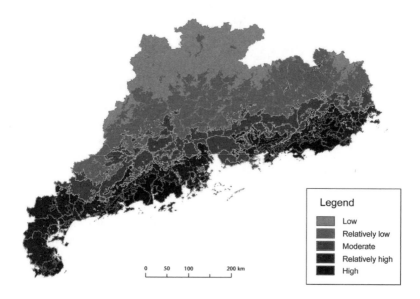

Legend

Low
Relatively low
Moderate
Relatively high
High

0   50   100   200 km

FIGURE 10.3 Typhoon risk zoning map of Guangdong Province (source: adapted from Du *et al.*, 2012)

coastal wetland ecosystems. In the last 15 years, the annual economic losses due to meteorological hazards averaged over CNY12.8 billion (GBP1.3 billion) – nearly seven times the loss levels of the 1980s – and the annual official death toll approaches 100 (Du *et al.*, 2012). Actual loss of life, property, assets and injury is likely to be higher than that reported due to losses incurred by migrants and other poor populations that do not have *hukou* and may not register their losses with the authorities. The differentiated impacts of such hazards depend on local socio-economic conditions. The most significant weather related hazards Guangdong faces, and their associated impacts, are show in Table 10.1.[2]

Increasing temperatures

Beyond tropical cyclones and their associated heavy rainfall and flooding, heat waves cause significant health and labour issues for the residents of Guangdong, as discussed in the case study of Chapter 7. Hot weather also speeds up the formation of smog, and Guangdong's annual total of low-air-quality days – when particulate pollution reduces visibility to less than 10 km – has increased by 16.4 days per decade over the last 50 years. Every hazy day raises the rate of respiratory infections by 15% and impacts those with cardiovascular issues while stunting children's respiratory development (Du *et al.*, 2013). Additionally, higher temperatures and heat waves are affecting agricultural yields and livestock morbidity and mortality in rural areas, impacting livelihoods and food security.

High humidity and temperatures, coupled with Guangdong's high population densities and the inability of urban infrastructure to keep pace with service demand (e.g. solid waste and sewage management), make it a perfect breeding ground for vector-borne diseases and microbial infection. The 2003 SARS outbreak originating in Guangdong made headlines worldwide and raised questions about how to prevent and control such epidemics, but with climate change multiplying public health threats, concerns range far beyond exotic viruses like SARS (Du *et al.*, 2013; see also Chapter 7). Guangdong's humid, subtropical climate encourages bacterial growth and infectious diseases, and its weather patterns, driven by the East Asian Summer Monsoon, are particularly sensitive to global climate change. Outside the Pearl River Delta, volatile weather may already be starting to overwhelm adaptive capacity in the health sector. Some underdeveloped areas have recently seen outbreaks of diseases like malaria and dengue fever, which had previously been eliminated or controlled locally, and have lower access to health services than urban areas, increasing the climate health risks of these rural populations.

Sea level rise

The sea level in the South China Sea has risen at an average annual rate of 2.7 mm in the last 30 years, with significant decadal variation and some areas

TABLE 10.1 Weather hazards common to Guangdong, 1961–2008, and their impacts

Hazard	Rates of change	Impacts
Temperature	Mean annual temperature increase of ~0.2°C per decade over the last 50 years, on par with the national average.	Higher energy use for cooling, impacts on air quality.
	Heat waves • The number of days in which the maximum temperature exceeds 35°C is significantly increasing after the 1970s, averaging 20 days per year by the late 1990s. • Extreme heat waves (daily maximum of 39°C) have occurred every year after 1999.	• High air pollution levels, increasing rates of respiratory illness and cardiac problems, particularly among elderly and chronically ill people (see Chapter 7). • Increasing rates of heat stress and heat stroke, particularly among elderly, children, labourers with insufficient cooling mechanisms and the chronically ill. • Higher rates of hospital admittance and death during heat waves.
	Cold snaps • Increasing variability in winter temperatures, with unprecedented severe cold snaps leading to snow and ice storms.	• Power outages and traffic congestion. • Damage to crops, fruit trees and urban canopy. Agricultural losses averages RMB3.8 billion (GBP383.8 million) per cold event. • Aquatic species death. • Danger to public safety due to transportation and heating issues, especially if cold snaps coincide.
Precipitation	• There have been no changes in annual precipitation between 1961 and 2008, but the incidence of drought and extreme rainfall is increasing.	• Impacts related to increasing variability in drought and heavy rainfall.

Extreme events   *Tropical cyclones*

- Total number of tropical cyclones has slightly declined, with an increasing trend in the number of storms reaching typhoon level.
- Tropical cyclone paths are becoming more erratic and difficult to predict.

- Increasing economic losses and infrastructural damage, largely due to urbanisation and concentrations of wealth along highly exposed, low-lying coastal areas.
- Persistent morbidity and mortality rates in spite of infrastructural protection improvements.

Heavy precipitation

- The number of days per year in which daily precipitation totals exceed 50 mm increased between 1961 and 2008.
- The total number of days of rain decreased over the same period, indicating that what precipitation occurs is increasingly falling as heavy precipitation events.

- Increased flooding due to more concentration rainfall events and inadequate sewerage and storm water drainage networks.
- Contamination of drinking water supplies and spread of overland pollution due to poor drainage.

Drought

- There has been a gradual increase in meteorological drought incidence in the Pearl River Basin between 1951 and 2008, with increases most pronounced after 1980.
- Agricultural droughts of different intensity are highly variable and show no trends.

- Agricultural and livestock losses.
- Decreasing water quality due to higher concentrations of pollutants and saline intrusion during low flow.
- Water shortages for domestic, industrial and agricultural purposes.

experiencing rates of rise up to five times more than the global mean for the past decade (Bindoff *et al.*, 2007; Cheng and Qi, 2007). The higher rates are largely attributed to thermal expansion, as the western Pacific Ocean responds to fluctuations in the El Niño Southern Oscillation. The rising ocean, together with uneven precipitation, allows saltwater to surge into coastal water supplies. In the last two decades, five severe saltwater intrusions poisoned the drinking water in the Pearl River Delta, raising the salinity above safe levels. Three such intrusions occurred in 2003, 2004 and 2005 (Figure 10.2). In 2005, levels of chloride (a salt) in the Guangchang pump station, which supplies 1 billion litres of water per day to the cities of Macau and Zhuhai, exceeded national safety standards for 38 consecutive days.

Sea level rise is also increasing the wave damage from tides and storms, eroding the coast and threatening to inundate key infrastructure, and altering the frequency of high water events. The frequency of high water events is directly related to the height of the sea level rise (Church *et al.*, 2008). Already, some high tides have exceeded the maximum level for which the Daya Bay nuclear power plant, the Huilai coal power plant, the Macao airport and the Huangpu seaport were designed. It is more difficult to drain all the storm water. Although height standards in building codes for flood control and drainage systems in Guangzhou and Shenzhen are constantly updated, infrastructure is in danger due to the combined impacts of soil compaction, sea level rise and increased wave destruction. Coastal erosion becomes increasingly severe. The coast along Maxietongguling Mountain (Zhanjiang City) has been eroded by 25 m in the last 40 years at an annual rate of 0.6 m.

As vulnerabilities shift and the frequency and intensity of both slow-onset (e.g. drought and gradual changes in temperature) and extreme (e.g. tropical cyclone and heat wave) climate events change for Guangdong, its climate change risk profiles are also being altered. In order to fully under the significance of some of these climate risks, the following section uses a case study approach to examine how different regions and populations of Guangdong have different risks.

Case study: climate change and potential future climate risk

According to the climate model BCC_CSM1.0, running the emission scenario combinations conducted for the ACCC I research programme (see Chapter 7), climate change is likely to alter seasonal and annual precipitation and temperature regimes in Guangdong, and to cause shifts in the frequencies and intensities of the extreme weather events to which the province is currently exposed. With relation to temperature, the following types of changes are likely over the period of 2071–2100 when compared with the baseline historical period of 1961–1990:

- increasing temperatures in all seasons, with average annual temperatures likely to rise 0.8°C by the 2020s and 1.8°C by the 2050s;
- greater rates of morbidity and mortality caused by a greater number of heat waves, coupled with heat island effects exacerbated by urbanisation;
- an increase in the number of days in which temperatures exceed 35°C by 90 to 115 days per year (compared with the average of only 19 days per year in 1961–1990); and
- a dramatic decrease in the number of cold days and nights during the winter season, by more than 70% by the later twenty-first century.

A number of changes in the timing and amount of precipitation are also likely. Extreme precipitation events are likely to increase in frequency and intensity, especially during the wet season (Figure 10.4). Overall annual precipitation is likely to increase due to the greater number of extreme precipitation events, though the incidence of drought is also likely to increase (not shown). The greater projected variability in sub-daily to seasonal precipitation is consistent with trends already being experienced within the province and with trends and projections for other provinces in China.

These shifts in the likelihood and intensity of slow-onset and extreme weather events, coupled with high differentials in variability discussed previously, will lead to significant climate risk for various populations and portions of Guangdong. Economic development, population and urbanisation rates are all projected to increase but, as the urban economies are projected to reach maturity around 2030, the influx of young migrants is likely to slow and the proportion of elderly people will start to rise (GDASS, 2011). Currently, the ratio of elderly to young people is lower than the national average, but the young labour force of the last 30 years is ageing and has become part of the elderly population after 2010. The proportion of elderly will further increase,

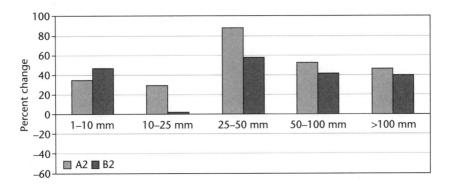

FIGURE 10.4 Projected percentage changes in precipitation at different thresholds in South China during 2071–2100 relative to 1961–1990 (source: Du *et al.*, 2012)

and the combined population of children and elderly is likely to constitute 35–40% of the total population by 2030 (GDASS, 2011).

Changing demographics and uncertainty about future socio-economic disparity, rates of ecological degradation and the resiliency of infrastructure imply the potential for an ongoing dynamic vulnerability for Guangdong. When combined with projections of likely shifts in the frequency and intensity of particular climate events for the province, the following climate change risk profiles emerge for various regions of the province (Table 10.2). The risks are projected to be most acute in the sectors where Guangdong is currently most vulnerable: coastal zones, disaster management, water resources and human health.

Coastal impacts

Mean sea level rise along coasts, including Guangdong's coast, is driven by both local projects (land use development, dikes and sea wall construction, etc.) and global climate factors (e.g. increased sea surface temperatures and multi-decadal climate oscillations) (Rhein *et al.*, 2013; Pelling *et al.*, 2013). The sea level along the coast of southern China is projected to rise by an additional 84–149 mm between 2010 and 2040 (Du, 2013). As a result of increased mean sea levels and continued alteration of the coastline, strong storm surges may become more frequent, impacting larger areas of low-lying regions. Islands and mud flats are likely to be inundated and salt water will intrude further inland, aggravating coastal erosion and salination of water supplies and contributing to continued degradation of mangroves and coral reefs. Without intervention, high tides could wash across 48 inhabited offshore islands of the Pearl River Delta, displacing residents and businesses. Mangroves and coral reefs, which help protect the coast from storms, will continue to weaken due to human activity (land conversion and pollution). Warmer sea surface temperatures and mean sea level rise could contribute to widespread coral and mangrove system die-offs (Du, 2013; SCCCAR, 2013). The warmer temperatures, when combined with terrestrial-based pollution (industrial, urban and agricultural), will also reduce water quality and trigger

TABLE 10.2 Future climate change risk for various regions of Guangdong

Region/climate change risk	Temperature rise	More heat waves	Sea level rise	More seasonal water shortages
South coastal regions	Medium	Medium	High	Medium
Pearl River Delta	Medium	High	High	High
North mountainous region	Medium	Medium	Low	High
Guangdong overall	Medium	Medium	High	High

eutrophication and red tides, contributing to fish mortality. These are already issues in the Pearl River Delta.

These changes affect coastal development and land use across the board, from regional planning and industrial layout to water safety, territorial security and tourism. In particular, engineering standards will have to be adjusted for coastal protection infrastructure, and consideration might have to be given to selectively allowing some areas to flood. Research shows that Guangzhou, Zhongshan, Zhuhai, Hong Kong and Macau are likely to be influenced by salt water intrusion during dry to normal rainfall years if mean sea levels rise by 100 mm, which may be possible by the end of the twenty-first century (Church et al., 2013; SCCCAR, 2013). Scenarios of mean sea level rise of around 300 mm (a hypothetical, worst-case scenario) would shorten the interval between severe saltwater intrusions by 50–60%, although this scenario is unlikely over the next century. The intertidal zone along the Guangdong coast may shrink by up to 23% if no infrastructural adjustments, ecosystem restoration, building restrictions or institutional measures are taken to protect the area. Rising sea levels will have negative impacts on regional planning and industrial layout, coastal typhoon storm surge and tide mitigation, and urban flood control and drainage. It will have additional ecosystem service, environmental degradation and infrastructure impacts in areas such as water quality, coastal protection projects, development and utilisation of land resources in south China (Church et al., 2013; SCCCAR, 2013). Marine and territorial security, and claims over marine resources, along with coastal tourism are also likely to be impacted.

Infrastructure and services impacts

To date, typhoons in the South China Sea have shown few changes in frequency and intensity. Continued sea surface warming and other climate-related changes are likely to produce more powerful and destructive storms (see Chapter 3). In recent years, tropical cyclone paths have become more erratic and difficult to forecast. It is possible that more super typhoons like Typhoon Sally – Guangdong's last 'super typhoon' that struck in 1996 – will happen more frequently. Even without climate change altering the intensity, frequency and paths of future cyclones, the damage associated with tropical storms is increasing as the coast is built-up and development intensifies; stronger typhoons combined with higher storm surges would have devastating impacts.

Disaster management systems in this province have historically emphasised disaster relief rather than disaster risk resilience and planning. Effective risk management is lacking, forecasts are not accurate enough and early warning services are poorly targeted and inadequate, relying on an information network that is frequently overwhelmed during events. Legal and governance systems for disaster management also fall short of the province's needs. There are no comprehensive laws or regulations on managing the range of weather, technical and other natural hazards that Guangdong experiences, and there is no leading organisation or other mechanism for coordination across sectors. Building plans, land use development and health services, among other areas, do not always take a multi-hazard planning perspective and, if they do, plans on paper do not always translate into action or enforcement. These institutional deficiencies further slow the flow of information and limit the government's ability to respond to risks accurately, rapidly and efficiently, or take more proactive resilience measures.

Water resource impacts

As described previously in this chapter and Chapter 4, significant demand and pollution pressures are being placed on China's water supplies, leading to widespread water shortages and loss of wetlands, surface and groundwater sources. Rising temperatures, coupled with socio-economic growth and urbanisation processes, are likely to increase water demand across the province. While projections indicate a potential increase in annual precipitation, largely due to increases during the wet season, the length of the dry season and the number of droughts are also likely to increase. More rain may bring a modest increase in surface water resources by the late twenty-first century (SCCCAR, 2013). Yet, shifting demands and resource priorities, environmental degradation and land use change may negate potential increases in surface supplies. These processes, along with sea level rise and warmer temperatures, will contribute to declining water quality and saline intrusion. Guangdong will experience more frequent seasonal water shortages and declines in water quality. Additionally, both increased flooding and drought will threaten the safety of water projects (Chen *et al.*, 2012) and can contribute to instability in power generation and electricity supply, triggering negative feedbacks for water and wastewater treatment.

Summary

Due to the socio-economic disparities between the rural and urban regions of the province, each is likely to experience different risks under a changing climate. Highly urbanised areas like the Pearl River Delta face higher heat wave risks than rural areas because of factors like the urban heat island effect and greater concentrations of elderly and very young populations that are less tolerant of heat. Rural areas, such as the mountainous counties in the north of the province, face greater risks of drinking water shortages in the future due to the combination of pollution, lower coverage of drinking water infrastructure than urban areas and the pressure of warmer temperatures and drought. These regional and population differences in Guangdong's current and future climate risk constitute its adaptation challenge, as well as presenting opportunities for shifting development and ecosystem management strategies that could improve its future climate resilience.

Adaptation challenges, opportunities and recommendations

In some ways, Guangdong is a miniature version of China. Rapid economic development, socio-cultural and environmental change processes and income inequality contribute to the dynamic and geographically diverse vulnerability and climate risk profiles of Guangdong's population. China is a vast country with different regional socio-cultural and economic characteristics and development levels. It faces various challenges from climate change that require responses specific to each region. Guangdong's experiences in trying to incorporate disaster risk reduction measures in land use and socio-economic development planning, and beginning to consider climate change adaptation processes, not only set examples for other Chinese coastal areas but also provide lessons for inland regions. Guangdong's existing measures for disaster risk reduction and near-term adaptation, such as policies, infrastructure and governance, offer opportunities to examine how such measures may reduce or aggravate future climate change risks, and what enhances or detracts from living conditions, social well-being, economic development and ecosystems management.

Guangdong's development is being visibly shaped by efforts to reduce greenhouse gas emissions. In 2010, it became China's first *Low Carbon Development Pilot* province, and it accepted challenging targets for lowering the energy intensity of its growth. In contrast, actions to respond to climate impacts and prepare for the future are far less evident. Nonetheless, the provincial government views climate change adaptation processes as important and prioritises their incorporation into many aspects of provincial life. It has started to tackle the issue by creating institutions and policies, supporting specialised research and cooperating and communicating with other governments.

Guangdong's main planning body, the provincial Development and Reform Commission (DRC), has set up a division on resource efficiency, environment and climate to define responsibilities of relevant departments, and a new regional climate change network for South China provides a platform for inter-departmental communication and cooperation. A provincial plan for addressing climate change through both mitigation and adaptation was issued in January 2011 (Guangdong Provincial Government, 2011a).

Research institutes in Guangdong have contributed regional findings to the process of formulating the 2013 *National Adaptation Strategy* (NAS). Researchers have also compiled assessment reports on climate change in southern China region and Guangdong Province. Institutions such as the Guangdong Climate Centre, the provincial Centre for Disease Control and Prevention and Sun Yat-Sen University are undertaking government-funded studies of specific climate impacts and adaptation needs (Guangdong Provincial Government, 2011b). Some of this knowledge is being shared through international and regional exchanges – with the United Kingdom and United Nations agencies, for example. In a collaboration between Guangdong, Hong Kong and Macao, the three governments take turns holding workshops on climate change and forecasting in the Pearl River Delta, and they have cooperated extensively in climate data sharing and disaster prevention.

Guangdong has taken some concrete steps toward improving disaster risk reduction measures but has yet to mainstream climate change considerations into policy areas beyond health, agriculture, water resource management or disaster risk reduction (Du *et al.*, 2012). It released its provincial *Climate Change Programme* plans in 2011, with a primary focus on understanding socio-economic vulnerabilities to sea level rise, the impacts of climate change on extreme events (e.g. typhoons and flooding), salt water intrusion and health issues. Primary disaster risk reduction activities being undertaken in the province include improved disaster forecast and early warning systems, particularly around coastal hazards like flooding and typhoons. Forecasting accuracy for heavy rainfall events and typhoons had improved by 12% and 18% respectively by 2010 when compared with 2005. Emergency management capacity is being strengthened, and an emergency health plan was formulated to protect public health against high temperatures, flooding and typhoons. A broader range of water resource management measures is being implemented, from restoring coastal ecosystems and imposing rural drinking water safety measures to the reinforcement of dikes and upgrading of pumping infrastructure to reduce waterlogging in low-lying areas.

Researchers in the province are urging the government to act upon and strengthen the *Provincial Adaptation Strategy*. Currently, the DRC is awaiting further policy guidance from the National Development and Reform Commission before undertaking broader adaptation planning and mainstreaming climate change considerations into other sectors. The NAS names Guangdong as a pilot province for the establishment of urban disaster response systems for typhoons and storm surges. The focus of this NAS theme is to strengthen the monitoring, early warning and risk management of urban disasters, building upon the measures that Guangdong is already undertaking. Additionally, the guidelines include calls for the development of multi-sector emergency plans and greater public outreach and capacity building through programmes to educate about urban typhoon defence that will be disseminated in schools and communities. To ensure that the existing strategy is implemented, new policies are required that incorporate adaptation assessments into industry standards, construction of major projects and regional development planning at all levels. In spite of the development of policies, programmes and research projects around disaster risk reduction, environmental protection and climate adaptation planning, much work remains at the local and provincial levels before concepts and practices around resilience are regularly incorporated into other areas. Industry regulations, regional development plans and infrastructure projects and construction do not yet always incorporate disaster risk reduction or climate change considerations, and they are sometimes at odds with environmental protection policies.

Finally, Guangdong is an economic powerhouse. Socio-economic development inequalities create large vulnerability disparities within the province. The 3.16 million people living below the UN poverty line in Guangdong – most of them in the mountain areas – face different climate risks and challenges than more financially stable urban dwellers. Rapid development without adequate planning or environmental protections exacerbates ecosystem degradation and pollution, locking some parts of the province into development pathways that are not resilient to climate change or other shocks. The provincial disparities greatly increase the difficulty of implementing adaptation measures (GDCC, 2013).

Summary

The dense cities clustered on the Pearl River Delta have no easy remedies for the rising seas at their doorstep; heat waves, air, water and land pollution; or growing demands placed on limited supplies of water and electricity. Unregistered migrants are particularly vulnerable because they cannot officially access social and health services or other amenities that would build their adaptive capacity. Rural areas lag behind in socio-economic and infrastructural development. All areas are facing significant pollution, ecological degradation and loss of ecosystem services, but they experience differentiated impacts on livelihoods and well-being due to disparities. These challenges make it difficult to develop a coherent set of adaptation planning processes, policies and measures in Guangdong that address the disparate vulnerabilities and risks throughout the province.

Guangdong is extremely important to the regional and national economy; it can ill-afford not considering environmental protections, socio-economic development and building climate resilience. The province has begun instituting policies to address these complex issues in the past decade, but still has not formulated specific climate change adaptation plans. Mitigation and efforts to reduce air pollution burdens have entered the policy and public spheres, but adaptation does not yet play a significant role in social and economic development or discourse. Adapting to climate change is a long-term, iterative learning process. Adaptive planning will not only require improving the capabilities of key departments and vulnerable groups, but building wider societal awareness of climate change, land use development and broader socio-economic implications and actions to reduce these. Moreover, concepts of effective adaptation planning require restructuring and improvements in current governance, and social and economic development models toward more transformational adaptation change (see Chapters 1 and 2). The *Twelfth Five Year Plan* period is a crucial one for Guangdong to take the lead in building a more resilient and flexible society. It is also represents a period of strategic opportunity to rethink ecological and socio-economic development pathways, and begin addressing inequalities within the province. This period affords opportunities for Guangdong to formulate and implement strategy and adaptive planning for climate change, though many challenges remain.

Notes

1 The central government instituted a central, planned economy when it came to power and was worried that massive migrations to urban areas in search of better economic opportunity would result in a shortage of agricultural labour and food security issues. They established a system of household registration, the *hukou* system, to confine people to their birthplace and limit economic migration.
2 Guangdong Meteorological Bureau provided data from 76 weather stations covering the period 1961–2008; CMA provided tropical cyclone data.

References

Azzam, R., Strohschön, R., Baier, K., Lu, L., Wiethoff, K., Bercht, A. and Wehrhahn, R. (2014) Water quality and socio-ecological vulnerability regarding urban development in selected case studies of megacity Guangzhou, China. In: Kraas, F., Aggarwal, M., Mertins, G. (eds), *Megacities: Our Global Urban Future*. Springer: Berlin, Germany.

Bindoff, N.L., Willebrand, J., Artale, V., Cazenave, A., Gregory, J., Gulev, S., Hanawa, K., Le Quéré, C., Levitus, S., Nojiri, Y., Shum, C.K., Talley, L.D. and Unnikrishnan, A. (2007) Observations: Oceanic climate change and sea level. In: Solomon, S., Qin, D., Manning, M., Chen, Z., Marquis, M., Averyt, K.B., Tignor, M. and Miller, H.L. (eds), *Climate Change 2007: The Physical Science Basis. Contribution of Working Group I to the Fourth Assessment Report of the Intergovernmental Panel on Climate Change*. Cambridge University Press: Cambridge, United Kingdom and New York, New York, USA.

Chen, J., Taniguchi, M., Liu, G., Miyaoka, K., Onodera, S., Tonkunaga, T. and Fukushima, Y. (2007) Nitrate pollution of groundwater in the Yellow River delta, China. *Hydrogeology Journal*. 15. pp. 1605–1614.

Chen, J.H. and Lin, S.J. (2013) Seasonal predictions of tropical cyclones using a 25-km resolution general circulation model. *Journal of Climate*. 26. pp. 380–398.

Chen, X. and R. Greene (2012) The spatial-temporal dynamics of China's changing urban hierarchy (1950–2005). *Urban Studies Research*, 2012. art. 162965.

Chen, X., Fang, C. and Li, X. (2012) *Assessment Report of Climate Change Impacts on Water Resources in Guangdong and Adaptation Measures*. Sun Yat-Sen University (ACCC I Technical Report).

Cheng, X. and Qi, Y. (2007) Trends of sea level variations in the South China Sea from merged altimetry data. *Global and Planetary Change*. 57. pp. 371–382.

Church, J.A., Clark, P.U., Cazenave, A., Gregory, J.M., Jevrejeva, S., Levermann, A., Merrifield, M.A., Milne, G.A., Nerem, R.S., Nunn, P.D., Payne, A.J., Pfeffer, W.T., Stammer, D. and Unnikrishnan, A.S. (2013) Sea level change. In: Stocker, T.F., Qin, D., Plattner, G.K., Tignor, M., Allen, S.K., Boschung, J., Nauels, A., Xia, Y., Bex, V. and Midgley, P.M. (eds), *Climate Change 2013: The Physical Science Basis. Contribution of Working Group I to the Fifth Assessment Report of the Intergovernmental Panel on Climate*

Change. Cambridge University Press: Cambridge, United Kingdom and New York, New York, USA.

Church, J.A., White, N., Hunter, J. McInnes, K., Cowell, P. and O'Farrell, S. (2008) Sea level rise and the vulnerability of coastal environments. In: Newman, P.W. (ed.), *Transitions: Pathways Towards Sustainable Urban Development in Australia*. CSIRO Publishing: Melbourne, Australia.

Ding, S., Chen, Y., Wu, H., Li, Z. and Feng, L. (2007) Analysis of poverty and vulnerability and its determinants in rural Hubei. Presented at the 6th PEP Research Network General Meeting, Lima, Peru.

Du, B. (1997) *The Impact of Sea-Level Rise on Major Vulnerable Coastal Regions in China and Counter-Measures*. Ocean Press: Beijing, People's Republic of China.

Du, Q. (2011) Mainland China boasts more than 20,000 billionaires, while Guangdong has the largest number of multimillionaires. *Oriental Morning Post*. [Online] 21 April. Available from: http://money.jrj.com.cn/2011/04/2113549794016-1.shtml. [Accessed: 11 June 2014.]

Du, Y. (2007) Guangdong climate change assessment report. *Guangdong Meteorology*. 29 (3). pp. 1–14.

Du, Y. (2013) *Adaptation Strategic Research Report, and Roadmap for South China*. Guangdong Climate Centre (ACCC I Technical Report).

Du, Y., Liu, J., Zhao, X., Zeng, Y., Chen, X., Liu, B., Fang, C., Li, X., Tang, L., Li, C., Hu, Y., He, J., Ai, H., Duan, H., Zheng, J., Wang, B., Wu, X. and Zheng, D. (2012) *Final Report on Climate Disaster Risk Assessment and Adaptation Strategies for Guangdong*. Guangdong Climate Center.

Du, Y., Wang, X., Yang, X., Ma, W., Ai, H. and Wu, X. (2013) Impacts of climate change on human health and adaptation strategies in south China. *Advances in Climate Change Research*. 4 (4). pp. 208–214.

Emran, M.S. and Hou, Z. (2013) Access to markets and rural poverty: Evidence from household consumption in China. *Review of Economics and Statistics*. 95 (2). pp. 682–697.

Fan, S. and Zhang, X. (2004) Infrastructure and regional economic development in rural China. *China Economic Review*. 15. pp. 203–214.

Fan, X., Cui, B., Zhao, H., Zhang, Z. and Zhang, H. (2010) Assessment of river water quality in Pearl River Delta using multivariate statistical techniques. *Procedia Environmental Sciences*. 2. pp. 1220–1234.

GDASS (Guangdong Academy of Social Sciences) (2011) *Guangdong Socio-economic Scenario Construction Building* (ACCC I Technical Report).

GDCC (Guangdong Climate Centre) (2011) *Climate Change and Disaster Risk Reduction Report* (ACCC I Technical Report).

GDCC (Guangdong Climate Centre) (2013) *Guangdong Adaptation Planning Report* (ACCC I Technical Report).

Guang, L. (2005) Guerrilla workfare: Migrant renovators, state power, and informal work in urban China. *Politics and Society*. 33. pp. 481–506.

Guangdong Provincial Government (2011a) *Notice on Issuing the Climate Change Programme of Guangdong* (Notice No. (2011) 5).

Guangdong Provincial Government (2011b) *Notice on Issuing Guangdong's Twelfth Five Year Plan on Science and Technology Development* (Notice No. (2011) 84).

Halbrendt, C., Tuan, F., Gempesaw, C. and Dolk-Etz, D. (1994) Rural Chinese food consumption: The case of Guangdong. *American Journal of Agricultural Economics*. 76 (4). pp. 794–799.

Kanbur, R. and Zhang, X. (2004) *Fifty Years of Regional Inequality in China: A Journey Through Central Planning, Reform, and Openness.* United Nations University. [Online] Available from: www.wider.unu.edu/publications/working-papers/research-papers/2004/en_GB/rp2004-050/_files/78091746406106311/default/rp2004-050.pdf. [Accessed: 1 December 2014.] (UNU-WIDER Research Paper No. 2004/50.)

Li & Fung Research Centre (2012) *Consumption in Guangdong.* [Online] Available from: www.funggroup.com/eng/knowledge/research/china_dis_issue103.pdf. [Accessed: 30 September 2014.]

Li, Z. (2007) Protection of peasants' environmental rights during social transition: Rural regions in Guangdong Province. *Vermont Journal of Environmental Law.* 8. pp. 337–376.

Liao, F.H.F and Wei, Y.D. (2012) Dynamics, space, and regional inequality in provincial China: A case study of Guangdong Province. *Applied Geography.* 35. pp. 71–83.

Liu, H. (2006) Changing regional rural inequality in China 1980–2002. *Area.* 38 (4). pp. 377–389.

Lu, S. (2012) *Guangdong Province.* Consulate General of Switzerland in Guangzhou. [Online] Available from: www.dfae.admin.ch/etc/medialib/downloads/edactr/chn/gua.Par.0015.File.tmp/Guangdong%20Province.pdf. [Accessed: 30 September 2014.]

Oxfam (2004) *Trading Away Our Rights: Women Working in Global Supply Chains.* Oxfam International: Oxford, United Kingdom.

Pelling, H.E., Uehara, K. and Green, J.A.M. (2013) The impact of rapid coastline changes and sea level rise on the tides in the Bohai Sea, China. *Journal of Geophysical Research: Oceans.* 118. pp. 3462–3472.

Rhein, M., Rintoul, S.R., Aoki, S., Campos, E., Chambers, D., Feely, R.A., Gulev, S., Johnson, G.C., Josey, S.A., Kostianoy, A., Mauritzen, C., Roemmich, D., Talley, L.D. and Wang, F. (2013) Observations: Ocean. In: Stocker, T.F., Qin, D., Plattner, G.K., Tignor, M., Allen, S.K., Boschung, J., Nauels, A., Xia, Y., Bex, V. and Midgley, P.M. (eds), *Climate Change 2013: The Physical Science Basis. Contribution of Working Group I to the Fifth Assessment Report of the Intergovernmental Panel on Climate Change.* Cambridge University Press: Cambridge, United Kingdom and New York, New York, USA.

Sicular, T., Yue, X., Gustafsson, B. and Li, S. (2006) *The Urban–Rural Income Gap and Inequality in China.* United Nations University. [Online] Available from: www.wider.unu.edu/publications/working-papers/research-papers/2006/en_GB/rp2006-135/_files/78091820194269436/default/rp2006-135.pdf. [Accessed: 1 December 2014.] (UNU-WIDER Research Paper No. 2006/135.)

Solinger, D.J. (1993) China's transients and the state: A form of civil society? *Politics and Society.* 21. pp. 91–122.

South China Climate Change Assessment Report Writing Committee (SCCCAR) (2013) *Decision-Makers' Summary and Executive Summary of the South China Climate Change Assessment Report (2012).* China Meteorological Press: Beijing, People's Republic of China.

Wang, B. and X. Liyun (2013) Ecological management of Beijing–Tianjin–Hebei urban agglomeration: The tragedy of commons and system solution. *Journal of US–China Public Administration.* 10 (10). pp. 970–981.

Wei, Y. (2007) Rural–urban migrant workers in China: The vulnerable group in cities. Presented at 6th Berlin Roundtables on Transnationality on Population Politics and Migration: The Interdependence of Migration Politics and Demography, 14–19 February 2007. Irmgard Coninx Stiftung: Berlin, Germany. Available from: www.irmgard-coninx-stiftung.de/87.html. [Accessed: 3 April 2014.]

Wisner, B., Blaikie, P., Cannon, T. and Davis, I. (2003) *At Risk: Natural Hazards, People's Vulnerability and Disasters*, second edition. Routledge: London, United Kingdom.

Wong, K.T.M., Lee, J.H.W. and Harrison, P.J. (2009) Forecasting of environmental risk maps of coastal algal blooms. *Harmful Algae*. 8. pp. 407–420.

Yao, S., Zhang, Z. and Hanmer, L. (2004) Growing inequality and poverty in China. *China Economic Review*. 15. pp. 145–163.

Yokoi, S. and Takayabu, Y. (2013) Attribution of decadal variability in tropical cyclone passage frequency over the western North Pacific: A new approach emphasizing the genesis location of cyclones. *Journal of Climate*. 26. pp. 973–987.

Zhang, H.X. (1999) Female migration and urban labour markets in Tianjin. *Development and Change*. 30. pp. 21–41.

Zhang, Q.F. and Donaldson, J.A. (2010) From peasants to farmers: Peasant differentiation, labor regimes, and land-rights institutions in China's agrarian transition. *Politics and Society*. 38. pp. 458–489.

PART IV

Adaptation planning and policy in China

11

UNDERSTANDING CLIMATE RISK AND BUILDING RESILIENCE

Research and policy approaches in China

Rebecca Nadin, Sarah Opitz-Stapleton and Jia Wei

Introduction

China's sheer size, vast population and competing development priorities (whose pathways often contribute to severe environmental degradation), as well as increasing economic disparity across regions, are among the many challenges facing China's current leaders. As documented in the previous chapters, climate change presents an additional stressor. China has been subject to floods, droughts and heat waves for millennia; these hazards are not new. What is new is how rapidly climate risks are changing for different groups of people and sectors. This is due to the unprecedented rates of change in multiple processes – socio-economic development, migration, land use change, pollution and urbanisation – occurring alongside increasingly more intense and frequent weather hazards and shifts in seasons. China's people and ecosystems are facing dynamic pressures that threaten the progress made in lifting large segments of the population out of poverty. It is within this challenging context that China's policy makers, businesses and citizens must manage climate risk and build resilience.

China faces similar difficulties to other countries in grappling with climate risk and adaptation as a 'wicked challenge'. As discussed in Chapter 1, developing climate risk management and adaptation strategies and polices is difficult for a number of reasons, including: limited data records; low financial, computational and research capacity for conducting and understanding integrated risk assessments; over-reliance on technological and engineering solutions; and the necessity of cross-sector policies and actions that do not sit conveniently within any one government agency or research discipline. Adaptation planning for policy making requires significant investment of both human and financial resources, and many countries currently lack capacity in core areas needed for adaptation. Ensuring successful long-term adaptation is complex, as it involves trade-offs between certain actions. Even with the best data and intent, the results can lead to policies and actions that create maladaptive futures. The challenge for China, an emerging world power, is how to approach the risks and opportunities presented by climate change while also addressing long-term socio-economic needs — particularly the needs of diverse vulnerable populations — in more sustainable ways, despite an uncertain climate future.

This closing chapter documents the evolution of Chinese climate adaptation planning efforts, from approaches in assessment research to institutional arrangements and policy. It does so by examining assessment research methodologies and attitudes toward the environment and natural resource use, both of which underpin current policy and planning decisions. The chapter provides an overview of key adaptation policies that China has instituted at national to provincial scales in light of research priorities and concerns, such as those documented in the other chapters. The chapter covers some of the ongoing challenges to national and provincial adaptation policy and planning. It also highlights, and concludes with, China's emerging South–South climate policy and cooperation efforts in moving forward with treating adaptation as an iterative, cooperative process.

Providing the evidence base for adaptation policy and planning in China: current approaches and focus

Traditions and concepts: humankind versus nature

In order to fully understand China's approach to managing climate risk, it is important to appreciate historical Chinese concepts of the ideal relationship between humanity and the natural environment. Whilst Daoism and Buddhism have preached harmony with and respect for nature, imperial China often pursued a command-and-control relationship with nature (Elvin, 1998). An example of this approach is the massive, centuries-old flood control infrastructure highlighted in Chapter 4. Control over nature is also a theme in Chinese mythology, with mythical heroes such as the Great Yu and Gong Gong taming floods and controlling China's mighty rivers. As Elizabeth Economy (2010, p. 15) notes, 'China's current environmental situation is the result not only of policy choices made today but also of attitudes, approaches, and institutions that have evolved over the centuries'. More recently — after the formation of the People's Republic of China — Chairman Mao Zedong believed that by understanding the laws of nature, humankind could overcome them. In his speech at the inaugural meeting of the Natural Science Research Society of the Border Region in 1940, he said, 'For the purpose of attaining freedom from nature, man must use natural science to understand, conquer and change nature, and thus attain freedom from nature' (Economy, 2010, p. 48). Newspapers of the time frequently ran headlines such as 'The desert surrenders' and 'Chairman Mao's thoughts are our guide to scoring victories in the struggle against nature'. Nature was viewed as existing for 'exploitation at best, and an enemy to be conquered at worst' (Economy, 2010, p. 29).

Massive geo-engineering projects such as the Three Gorges Dam, first suggested by Sun Yat-Sen in 1919, is one of several such projects, another example being the South–North Water Transfer project, that were planned and developed under Chairman Mao Zedong. Mao saw the need to build a dam at the Yangtze River for flood control purposes and eventually electric power generation. Moreover, he believed that building the Three Gorges Dam would illustrate China's strong engineering capabilities in a period when China was isolated from the West. Following Mao's death in 1976, discussions about the feasibility of the project continued for another decade, largely among a few competing ministries and experts. In 1992, pushed by the then-Premier Li Peng, the project was rubber-stamped by the National People's Congress. Given public and scientific opposition to the dam due to environmental, economic and social impacts (Hvistendahl, 2008; Li *et al.*, 2001; Wu *et al.*, 2004), the decision to go ahead was clearly a political one. From the highest level of the Chinese government, developing a scientific approach to delivering China's development goals has been clearly advocated through high-level ideological campaigns such as Hu Jintao's 'Scientific Outlook on Development' (Hu, 2007). China is not alone in following a resource-depleting, rather than symbiotic, relationship with nature; this has been a common approach in the development pathways of many nations. What is unique is the role this relationship has played in establishing and exercising Chinese political power and ideology. To a certain extent this historical legacy continues to shape China's approach to adaptation planning, from risk assessment research to policy priorities and approaches.

The evidence base for adaptation policy and planning

In order to inform decision making, the evidence required must include 'decision determinants'. Developing national and provincial adaptation policy certainly requires a substantial amount of scientific and biophysical data, but also (and sometimes more importantly) socio-economic, environmental and political determinants – the other drivers of change. Some of the inherent challenges facing policy makers include: how to prioritise climate change issues within a range of competing political and developmental priorities; how to assess and integrate social and biophysical vulnerability and risk; how to assess the potential trade-offs, synergies and consequences of various choices; and how to provide information in a manner that builds public awareness, capacity and willingness to participate in adaptation initiatives. In China, providing the answer to these questions has traditionally been the responsibility of its universities and ministry-affiliated research institutions. Many of the researchers at these institutions are physical scientists and engineers whose academic background and experience, combined with the historical belief that humankind can overcome nature, have contributed to China's policy makers[1] viewing climate impacts assessments, risk mapping and adaptation needs as technical issues that can be tackled on a sector level (as reflected in the research priorities of the chapters in Part II). As demonstrated throughout this chapter, this approach has brought both benefits and challenges for adaptation policy and planning.

China began to research and assess the impacts of climate change in earnest through a nationally coordinated programme during the *Eighth* (1991–1995) and *Ninth* (1996–2000) *Five Year Plan* periods. More recently, China has started to build an extensive national research assessment programme, including the publication of *National Assessment Reports on Climate Change* (2007 and 2012), commissioned by the National Climate Change Coordination Committee. These priority sectors also receive a considerable amount of attention and funding from other government organisations and programmes, including the National Natural Science Foundation of China, the National Key Basic Research Development Programme (within the Ministry of Science and Technology) and the Inner Mongolia Meteorological Bureau.

In an attempt to provide policy-relevant scientific evidence and advice to the government, the informal National Advisory Committee on Climate Change (NACCC) was formed in 2005 by some of the country's top scientists. In 2007, the NACCC was granted official status under the National Leading Group. The role of the NACCC has been to coordinate scientific research on climate change, act as China's equivalent of the IPCC, and provide advice on the 'most fundamental, general and important aspects of China's climate change policy' (Wübbeke, 2013, p. 15). The creation of the NACCC can be regarded as a definite step towards providing the evidence base for China's domestic adaptation policy making. Certainly, in recent years, as highlighted in some of the sector chapters of this book, there has been a significant body of research focused on providing broad structural policy recommendations for climate change adaptation from a range of government institutions (Guo *et al.*, 2008; Xie *et al.*, 2009; Liu *et al.*, 2010). The Ministry of Science and Technology, the Chinese Academy of Sciences and the Chinese Academy of Agricultural Sciences have all drafted policy recommendations for the *National Assessment Reports* and the *National Adaptation Strategy* (NAS), published in 2013. China's National Natural Science Foundation and the National Key Basic Research Programme are also focused on creating a framework or structure for policy recommendations. Yet, a critical issue for future adaptation policy and risk mapping is the focus of the assessment research used to provide the evidence base for such recommendations.

As discussed in Chapter 1, there are two general approaches – biophysical and social – to assessing vulnerability and risk in a changing climate (Dessai and Hulme, 2004; Noble *et al.*, 2014) and providing evidence for adaptation policy recommendations and planning. The general approach in such assessments has been to downscale projections from multiple climate models to produce regional or local future climate scenarios that are then fed into biophysical impact models, such as crop yield or water resource models. From this phased approach, climate change impacts and risks for key sectors such as agriculture, animal husbandry and water resources are extrapolated, shifts in hazards like drought estimated, and various adaptation options and policies recommended. China, like many countries, has tended to take an impacts-based approach to adaptation policy and action which draws on its extensive physical science and engineering expertise and research (Moser, 2009; Hart *et al.*, 2012). Consequently, China's national and sector adaptation priorities and policies have tended to be based on a narrow view of climate change adaptation as one of disaster risk reduction and management in sectors like agriculture or water management (see Part II of this book). The result is that many of the climate risk policy recommendations call for and support engineering or technology-based adaptation actions (e.g. new water projects to 'control' flooding and drought, cloud seeding or shifting crop varieties to more drought and heat tolerant types) to the neglect of understanding societal implications or measures.

Research in non-traditional areas, such as the impact of climate change on human health, has only recently started to receive attention from Chinese scholars and funding from the government. Concern and increasing research attention are finally being paid toward understanding the relationships between climate, land use and development patterns and vector-borne diseases like dengue fever and schistosomiasis or heat stress (Yang *et al.*, 2010; Lu *et al.*, 2010). Chinese health-climate research still relies heavily on international sources, primarily literature reviews or overviews of the general state of understanding of the impact of climate change on human health (Zhou, 2006). Previous research has generally not been specific to China, but − as highlighted in Chapter 7 − it is starting to emerge.

Research into the impacts of climate change on social stability and harmony is also still limited. Leading scholars such as Lin Erda, a member of the Chinese People's Political Consultative Conference (CPPCC) Standing Committee and contributor to the Intergovernmental Panel on Climate Change (IPCC), has expressed his concern regarding climate change impacts on agricultural output and rural development. In the medium- to long-term, severe shortages in food, water and energy supplies could occur, which could potentially be a threat to social stability and national security (Freeman, 2010; Beddington *et al.*, 2011; Hung and Tsai, 2012). Social stability has been considered in relation with other factors, such as economic stability, food security and political stability, but such studies are generally quite broad (Liu *et al.*, 2006). Research into specific climate change impacts is just emerging (Werz and Reed, 2014; Moore, 2009).

Migration is a strong force shaping China's social, cultural and economic futures; it is driving rates of urbanisation and land use change (see Chapters 6,

8 and 9). Research on disaster-forced migration or climate change impacts on planned migration have only recently started being published and tend to deal with definitions and characteristics (Hu and Shu, 2010; Shi *et al.*, 2009). There is research concerning disaster-forced migration, but this is general and does not make the connection to climate change; or, if there is a connection made, it is based on historical data and concerns major social migration patterns from the past (Wang *et al.*, 1996; Zhang and Wu, 1999). While some of the migration is planned, like Ningxia's ecological migration programmes (see Chapter 8), many households are migrating to cities within their province or in neighbouring provinces without government intervention (see Chapters 2, 9 and 10). There is quite a bit of research on migration push-pull factors and its potential implications for China (Shi *et al.*, 2009; Fan, 2003; Wang *et al.*, 2011), but this research does not investigate the potential of climate change as a push factor and has yet to be integrated into the socio-economic and bio-physical assessments that are informing adaptation policies. Clearly, this is still a nascent topic in Chinese scholarship and its future course is unpredictable, depending on both China's policy directives and the prevalence of disaster-forced migration.

China's social research capacity to inform adaptation policy regarding social vulnerability remains weak, particularly in how different vulnerabilities among groups of people and economic sectors give rise to disparate climate risks. This is because Chinese social science research for adaptation planning tends to focus more on assessing the economic impacts of existing hazards and potential climate changes on livelihoods, production and sectors – but it does not yet fully account for social or cultural behaviours influencing, or being influenced by, climate change. Social science research on the potential impacts of various policies (e.g. agriculture, ecological compensation or large-scale infrastructure development) on social vulnerability does not currently have a significant influence on adaptation planning and policy development within China.

Socio-economic and cultural processes like the ones mentioned above are core determinants of China's future development pathways, and they will shape its future vulnerabilities. These attitudes and methodologies have, to a certain extent, already shaped both its development pathways and its approaches toward adaptation planning and policy. A strong focus on biophysical impacts, engineering or technology-based approaches is unsurprising, as China's strong physical science capacities are juxtaposed with weaker capacity in social science research for adaptation policy and planning.[2] With current Chinese adaptation assessment research focusing predominantly on estimating future biophysical impacts and understanding shifts in seasons and hazard (extreme and slow-onset) intensity and frequency, understanding people's vulnerability and climate risks remains limited. Whilst there is growing awareness of the climate change impacts on socio-economic systems, work to develop comprehensive socio-economic vulnerability profiles in this area is just emerging. More detailed assessments of biophysical and socio-economic impacts on livelihoods, production and infrastructure, and the planning and construction of major projects, are needed to inform and prioritise potential response strategies. Resulting adaptation policies and plans do not yet adequately account for social implications or feasibility.

The next section provides an overview of key institutional arrangements and adaptation policies that China has instituted at different levels in light of the aforementioned research priorities and concerns.

Chinese government institutional arrangements and policies relating to adaptation

In addition to a multidiscipline evidence base to support decision making, building a climate resilient society requires institutional arrangements and robust polices to manage current and future climate risk. This is a challenging proposition for any nation and China is no exception. China's leadership faces the challenge of devising adaptation policies and actions that address the needs and vulnerabilities of both highly urbanised and underdeveloped rural areas. Simultaneously, it must adapt to climate change in a manner that is more proactive than reactive to disaster impacts. Since 2006, the publication of the *National Assessment Report on Climate Change* and an increase in extreme weather event impacts around the country have led to the central government seeking to develop institutional and policy approaches for addressing emergent climate risks.[3] This section aims to provide an overview of the evolution of China's government institutions and domestic adaptation policy through the lens of basic national polices, communications and provincial government policy documents. This section does not cover China's policy approach to adaptation within the international climate change negotiations, but it does offer a brief overview of China's emerging climate change South–South cooperation strategy.

Adaptation institutional arrangements

In response to the 1992 United Nations Framework Convention on Climate Change (UNFCCC), the Chinese government began to set up institutional mechanisms to provide the expertise and information needed to support policy making, as well as cross-ministry mechanisms and technical bodies to coordinate work across sectors. Initially, the State Meteorological Administration (SMA, now the China Meteorological Administration under the State Council) was responsible for climate change-related issues (primarily mitigation and climate analysis and projection research). The SMA was a key player in the coordination of China's early climate change research and its participation in the IPCC and other international scientific programmes, and it was responsible for the implementation of China's UNFCCC commitments post-ratification.

In 1998, responsibility for climate change issues within China was given to the State Development Planning Commission, now the National Development and Reform Commission (NDRC). The NDRC is China's macro-level economic planning body whose primary task is formulating and implementing medium- and long-term national and social development plans. To this end, the NDRC, with input from line ministries, is also responsible for the drafting and submission of China's *Five Year Plans* for national economic and social development to the National People's Congress on behalf of the State Council. It is a powerful body with wide-ranging responsibility for major economic development and fiscal and financial management in China. This responsibility shift to the NDRC reflected changing perceptions about the importance of climate change from a principally scientific concern to an economic development and political issue (Heggelund *et al.*, 2010). As understanding of the complex nature and seriousness of climate change and its implications for China grew, further shifts in governmental institutions and roles occurred.

In 2003, the National Coordination Committee on Climate Change (NCCCC) was established under the State Council, although it is housed in and chaired by NDRC (Held *et al.*, 2011). The NCCCC's primary work focused on the formulation and coordination of climate change-related policies and measures, and providing guidance to the central and local governments' responses to climate change. In order to fulfil China's commitment under the UNFCCC, the NCCCC organised the work on the compilation of the *Initial National Communication on Climate Change of the People's Republic of China* and presented the report to UNFCCC at the tenth session of the Conference of the Parties (COP 10) in December 2004 (NDRC, 2004).

In 2007, the NCCCC was replaced by the National Leading Group to Address Climate Change, which was chaired by then Premier Minister Wen Jiabao. The role of the Group is to coordinate 27 different government agencies and – much like that of its predecessors – to make major decisions and to coordinate national actions on climate change. It has considerably strengthened capacity and decision-making power compared to previous incarnations (Held *et al.*, 2011). The inter-ministry nature of the group demonstrates that Chinese leadership understands the importance of taking a cross-sector approach to responding to climate change (see Figure 11.1).

Also in 2007, China elevated the status of climate change within the NDRC from an office to a department. The principal responsibilities of the Department of Climate Change within the NDRC are to:

- comprehensively analyse climate change impacts on economic and social development and organise the formulation, coordination and drafting of major climate change strategies, planning and policies;

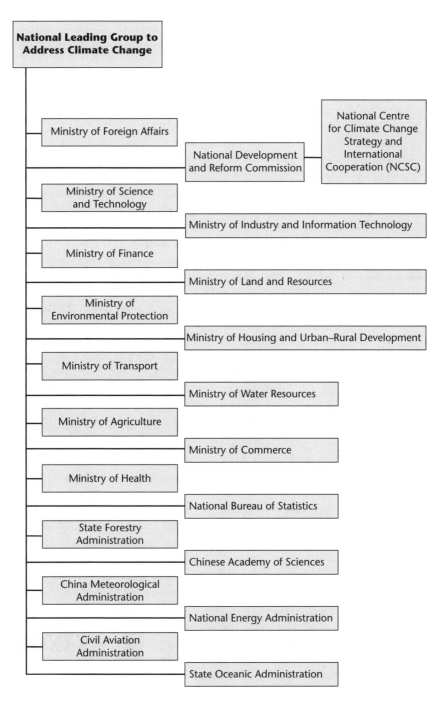

FIGURE 11.1 The structure of the National Leading Group to Address Climate Change (source: NDRC, 2014)

- take the lead in fulfilling China's commitment to UNFCCC and in organising participation in and leading discussions in joint international climate change negotiations;
- coordinate international climate change cooperation and capacity-building work;
- organise the implementation of Clean Development Mechanism related work; and
- undertake the routine work of National Leading Group on Climate Change.

The initial rationale for the establishment of China's climate-related institutional arrangements was primarily to facilitate China's emissions reduction efforts and manage its international responses. However, the need for these institutions to take into account adaptation issues is increasingly evident.

The overall planning of national and provincial adaptation work is the responsibility of NDRC. The Department of Climate Change within the NDRC reports to the Office of National Climate Change Leading Group. It is composed of five divisions: the Division of Strategy and Planning; the Division of General (and Comprehensive) Affairs; the Division of Domestic Policies and Compliance; the Division of International Policies and Negotiations; and the Division of International Cooperation. Whilst there is no specific division dedicated to adaptation, the department does have officials assigned to work on adaptation policy formulation and coordination, including South–South cooperation on climate change.

However, other ministries and administrations, such as the Ministry of Agriculture, Ministry of Water Resources, Ministry of Health, Ministry of Housing and Rural Development, China Meteorology Administration, State Forestry Administration and State Oceanic Administration participate in adaptation planning, consultation and preparation. They are supported by a number of decision support agencies, including the National Climate Centre, Chinese Academy of Agricultural Sciences, Chinese Academy of Social Sciences and the Economic Development Research Centre of the Provincial Development and Reform Commission.

As the principal agency responsible for adaptation work, the NDRC has set a number of priorities for itself in supporting national- and local-level processes. The first priority for the NDRC is to continue to advocate for climate adaptation and sustainable development, and to ensure that they are mainstreamed within the *Five Year Planning* process. NDRC's second priority is to secure ongoing funding for implementation of adaptation plans from the Ministry of Finance (see the finance section of this chapter, p. 315) and international platforms such as the Strategic Climate Fund (SCF), the Special Climate Change Fund (SCCF),[4] and to seek grants from, and continue to build international cooperation platforms with, developed countries. Perhaps the most important priority for NDRC is to raise the profile of adaptation and strengthen capacity for implementation at the provincial levels.

Presently, climate adaptation is not universally seen as a priority task for provincial leaders; this is perhaps a reflection of historical national policy foci of mitigation and energy efficiency efforts at the local level. As a result, while many provinces have pilot programmes for low carbon or clean development mechanism development within their *Five Year Plans*, limited attention has been given to adaptation. For example, although some sectoral agencies in Yunnan are engaged in adaptation-related activities (e.g. crop breeding), there is no integrated planning at the provincial level. Instead, the focus of Yunnan Development and Reform Commission has been on implementing low-carbon development activities, and adaptation has not been a priority. This is beginning to change, as some provinces (including Yunnan) have been listed pilot provinces in the NAS (NDRC, 2013).

The development of national adaptation policy

Internationally, China has advocated mitigation and adaptation with equal emphasis; domestically, however, much of the focus of China's climate policy has been largely on mitigation. This focus on emissions reduction is in line with Beijing's desire for greater energy security and the need to build a more energy-efficient growth model. Perhaps reflecting the growing importance of adaptation within the international climate negotiations, including China's position within the G77 (in which adaptation is a critical area of discussion) and the deepening understanding of China's own domestic vulnerability, the need for comprehensive adaptation polices has started to move up the domestic political agenda since 2009. The need for national and provincial policy processes also reflects greater focus on climate change adaptation financing in the international climate change negotiations, as well as deeper understanding by the central government leaders of the true economic costs of climate change for core sectors.

Before reflecting upon China's climate change (and, more specifically, adaptation) policy development, it is useful to examine what is meant by policy. In the academic literature and government documents, terms such as *plans*, *strategies* and *policies* are often used interchangeably, but they may in fact have different levels of scope, purpose and legal enforcement. Policy can be 'substantive', stating what a government intends to do, or 'procedural', indicating how something will be done and who will do it. The reality in China is that whilst policy can be a combination of 'substantive' and 'procedural', it is often more a set of guiding principles or general direction than it is prescriptive. This is certainly true of its adaptation policy at the present time. China's climate change polices should be viewed as basic national policies designed to address long-term problems in China's economic and social development in the short to mid-term (within the next 5–30 years).

*China's Agenda 21 White Paper: China's Population, Environment and Develop-
ment in the 21st Century* (referred to hereafter as 'Agenda 21') was released in
1994 and marked the first of China's policies to examine sustainable development through the lens of climate change. It set out policy for long-term sustainable development and is still considered to be China's overall guideline for
national development (PRC State Planning Commission and PRC State
Science and Technology Commission, 1994). It was also the first official
document to declare support for climate change impact research, and it established the basis of current research efforts. Since 1994, China has published a
number of white papers, national communications and policy documents relat-
ing to climate change. While the majority of these instruments (with the exception of the NAS) are not adaptation policy documents specifically, they indicate
a greater scientific understanding by policy makers of both the observed and
future biophysical impacts of climate change, as well as potential required
adaptation measures. Some notable examples are listed in Table 11.1.

China's National Adaptation Strategy

Building upon all of these previous efforts, China released its NAS in 2013 at
COP 19 in Warsaw, Poland. It is the result of more than two challenging years
of work by 12 ministries and government agencies, including the China Meteorological Agency and Ministry of Agriculture, and was coordinated by the
NDRC. The NAS is arguably the most important Chinese policy to date
related to climate adaptation efforts in the country, because it provides the
macro-policy framework for the drafting of *Urban and Provincial Adaptation Plans*
and moves China's adaptation response beyond assessment to the development
of implementable policies. No simple association can be made between socio-
economic status or regional economic development and levels of vulnerability
or risk. However, the NAS is an attempt at the policy level to provide a framework and set of guiding principles for provincial governments and line ministries. However, NDRC officials are keen to emphasise that the strategy is not
a plan, but rather an outline of work that will take time to implement (Sun,
2014).

As seen throughout this book, uneven development and regional diversity
make it impossible for China to approach adaptation on a solely national level.
As previously discussed in Chapters 8 and 9, levels of vulnerability and climate
risk are highly disparate even within a province. Thus, the NAS represents a
monumental effort to provide guidance at a number of administrative levels
while affording each level the flexibility it needs to modify policies, actions and
principles according to specific local contexts and capacities.[5] The NAS also
treats adaptation planning as a learning process at multiple levels, having designated a number of provinces and autonomous regions as pilots for testing practices and recording experiences related to adaptation measures in the sectors

TABLE 11.1 Notable Chinese white papers, national communications and policy documents related to climate change

Initial National Communication on Climate Change of the People's Republic of China (2004)	First assessment report on observed and projected climate change impacts on water resources, agriculture, terrestrial ecosystems and coastal zones.
1st and 2nd *National Assessment Report on Climate Change* (2006 and 2011)	Broader assessment of climate change impacts on ecosystems and socio-economic development, including human health issues, impacts on major development projects and energy security. Reports also examine regional impact disparities due to geographic and socio-economic variance.
National Climate Change Programme (2007)	Policy document outlining China's specific objectives, key action areas, and policies and measures to address climate change to 2010. The programme also emphasised targeted local mitigation and adaptation actions.
Eleventh Five Year Plan (2006–2010)	The Ministry of Science and Technology releases a report summarising new knowledge on key vulnerable sectors – agriculture, water resources, forestry, human health, biodiversity, urban development, environmental protection – and tasks and action plan recommendations for adaptation, as well as potential challenges.
Twelfth Five Year Plan (2011–2015)	National goals for sustainable development are released that prioritise adaptation alongside mitigation for the first time.
National Plan for Climate Change (2014–2020)	The plan provides guidance to assist China in meeting its 2020 Copenhagen commitments and outlines adaptation efforts through to 2020. ACCC I is cited as a successful example in the field of adaptation.
National Adaptation Strategy (2013)	Main Chinese policy related to climate adaptation efforts in the country. It provides the macro-policy framework for the drafting of Provincial Adaptation Plans (PAP).

outlined. China has a long history of using pilot projects to test programmes and policies in some areas before modifying and scaling them to the rest of the country, and the NAS continues this tradition. Pilot provinces include: Chongqing (Three Gorges area), Guangdong, Guangxi, Hainan, Hebei, Heilongjiang, Inner Mongolia, Jiangxi, Jilin, Ningxia, Shanghai, Sichuan and Xinjiang. Each pilot has a specific sector focus, which means guidance and support from relevant line ministries is also required. The strategy further divides the country into regions, with a critical focus on urban areas, agriculturally important regions and ecological zones currently most threatened by degradation or deemed extremely vulnerable to climate change, such as the northern sand shelterbelts.

This high-level policy document identifies the guiding objectives, priority work areas and pilot provinces in which various adaptation policies and actions are to be trialled by 2020. The overall strategic objectives of the NAS focus around building China's adaptation capacities and responses. The first objective of the NAS calls for 'anticipatory' adaptation approaches that encompass more capacity building and vulnerability reduction in at-risk populations and the climate-sensitive sectors of the primary work areas (listed below). Under this objective, enhanced monitoring networks and early warning systems to reduce losses caused by extreme events and climate change are to be strengthened. It also calls for more locally targeted and relevant adaptation measures that account for regional differences in socio-economic development, technical capacity and environmental conditions. In recognition of some of the limits of current institutional arrangements, the second objective of the NAS focuses on enhancing synergy and collaboration between different ministries, agencies, research institutes and community networks at various scales and across sectors. As discussed in several chapters, lack of coordination and communication between these different adaptation stakeholders has been problematic in previous adaptation and disaster risk reduction efforts. The final objective mandates the facilitation of broad engagement, from increasing public awareness and capacity building to enhancing international cooperation at various levels, including strengthening South–South cooperation.

The strategic objectives of the NAS are to be realised through three primary work areas: strengthening capacities to address climate change risks in the priority sectors of agriculture, water resources, forestry and ecological systems, tourism, human health, coastal zones and maritime waters and other industries; elevating the importance of disaster risk reduction and mitigation; and reducing economic losses and human and asset damages triggered by extreme weather events and shifting climate. These three primary work areas are reflected in the research conducted for the chapters in Parts II and III of this book.

Under the NAS, the NDRC and provincial and local development and reform authorities (DRCs) are responsible for the organisation and coordination of the National Adaptation Strategy, Urban Adaptation Plans and PAPs and mainstreaming these within the *Five Year Planning* process. The NAS provides guidance on policies and institutional arrangements to local governments, agencies and authorities for adaptation to climate change. It mandates them to align existing policies and institutions to the strategy, develop work mechanisms, funding policies, technical support and international cooperation systems to ensure adaptation actions. Through the NAS, China's ministries and provinces are required to develop PAPs, making provincial adaptation planning compulsory and moves China's adaptation responses from a strategic level to one of implementation.

Provincial adaptation planning

The NAS requires provinces, autonomous regions, municipalities and the Xinjiang Production and Construction Corporation to develop provincial climate change adaptation action plans in accordance with the principles laid out in the national strategy, and to oversee their implementation. It is recognised that a number of ministries and research institutions from a variety of sectors such as environmental protection, water, agriculture, health, forestry, coastal zones and meteorology will need to work together. Some provinces have already established provincial leading groups, headed by the provincial governor and consisting of all the heads of provincial government organisations including local Development and Reform Commissions (DRCs), Environmental Protection Bureaus, Metrological Bureaus and Financial Bureaus (NDRC, 2012). The provincial leading group takes responsibility for implementing national climate change policies and drawing up work plans for relevant agencies to act. For example, Inner Mongolia has set up a provincial climate change leading group in which 26 provincial departments are represented. Inner Mongolia Meteorology Bureau has also set up a Climate Centre, which houses an Ecology and Agriculture Climate Centre. Inner Mongolia University often plays the role of 'think tank' for the provincial DRC. Within specific sectors, however, other provincial institutes may be preferred sources of policy advice.

The provincial and regional DRCs, with guidance from NDRC, are now expected to play a key role in developing and implementing provincial adaptation action plans. The DRCs will coordinate the assessment research, identify priority areas and make recommendations for adaptation policies and actions to address those; the combined information will be submitted as plans to the provincial government. The provincial government is then responsible for deciding what options to issue (either on behalf of provincial government or in the name of development and reform commission) as policy, and what to implement.

China's administrative framework is particularly relevant in terms of policy making and implementation from the central government down to the local level. It is easy to regard administration in China as a simplistic model of top-down governance. Certainly, the *Five Year Planning* process and ten-year leadership cycles facilitate top-level policy making. However, regional differences and provincial administrative systems make implementation of top-level policies difficult. The coordination and implementation of national and provincial polices across administrative divisions can be convoluted, involving numerous actors. At the local level there are prefectures, autonomous prefectures, autonomous counties and county level administrations, which means the provincial government also requires the support of the prefecture level for implementation.

The entire provincial adaptation planning process is expected to occur over an 18-month time period, from applying for approval to initiating the plan to submission to the provincial government for approval. Many provinces are beginning preparations for the *Thirteenth Five Year Plan* (2016–2020), with some (like Guizhou) beginning work on its PAP in 2014. Table 11.2 highlights some of the adaptation-related policies and planning that has been occurring in select provinces.

Adaptation is not being uniformly addressed or integrated by the provinces into their *Five Year* socio-economic development policies or planning. The NDRC acknowledges that many provincial and local officials lack capacity for adaptation planning processes and, as such, will be responsible for strengthening local capacity, especially in vulnerability and risk assessment and moving from these to policies and planning. It aims to support the provinces through training, multimedia communication and study visits. These provincial-level challenges are discussed in greater detail in subsequent sections. However, some provinces, like Ningxia and Inner Mongolia, are further along than others. This is why those two provinces featured so strongly throughout this book (see Chapters 5, 6, 8 and 9). Both provinces are addressing climate change adaptation within their existing planning systems, although Inner Mongolia's plan also accounts for mitigation, which remains a dominant concern outside of animal husbandry and grassland management. These two provinces' policies and activities around climate adaptation planning, policies and actions are detailed in the aforementioned chapters.

TABLE 11.2 Climate adaptation-related policies and plans in select provinces

Ningxia	Inner Mongolia	Jilin
Eleventh Five Year Plan is concerned with increasing disaster risk.	2010 *Autonomous Region Implementation Plan on Climate Change* with focus on grassland management and disaster risk reduction.	2008 *Climate Change Plan*, with climate change leading group investigating adaptation and mitigation. Adaptation still limited – focus of disaster risk reduction.
2009 *Ningxia Climate Change programme.*		
Twelfth Five Year Plan includes climate change in key sectors – ecological migration, development, water resources, and weather-disaster monitoring and risk reduction.	Climate adaptation funding only mentioned in meteorology sector of the *Twelfth Five Year Plan.*	No explicit adaptation plan, climate change integrated into sector *Five Year Plans* like agriculture (e.g. efficient irrigation, crop varieties).
NAS asks Ningxia to focus on ecological migration to reduce population pressures, introduce climate-resilient livelihood practices in ecologically vulnerable areas.	Multiple policy statements stressing need to improve agro-meteorology services, disaster risk monitoring and assessment of climate change impacts.	NAS asks Jilin to improve 'blackland' soil conservation and soil fertility restoration in major grain producing areas.
	NAS asks Inner Mongolia to protect and restore degraded grasslands, promote resilient animal husbandry practices.	

Jilin province does not have an explicit adaptation plan but integrates climate change concerns in its *Five Year Plans* in each sector (e.g. plans for agriculture that highlight adaptation options such as varietal breeding and water-saving irrigation). Perhaps reflecting some of the capacity issues regarding adaptation planning, the plans for Jilin were reportedly drafted within one week by biophysical scientists with no economics or social research input.[6] The focus of the NAS for Jilin is on peatland conservation. Other provinces listed as pilots within the NAS are at various stages of adaptation planning, and coordinating ministries and research institutes to generate the information are needed to support policies.

Domestic adaptation financing

Building a climate-resilient society requires financial capital and robust management systems to allocate and manage adaptation finance; these arrangements are led by the NDRC and Ministry of Finance within China. Within the Ministry of Finance, the Economic Construction Department is responsible for working with NDRC and other ministries on formulating investment policies, and provides recommendations on annual budget and earmarked expenditure for climate-related investment projects (mostly involving purchase of long-term physical assets, capital improvement and the rehabilitation of physical assets that enhance or extend their useful life. Other departments involved include the Budget Department and the Treasury Department. In addition to the Climate Change Department, there are a number of departments within NDRC that are involved in mobilising climate-related public finance:

- The Department of Fixed-Asset Investment is in charge of coordinating with relevant ministries in drafting plans for the central government to invest in fixed assets in the area of climate change.
- The Department of Resource Conservation and Environmental Protection is responsible for providing recommendations on arranging central government finance for resource conservation and environmental protection.
- The Finance Department is involved in ascertaining the total size and the use of climate-related construction budget and different subsidies.

At the international level, China has made its position clear that funding, technology and capacity-building for developing nations should be supported by developed countries. On a domestic level, it is increasingly evident that China's adaptation needs cannot be met within current budget frameworks. A recent report by the Climate Group (2013, p. 7) concluded that

> China's public investment in climate change related activities represents a significant proportion of total spending. In 2012, it was estimated that US$26 billion of public funds were spent, accounting for 20% of the total volume of nationwide climate related investment.

The central government recognises the need for increased financial resourcing to build a robust and climate-resilient society and economy. The NAS outlines a number of fiscal and financial policy support priorities, including:

- the availability of public financial resources to ensure a reliable source of funding for state-level adaptation actions, consisting of:
  - ○ increased financial support for adaptation capacity building and major technological innovations and completion of adaptation tasks in key fields and regions;
  - ○ clarification of jurisdiction and responsibility for adaptation to climate change to determine the expenditure responsibilities between central and local authorities; and
  - ○ an appropriate exemption of economically underdeveloped regions from adaptation financial expenditure burdens by way of existing policies and funding channels.
- climate finance markets to encourage the development of climate-related services and products and applicable tax incentives, which might entice various market players to engage more in adaptation;
- risk-sharing mechanisms to support the development of insurance products in agriculture, forestry and other fields and related insurance operations; and
- a platform to manage international adaptation funding facilitating the use and management of funds for international cooperation.

However, the total volume of public finance to be committed remains uncertain over the short to medium term. The NDRC has informally disclosed that around US$160 billion of public investment will be made across the *Twelfth Five Year Plan* period (2011–2015), which is expected to leverage an additional US$634 billion in capital. However, the precise arrangements for raising these funds – and how they will be used – remain unclear.

Beijing has been contributing funds to climate change, but it is unclear how much and how these public funds will be used for adaptation. As discussed throughout this book, China has started to move towards the development of sectorial, provincial and national adaptation polices. However, implementation has been slow due to limited financial inputs from central government. For example, the *Emergency Response Law of the People's Republic of China* implemented in 2007 explicitly outlined the principle of providing an insurance system against natural disaster loss backed by the state's financial allocations. Unfortunately, the *Emergency Response Law* was hamstrung by the lack of necessary funds. While China has sought funding for technical assistance from a number of developed countries and has also applied for and received funding for adaptation projects from the Global Environment Facility, this amounts to only a few million dollars, rather than the hundreds of millions needed.

At present, there are no specific adaptation funds available to provinces. For example, in Jilin and Inner Mongolia, where adaptation needs and costs could potentially place an increased burden on already indebted provincial govern-ment budgets, no specific funding for adaptation assessments or planning can be identified. As a result, provinces are utilising other funding streams for adaptation-related work. This funding comes from a variety of channels such as national research funding (usually administered by the Ministry of Science and Technology or its affiliated institutions) and money allocated under the *Five Year Planning* budgets.[7] In Inner Mongolia, climate change adaptation related funding is only mentioned in the Inner Mongolia Meteorology *Twelfth Five Year Plan*, including impact assessments and adaptation assessments as well as climate services. This implies that funding for provincial agencies and research institutes will be available for this research.

An important development is that the Ministry of Finance's 2015 budget now contains a specific line for climate change. Prior to 2015, climate change had not been mainstreamed into the budgetary process. It is still unclear how available funds will be divided between mitigation and adaptation activities and needs. There is also no national definition for climate expenditure, making tracking resources allocated for financing climate-related efforts difficult. In addition, there is no mechanism at present for gathering climate finance statistics from central and provincial government departments that would allow tracking and monitoring of spending of funds, which have not been categorised under special climate accounts in the national budget. How China finances its adapta-tion response is one of the ongoing adaptation challenges for Beijing.

Ongoing challenges to national and provincial adaptation planning

As highlighted throughout this book, China is one country with disparate adaptation needs, profiles and responses. Though it has made significant progress in recent years in building its capacity to respond to climate change, a number of challenges on multiple levels of governance remain to developing and imple-menting adaptation policies and actions. These challenges are openly acknow-ledged by NDRC and are listed as priority concerns in the NAS. Examples of some challenges are documented in Table 11.3 and are detailed further in the sections following.

Data and knowledge gaps

As discussed earlier in this chapter, China's largest data and knowledge gaps lie in socio-economic and policy analysis and information. Because of this, the social, policy and economic aspects of adaptation have received less research attention. Consequently, reliable data on social vulnerability indicators or

TABLE 11.3 Some adaptation planning-to-policy development and implementation challenges at national and provincial levels. These challenges were mentioned during interviews and discussions with the NDRC, research institutions and provincial policy makers

Data and knowledge gaps	• Lack of access to user-friendly climate scenario data • Lack of socio-economic impact data and cost–benefit analysis of adaptation measures at both macro and micro levels • Lack of funding for integrated climate risk research • Limited understanding of climate risk beyond biophysical impacts
Communication challenges	• Scientist to end user • Misunderstanding of policy cycles and decision maker needs
Weak local capacity	• Uncertainty among provincial decision makers regarding the scope and severity of climate change impacts, and underlying vulnerability conditions • Institutional, governance and regulatory weakness • Lack of provincial adaptation-specific finance

disaster losses are lacking at some levels. Cost analyses of adaptation measures, especially in the agriculture sector, present another gap.

Deficiencies remain in assessing how local communities and governments make decisions regarding adaptation; understanding community-based knowledge and experiences around impacts and autonomous adaptation measures; and integrating these into provincial or higher policy levels. In the past, the traditional knowledge and experiences of the land and the environment by ethnic minority groups was not considered scientifically sound by researchers or policy makers. Things are changing slowly, as seen in the chapters on Ningxia and Inner Mongolia (Chapters 8 and 9), with more emphasis now being placed on engaging such groups in adaptation processes. However, a systematic analysis of existing local adaptation knowledge, traditional ecological knowledge and practices and household- and community-level opportunities and constraints is still needed to inform policies from the local to national levels. Finally, the lack of policy research to understand the design and fit of processes and institutional arrangements for mainstreaming adaptation into development makes it difficult for decision makers to know what strategies are relevant and effective at different entry points.

Though many efforts have been made to increase data and knowledge gaps in vulnerability and risk assessments in order to craft adaptation policies and options, significant gaps remain. In remote areas, meteorological and environmental monitoring are limited, as are data records for assessing hazard trends, losses and damages. Socio-economic data collected at the local level is not always consistent with provincial or national level aggregate data in certain regions; historical data is even more lacking (Zhou *et al.*, 2014). Beyond data and assessment gaps, much of the emergent information from the assessments is still too complex to be readily integrated into provincial- or local-level adaptation planning efforts, let alone understood or communicated to certain decision makers or the general public.

Communicating challenges

Some of the data and knowledge gaps are due to critical communication gaps that exist between the central government, social and physical scientists, provincial and local governments and the general public. These communication issues are not unique to China; many are similar to those in other countries (Opitz-Stapleton *et al.*, 2010; Pennesi, 2007). Historically, scientific institutions like climate information providers tended not to work across scientific disciplines, causing unfamiliarity with research methods, terminology and methods of data interpretation from other disciplines (Bray and von Storch, 2009; Gay and Estrada, 2010). Scientists are also often used to providing a range in their estimates of future projections, scenarios and impacts that represent uncertainty, and they are occasionally wrong in their estimates of actual climate impacts. Lack of consistency between scientists in different disciplines in communicating information and uncertainty can be confusing to policy makers and non-technical stakeholders, hampering adaptation efforts.

At the same time, low science literacy among some policy makers and the general public means that information may not be perceived as relevant or may be considered contradictory and unreliable. Scientists themselves, in conducting highly specialised research, are frequently unaware of linkages to other fields, policy processes or how to relate their work to public needs and concerns. Clearer distinction between what is relevant and effective at different entry points is still needed. For example, provincial planning requires expert consultation with high-level decision makers and integration into existing planning cycles; detailed vulnerability and risk assessment may be unrealistic due to local capacity and the timing of policy cycles. It also means that the scientific evidence base offered for crafting adaptation policies is sometimes too narrow, and the resulting policies themselves are limited. Furthermore, monitoring and evaluation systems to test the efficacy of policy-ready adaptation recommendations is currently lacking at the science–policy interface.

Provincial decision maker capacity

The NDRC acknowledges that many provincial and local officials do not understand the differences between mitigation and adaptation, or understand the potential impacts of climate change within their areas or how local contexts give rise to different vulnerabilities and risks for different groups of people or sectors. Some of this low capacity is due to data and knowledge gaps, especially the lack of integrated social and biophysical vulnerability and risk assessments or the ability to conduct them. Even when presented with data and information, capacity to understand them and using them to formulate policy varies among decision makers. NDRC also recognises the importance and need to promote the NAS to relevant line ministries.

Uncertainty amongst provincial decision makers regarding the scope and severity of climate change impacts is also an issue. Many of these leaders have a difficult time understanding the uncertainty in climate change impacts. Some do not understand the linkages between socio-economic and ecosystem development trends (altering vulnerabilities), rates of urbanisation and land use change (increasing exposure to hazards), and shifting climate that give rise to climate risk and cause specific impacts (see Chapter 2). Local-level decision makers in particular grapple with understanding the uncertainty in climate projections or scenarios of future socio-economic growth and ecosystem changes, and how the range of potential impacts varies according to assumptions in these future scenarios.

NDRC aims to formulate, in collaboration with local governments, a *Local Action Guidance for Climate Change Adaptation*. Under the NAS, NDRC will be responsible for strengthening local capacity (especially in conducting integrated social and biophysical vulnerability and risk assessments and linking their outcomes to adaptation planning) through training, communication and study visits.

Institutional, governance and regulatory weaknesses

Institutional, governance and regulatory weaknesses still present significant challenges for China in developing comprehensive adaptation responses. Despite the focus given to coordination in the NAS, the lack of practical governance coordination and integration among government sectors remains a major challenge for managing climate risk in China at national and provincial levels. Particularly, little is known with relation to the processes and institutional arrangements for mainstreaming adaptation into development at county and local levels.

At present, there is still insufficient coordination, lack of cooperation between ministries, and sometimes overlapping mandates, resulting in inefficient resource deployment and overlap. This is limiting the sharing of relevant information and lessons learned across ministries and serving as barriers to integrating adaptation into larger policy frameworks. For example, synergies between the current climate change adaptation initiatives of line ministries need to be developed. In addition, weak legal and regulatory frameworks to support financial investment, taxation and risk transfer mechanisms, combined with the absence of clear objectives for local adaptation policies and actions, mean synergistic adaptation planning continues to be slow and complex.

Lack of adaptation-specific finance

While there is no systematic estimate of the funding needed to support climate adaptation in China, there is broad consensus that increased capital investment is needed, including the establishment of national and provincial funds for developing and implementing regional adaptation plans. While funding is available, at present it is ad hoc and tied to priority sectors identified in the *Twelfth Five Year Plans*, making it hard for provinces to conduct comprehensive cross-sector and integrated vulnerability, risk and impact assessments and move from these to implementing appropriate policies and actions.

There is currently no national definition on climate expenditures, making it difficult to track resources allocated for financing climate-related efforts. Additionally, there is no mechanism for gathering climate funding statistics from central and provincial government departments that would allow tracking and monitoring of funds not categorised under special climate accounts in the national budget. The Ministry of Finance's 2015 budget now indicates a clear amount dedicated to climate change, but how these funds will be allocated between mitigation and adaptation related activities and needs are unclear.

In summary, China faces a number of challenges in adaptation planning processes, particularly at the provincial and local levels. The capacities and priorities of assessment researchers and policy makers, along with limited data and resources, mean that understanding of the linkages between socio-economic, cultural, policy, environmental and climate change processes is weak. Of particular concern is the current failure to adequately investigate or incorporate the perspectives of communities or how socio-cultural processes and behaviours shape, and are shaped by, climate risks and development pathways. Because of this, many provincial- and local-level policy makers have a hard time conceptualising climate risks, tending to focus on technological and engineering solutions, and have difficulty mainstreaming adaptation considerations into broader development plans. Funding mechanisms and clarity about these continues to be lacking at all levels and serve as barriers to developing adaptation policies and actions. Yet Chinese researchers and policy makers acknowledge these barriers and seek ways to address them in future iterations of adaptation planning, from assessments to policies and actions.

China's emerging South–South climate policy and cooperation

Despite its adaptation challenges, funding and knowledge on climate change adaptation is flowing out of China through its developing South–South cooperation strategy (Simpson et al., 2012). South–South cooperation between China and other developing countries is not a new concept. It has been underway since the 1950s via bilateral cooperation, academic exchanges, aid, institutions and programmes.[8] However, climate change and, more specifically, adaptation are emerging areas of cooperation.

Since COP 15 in 2009, in response to the criticism China received regarding its handling of the negotiations as well as its evolving role in the global climate change arena and emerging economic power status, the central government has started to establish policies for South–South collaboration in climate change. China's *White Paper on Climate Change 2012* clearly states that South–South cooperation (SSC) to address climate change has become a priority area, and this is also echoed in the NAS.

In recent years, Chinese leaders have expressed the need for climate change SSC. In 2011, Xie Zhenhua, Vice Chairman of the National Development and Reform Commission announced four major areas of SSC at COP 17 in Durban: adaptation; promotion of climate change adaptation technology; dissemination and donation of technology in energy conservation, water conservation and renewable energy to small island states and least developed countries; and continuation of capacity building programmes for developing countries (Hsu, 2012).

In 2012 at Rio+20, Premier Wen Jiabao pledged CNY200 million (GBP20.2 million) for a three-year international project to help small island states and least developed countries to tackle climate change. He also said that China would donate US$6 million to the trust fund of the United Nations Environment Programme (UNEP) to help developing countries to improve their capacity of organising projects and activities of environmental protection (Xinhua, 2012). This was followed in 2014 with China and UNEP signing a high-level agreement to boost South–South cooperation on climate change adaptation to assist countries of the global South to combat climate change (Za, 2014). At the 2014 New York Climate Summit, Executive Vice Premier Zhang Gaoli announced a doubling of annual funding for South–South cooperation, which is expected to be CNY140 million, and establish the South–South Cooperation Fund on Climate Change (IISD, 2014). In addition to this commitment, China will provide US$6 million to support the UN Secretary General in advancing the South–South cooperation in tackling climate change. The decision on which multilateral agency will manage this fund has not yet been taken.

The NDRC is China's designated agency for South–South cooperation on climate change; however, it is a domestic agency with little experience in this area. The current focus of much of the agency's outreach is the export of climate-friendly technologies to developing countries. For example, China has donated 900,000 energy-efficient lights and more than 10,000 energy-efficient air conditioners. At present, China currently does not have a specific strategy for its South–South cooperation on climate change. The NDRC's National Centre for Climate Change Strategy and International Cooperation (NCSC) – China's first national-level think tank – has been assigned the task of drafting a strategy for China on SSC and climate change.

Currently, China has inadequate capacity to carry out South–South projects in the area of climate change that fully complement other developing countries' national plans. This is due in part to the absence of a comprehensive policy, but also to the majority of support to South–South countries being in the form of equipment or limited training for personnel. Many of the South–South projects are not demand-driven, nor do they reflect the needs of recipients. Most of China's SSC works are bilateral in nature, with projects initiated in China to strengthen SSC on climate change. According to China's climate change white paper, *China's Policies and Actions for Addressing Climate Change 2013*, NDRC has established cooperation with 41 developing countries and signed Memoranda of Understanding on Providing Foreign Aid to Address Climate Change with 12 developing countries, including Grenada, Ethiopia, Madagascar, Nigeria, Benin and Dominica.[9] From a global perspective, China is a very important player in SSC. Despite limitations in complementing other countries' development and adaptation priorities, China has extensive experience to share in both mitigation and adaptation, including disaster risk reduction and relief. Time and further experience in engaging with other countries around SSC will improve China's capacity in mainstreaming climate change adaptation considerations into cooperation initiatives.

Summary

Climate change is gradually being recognised as a key factor restricting the economic and social development of China. As such, adaptation is beginning to be seen as an integral part of China's sustainable development and essential for safeguarding economic and social progress. This book has documented that adaptation is not simply a technical issue; it must become an integral part of social and economic growth and the development of a country. Chapters 2, 8 and 9 in particular show that the climate risks faced by China's many populations and sectors, like pastoralism and grassland management, are as much due to the culmination of many dynamic social and biophysical vulnerability factors as they are to exposure to increasingly frequent and severe extreme weather events and overall shifts in regional climates.

Many adaptation problems and their response measures are related to changing social and economic behaviours and norms; focusing primarily on technological or engineering solutions is insufficient for building climate resilience. Some examples of social adaptation include requiring changing the location or intensity of an economic activity or settlement, the type of livelihood and settlement occurring at a particular place and the introduction of new social policies and programmes. Addressing the adaptation challenge in any country requires a concerted and focused effort involving organisations, agencies and institutions at multiple levels and from all sectors. It will also involve the general public and those institutions that support and inform them (e.g. media).

Adaptation policy and planning is complex; this book discussed some of the issues facing China in particular around this topic. Implementing planning, policies and actions are concurrently technical, political, economic, legal and development issues. On the surface, China's understanding of climate risk and its capacity to build climate resilience appears high, with a strong science base, a long history of dealing with drought and a central planning structure to ensure institutional coordination. In reality, the challenge facing China's leadership is somewhat greater – from conducting and integrating biophysical and social vulnerability and risk assessments and connecting the information from these to policy priorities and time frames, to developing and implementing policies and actions at a variety of scales. Despite these challenges, China is continuing to move forward with adaptation planning, from assessment to policy and action, and learning from and building upon previous efforts. In its *Twelfth Five Year Plan*, China has, for the first time, dedicated an entire chapter to climate change, with equal emphasis on both mitigation and adaptation. It is not yet known exactly what the *Thirteenth Five Year Plan* will bring in the area of climate change, but it is likely to result in further strengthening and mainstreaming of climate change considerations into all policies.

China's climate change challenges and adaptation policies also present opportunities for the international community, though a detailed discussion on China–international climate change issues was beyond the scope of this book. China must prepare for increased natural resource stress by using evidence-based adaptation planning in core sectors such as water, agriculture and energy in order to ensure the implications for traded goods, supply chains, migration and international relations are positive. For example, glacial retreat, wetland evaporation and shifting precipitation and temperature patterns will also have impacts on the water supply of the Yangtze, Yellow and Lancang rivers, which could have wider political, development and strategic implications for downstream countries. As a result, climate change impacts and response measures are both a national and a regional issue and should be an integral part of the broader development agenda (Keskinen *et al.*, 2010; Renaud and Kuenzer, 2012). Forming partnerships among countries of the region to develop common goals and commitments and share resources and knowledge to plan response strategies is necessary for a sustainable future.

While the physical impacts of climate change are complex and not completely predictable, many countries face similar risks and vulnerabilities from higher average global temperatures, rising sea levels, extreme events, climate variability and loss of agricultural land and fresh water (IPCC, 2014). Forming partnerships and international networks to facilitate collaboration in adaptation research and knowledge sharing to reduce risks, build resilience and develop adaptive pathways are important for China and the international community as a whole.

Going forward, it is therefore crucial for China not only to develop new national adaptation strategies and polices but also to review existing policies targeting such vulnerable groups as migrant workers, women in rural areas and children, and to propose recommendations on building up adaptive capacity. Adaptation planning is truly an iterative, and hopefully an increasingly participatory, process within China.

Notes

1 Scientists and engineers also dominate many of China's top political positions, including current President Xi Jinping, who has an undergraduate degree in chemical engineering.

2 This is in part due to the fact that traditionally, social science research in China has primarily provided the evidence base and academic framework to support government ideological campaigns or thinking.

3 In addition to China's own domestic research, its scientists' participation in international research such as the IPCC has also contributed to increased domestic policy-maker understanding and awareness.

4 The Strategic Climate Fund (SCF) will provide financing to pilot new development approaches or to scale-up activities aimed at a specific climate change challenges through targeted programmes. The SCF is part of the Climate Investment Funds (CIF) established by the World Bank jointly with the Regional Development Banks (AfDB, AsDB, EBRD and IDB) in July 2008 to promote international cooperation on climate change and support progress towards the future of the climate change regime. The Special Climate Change Fund (SCCF) was established in response to guidance received from COP 7. It is designed to finance activities, programmes and measures related to climate change that are complementary to those funded through the climate change focal area of the Global Environmental Facility.

5 As detailed in the chapters in Part II, the Ministry of Water Resources and the Ministry of Agriculture have developed some sector-based adaptation polices. NDRC's annual report, *China's Policies and Actions on Climate Change 2014*, documents that a number of other ministries have also started to develop climate adaptation related polices, including: *Guiding Opinions on Strengthening the Development of Disaster-Relief Equipment* (Ministry of Civil Affairs), *Design Code for Outdoor Drainage* (Ministry of Housing and Urban-Rural Development); and the *Provincial Island Protection Plan* (State Oceanic Administration). Eight provinces (Liaoning, Hebei, Shandong, Jiangsu, Zhejiang, Fujian, Guangdong and Guangxi) have approved their own version of the scheme.

6 Information provided at ACCC I meetings in Jilin.

7 Based on publicly available data and personal interviews with provincial governments in Guangdong, Inner Mongolia, Jilin and Yunnan.

8 Examples of programmes and exchanges include the Chinese Academy of Science and Technology for Development, the China Council for International Cooperation on Environment and Development, the Forum on China–Africa Cooperation, the Technology Manuals published by the Chinese Ministry of Science and Technology and partners, and the Network/Platform for International Science and Technology Cooperation launched by the China Science and Technology Exchange Centre and partners.

9 For example, the China–ASEAN New and Renewable Energy Utilization International Technology and Cooperation Forum was hosted by the Ministry of Science and Technology, the Ministry of Foreign Affairs and other departments to promote exchanges and communication between China and ASEAN countries. NDRC and the State Oceanic Administration also implemented a South–South cooperation research project on maritime disaster monitoring and early warning system within the framework of climate change. The English version of the *Guide for Building the*

Capabilities of Developing Countries' Marine Disaster Monitoring and Early Warning was drafted and seminars on developing countries' marine disaster monitoring and early warning technologies were held in Xiamen. It provided training to 16 students from nine developing countries, including Cambodia and Indonesia. The Seminar on Monitoring Deforestation and Land Degradation and Evaluating South–South Cooperation within the Climate Change Framework was held by China's State Forestry Administration. Technology training to professionals from developing countries on the relationship between climate change and extreme weather and climate events was offered by China's Meteorological Administration. It also provided training on early warning systems for various disasters and climate service system.

References

Beddington, J., Asaduzzaman, M., Clark, M., Fernández, A., Guillou, M, Jahn, Molly, Lin, E., Mamo, T., Bo, N., Van Nobre, C.A., Scholes, R., Sharma, R. and Wakhungu, J. (2011) *Achieving Food Security in the Face of Climate Change. Final Report from the Commission on Sustainable Agriculture and Climate Change.* CGIAR Research Program on Climate Change, Agriculture and Food Security (CCAFS): Copenhagen, Denmark.

Bray, D. and von Storch, H. (2009) 'Prediction' or 'projection'? The nomenclature of climate science. *Science Communication.* 30. pp. 534–543.

Climate Group (2013) *Shaping China's Climate Finance Policy.* The Climate Group: Beijing, People's Republic of China.

Dessai, S. and Hulme, M. (2004) Does climate adaptation policy need probabilities? *Climate Policy.* 4 (2). pp. 107–128.

Economy, E. (2010) *The River Runs Black: The Environmental Challenge to China's Future.* Cornell University Press: New York, New York, USA.

Elvin, M. (1998) The environmental legacy of imperial China. *China Quarterly.* 156. pp. 733–756.

Fan, C.C. (2003) Rural–urban migration and gender division of labor in transitional China. *International Journal of Urban and Regional Research.* 27 (1). pp. 24–47.

Freeman, D. (2010) The missing link: China, climate change and national security. *BICCS Asia Paper.* 5 (8). pp. 1–30.

Gay, C. and Estrada, F. (2010) Objective probabilities about future climate are a matter of opinion. *Climatic Change.* 99. pp. 27–46.

Guo, M., Xie, L., Cao, M. and Liu, E. (2008) Policy and impacts of climate change on agricultural production and agricultural development. *Agricultural Economics.* 10. pp. 8–10.

Hart, J.A.F., Grifman, P.M., Moser, S.C., Abeles, A., Myers, M.R., Schlosser, S.C. and Ekstrom, J.A. (2012) *Rising to the Challenge: Results of the 2011 Coastal California Adaptation Needs Assessment.* University of Southern California Sea Grant: Los Angeles, California, USA. (USCSG-TR-01-2012.)

Heggelund, G., Andresen, S. and Buan, I.F. (2010) Chinese climate policy: Domestic priorities, foreign policy and emerging implementation. In: Harrison, K. and Sundstrom, L.M. (eds), *Global Commons, Domestic Decisions: The Comparative Politics of Climate Change.* MIT Press: Cambridge, Massachusetts, USA and London, United Kingdom.

Held, D., Nag, E.M. and Roger, C. (2011) *The Governance of Climate Change in China. LSE Global Governance Working Paper WP 01/2011.* [Online] Available from: www.

lse.ac.uk/globalGovernance/publications/workingPapers/climateChangeInChina.pdf. [Accessed: 4 February 2015.]

Hsu, A. (2012) *China Promotes South–South Cooperation in Durban.* ChinaFAQs: The Network for Climate and Energy Information. [Online] Available from: www.china-faqs.org/blog-posts/china-promotes-South-south-cooperation-durban. [Accessed: 2 February 2015.]

Hu, J. (2007) *Hold High the Great Banner of Socialism with Chinese Characteristics and Strive for New Victories in Building a Moderately Prosperous Society in All.* PRC Central Government. [Online] Available from: www.china.org.cn/english/congress/229611.htm. [Accessed: 9 December 2014.]

Hu, S. and Shu, B. (2010) The analysis on the boundary personality of externally migrated geologic hazard emigrant victims. *Northwest Population.* 3 (31). pp. 17–21.

Hung, M.T. and Tsai, T.C. (2012) Dilemma of choice: China's response to climate change. *Revista Brasiliera de Polꞔtica Internacional.* 55. pp. 104–124.

Hvistendahl, M. (2008) China's Three Gorges Dam: An environmental catastrophe? *Scientific American.* [Online] 25 March. Available from: www.scientificamerican.com/article/chinas-three-gorges-dam-disaster/. [Accessed: 4 February 2015.]

IISD (International Institute of Sustainable Development) (2014) Summary of Climate Summit 2014: 23 September 2014. *Climate Summit Bulletin.* [Online] 172 (18). pp. 1–19. Available from: www.iisd.ca/download/pdf/sd/crsvol172num18e.pdf. [Accessed: 4 February 2015.]

IPCC (2014) Climate Change 2014: Impacts, adaptation, and vulnerability. Part B: Regional aspects. In: Barros, V.R., Field, C.B., Dokken, D.J., Mastrandrea, M.D., Mach, K.J., Bilir, T.E., Chatterjee, M., Ebi, K.L., Estrada, Y.O., Genova, R.C., Girma, B., Kissel, E.S., Levy, A.N., MacCraken, S., Mastrandrea, P.R. and White, L.L. (eds), *Working Group II Contribution to the Fifth Assessment Report of the Intergovernmental Panel on Climate Change.* Cambridge University Press: Cambridge, United Kingdom and New York, New York, USA.

Keskinen, M., Chinvanno, S., Kummu, M., Nuorteva, P., Snidvongs, A., Varis, O. and Västilä, K. (2010) Climate change and water resources in the Lower Mekong River Basin: Putting adaptation into the context. *Journal of Water and Climate Change.* 1 (2). pp. 103–117.

Li, H., Waley, P. and Rees, R. (2001) Reservoir resettlement in China: Past experience and the Three Gorges Dam. *The Geographical Journal.* 167 (3). pp. 195–212.

Liu, E., Xie, L., Zhao, H., Cao, M. and Guo, M. (2010) On the adaptation ability and construction problem of climate change on agriculture. *Agricultural Economics.* 1. pp. 3–5.

Liu, Z., Zou, J. and Yu, H. (2006) Impacts and responses to socioeconomic effects of climate change in China, using Wuhan as an example. *Advances and Policies in Technology.* 11. pp. 89–92.

Lu, L., Lin, H. and Liu, Q. (2010) Risk map for dengue fever outbreaks based on meteorological factors. *Advances in Climate Change Research.* 6 (4). pp. 258–264.

Moore, S. (2009) Climate change, water and China's national interest. *China Security.* 5 (3). pp. 25–39.

Moser, S.C. (2009) Governance and the art of overcoming barriers to adaptation. *Magazine of the International Human Dimensions Programme on Global Environmental Change.* 3. pp. 31–36.

NDRC (PRC National Development and Reform Commission) (2004) *The People's Republic of China Initial National Communication on Climate Change.* Executive

Summary. PRC National Development and Reform Commission: Beijing, People's Republic of China.

NDRC (PRC National Development and Reform Commission) (2012) *China's Policies and Actions for Addressing Climate Change 2012*. PRC National Development and Reform Commission: Beijing, People's Republic of China.

NDRC (PRC National Development and Reform Commission) (2013) *China's Policies and Actions for Addressing Climate Change 2013*. PRC National Development and Reform Commission: Beijing, People's Republic of China.

Noble, I.R., Huq, S., Anokhin, Y.A., Carmin, J., Goudou, D., Lansigan, F.P., Osman-Elasha, B. *et al.* (2014) Adaptation needs and options. In: Climate Change 2014: Impacts, Adaptation, and Vulnerability. Part A: Global and Sectoral Aspects. In: Barros, V.R., Field, C.B., Dokken, D.J., Mastrandrea, M.D., Mach, K.J., Bilir, T.E., Chatterjee, M., Ebi, K.L., Estrada, Y.O., Genova, R.C., Girma, B., Kissel, E.S., Levy, A.N., MacCracken, S., Mastrandrea, P.R. and White L.L. (eds), *Contribution of Working Group II to the Fifth Assessment Report of the Intergovernmental Panel on Climate Change*. Cambridge University Press: Cambridge, United Kingdom and New York, New York, USA.

Opitz-Stapleton, S., Guibert, G., MacClune, K., MacClune, K., Sabbag, L. and Tyler, S. (2010) *Only Death is Certain, Yet You Still Get Out of Bed in the Morning. Observations on the Use of Climate Information in Adaptation and Resilience Practice*. Climate Resilience in Concept and Practice: ISET Working Paper 2. ISET: Boulder, Colorado, USA.

Pennesi, K. (2007) Improving forecast communication: Linguistic and cultural considerations. *Bulletin of the American Meteorological Society*. 88 (7). pp. 1033–1044.

PRC State Planning Commission and PRC State Science and Technology Commission (1994) *China's Agenda 21: White Paper on China's Population, Environment, and Development in the 21st Century*. PRC State Planning Commission and PRC State Science and Technology Commission. [Online] Available from: www.acca21.org.cn/ca21pa.html. [Accessed: 14 November 2014.]

Renaud, F.G. and Kuenzer, C. (eds) (2012) *The Mekong Delta System: Interdisciplinary Analyses of a River Delta*. Springer: Dordrecht, Germany.

Shi, G., Deng, D. and Zhou, J. (2009) Problems, classification and characteristics of disaster-forced migration. *Journal of Hohai University*. 11 (1). pp. 20–24.

Simpson, M.C., Cole, M.J., Harrison, M., Tyldesley, S., Madangombe, W., Carter, S., Hutchinson, N., King, D.A., New, M. and Gibbons, H. (2012) *China and South–South Scoping Assessment for Adaptation, Learning and Development (CASSALD)*. Adapting to Climate Change in China I (ACCC I) Programme: Beijing, People's Republic of China.

Sun, Z. (2014) *Update on the National Adaptation Strategy*. International Workshop on Urban Adaptation convened by Ministry of Housing and Rural Development.

Wang, X., Huang, J., Zhang, L. and Rozelle, S. (2011) The rise of migration and the fall of self employment in rural China's labor market. *China Economic Review*. 22. pp. 573–584.

Wang, Z., Zheng, P. and Zhou, Q. (1996) The impact of climate on the society of China during historical times. *Acta Geographica Sinica*. 51 (4). pp. 330–339.

Werz, M. and Reed, L. (2014) *Climate Change, Migration, and Nontraditional Security Threats in China: Complex Crisis Scenarios and Policy Options for China and the World*. Center for American Progress: Washington, DC, USA.

Wu, J., Huang, J., Han, X., Gao, X., He, F., Jiang, M., Jiang, Z., Primack, R.B. and Shen, Z. (2004) The Three Gorges Dam: An ecological perspective. *Frontiers in Ecology and the Environment*. 2 (5). pp. 241–248.

Wübbeke, J. (2013) China's climate change expert community: Principles, mechanisms and influence. *Journal of Contemporary China*. 22 (82). pp. 712–731.

Xie, L., Guo, M., Liu, E. and Zhang, W. (2009) Actions and prospects for adapting agriculture to climate change. *Rural Economy*. 12. pp. 35–36.

Xinhua (2012) Full text of Wen Jiabao's speech at the United Nations Conference on Sustainable Development. *Xinhua*. [Online] 21 June. Available from: www.gov.cn/ldhd/2012-06/21/content_2166455.htm. [Accessed: 4 February 2015.]

Yang, K., Pan, J., Yang, G., Li, S., Xu, Y. and Zhou, X. (2010) Projection of the transmission scale and intensity of schistosomiasis in China under A2 and B2 climate change scenarios. *Advances in Climate Change Research*. 6 (4). pp. 248–254.

Za, M. (2014) New China-UNEP agreement to boost South–south cooperation on climate change adaptation. *UN Environmental Programme*. [Online] 10 May. Available from: www.unep.org/NewsCentre/default.aspx?ArticleID=10854&DocumentID=2788. [Accessed: 2 February 2015.]

Zhang, Z. and Wu, R. (1999) Climatic changes of Little Ice Age and its social effects in China. *Exploration of Nature*. 18 (1). pp. 66–70.

Zhou, Q. (2006) Advance in the effects of climate change on environment and health. *Journal of Meteorology and Environment*. 22 (1). pp. 38–44.

Zhou, Y., Li, N., Wu, W., Wu, J. and Shi, P. (2014) local spatial and temporal factors influencing population and societal vulnerability to natural disasters. *Risk Analysis*. 34 (4). pp. 614–639.

INDEX

Page numbers in *italics* denote tables, those in **bold** denote figures.